WITHDRAWN

ANDREW MARVELL: THE CRITICAL HERITAGE

THE CRITICAL HERITAGE SERIES

GENERAL EDITOR: B.C. SOUTHAM, M.A., B. LITT. (OXON.)

Formerly Department of English, Westfield College, University of London

For a list of books in the series see the back end paper

ANDREW MARVELL

THE CRITICAL HERITAGE

edited by

ELIZABETH STORY DONNO

Department of English and Comparative Literature
Columbia University, New York

ROUTLEDGE & KEGAN PAUL
LONDON, HENLEY AND BOSTON

First published in 1978
by Routledge & Kegan Paul Ltd
39 Store Street,
London WC1E 7DD,
Broadway House,
Newtown Road
Henley-on-Thames,
Oxon RG9 1EN and
9 Park Street,
Boston, Mass. 02108, USA
Set in Monophoto Garamond
by Thomson Press (India) Limited, New Delhi
and printed in Great Britain by
Weatherby Woolnough
Copyright Elizabeth Story Donno 1978

British Library Cataloguing in Publication Data

Andrew Marvell, the critical heritage.— (The critical
heritage series).

1. *Marvell, Andrew—Criticism and interpretation*
—Addresses, essays, lectures
I. Donno, Elizabeth Story II. Series
821'.4   PR3546   78–40044

ISBN 0 7100 8791 8

To

WILLIAM NELSON

he nothing common did or mean

General Editor's Preface

The reception given to a writer by his contemporaries and near-contemporaries is evidence of considerable value to the student of literature. On one side we learn a great deal about the state of criticism at large and in particular about the development of critical attitudes towards a single writer; at the same time, through private comments in letters, journals or marginalia, we gain an insight upon the tastes and literary thought of individual readers of the period. Evidence of this kind helps us to understand the writer's historical situation, the nature of his immediate reading-public, and his response to these pressures.

The separate volumes in the *Critical Heritage Series* present a record of this early criticism. Clearly, for many of the highly productive and lengthily reviewed nineteenth- and twentieth-century writers, there exists an enormous body of material; and in these cases the volume editors have made a selection of the most important views, significant for their intrinsic critical worth or for their representative quality—perhaps even registering incomprehension!

For earlier writers, notably pre-eighteenth century, the materials are much scarcer and the historical period has been extended, sometimes far beyond the writer's lifetime, in order to show the inception and growth of critical views which were initially slow to appear.

In each volume the documents are headed by an Introduction, discussing the material assembled and relating the early stages of the author's reception to what we have come to identify as the critical tradition. The volumes will make available much material which would otherwise be difficult of access and it is hoped that the modern reader will be thereby helped towards an informed understanding of the ways in which literature has been read and judged.

B.C.S.

Contents

CONTENTS

CONTENTS

Preface

To a twentieth-century reader who thinks of Andrew Marvell in terms of poetic achievement, the history of his literary fortunes may occasion surprise. The single edition of the poetry published in the seventeenth century, and posthumously at that, had its promptings in his reputation as a witty satirist and incorruptible patriot. Established during the last few years of his life and lasting for nearly two centuries, this reputation was primarily determined by the impact of the controversial writings in prose. Editions in the eighteenth century did indeed keep the poetry in public view, but the same motivation for publication continued to obtain, as the assertions of the editors, together with their inclusion of the letters and prose pieces, attest. In order to trace the development of Marvell's reputation chronologically, comments on the works which determined this public image appear first. To establish a context for them, a summary of each controversy introduces the comments; to elucidate often remote topical allusions, some notes are appended.

The remaining critical items focus on the emergence of the poet, first in conjunction with the persistent image of satirist and patriot, then within the double frame of his achievement as poet and prose writer. Finally, at the end of the nineteenth century and the beginning of the twentieth, comes the singular stress on his achievement as poet.

E.S.D.

Acknowledgments

The author and publishers are grateful to the following for permission to reproduce copyright material:

Associated Book Publishers Ltd for A. Clutton-Brock, *More Essays on Books*; Faber & Faber Ltd and Mrs Valerie Eliot and Harcourt Brace Jovanovich, Inc. for T. S. Eliot, *Selected Essays*, copyright 1932, 1936, 1950 by Harcourt Brace Jovanovich, Inc.; renewed, 1960, 1964 by T. S. Eliot. Reprinted by permission of Harcourt Brace Jovanovich, Inc.; The Huntington Library, San Marino, California, for Nos 1, 3, 6, 9, 12, 16, 17, 19, 20, 22, 23, 31, 32, 33, 34, 36, 39, 42, 43, 46, 48, 53, 62, 66; Macmillan London and Basingstoke for Augustine Birrell, *Andrew Marvell*; Macmillan Publishing Co. Inc., New York, and the Executors of George Saintsbury Deceased for George Saintsbury, *A Short History of English Literature*; John Murray (Publishers) Ltd for extracts from the *Cornhill Magazine* and the *Quarterly Review*; *New Statesman*, London, for Matthew Arnold's letter to Sainte Beuve, reprinted in the *Athenaeum*, J. Stuart's review in the *Athenaeum* and T. S. Eliot's review in the *Nation and Athenaeum*; the *North American Review* for Francis L. Bickley's essay; Oxford University Press for Herbert J. C. Grierson, *Metaphysical Lyrics and Poems of the Seventeenth Century*; the *Spectator* for reviews by W. D. Christie and Lytton Strachey; the *Times Literary Supplement* for the unsigned review, No. 91a.

Note on the Text

In general, the copytext is that of the earliest printing, with abbreviations and contractions expanded, modern typographical conventions followed, and insignificant printing errors corrected. For texts originally printed in italic with proper names in roman, a reverse procedure has been followed. Selected original notes are indicated by asterisks, explanatory notes by a numerical sequence. Place of publication is indicated only when it is other than London.

In place of long quotations from Marvell's writings, bracketed references have been inserted, keyed to the following editions:

Grosart	*The Complete Works in Verse and Prose of Andrew Marvell*, ed. A. B. Grosart, 4 vols, Fuller Worthies Library, 1872–5
Poems; Letters	*The Poems and Letters of Andrew Marvell*, ed. H. M. Margoliouth, rev. Pierre Legouis with the collaboration of E. E. Duncan-Jones. 2 vols, Oxford, 1971
R T I and *II* or Smith	*The Rehearsal Transpros'd* and *The Rehearsal Transpros'd the Second Part*, ed. D. I. B. Smith, Oxford, 1971

Introduction

In 1753 Andrew Marvell was styled the 'poet laureate of the
dissenters,' otherwise known as 'fanatics'; in 1901 he was styled
the 'laureate of grass and greenery.'¹ Each phrase aptly sums up
public response to the man and his works within their eras; in
conjunction, they sharply point up the alteration in response that
took place in the years between. The first designation is apt, not
because it defines Marvell's literary achievement but because it
reflects, as well as projects, his literary status for nearly two centuries. The 'poet laureate of the dissenters' did not write poetry on
the theme of religious dissent (except perhaps for 'Bermudas'
which was later so interpreted and the anti-prelatical portion of
'The Loyal Scot,' if it is his), but he did write prose pamphlets that
were to mark him out as an intrepid opponent of the ecclesiastical
and political establishment. From the last decades of the seventeenth until the last few decades of the nineteenth century, he was
to be acknowledged in metaphoric terms as *the* laureate of dissenting opinion. However odd it may seem to twentieth-century
enthusiasts, his reputation as a poet was to remain in inverse relation to his general reputation almost throughout this period.

While early documentary material of the poetry is scant, its very
paucity, whether printed or manuscript, can be taken as revelatory
of Marvell's attitude toward his craft. Of the ten selections published during his lifetime, he chose to acknowledge only five
either by name or by initials, and each of these is occasional in
nature. The earliest stems from the period at Cambridge when he
contributed verses to a congratulatory volume on the birth of a
royal child in 1637; the latest that can be dated is the commendatory poem on *Paradise Lost* which he contributed to the second
edition of Milton's epic in 1674. The remainder (apart from the
dubious and not so dubious post-Restoration satires) were probably written early in his career before the assuming of his parliamentary duties in 1659–60, with certain pieces lending themselves

to fairly precise dating because of their occasional nature: 'Tom May's Death,' for example. Others can only be tentatively allocated to likely periods of composition: the period of travel abroad following his education at Cambridge, the return to London and sojourn antedating the short period spent in Yorkshire as tutor to Mary Fairfax, the short period spent at Eton as tutor to Cromwell's ward, and the equally short period spent as a Latin secretary in the Cromwellian regime.

None the less, this period of poetic activity (nearly forty years on the basis of first and last dates; more likely fewer on the basis of the smallness of the canon) covers a long span of time in contrast to that obtaining for the prose pieces. All occasional in nature and all but one of them published anonymously or pseudonymously, the prose pieces appeared within the space of five and a half years. Yet in spite of their disclaimer of authorship and their topical character, these were the works that were to establish Marvell's long-lived reputation as witty satirist and incorruptible patriot, with its corollary as the conscientious MP from Hull.[2] More than two centuries were to pass before his reputation was established as, primarily, that of a lyric poet.

The critical materials included here have been ordered to reflect this changing reputation: first, the contemporary reactions to the prose works (with their occasional acknowledgment that he was a poetaster if not a poet) are followed by the later criticism of these works, extending chronologically to 1894, after which they all but drop from consideration. Then the gradual emergence of the poet is traced, along with the continuing emphasis on his image as satirist and patriot, up to 1845.[3] In the course of the nineteenth century, concern for that image, on the one hand, and the poet and prose writer, on the other, is seen to fluctuate, gradually giving place to a somewhat uneven recognition of his dual literary achievements. Finally, during the last decade of that century and the first two of the twentieth, a reassessment comes. Though not invariably favourable, in its concentration on the lyric poetry it notably anticipates the kinds of literary concern so markedly characterizing Marvell criticism after 1921, the tercentenary of his birth and the terminal date for this survey. In view of the kind of literary evaluation accorded during his lifetime, such a reassessment could equally well be termed a 'reversal' or a 'discovery.' In view of the evaluation of his writings after his death, it represents a radical shift

2

in political and literary values. From either aspect it is significant in pointing the way to the current esteem for Marvell as poet.

However aggrandizing this tardy recognition may seem to literary sensibilities in this the tercentenary of his death (and it seemed so to a reassessing critic even in 1901; see No. 86), the fact remains that the poetry Marvell chose to acknowledge (or not to acknowledge on its publication) never disappeared from view once it was printed. His public image simply eclipsed it. That this should have been so is not surprising when belletristic writings are seen in historical perspective.[4] Ascertainably responsive to classical, contemporary, and near-contemporary writers in his fine-honed and essentially 'literary' poems, Marvell none the less deliberately chose to renounce their publication, electing instead an outlet in the propagandistic underground. He seems, as a result, a puzzling 'dimorphic' figure, one seemingly representative of the Renaissance that preceded him and anticipatory of the journalistic age that followed, albeit it too had its roots in a Renaissance milieu.

Bits and pieces of biographical allusion tend to support this Janus-like aspect of essentially private poet and public gladiator.[5] On the one hand, there is the delineation of the solitary poet, drinking liberally from his bottles of wine—after becoming an MP it was to be the ale furnished by his constituency—with the intent, as John Aubrey put it (No. 28), 'to refresh his spirits and exalt his muse.' On the other hand, there is the delineation of the habitué of the coffee house, along with—as an opponent put it—the loiterer about Lincoln's Inn Fields and Charing Cross where political 'farces and drolls' were daily enacted.[6]

Equally puzzling to biographical commentators was how the MP from Hull managed to support himself during his nearly twenty-year tenure in parliament, a puzzlement that gave rise to his denigration as the last in his period to accept parliamentary wages, apparently 6s. 8d. per diem when parliament was in session (see No. 41). This implication of material dependency does not altogether square with the image of the incorruptible patriot. Does its prevalence, beginning in the seventeenth century with Wood (No. 10), Parker (No. 22), and Aubrey (No. 28) and frequently repeated up until 1895 (No. 82), reflect partisan politics, or does it reflect the difficulty that even partisans of a historical approach find in attempting to reconcile the engaged polemicist with the disengaged poet? Whatever the answer, as an acknowledged legislator (as well as an unacknowledged one in Shelleyan terms), Andrew Marvell was to project a dichotomized figure to successive generations.

II THE SEVENTEENTH AND EIGHTEENTH CENTURIES

In an age when satiric wits—in verse and prose—and pamphleteers—anonymous, pseudonymous, and otherwise—were equally prolific, it is notable that in Marvell's case prose anonymity yielded to detection more readily than poetic. An example of his satiric verse, 'The Character of Holland' (ll. 1–100), was published anonymously in 1665 and again in 1672, but it was not to be ascribed to him until after his death. In contrast, the anonymous appearance in 1672 of the first part of the *Rehearsal Transpros'd* was immediately to elicit a half-dozen replies (along with a number of later comments) demonstrating that the author's identity was well known. The inevitable pun on his surname, by supporters and opponents alike, and the syncopation of his given name to Merry-andrew—a mountebank's assistant—by opponents alone, support his authorship, and Marvell himself confirmed it late in 1673 when he appended his name to the second part and took cognizance of these half-dozen replies in his text.

Directed against the high-churchman Samuel Parker—'that venal apostate to bigotry,' as he is called in 1819 (No. 43)—these two parts of the *RT* served to determine not only Marvell's reputation as witty satirist but also his way of capitalizing on current theatrical productions. For this his first flyting, he appropriated the designation 'Mr. Bayes' from the major character in Buckingham's farce *The Rehearsal* in order to ridicule his ecclesiastical opponent. For his second flyting in 1676 with Francis Turner (Master of St John's College, Cambridge), he appropriated the designation 'Mr. Smirke' with similar intent, deriving the name this time from a minor character in Sir George Etherege's *The Man of Mode*. The authorship of *Mr. Smirke: Or, the Divine in Mode*, as Marvell entitled his pamphlet, was again recognized despite the pseudonymous 'Andreas Rivetus, Junior' on the title page.

For his third and most seriously intended polemic of 1677, he ignored literary and theatrical allusions altogether, calling his work *An Account of the Growth of Popery and Arbitrary Government* in a conjunction of terms that were destined to become religious and political watchwords. Of his five pamphlets, this was considered the most inflammatory. For some years after his death, the Tory journalist Roger L'Estrange (No. 17) continued to allude to it as a propaedeutic for revolutionary action, declaring that both the Earl of Shaftesbury and Marvell must either have been privy to the Popish Plot or 'jumped in opinion with all the fanatics that came after them, for the ruin of the government'; 'for never,' he continues, was 'a truer image drawn of one thing from another, than the model that was taken from this book of Marvell's, and made use of in all that followed' (*Observator*, 9 February 1683). In a gesture underscoring its timeliness, Robert Ferguson the Plotter published the *Second Part of the Growth of Popery and Arbitrary Government*, one that began where the former left off, 'viz. from the year 1677 unto the year 1682' in an edition that was paginated to continue Marvell's. Also in 1682, Dryden associated a later inflammatory pamphlet, the three-part *No Protestant Plot*, with Marvell's earlier piece, describing the third part vindicating the Earl of Shaftesbury (incorrectly) as stolen, 'much of it,' from the 'dead author's *Growth of Popery*' (No. 21). As a result of this sense of its political relevance, during the early years of the next century historians continued to denigrate or commend it according to their Whiggish or Tory propensities (see No. 24).

Though his last pamphlet (a defense of John Howe), published only four months before his death and the only one unredeemingly devoted to theological matters, evoked no extended early comment that I have discovered (for examples of later comment, see Nos 25, 26), the other four evoked a sufficient abundance—this is in marked contrast with the poetry. Such a disparity of response can be accounted for simply by the facts of publication. Of the acknowledged and unacknowledged prose pamphlets, four went through a number of editions before the end of 1678, the year of Marvell's death, while the single edition of the collected poems in the seventeenth century appeared posthumously (1681), under the auspices of his former housekeeper purporting to be his widow.[7] Motivation then, as for the later editions discussed below, was the desire to capitalize on Marvell's political reputation. This easy availability of four texts dealing with topical matters that were handled with wit or bravado does much to account for the seventeenth-century, as well as the later, emphasis on the polemicist in prose.

A contributing factor that helps to explain how the image of the incorruptible patriot developed, and accounts for its survival long after the pamphlets ceased to have topical interest, relates to difficulties attendant on their publication. The first part of the *Rehearsal Transpros'd* was initially published without license, inhibited from being sold, and then authorized at the direction of King Charles II, while the second part conspicuously displayed on its title page the threat (signed by one 'J.G.'; see No. 4) that the author of any libel directed against Dr Parker could expect to have his throat cut. The pseudonymous publication of *Mr. Smirke* resulted in the imprisonment of the bookseller who confessed to receiving the papers from Marvell and arranging for their printing without license; and, finally, the anonymous publication of the 'scandalous' *Growth of Popery*, as it was labeled, resulted in the offer of a sizable reward for information relating either to its author or its printer. Although Marvell seems to have escaped personal reprisal in each instance, his sudden death in August 1678 gave rise to the notion of foul play. The aura of political intrigue surrounding him was thus to generate a number of popular 'fictions,' with the result that his charismatic image came to overshadow his literary achievement.[8]

Given this political cast, it is not surprising that when Thomas 'Hesiod' Cooke (No. 33) readied a second (two-volume) edition, including poems, letters, and verse satires, in 1726, his motivation was essentially political: 'My design in this,' he declares, 'is to draw a pattern for all freeborn Englishmen in the life of a worthy patriot, whose every action has truly merited to him, with Aristides, the surname of "the Just."' The issuing of this edition again in 1772 was followed four years later by that of Captain Edward Thompson (No. 38) in three handsome folios. It was to make available additional letters, including the ones to the Hull Corporation which reveal Marvell in his parliamentary role, and additional poems, not all of them by Marvell; but for the first time—following on their cancellation from the 1681 Folio—the three major poems on Cromwell were made available to the reading public. Again the motivation was essentially political: 'One of my first and strongest reasons for publishing the works of

Marvell,' Captain Thompson announces in his preface, 'was the pleasing hopes of adding a number of strenuous and serious friends to our Constitution.'

In between the editions of Cooke and Thompson, another had been projected. In 1756 the admiring Thomas Hollis secured a portrait of Marvell which he then had engraved and distributed 'to his friends and fellow-patriots; and to some, perhaps, who were neither.' In 1765 he was endeavouring to interest the printer William Bowyer in a new edition of the works; two years later, he was seeking to enlist a collector of libertarian tracts to explicate the difficult passages. Bowyer, however, declined to undertake the project, 'not from any dislike to the works of Marvell,' Hollis's editors explain, but from an apprehension that he might not recoup his expenses.[9] Whatever the case, the point needing emphasis is that, despite the partisan motivation, despite the literary and extra-literary accruals to his writings, there were indeed four appearances of the collected poems in under a century. Compared with the scant availability of the works of any number of Renaissance poets, this is a notable record.

Though eighteenth-century biographical dictionaries and encyclopaedias identify Marvell as an 'ingenious writer' or a 'witty droll,' they tend, not surprisingly, to stress his political character, referring to his Latin verses, to the verses on *Paradise Lost* or to 'Flecknoe' when they refer to his poetry at all.[10] In the ten-volume *General Dictionary, Historical and Critical*, translated from Pierre Bayle and augmented by Bernard, Birch *et al.* (1734–41), he is designated, in a reflection of tenuous Continental esteem (see No. 35), an 'ingenious English writer.' In 1748 (*Biographia Britannica*, he is called a 'witty droll'; in 1769, James Granger (*Biographical History of England*, II, ii) classifies him under the category of 'Poets and other ingenious Persons' but stresses his patriotic character; in 1770, Joseph Towers (*British Biography*, VI) includes a single reference to his 'satires and other poetical compositions.'

He is not included in the first edition (1768–71) of the *Encyclopaedia Britannica* (though Milton figures in an article on composition). In the second (1777–84), he is called an 'ingenious writer.' In the third (1788–97), the terse statement 'also Poems and Letters' is added to a mention of some of the prose. Not until the eighth edition (1853–60) is there to be a critical comment on the poetry:

'besides his controversial and political services, Marvell had
written some minor poems of great tenderness, fancy, and beauty,
which were deservedly popular [!]. His lyrical stanzas on the
sailing of the emigrants for Bermudas, *Safe from the Storms and
Prelates' Rage*, form one of the finest strains of the Puritan muse.'
Despite this late recognition, the single most influential, if succinct,
evaluation of the Marvellian poetic style in biographical dictionaries, that of John Aikin, came at the turn of the eighteenth
century (see No. 39).

On the other hand, nine of the lyrics had appeared in Tonson's
(or Dryden's) popular *Miscellany*, published in 1716 and reprinted
in 1727, some in abbreviated form. Silent improvement of the
texts by abridgment without ellipsis, by alteration of line order,
and by verbal emendations was to remain a constant until well
into the twentieth century.[11] Equally, the popularity of a small
number of poems in a small canon was to remain a constant even
after the beginnings of reassessment.

In addition to the verses in Latin, one or another of the lyrics
like 'Eyes and Tears' or 'The Nymph' or the 'Dialogue Between the
Resolved Soul and Created Pleasure' received occasional printing
or comment (see, for example, Nos 34, 35), and in his life of
Dryden Samuel Johnson did see fit to include six lines (17–22)
from the commendatory verses on *Paradise Lost* (with two 'im-
provements'); still, he was several times to be charged with having
inadvisedly omitted Marvell from the bead-roll of English poets.
One of the explanations offered for this exclusion from the *Lives
of the Poets* was on the alleged grounds that the selection was
dictated by a bookselling syndicate rather than by Johnson
himself. It was, none the less, judged to be an irresponsible action
in 'a work which bore so close a relationship to the honour of his
country.'[12] Another explanation offered was his strong antipathy
to Marvell's politics, an antipathy overcome in the case of Milton
because of his stature as an epic poet.

A curious critical correlative to Marvell's image as the laureate
of dissenting opinion was the notion first enunciated by Giles
Jacob in 1720: what was most to Marvell's 'honour,' he affirmed,
and above his own several poetical 'performances,' was 'his being
the first that found out the beauties of Milton.'[13] Though attribut-
able no doubt in part to the MP from Hull's open defense of Milton
(publicly reported by Edward Phillips in 1694) and in part to his

published remarks in the *RT II* (p. 312), this easy blending of political and critical attitudes also reflects the early (but not later) esteem accorded to the commendatory verses on *Paradise Lost*. Despite his desire to credit Dryden with the honor, John Dennis admitted Marvell's (and Dr Barrow's) early championing of Milton's epic.[14] Both Cooke and Thompson proclaimed it, with the result that the notion filtered into the nineteenth century to be reported by others. It was being repeated in England in the *Civil Service Handbook of English Literature* as late as 1874 and in the United States in the comments of a dull Lutheran divine as late as 1877 (No. 76).

During the last decades of the seventeenth century and throughout the eighteenth, Marvell's charismatic image as witty satirist and incorruptible patriot bears out John Ormsby's observation that had he been less brilliant as a patriot, he would have been more conspicuous as a poet (No. 71). Both the geographical range and longevity of this image can be illustrated by two examples from the United States. In 1698 Cotton Mather was prompted to include in his *Eleutheria* a long, if telescoped passage from the 'witty' Marvell's *RT I*; nearly one hundred and fifty years later, James Russell Lowell (No. 41c) disdained to compare the patriot Marvell with an example of the home-bred variety—a former president of the United States currently serving in the House of Representatives—because of the 'vast deal of humbug' in John Quincy Adams's reputation and because he was not 'well seen in the very ABC of freedom.'

III THE NINETEENTH AND TWENTIETH CENTURIES

I TO 1890

In a reflection of a developing esthetic, the inciter of the 'Pope and Bowles' controversy, William Lisle Bowles (No. 42) saw fit to include comments on some lines from Marvell in the notes to his edition of *Windsor Forest* (1806); while acknowledging the abundance of 'conceits' and 'false thoughts,' he was among the very first to characterize Marvell as 'an accurate descriptive rural poet' and surely the first to excerpt lines from 'Appleton House' as an

9

example. The measure of change in sensibilities that occurred
during the nineteenth century is indicated by the easy incorporation
of these remarks into the Victorian edition of Pope (Elwin and
Courthope, 1871–89). Following Bowles, the brief comments and
quotations included in the popular journalism of Lamb (No. 44),
Hazlitt (No. 45), and Leigh Hunt (No. 46), taken together with the
inclusion of four of the lyrics in the anthologies of George Ellis
(1801) and Thomas Campbell (1819, No. 43), helped to make
Marvell's name somewhat familiar to the reading public.[15]

But it was the appearance of a two-part article by an anonymous
writer in 1824–5 (No. 47) that signaled the trend toward poetic
concern. Continuing to stress the 'British Aristides' as the 'great
exemplar of public and private integrity,' the writer none the less
deliberately discounts the prose in order to emphasize the poetry,
selecting thirteen of the poems for quotation and comment;
notably, 'The Character of Holland' is the only satire included.
(Also at this time Hazlitt included eight of the lyrics in his *Select
British Poets*, an anthology transatlantic in its appeal.[16]) As a result,
when John Dove, 'a Whig and a dissenter' (see No. 50), published
the first single life of Marvell in 1832, though 'pillaging' this and
other sources, he included seventeen of the poems as well as extracts
from the prose, while Hartley Coleridge, who unblushingly
plagiarized Dove, included seven in one of the versions of his *Life*
which appeared as an individual biography under the imprint of
two different Hull publishers in 1835. The other version had
appeared in the same year as Dove's as part of the *Worthies of
Yorkshire and Lancashire*; though also indebted to Dove, this
version relied on the letters to a greater degree with a consequent
greater stress on Marvell's patriotic and parliamentary character.
It was to appear under many different titles and imprints until the
posthumous edition, entitled the *Lives of Northern Worthies*,
appeared in 1852, edited by his brother. By means of these biographical accounts, though significantly now dressed with
examples from the poetry, the image of the patriot and wit maintained its attraction; it was, however, increasingly being enhanced
with romantic fictions in tacit acknowledgment either of the
prevailing esthetic or of the declining appeal of a writer seen mainly
as one committed to the political scene (see No. 51b). (In contrast,
Landor's earlier 'imaginary conversations,' 1824–9, involved

Marvell with other public figures: Henry Marten, Parker, and Milton.)

Twelve years after Dove's *Life* appeared, Henry Rogers wrote a long review-article on it (his tardy consideration perhaps having been prompted by a developing interest in Marvell as the champion of John Howe whose works he had edited [see No. 25]); although commenting sharply on Dove's reliance on earlier sources, he ignored Coleridge's more flagrant borrowings (see No. 57). During the same period when Rogers published his influential review—it was to be incorporated, with due acknowledgment, in the first American edition of the poetry in 1854 and the first since Captain Thompson's in 1776—George Craik (see No. 58) also included Marvell in his equally influential *Sketches of the History of Literature and Learning* (1844–5), with quotations from the lyrics (and the post-restoration satires) but none from the prose.

By mid-century, then, the tide of opinion was showing a persistent undertow of poetic concern in both England and America. Indeed the Americans may be said to have responded the more enthusiastically. In 1836 Edgar Allan Poe (No. 54) singled out 'The Nymph' for extensive comment in a review of S. C. Hall's *Books of Gems* (No. 53). In 1848 John Greenleaf Whittier (No. 60), attracted both by the political image and by the poetry, published an essay with excerpts, including the 'splendid Ode to Cromwell' in its entirety since it was 'not generally known.' An advocate of seventeenth-century poetry as early as 1828, Ralph Waldo Emerson (No. 48) not only introduced lines from 'The Mower Against Gardens' into a lecture given before an agricultural society, but also showed his admiration in some of his own lyrics where, in the words of Oliver Wendell Holmes, the influence of Marvell is 'plain to every reader.' And in 1854 James Russell Lowell added a brief but pointed evaluation to Rogers's biographical account in the 'very elegant' American edition which was to have a dozen printings in the United States and England, some editions including Milton's poetry as well.

Random anthologies having made some of the poems well known, these were to be climaxed by the three most popular: Gilfillan's (1860), Palgrave's (1861), and Archbishop Trench's (1868); Trench, in fact, excluded 'Bermudas' from his *Household Book of English Poetry* because it had already found its way into so

11

many modern collections (an exclusion that H. J. Massingham was to follow on the same grounds when compiling his *Treasury of Seventeenth-Century English Verse* in 1919). Somewhat surprisingly, Matthew Arnold was first to encounter the 'Horatian Ode' in Palgrave, but he can be credited at least with having introduced it to Sainte Beuve (see No. 69), who, in turn, introduced it to a French audience. Thus at the end of that anthologizing decade the time was opportune for the appearance of the first judicious survey of the man *and* his work—that of John Ormsby in an unsigned essay in the *Cornhill Magazine* (No. 71).

In the remaining years before 'poetic reassessment,' it was the writers, as opposed to the critics, who kept the poetic Marvell in public view. In 1870 James Russell Lowell incorporated admiring comments on the Cromwell poems in his essay on Dryden (No. 72). In the next year or so, an enormously popular anthology—*A Library of Poetry and Song, Being Choice Selections from the British Poets*—appeared under the name of William Cullen Bryant and included three of the lyrics under appropriate rubrics; though Bryant was not himself responsible for the classification and arrangement, they had all passed his 'cultured criticism,' including, one presumes, the textual alterations. According to the 1874 printing, this anthology proved so popular that a twentieth edition was called for within six months of the first. *Parnassus*, an anthology based on his commonplace book by still another American—Ralph Waldo Emerson, mentioned earlier—appeared in 1875 and included five of the lyrics, again classified under rubrics and again with textual alterations.

A few personal comments by English writers at this time indicate that the poet was being read, if only in the various anthologies. In a letter of 1872, the translator of the *Rubáiyát*, Edward FitzGerald (No. 74) termed him an 'old favourite'; in 1879, in an exchange with R. W. Dixon, Gerard Manley Hopkins, while admitting that he knew Marvell only from extracts, described him as a 'most rich and nervous poet.' In the following year, interestingly, the 'measure and music' of Hopkins's verse were found, according to an unidentified reviewer, to recall that of Marvell's.[17] And, finally, the poet laureate, as Tennyson's son and his close friend F. T. Palgrave record (No. 78), admired the poems, including the one—'To His Coy Mistress'—deliberately excluded from the most popular of all nineteenth-century anthologies, that of Palgrave himself.

12

II POETIC REASSESSMENT 1892–1921

During the opening years of the period of reassessment, there was a surge of conflicting opinions. On the one hand, some few poems—all those 'worth more than a single reading,' as one J. Stuart put it in 1892 (No. 80)—were much admired. On the other, there was a distinct falling off of interest in the prose works, with the *RT* and *Mr. Smirke* being described as 'peculiarly distasteful,' combining the 'characteristics of tedium, dullness, and scurrility to a perfectly phenomenal degree.' (*The Growth of Popery* had long since disappeared from public concern.[18]) Equally, there was a falling off of the image of the incorruptible patriot, with Alice Meynell (No. 84), for one, commenting on the 'portly dulness of the mind' that could term Marvell the 'British Aristides,' a narrow reflection on the efforts of Thomas Cooke whose two printings of the poems and letters had been 'pillaged' by so many others.

A compensation of sorts was the developing realization that as a result of his public commitment there had been 'the loss of a great English poet' (No. 79). Exactly how that lost poet should be categorized remained critically uncertain. Was he classic or romantic, metaphysical or Augustan, Cavalier or Puritan, or—in witness now to the impact of the 'Horatian Ode' rather than to the controversial works—republican or royalist? Almost invariably he was viewed, in the words of a critic of the period (No. 100) as 'dimorphic,' a view which well accords with that of Marvell's contemporaries who, in an appropriation of his own diction, had described his 'wit and polity' as 'unhoopable' (see Nos 5, 20).

The question of his literary status was equally uncertain, one reviewer asserting in 1905 (No. 91a) that he was of scant importance because he had had no influence on his contemporaries and had founded no school of verse, while others only too readily associated him with other 'great' poets, including him, not in the 'narrow sense' but 'in the wider and more usual sense,' among 'some five-and-twenty great English poets' (No. 102).

Despite Marvell's small canon of poems, a persistent recognition of his poetical versatility is to be sensed in the widely divergent remarks of commentators who endeavoured throughout the century to 'place' him. Some critics early on had linked him with his contemporaries—with Donne, Jonson, Lovelace, Suckling,

Cowley, Waller, Herbert, Herrick, and the Milton of the lyrics—
or had endeavoured to pinpoint him as a synthesis of differing
literary strains—a blend of Donne and Milton, of Donne and
Butler, of Jonson and Herrick, of Crashaw and Vaughan. As the
esthetic of the century solidified, others linked him with *their*
contemporaries and near contemporaries, crediting him with
having sounded 'certain notes' (No. 96) not to be heard again until
the days of—Cowper, Crabbe, Clare, Wordsworth, Coleridge,
Keats, Shelley, Meredith, Hopkins, and Hodgson. (Even when the
prose works were still of concern earlier in the century, there had
been a comparable urge to see in the Marvellian style influences
on, as well as anticipations of, Burke, Junius, Swift, Addison, and
Steele.) Such a plethora of literary associations may account for
Stuart's jaundiced comment in 1892 that the poems were often
'monstrously overrated,' the work of a man with 'scarce a spark of
originality.' Yet in that same year, A. C. Benson (No. 79) offered a
diametrically opposite view, declaring that Marvell 'does not seem
to imitate, he does not even follow the lines of other poets'; except
for a scattered instance or two, 'never,' he continues, 'does he
recall or suggest that he has a master.'

As a result of these divergent opinions (indicative as well of an
emerging new literary attitude), some of the poems were devalued,
some maintained their established rank, and some came into new
prominence. The early satires were among those being devalued.
Whereas in 1848 Whittier asserted that there was nothing in its
way superior to 'The Character of Holland' and *c.* 1887 Tennyson
professed to having made Carlyle laugh for half an hour at the
reading of one line, it was considered by 1897 a 'heavy-handed
squib' (No. 83); while acknowledging it as the 'most amusing' of
the satires, Stuart, even earlier, termed both 'Flecknoe' and 'Tom
May's Death' 'unreadable.'

Poems continuing to maintain their popularity were those that
had been anthologized: 'Bermudas,' 'The Garden,' 'The Nymph,'
the 'Horatian Ode,' etc; while those beginning to come into their
own include the dialogues, the Mower poems, and the Cavalier
lyrics like 'The Fair Singer,' 'Music's Empire,' and, especially,
'To His Coy Mistress.' Doubted in 1832 as to whether it was
really by Marvell, excluded by both Palgrave and Trench on
account of its doubtful propriety, 'To His Coy Mistress' had,
however, impressed such critics as Craik and Ormsby as early as

14

1845 and 1869 (and Hazlitt even earlier). It was to come into its own in the decades of reassessment, even though the 'Affable Hawk' Desmond MacCarthy was to point out in 1922 that neither Edmund Gosse nor J. C. Squire, two of the contributors to the *Tercentenary Tributes*, had seen fit to mention Marvell's 'best and most surprising poem.'[19]

None the less a change in sensibilities had gradually been taking place. Well documented by J. E. Duncan in his study of the *Revival of Metaphysical Poetry*, it was ushered in, in part, by the much maligned Grosart (see, for example, Nos 81, 96), who, in Duncan's words, was 'one of the first critics to discover in metaphysical poetry a dynamic process in which thought and feeling were merging into one another.'[20] Equally important, since there must be texts before there can be appreciation, during the 1870s and 1880s Grosart elected to edit not only Marvell but also Donne, Cowley, Herbert, and Crashaw. Other important editions were Sir Herbert Grierson's two-volume Donne in 1912 and his one-volume *Metaphysical Lyrics and Poems* in 1921 wherein he announced that 'at his very best' Marvell was a 'finer poet' than either Donne or Dryden, a far cry from the eighteenth-century notion that Marvell's major literary contribution had been to discover 'the beauties' of Milton.

Despite the evidence provided by the increasing availability of texts, T. S. Eliot is the one most often credited with having ushered in the new appreciation of the poet, purportedly a result, first, of his account of Marvell in the *Times Literary Supplement*, which was to become a selected essay and one he himself elected to print twice, and, second, of his later review of Grierson, which was also to become a selected essay. A look at the critical evidence suggests something else.

With examples of historical criticism such as make up this volume—more revelatory, it seems, of the cultural context than of the writings dealt with—one may well be struck by the repetitive factor or what, in harsher terms, might be called plagiarism. In the case of Marvell this situation obtains on three specific counts.

First, it obtains in respect to the handling of the texts, a matter relating both to their derivation from preceding editions and to editorial preferences, typical phenomena until recent times. One striking example of this persistence of emendation is the reading 'claps' for 'combs' in line 55 of 'The Garden.' Introduced as early as 1716 in Tonson's *Miscellany*, it was to persist even after G. A. Aitken had recourse to the Folio and restored 'combs' in his 1892 edition. For example, Sir Francis Meynell, who edited Marvell in 1918, notes that his mother (No. 84), in preparing her anthology *The Flower of the Mind*, was given the reading 'claps' by F. T. Palgrave, and he comments: 'he would not (and he could not) have invented a phrase, an image, a movement so much more lovely, and lovely with the very gesture of the poet and of his century.' Did he, Sir Francis wonders, perhaps see one of Marvell's manuscripts which was discovered and then lost? (*Henry Vaughan the Silurist and Andrew Marvell*, p. 58)

When undertaking to publish Marvell in 1726, Thomas Cooke showed a certain conscientiousness about the texts, at least to the extent of consulting Marvell's relatives, but he too emended some of the poems in conformity with prevailing taste. Either because of prevailing taste or because of his own indolence or even inadvertence, in preparing his edition Captain Thompson followed his example, so that eighteenth-century emendations, together with those acceptable to various nineteenth-century anthologists, were to have a long perpetration. This might be called the plagiarism of received texts.

Second, the situation obtains in respect to the biography, a more understandable phenomenon in that popular and apocryphal stories tend to cluster around a likely figure in anecdotal, derivative accounts. Moreover, to associate one historical personage with another provides a shorthand of signification that may come to have the weight of tradition. Instances are Cooke's metaphor of Marvell as the 'British Aristides' and Thompson's comparison of him with the unnamed Roman general content with his plate of turnips; first specified by Disraeli as 'Curtius' through either a misprint or a slip, this 'unclassical' comparison was to be frequently invoked. On the other hand, the biographies of Dove and Coleridge, replete with unacknowledged borrowings, invite the charge of plagiarism. Others, like the sketches of Mrs S. C. Hall or the biography of E. P. Hood (1853), represent wayward growths grafted to received accounts.

Third, the situation obtains in reference to critical aperçus, where the repetitive factor may be accounted for on several grounds. As pointed out earlier, the concise statement on Marvell's poetry in Aikin's *General Biography* (1799–1815) was frequently repeated—

for instance, by John Gorton, whose *General Biographical Dictionary* appeared in 1851 and was to be reissued many times—so that the judgment itself passed into general currency. Lamb's 'witty delicacy' is another sort of example, somewhat akin to the historical comparison. Used to describe 'The Garden,' in however brief an account of that poem (No. 44), the phrase was considered so 'classical' by the turn of the century (No. 86) that it became almost mandatory to repeat it, although generally with acknowledgment, at least by quotation marks. Capping the period of poetic reassessment, Eliot provides an interesting example of still another sort, as a brief consideration of his comments on Marvell should demonstrate (No. 103).

An essential aim in his essay is the attempt to define 'wit.' Early on, he offers the well-known asseveration, set forth in conjunction with a mention of the 'Horatian Ode,' that it is 'a tough reasonableness beneath the slight lyric grace.' J. E. Duncan has suggested that his expression may have been inspired by Craik's phrase 'the union of force and grace' (applied to 'To His Coy Mistress,' No. 58). Closer in time, one may note, is A. C. Benson's use of the phrase 'force with grace' to decribe the 'Horatian Ode' (No. 79).

When speaking of 'To His Coy Mistress,' Eliot remarks that 'the poem turns suddenly with that surprise which has been one of the most important means of poetic effect since Homer.' Later on, when speaking of 'Clorinda and Damon,' he again remarks on its element of surprise, adding that Poe considered it to be of the highest importance. Here again one might note Benson's observation that the 'strength of [Marvell's] style lies in its unexpectedness.' Or, equally, one might note Francis L. Bickley's remarks on 'the gift of sudden inevitability,' which, as he points out, represents Arnold's distinction between 'classic' and 'romantic' (No. 96).

Again, in connection with 'To His Coy Mistress,' Eliot comments on the way in which the wit is fused into the imagination and characterizes it now as an 'alliance of levity and seriousness (by which the seriousness is intensified).'[21] Consequently, he observes, in such poetry there is a 'very narrow' difference between imagination and fancy.

The 'equipoise' or 'balance and proportion of tones'—its 'internal equilibrium'—is the result, he concludes, of Marvell's finding the 'proper degree of seriousness for every subject he treats,' never 'taking a subject too seriously or lightly.' It is this quality that makes him a 'classic.' These comments, which have been frequently parroted, may be compared with those made, in briefer compass, as early as 1854:

... whenever [Marvell] surrendered himself to his temperament, his mind sought relief in wit, so sportful and airy, yet at the same time so recondite, that it is hard to find an instance in which the court, the tavern, and the scholar's study are blended with such Corinthian justness of measure. Nowhere is there so happy an example of the truth that wit and fancy are different operations of the same principle. The wit is so spontaneous and so interfused with feeling that we can scarce distinguish it from fancy; and the fancy brings together analogies so remote that they give us the pleasurable shock of wit.

The mind of the poet, James Russell Lowell concludes, presents the 'rare combination of wit with the moral sense' (No. 64).

One can see in this constellation of critical aperçus a basis for Eliot's element of surprise, for the 'alliance of levity and seriousness,' for the 'very narrow' distinction between imagination and 'witty' fancy, for the 'equipoise' or 'balance and proportion of tones,' and for the fusion of thought and feeling which was to make its appearance in the essay on the metaphysicals.

Whether Eliot was (or was not) acquainted with any or all of these critical judgments is not, in my estimation, the significant point.[22] What is significant is the fact that his criticism of Marvell and the metaphysical poets is not so much an innovation as it is a bringing together of opinions that had long been current. One might call this the plagiarism of received ideas.[23] It is this fact, I think, rather than the originality or novelty of his views, that accounts for his influence on subsequent Marvell criticism. As selections in this volume attest, changes in sensibility are inevitably gradual and cumulative. Like Ormsby's for his era, it was Eliot's achievement to enunciate what had oft been thought and to do so at an opportune time.[24]

Such instances of similar evaluations—and others could be adduced—indicate that in spite of individual aberration, a consensus of critical response was developing. It was left to the period after Marvell had come into his own as a lyric and, above all, a 'philosophic' poet to fragment that response by increasingly idiosyncratic interpretations.

III 1921–76

In the decade of Eliot's two influential pieces, there were also two influential textual and biographical publications. First, H. M. Margoliouth's well-annotated edition of Marvell's *Poems*, including the post-Restoration satires variously attributed to him, and the *Letters* (Oxford, 1927). In terms of the canon, this edition follows directly in the Cooke-Thompson (but not the American Lowell's) tradition. In terms of the text, Margoliouth offered a new approach by abstaining from preferential readings and relying on the Folio (apart from the missing conclusion to 'A Poem Upon the Death of O. C.,' where, necessarily at that date, he relied on Thompson). In the slightly revised edition of 1952, he took note of the recovered Popple manuscript (*Eng. poet. d.* 49) used by Thompson and recently acquired by the Bodleian. Not until the third edition, revised by Pierre Legouis with the collaboration of E. E. Duncan-Jones in 1971, were the readings of that manuscript even to be recorded. Second, there was Legouis's biographical and critical study, *André Marvell: poète, puritain, patriote* (Paris–London, 1928), an exhaustive treatment of the man and the writer and an invaluable source for its references to Marvell's later reputation.[25] The shortened corrected English version, prepared by Legouis in 1965 (Oxford), reprinted in 1968, remains the standard biography.

A somewhat later 'recovery' of the post-Restoration satires is indicated by their being included in the *Poems on Affairs of State*, under the editorship of George deF. Lord (New Haven, 1963). Such inclusion can perhaps be seen as an ironic 'reversal' of nineteenth-century attitudes in that the editor may now have been prompted to attribute satires to Marvell on the grounds of his ascendant fame as lyric poet. A particularly valuable recovery of the prose was the 1971 Oxford edition of the *RT*, edited in accord with modern standards and annotated with skill.

From the 1930s on, critical fragmentation developed, the result, in part, of an acceptance of the variety of kinds—pastoral, country-house poem, panegyric, etc.—exemplified in the small canon. Further, it came to seem as if in certain poetic instances Marvell deliberately had decided to 'summarize and surpass' the achievements of his predecessors.[26] Concomitant methodologies supported these realizations. Along with what Eliot dubbed the 'lemon-squeezer' type of criticism, *explication de texte* became an operational procedure, with consequent concern for the paradoxes, ironies, and complexities of his poetic style—the result, it was discovered not only of his confounding verbal and grammatical usage but also of his commingling seemingly opposed attitudes. An allied approach had been tirelessly ushered in in 1930 by William Empson with his *Seven Types of Ambiguity* (though in the revised edition of 1947, he was to reduce his analysis of Marvell's use of the conceit with 'the beginnings of its decay' in 'Upon the Death of Lord Hastings' and its 'blurring' in 'Eyes and Tears').

Historical critics, in turn, sorted themselves into compartments, signaled by their multiple points of departure, with the result that some of them frequently seemed to go beyond an approach that on its own terms stresses literary contexts within the social and political confines of a particular era. First of all, there were those who endeavoured to place Marvell within a particular literary tradition, the rhetorical, for example, where he was considered as having employed common Renaissance techniques—rather than sounding certain notes not to be heard again until the nineteenth century. Or he was placed, stylistically, with the 'sounders' of the metaphysical or the Cavalier or the baroque mode.

There were also the 'source hunters and echo hearers,' as John Carey has neatly labeled them, a very large and disparate group of commentators. They break down into those tending to a 'history of ideas' approach, tracing certain concepts back to a welter of would-be philosophic sources—hermetic, neo-Platonic and neo-Plotinian—and those finding precedents and analogues in classical, medieval, and Renaissance literature. As with H. M. Margoliouth earlier (see No. 99), J. B. Leishman in his posthumous *Art of Marvell's Poetry* (1966) was to point up one of the most tantalizing aspects of Marvell's technique with the suggestion that in some instances he may have been undertaking a witty response to a particular poem. All too obviously, it appeared, Marvell had appropriated phrases from his contemporaries to incorporate or adapt, a procedure raising questions as to whether a borrowing represented common idiom or subtle twist, an unconscious or a conscious echo recollected in tranquillity. If the latter, how its function as an internal comment can be demonstrated has yet to be made clear.[27] Other historical critics addressed themselves to the religious and political scene, coming up with a Puritan or a

Cromwellian poet (despite Marvell's own minimizing of his role in *RT II*, p. 203), and in the process perhaps scanting the complexities of a prose writer who could be seen by others as a 'trimmer,' 'non-conformist,' or a 'semi-Arminian.'

A final group employing something of a historical approach were the allegorists. Legion in number, as unresponsive to tonal nuances as to literal statement, they saw a Marvell far removed from Eliot's witty and urbane poet working within the tradition of Latin culture. Instead they viewed him as one so wounded by the fall that he was compelled to reflect on the post-lapsarian state of the world in the slightest of his lyrics as well as the longest of his poems. For these commentators, Marvell (so Thomas Fuller might have put it) had evidently drunk more of the waters of Jordan than of Helicon.

As a result of these related and disparate approaches, the last fifty-odd years reveal no critical consensus, despite the varying depths and eddies that have been probed. What has been revealed is a prime concern for the poetry and, to a happier degree than in the later nineteenth century, some concern for the prose. Validation of some or all of the approaches adopted awaits the appearance of a synthesizing critic who, speaking at a time opportune for the last quarter of the twentieth century, may perhaps hoop together that dimorphic figure, the poet and the polemicist in prose.

NOTES

1 In 1753 by Edmund Carter (*History of the University of Cambridge*), p. 323; in 1901 by H. C. Beeching (see No. 86). Quotations in the Introduction have been modernized.

2 Though undoubtedly the post-Restoration verse satires variously attributed to Marvell had a share in the later dissemination of this image, it is impossible to document his authorship, since the attributions date anywhere from eleven to nearly a hundred years after his death. As a consequence, commentary on them has generally been discounted in the pages that follow except for 'The Last Instructions to a Painter,' 'The Loyal Scot,' and the epigrams on Blood's stealing the crown (in Latin and English) which offer some evidence for his authorship.

3 Whatever the private applause, two instances of publishers' shifting of early examples of Marvell's occasional verse ('To His Noble

Friend Mr Richard Lovelace' and 'Upon the Death of Lord Hastings') afford evidence that in 1649–50 his name had a certain poetic
cachet, at least in Cavalier circles. In the one case, his contribution
was shifted from a position near the middle of the volume to pride
of place at the beginning in some copies; in the other, to a position
nearer the beginning in the second issue.

4 In the introduction to his useful collection of critical appraisals
(Penguin Critical Anthologies, Harmondsworth, 1969), John Carey
compares the neglect of Marvell's poetry with the neglect of
Vermeer's painting, accounting for both on what he terms 'literary'
and 'painterly' terms. Despite a certain validity, this explanation
discounts the lack of publication in Marvell's lifetime. Before there
can be readers, there must be texts. How much historical acclaim did
a superlative lyricist like Thomas Campion receive before the first
edition of his works in 1889?

Further, it discounts the slight value assigned to lyrical poetry and
to its critical evaluation in earlier periods. In 1912, for example, the
American Edward B. Reed could announce that his was the first
history of English lyric poetry (No. 95). The new critical attitudes
developing in the course of the nineteenth century led to new
methodologies which culminated in those of the New Critics; the
emphasis on poems as artifacts introduced a difference, if not in
principle, in critical practice.

5 In 1880, Goldwin Smith was struck by the 'depth of poetic feeling'
in 'The Garden' that is wonderful to find 'in a political gladiator'
(*The English Poets*, ed. T. H. Ward, 1908 edn, II, p. 382). Even in his
own time he was called a 'gladiator' and a 'fencer' (see No. 22).

6 Richard Leigh (No. 1) calls him a coffee-house virtuoso (pp. 34ff.);
Bishop Parker (No. 2) describes his loitering about Lincoln's Inn
Fields and Charing Cross. For the daily enactment of 'farces and
drolls' on political topics, see *Calendar of State Papers, Domestic,
1672–3*, p. 148.

7 Two anonymous pamphlets (*A Letter from a Parliament-Man to His
Friend* and *A Letter from a Person of Quality to His Friend in the Country*,
both 1675), taken as indicative of the compatibility of Marvell's
political ideas with those of the Earl of Shaftesbury, were on occasion attributed to him by contemporaries (see No. 17). Two others
(*A Seasonable Argument*, 1677 [see Nos 17, 75] and *Flagellum Parlia-
mentarium*, not printed until 1827) have also on occasion been attributed to him, the latter eliciting a long article by F. G. Walters, who
purported to find evidence of the 'same fine Roman hand' in both
(*Gentleman's Magazine*, 289 [1900], pp. 57–66).

8 The most often repeated is the account of his refusal of a bribe from

22

Lord Danby, an account that becomes successively particularized, beginning with the poet's need to borrow a guinea (1726) to his dining on a shoulder of mutton, with his servant boy Jack (in 1859 he was to be renamed 'Buttons'), later putting the bone to broil (1754). Others relate to the merry monarch's delight in his company, the secret visits of Prince Rupert, and, among the elaborations of the nineteenth century, his seduction by court beauties, surveillance by spies, and waylaying by ruffians. A contrary, if equally romantic, fiction is set forth by Mark Noble in 1806 when he asserts that Marvell had no enemies, that the court which he opposed loved the man, and that all parties reverenced him (*Biographical Dictionary*, II, p. 225).

9 Francis Blackburn and others, *Memoirs of Thomas Hollis*, 1780, pp. 97, 361–3.

10 Perhaps in a kind of tribute to the 'garden poetry,' the Rev. Robert Banks of Hull described Marvell in 1708 as 'poet and botanist' as well as 'sometime burgess in Parliament' (*Letters of Eminent Men Addressed to Ralph Thoresby*, 1832, II, p. 102).

11 Two such long-lived emendations begin as early as 1716 with Tonson's inclusion of nine of the lyrics in his *Miscellany*; these alterations were silently adopted by Cooke, then by Thompson, and subsequently by numerous others.

12 Henry Headley, *Select Beauties of Ancient English Poetry*, 1787, I, pp. xxx–xxxi.

13 *An Historical Account of the Lives and Writings of Our Most Considerable English Poets*, II, p. 98. For an account of Milton's early literary status, see *Milton's Contemporary Reputation* (Columbus, Ohio, 1940) by W. R. Parker. Supportive of the scant attention historically accorded to lyric poetry is Parker's conclusion that, apart from the (three) printed tributes in the 1645 *Poems*, 'no printed or manuscript allusions' to the minor English poems seem to exist (p. 24).

14 *Original Letters*, 1721 (2 vols in one), p. 75.

15 Ellis included 'Daphnis and Chloe' and 'Young Love' (both in part) in the second edition of his *Specimens of the Early English Poets*, while Campbell included 'Bermudas' (entitled 'Emigrants') and 'The Nymph' in part, 'Young Love' in its entirety.

16 Oliver Wendell Holmes recalls the time, *c.* 1826 or 1827, when Emerson's younger brother came into his study, picked up his copy of Hazlitt's *British Poets*, and turning at once to a poem of Marvell's read it aloud (*Ralph Waldo Emerson*, American Men of Letters series, ed. Charles Dudley Warner, Boston, 1885, p. 21).

17 *Correspondence of Gerard Manley Hopkins and Richard Watson Dixon*, ed. C. C. Abbott, 1955, p. 23. *St James's Gazette*, 8 September 1880.

18 An anonymous article on the prose (No. 87) and a pedestrian one by W. D. Taylor (*Queen's Quarterly*, 22 [October–December 1914], Kingston, Ont., pp. 113–25) are instances of rare concern for the prose in the period of reassessment.

19 *New Statesman*, 2 April 1921, p. 757. This may be contrasted with the amusing situation in 1890 when (like Prufrock) Robert Louis Stevenson recalls lines 41–2 (in order to make a critical point on Kipling's copiousness and haste) in somewhat imperfect fashion: 'He should shield his fire with both hands "and draw up all his strength and sweetness in one ball" ("Draw all his strength and all His sweetness up into one ball"? I cannot remember Marvell's words' (*Letters*, ed. Sidney Colvin, 1911, III, p. 270).

20 First published 1959, repr. New York, 1969. See ch. V, 'The Metaphysical Revival: 1872–1912.'

21 Cf. Ormsby's observation in 1869, also in relation to 'To His Coy Mistress,' on Marvell's 'trick—if anything so obviously natural and spontaneous can be called a trick—of passing suddenly from a light, bantering, trivial tone, to one of deep feeling, and even … of solemnity' (No. 71). Or H. J. Massingham's citing the 'imaginative gravity' to be found in 'To His Coy Mistress' in an essay that appeared two days after Eliot's (No. 100).

22 Presumptive evidence for his knowing the critical remarks in an edition that was printed a dozen times in the United States and England might be its printing of line 769 of 'Appleton House' as 'And now the salmon-fishers moist' which is what Eliot prints, whereas the Folio reads 'But.' This reading, however, is also to be found earlier in Thompson's edition (on which Lowell's is based) and later in Aitken's (1892).

23 In the introduction to a collection of 'Modern Judgements' on Marvell, Michael Wilding, like J. E. Duncan before him, acknowledges that the metaphysicals were not 'rediscovered' by Eliot (interestingly, Eliot does not use the term 'metaphysicals' until his review of Grierson), but he comments that the earlier elements found in his criticism had been 'less emphasized in their original contexts' (1969, p. 36). This protective attitude—if that is what it is—can be compared with that of Henry Rogers's ignoring of Hartley Coleridge's reliance on Dove in the many issues of his versions of the *Life* while chastizing Dove for his reliance on earlier authors in the single printing of his biography.

24 His critical influence was abetted of course by his later reputation as a poet, but, as the heavy body of subsequent criticism of Marvell's poetry shows, the time *was* opportune; despite Eliot's later revisionist tendency, criticism continued unabated. For his altered view of

Marvell's poetry, see No. 103 Note.

25 In addition to the later surveys of Carey and Wilding already mentioned, there is a 1975 bibliography of 'Recent Studies in Marvell' by Gillian Szanto in *English Literary Renaissance* V. 2, pp. 273–86.

26 Joseph H. Summers, Introduction to *Marvell* in the Laurel series (New York, 1961), p. 13.

27 The question of borrowings in Renaissance literature poses many problems. For the sixteenth century, source hunters, particularly in the 1930s and 1940s, tended to assume that the lesser borrowed from the greater. As Shakespeare's borrowings from minor writers indicate, this is not self-evident. Uninformed as we are as to the impact of publication on the immediate literary scene, it is impossible to know whether an appropriation served to indicate a knowing reference to a current literary piece, a reflection of *imitatio* directed to a purposed end, an overt tribute to a contemporary—rival or friend—or, simply, a bold filching.

With Marvell, the case seems even more complex since it would appear that he wrote for his own gratification, 'drinking liberally by himself to refresh his spirits and exalt his muse.' To utilize a 'conscious' borrowing for an audience of one would seem an example of super-subtlety (but not impossible for an 'unhoopable' figure).

POLEMICIST IN PROSE: CONTEMPORARY AND LATER COMMENTS

1673–1894

A *With Samuel Parker*

Samuel Parker, later Bishop of Oxford (see No. 2), had been born and bred a Puritan, and Marvell was first to encounter him *c*. 1662 at the home of their common acquaintance John Milton. Having taken orders in the Anglican church in 1664, he then became a high-churchman and vigorous opponent of the nonconformists. It was following on his publication of three works—*A Discourse of Ecclesiastical Polity* (1670, which was answered by the dissenting minister John Owen); *A Defense and Continuation of the Ecclesiastical Politie* (1671, attacking Owen); and the 'Preface' to Bishop Bramhall's *Vindication of Himself* (1672)—that Marvell, although a layman, chose to enter the controversy with his two-part *Rehearsal Transpros'd*, deriving his title and the nomination of 'Mr Bayes' (originally for Dryden among others) from the Duke of Buckingham's farce *The Rehearsal* (performed 1671).

The unlicensed first part, published anonymously in the autumn of 1672 with a mock imprint, elicited a half-dozen replies, all of which Marvell alludes to in the second part (pp. 174–6). Despite its anonymity, the identity of the author was clearly recognized, as the punning allusions in the replies to it attest. Part Two, published over Marvell's name in 1673, effectively silenced Parker.

1.   Richard Leigh on the
Rehearsal Transpros'd

1673

Richard Leigh (1649–1728?) is identified as a sometime commoner of Queen's at Oxford and afterwards a player at one of the theatres in London. His lively counter-attack, very much in the manner of his opponent, is entitled *The Transproser Rehears'd: or the Fifth Act of Mr. Bayes's Play.* It was published anonymously at Oxford, 1673.

Extracts from pp. 2–10, 29–33, 40–3, 55, 132–4.

I say, this great Author (of *Playbills*) having in conformity to his promising Title *Transp[r]osed the Rehearsal*, or at least all of Mr. *Bayes* his Play extant, *four Acts.* I thought it was great pitty so facetious and Comical a work should remain incompleat, and therefore I have continued it on, and added the *Fifth*, the Argument of which, and its dependance on the other *Four*, I shall give you an account of after a preliminary examination of the Characters and Plot in our Authors *Transp[r]os'd Rehearsal.*

But before I proceed to either of these, it will not be unnecessary to consider on what bottom he has erected his Animadversions, and this I find to be no other then the Preface to Bishop *Bramhalls* Vindication, which is as much as to say, here is a House wrought out of a Portal. 'Tis pretty I confess, and exceeds the power of common Architects. But what follows is more strange, that 100. pages (the Preface is no more by his computation) should be foundation sufficient enough to support his mighty *Paper-building* of 326.

Now 'tis very probable, that which gave the principal hint to our Authors *Rehearsal Transpros'd*, was the near accord he observes betwixt the Preface [of Parker] and Mr. *Bayes* his Prologue, *P.* 14. [*I*, p. 9] and here, I cannot but applaud his admirable dexterity that could extract four Acts of a *Farce*, from a single Prologue, but such is the singular felicity of some Animadverters, (and of ours amongst the rest) in their illustrating of Authors, that they have heighten'd and refin'd some of their Notions, not only above all others, but above even the intentions of the dull Authors themselves; A rare Art! and followed so well by some of our Translators of *French* Farce, that some of them have been luckily mistaken for Authors. For instance, the Writer of the Preface had said, *He could not tell which way his Mind would work it self and its thoughts* [*I*, p. 7, from Parker's *Preface* A2^v]; now this our *Improver of Verity* [*I*, p. 13], according to his peculiar excellence, *P.* 12. [*I*, p. 7] resolves into Prince *Volscius*[1] his Debate betwixt Love and Honour, and tells you more of the Authors mind in Verse, than he could do himself in Prose. And this feat is perform'd by no other Magick then *Regula Duplex*, turning Prose into Verse, and Verse into Prose *alternativè*. See what Miracles men of Art can do by *Transversing Prefaces*, and Transprosing Playes.

But to go on with our *Prologue*, (so the Animadverter will warrant me now to call the *Preface*) our Critick hath found a flaw in it, and what's that? It has no *Plot*. How, a *Prologue* without a *Plot*! It is impossible, tis a cross-graind objection this, and not easily evaded, had not our Critick plaid Mock-Apologist and answered himself, *P.* 11. [*I*, p. 7] *the Intrigue was out of his head*,[2] which is very civil I gad.

Another weighty exception against our *Prologue* is, that it is written in a Stile, *part Play-Book, and part Romance, p.* 22. [*I*, p. 12]. (Which of these two is Gazett, for that the Animadverter says, is our Authors Magazine [*I*, p. 11]); this is more unpardonable than the former; for what can be a higher *Indecorum* than a *Prologue* written in *Play-Book* stile. But that we may the better understand the pertinency of this Remarque, we must desire the Reader to observe, That the Writer of the Preface had said, *That the Church of* Ireland *was the largest Scene of the Bishops Actions* [*I*, p. 12, from Parker's *Preface* A3^v]. Now it will go very hard, but this Passage will be condemn'd for one guilty word or two; for Histories are *Playes* without *Scenes*, and without *Action*; and these two words being neither of the *Historians* Profession, nor *Divines*: the Bishops Historian must of necessity be cast, unlesse he have any hopes of benefit of Clergy; however we hope before Sentence be

[1] Character in *The Rehearsal* (1672), III. ii.
[2] Derives from *The Rehearsal*, I. i.

past, the Animadverter will inform us, what words are of the Clergy, and what of the Layity, which in Holy Orders and which not; and then their several Divisions, which *Catholick*, and which *Schismatical*; and amongst them, which *Classical, Congregational,* and of inferiour *Sects*; whether for *Church of Ireland* he would read *Congregation*, for *Scene, Diocess* or *Pulpit*, and for *Actions, Spiritual Excercises* or *Labours*.

But if at last the Animadverter intend, by *Play-Book-Stile*, whatever is written above the common elevation, unlesse he would have the Priest and the Poet write in two distinct Languages; I see no reason to allow him, that the Priest should make use of a less refin'd and polisht Stile than the Poet. If after all this, any one should be so impenitently inquisitive, as to demand a reason why our *Prologue Critick* would have a *Prologue* with a *Plot*, and not written in *Play-Book-Stile*, he will answer him, no doubt, because 'tis *New*.

From the Prologue, pass we to the *Rehearsal Transpros'd*, in which the Characters, the Action, and the Humour offer themselves to our consideration. The principal person concerned in this Farce is Mr. *Bays*, whom our *Transproser* makes to be of the same Character with the Writer of the Preface; for which he alledges these following reasons, *pag.* 15, 16 [*I*, pp. 9–10] ....

Now though the foregoing Paralell betwixt *Ecclesiastical Mr. Bays*, & *Mr. Bays* in the *Rehearsal* be so exact, that it were hard to distinguish betwixt *Mr. Bays*, and *Mr. Bayes*, had not one writ a Preface, and the other a Play; Yet because in the nearest resemblances of Twins, 'tis not impossible to trace some marks of distinction and *House-wives* there have been upon Record, so expert, as to discern a difference even in Eggs, so as they never mistook one for another; we shall endeavour to shew, that these two are not so alike, but that they are as unlike too; nay most unlike in their nearest resemblances.

First, Then our *Trans-proser* craves leave to call the Writer of the Preface *Mr. Bays*, because *he hath no name, or at least, will not own it*; from whence, we may infer, That every *Anonymus* Author may be as well call'd Mr. *Bays*, as this Writer. And what may we then think of the Gentleman himself, who would be Gossip to all the nameless Off-springs of the Press, and yet has not fathered his own Bastard; but let him learn to Christen his own Brat first, before he gives Nick-names to others; for who can endure that he should undertake, as Godfather, for anothers child, that leaves his own to the Parish; Had not his brain been delivered of this *By-blow*, without the Mid-wifery of an *Imprimatur*; the *Printer* and the *Stationer* at least, would have appear'd as *Sureties* for the Childs behaviour, and the Issue might have been judg'd legitimate, though the Father were not publickly known.[1] But now that the Infant has crept into the World without a lawfull Father, without Gossips, nay, without a name (or what is all one, without a name of its own) we cannot but expostulate with Fate; as Prince *Pretty-man*[2] much upon the like occasion.

> *Was ever Child yet brought to such distress!*
> *To be, for being a Child, made Fatherless.*

Though every Nurse can readily point to *Daddy's* Eyes and Mouth, in the little Babies face, as if the dapper Stripling were to be heir to all the Fathers features; and a Dimple, or a Mole, if hereditary, were better Titles to an In-Heritance, than Deeds and Evidences. Yet none certainly was ever born with fairer Marks than this. For it is stigmatiz'd in the Fore-head, and bears in the Front the legible Characters of a *well-meaning Zealot*.

And thus much in consideration of the first Reason, that induc'd the Animadverter to call the writer of the Preface *Mr. Bayes*, because he hath no name: for which reason he might as well have cal'd him *Bayes Anonymus* in imitation of *Miltons* learned Bull (for that Bulls in *Latin* are *learned* ones, none will deny) who in his Answer to *Salmasius*, calls him *Claudius Anonymus*.

The second Reason is, Because he would avoid *Tautologies* and distastefull *Repetitions of one word*; and to avoid this, he has taken a sure course; for since his own Invention could not supply him with variety of names, he has run over the *Dramatis Personae* of the *Rehearsal*; and because Mr. *Bays* alone was not sufficient for his purpose, he has made bold with Mr. *Thunderer*, *Draw-can-sir* and *Prince Volscius*. These Titles he has confer'd on our Author in consideration of his Dignity, as he is a Clergy-man of *Honour*.

If Mr. *Bayes* (as you tell us, *pag.* 17. [*I*, p. 10]) was more *civil* then to say *Villain*, he might have taught his actors better manners. All these, (besides the two last verses of the event of the Battle)

[1] Copies of the second issue of *RT I* omitted the burlesque imprint, simply giving date and place of publication.
[2] Character in *The Rehearsal*.

you have diligently Collected, and for the most part faithfully
transcribed, unless in these last recited, where for *Gonsalvo* in the
Rehearsal, you have put in *Valerio*,[1] and by the alteration of that
one word, have made it your own, just so Mr. *Bayes* us'd to do
with many a good notion in *Montaign* and *Seneca's* Tragedies: yet
though your Title promise us so fairly, you have not *Transpros'd*
three whole Verses in all your Book. But be it the *Rehearsal Transpros'd*, or *transcrib'd*, or if you will, *Reprinted*, for your Pamphlet
is little else but a *second Edition* of that *Play*, and Mr. *Hales* his
Tract of *Schism*:[2] though methinks you might have so much
studied the Readers diversion, and your own, as to have exercised
your happy talent of *Rhyming*, in *Transversing* the Treatise of
Schism, and for the Titles *dear sake* you might have made all the
Verses rung *Ism* in their several changes. I dare assure you Sir, the
work would have been more gratefully accepted than *Donns Poems*
turn'd into *Dutch*, but what talk I of that, then *Prynnes Mount
Orguil*,[3] or *Milton's Paradise lost* in blank Verse. But as it is, you
give as quotations of whole Books, like him who wrote *Zabarella*
quite out from the beginning to the end, professing it was so
good he could leave none behind[4] (how like is this to our Transcri-
ber, *yet whatsoever I omit, I shall have left behind more material passages*,
before his Edition of *Hales*, p. 176 [*I*, p. 79]). It is no absurdity now
to say, your Text is all Margent, and not only all your Dishes, but
your Garnish too is *Pork*.[5] And thus much for your *Regula Duplex*,
changing Prose into Verse, and Verse into Prose, that's your first
Rule. Your second Rule, is the rule of Observation or Record, by
way of Tablebook. . . .

This is his Diary, in which our small Historian registers the
proceedings of every Suburb Tumult; in this he summs up all the
Billinsgate Debates and Conferences. 'Tis his scolding Common-
place-book, which acquaints him with all the Moods and Figures
of Railing; here he has all the terms of that Art which *Smectimnuus*,

---

[1] From the original version of Sir William D'Avenant's *The Seige of Rhodes* (1656), the first
attempt at English opera.
[2] Published 1642.
[3] A verse description of his imprisonment for theological controversy at Mt Orgueil Castle
in Jersey.
[4] Francesco Zabarelli (1533–89) of Padua wrote a commentary on Aristotle; like Duns
Scotus, his name became generic for one providing useless knowledge.
[5] *I*, p. 142; deriving from Livy (trans. P. Holland, 1600, p. 916), the story is explained in
RT II (pp. 307–8).

Marchamont Needham,[1] *J. Milton,* or any other of the Professors ever thought of, for there is a certain form & Method in this as well as all other Arts; but yet, our Author being a well-wisher to the Railers, to encourage those that have any inclination this way, to improve that faculty, assures them. *Pag.* 261. [*I*, p. 117] *That the secret is not great, nor the Process long or difficult, if a man would study it* (and though in other things your knowledge may be above his, you may believe him in this, he hath made it his business). *Every Scold hath it naturally. It is but crying Whore first, and having the last word.* Next he instructs his Pupil in the several kinds of Railing; for besides the Common scurrilous way of calling men *Buffoons,* Brokers, &c. *p.* 2 [07]. [*I*, p. 93] *pag.* 106. [*I*, p. 49] in which he is so expert, that I am confident, that Fellow in *Plutarch,* that busied himself to find out how many several ways the Letters in the Alphabet might be rang'd, tranpos'd & alter'd,[2] could not invent more changes of the Letters, than he has in instructing them to scold; There is yet another by which dumb men may be taught to rail, that is by Signs, (for there is a Language of the Hand and Head.) This is *pag.* 160. Where he tells us of an *incorrigible Scold, that though she was duck'd over head and ears under water, yet stretch'd up her hands, with her two thumb-nails in the Nit-cracking posture, or with two fingers divaricated, to call the man still in that language, Lowsy Rascal, and Cuckold.*[3] It is a pretty Tale, I confess, but so miserably foisted in, that whoever will consult the fore-cited *Page,* cannot but allow with me, that our Disputant is better capacitated to maintain an *Argument* (in his own Phrase) with a rude bustling Carman, or a Porter in the street, then with an *Ecclesiastical Politician.*

Thus having rais'd and rang'd in order his Martial *Phantomes,* he sets them a fighting through all the Tropes and Figures of Rhetorick. He knew this way of resolving controversie into *Ecclesiastical Combat,* and deeds of Chivalry, would delight, amuse, and all that: Besides he had a politick fetch or two in it, for these Warlike *Notions,* and arm'd *Ideas* being terrible to him,

---

[1] Smectymnuus was the title of a cabal of Presbyterians, twice defended by Milton. A Cromwellian journalist, Nedham (see No. 18) was called by his contemporaries 'three-piled apostate.'

[2] Xenocrates, cited in 'Symposiaques,' Bk VIII, Ninth Question of the *Moralia,* trans. P. Holland, p. 782.

[3] *I*, pp. 72–3; derived from Montaigne's *Essays,* II, 32.

he conceived they would be no less to others, and that no ans-
werer would have the courage to engage such a *Rhetorical Souldier*,
unless he were able to give him battell in all the Metaphors of War.
But alas, it is not every Fight in Puppet-Shows strikes a terrour in
the beholders, nor are Armies figured, in the imagination, so
dreadfull.

And though I will not deny, that these hostile *Shapes* and
Military *Figures*, which our Romancer had quarter'd in the three
Ventricles of his Capacious Brain (his *Memory, Fancy* and *Judgement* being transform'd into Fortification and Garrison) might
raise such tumults in his Sconce, & so far invade his civil Peace,
as to make the Gentleman startle at his own dreams: yet to those
who consider that these are but the fumes of Melancholy, such
Visionary Battalia's are no more frightful than those fighting
Apparitions; which Exhalations raise in the Clouds. But to indulge our Author in the love of his *Chimerical* conceits, struck
blind with his own daz'ling *Idea* of the *Sun*, and admiring those
imaginary Heights which his fancy has rais'd Since even timerous
Minds are Couragious and bold enough to shape prodigious
Forms and Images of Battels; & dark Souls may be illuminated
with *bright* and shining thoughts. As, to seek no farther for an
instance; the *blind* Author of *Paradise lost* (the odds betwixt a
Transproser and a *Blank Verse Poet*, is not great) begins his third
Book thus, groping for a beam of *Light*.

> Hail, holy Light, Off-Spring of Heav'n
> first born,
> Or of th' Eternal Coeternal beam.

And a little after,

[Quotes ll.21-6.]

No doubt but the thoughts of this *Vital Lamp* lighted a *Christ-
mas* Candle in his brain. What dark meaning he may have in
calling this *thick drop Serene*, I am not able to say; but for his
Eternal Coeternal, besides the absurdity of his inventive Divinity,
in making *Light* contemporary with it's Creator, that jingling in
the middle of his Verse, is more notoriously ridiculous, because
the *blind Bard* (as he tell[s] us himself in his Apology for writing
in blank Verse) studiously declin'd Rhyme as a *jingling sound of
like endings*. Nay, what is more observable, it is the very same fault,

THE CRITICAL HERITAGE

which he was so quick-sighted, as to discover in this Verse of
Halls Toothless Satyrs.

> *To teach each hollow Grove, and shrubby-Hill.*
> [*His Defiance to Envy*, l. 81]

This, *teach each*, he has upbraided the Bishop with in his *Apology*
for his *Animadversions on the Remonstrants Defence against Smectymnuus.*[1]

You see Sir, that I am improved too with reading the Poets,
and though you may be better read in Bishop *Dav'nants
Gondibert*;[2] yet I think this *Schismatick* in *Poetry*, though *non-
conformable* in point of Rhyme, as authentick ev'ry jot, as any
Bishop Laureat of them all.

Every Age is not constellated for Heroes; such Prodigies are
as rarely seen as a *New-star*, or a *Phoenix*. Once, perhaps in a
Century of years, there may arise a *Martin-Mar-Prelate*, a *Milton*,
or such a *Brave* as our present Author. Every day produces not
such Wonders.

But enough of these two loathsome Beasts [Milton, Marvell],
and their spitting and spauling. Now what think you of washing
your mouth with a *Proverb* or two. For I cannot but remark this
admirable way he has of Embellishing his Writings [with]
Proverbial-Wit. As for instance. *One night has made some men Gray*,
pag. 144. [*I*, p. 65] and *better come at beginning of a Feast, then latter
end of a Fray*: pag. 166. [*I*, p. 75] Which (to express them Proverbi-
ally) are all out as much to the purpose as any of *Sancho Pancha's* Proverbs. For the truth of this Comparison, I shall only appeal to
the *Leaf-turners* of *Don Quixot*. Some there are below the Quality
of the *Squires* Wit, and would better have become the Mouth of
his Lady *Joan*, or any old *Gammer* that drops Sentences and Teeth
together, As (speaking of his own Tale of the-*Lake Perillous*,)
he saith in its Applause, this Story *would have been Nuts to Mother
Midnight*, pag. 56. [*I*, p. 27] and *pag.* 142. [*I*, p. 65] *A year, nay an*

---

[1] The remarks appear in the second of Milton's defenses, *An Apology for Smectymnuus*
(1642), Sect. X. *The Animadversions*, published a year earlier, include his well-known
comment on the impropriety of 'Toothless Satyres.'
[2] A moderate Calvinist, John Davenant (1576–1641) was Bishop of Salisbury; Sir William
D' Avenant (1605–68), was the author of the romantic epic *Gondibert*.

instant at any time of a mans Life may make him Wiser. And his Adversary hath, *like all other fruits his annual Maturity.* Though there is one sort of *Fruit trees* above all the rest, that beats with its *fruit,* a signal Hieroglyphick of our Author; and that's a *Medlar*: A *Fruit* more remarkable for its *annual maturity,* because the same also is an *annual rottenness.*

As for his wonderful Gift in Rhyming, I could furnish him with many more of the *Isms* and *Nesses* [*I*, pp. 83, 86], but that I should distast a *Blank Verse* Friend of his, who can by no means endure a Rhyme any where but in the middle of a Verse, therein following the laudable custom of the *Welsh Poets.* And therefore I shall only point at some of the *Nesses,* the more eminent, because of the peoples Coinage; and of a Stamp as unquestionable as the *Breeches,* and so far more legitimate then any that have past for currant since the People left off to mind words (another Flower of their Crown which they fought for, besides *Religion* and *Liberty*) they are these, *One-ness, Same-ness, Much-ness, Nothing-ness, Soul-saving-ness*; to which we may add another of our Authors own, *Pick-thank-ness*; in which word (to keep our Rhyme) there is a peculiar *Marvelousness.*

2. Samuel Parker's first response

1673

Having served as a chaplain to Archbishop Sheldon, Samuel Parker (1640–88) was appointed to the archdeaconry of Canterbury in 1670 and ultimately to the bishopric of Oxford (1686). Pricked by the satiric barbs of *RT I*, he was quick to answer in virulent fashion, and by May 1673 Marvell had seen some three hundred of its more than five hundred pages and described it as 'the rudest book . . . that ever was publisht (I may say), since the first invention of printing' (*Letters,* p. 328).

Calling Marvell 'a true whelp of Old Martyns,' perhaps following up a hint in Richard Leigh, Parker, in a 'lucky hit,' attempts to place him in the tradition of the Martin Marprelate controversial style.

Extracts from *A Reproof to the Rehearsal Transprosed, in A Discourse to its Authour*, 1673: To the Reader, A2; pp. 113, 226–7, 268–71.

When I first condemn'd my self to the drudgery of this Reply, I intended nothing but a serious Prosecution of my Argument; and to let the World see that it is not reading Histories, or Plays, or Gazzets, nor going a Pilgrimage to *Geneva*, nor learning French and Italian, nor passing the *Alps*, nor being a cunning Gamester that can qualify a man to discourse of *Conscience* and *Ecclesiastical Policy*; in that it is not capping an Argument with a story that will answer it, nor clapping an Apothegm upon an Assertion that will prove it, nor stringing up Proverbs and Similitudes upon one another that will make up a Coherent Discourse. And for a great while I kept close to my resolution, and contented my self to expose the man's Ignorance, without laughing at it: But he is all along so ridiculous, that at last Flesh and Blood could not refrain from being a little pleasant with him. And *as it chances it happens not unluckily*, for I hope I have hereby given an Example, how it is possible to be *serious* and merry *with a Buffoon without violating the Laws of Decorum*, and to discourse with a Clown *as long time* as *I have been writing* without being rude or angry.

This was the summe not of all old *Martyns* Buffoonery, but of all the serious part of the old-*Elsibeth* Puritanism. But as *Martyn* was just such another Wit as you, so are you just such another fool as *Martyn*, that as despicable as you make your self when you would play the Monkey, are ten times a more ridiculous sight when you would look serious.

As for the remainder of your Book, it is all such course and unserviceable rubbish, that it is not worth the sifting, it is all such loose and empty talk, as is as applicable to confute any other Book in the world as mine, in so much that I might, if it would but have recompenced the pains, have turn'd three parts of your own

Pamphlet upon it self. As all your profest fooling either by way
of Similitude or Rithm or Story; your playing upon single words,
your confusing introductions and transitions, your smutty imagi-
nations, your general and insolent censures, with abundance more
of such bold and immodest stuff, that though it signifies nothing
by it self, yet is almost enough to beat any modest man out of
countenance by pure force of brow and confidence. But in answer
to your Ribaldry I can only blush and say nothing; and as for
your rude and uncivil language, I am willing to impute it to your
first unhappy Education among Boat-Swains and Cabin-boys,
whose phrases as you learn'd in your Childhood, so it is not to be
expected you should ever unlearn them by your Conversation
with the Bear-herds of *Barn*, the Canibals of *Geneva*, the Boys and
Lackeys at *Charing-Cross*, and in Lincolns-Inn-fields.

But yet however you may assure your self that he [Samuel Butler,
author of *Hudibras*] will never take any notice of such a despicable
yelper as you, unless with a Dog-whip. Thou Prevaricatour of
all the Laws of Buffoonry, thou dastard Craven, thou Swad, thou
Mushroom, thou Coward in heart, word, and deed, thou *Judas*,
thou Crocodile, thus (though it were in thy greatest necessity) after
having profess'd wit and rithm these fifty years, to snivle out such
a whining submission in publick is past all precedent of Cowardize
from the Trojan war to this very day; but that thou shouldest do it
of thy own accord and without any provocation is more sneaking
than the flattery of a Setting-dog. Thou shalt wear a Collar, and thy
name shall be *Trey*.

And so we arrive at the Character of a Noble-man's Chaplain;
for having heretofore (among other your juvenile Essays of
Ballads, Poesies, Anagrams and Acrosticks) laid out your self
upon this Subject also, and your Papers lying useless by you at
this time when your Muse began to tire and set, it might be very
convenient to fill up twelve pages with this Character whilst she
baited and recover'd Breath. But the greatest part of it is so very
trite and vulgar, that none but a superannuated Wit would ever
have accepted of such outworn and old fashion'd Jests. And the
rest of it so Gargantuan and Legend-like, *v[erbi] g[ratia] the raising
of a mans Hypocondria into the Region of his Brain, his being lifted up
into the Air so high as to crack his Scull against the Chappel Ceiling*
[*I*, pp. 30, 31], with a deal more of such wild and incredible Stuff,

that I shall wave it all because I am sure it is impossible that Kings should ever make use of such idle and extravagant stories. And if I would study revenge I could easily have requited you with the Novels of a certain *Jack Gentleman* that was born of pure Parents, and bred among Cabin-boys, and sent from School to the University, and from the University to the gaming Ordinaries, but the young man being easily rook'd by the old Gamesters, he was sent abroad to gain Cunning and Experience, and beyond Sea saw the Bears of *Bern*, and the large Race of Capons at *Geneva*, and a great many fine sights beside, and so return'd home as accomplish'd as he went out, tries his fortune once more at the Ordinaries, plays too high for a Gentleman of his private condition, and so is at length cheated of all at Picquet. And so having neither Money nor employment, he is forced to loiter up and down about *Charing-Cross* and in *Lincolns-Inn fields*, where he had leisure and opportunity to make Remarques (among other Subjects) upon the wheel of Fortune, from whence with the help of a little skill in Mathematicks he at length makes out this new and important discovery in Politicks, *as a straight line continued grows a Circle, even so Power infinitely extended becomes Impotency* [I, pp. 92–3]. Which with many more of his choicest Observations he at length discharges into a certain Book call'd the *Rehearsal*, which as soon as you have finisht this, I would willingly recommend to your perusal, that you may see how much pains a witty man may take to make others merry and himself ridiculous. Where you will meet with many more that perhaps you will think but idle stories, but Kings know how to make use of them. For how modestly soever the Author may speak of his own private condition and breeding, his Memoires will be very serviceable to the instruction of Princes.

3. Edmund Hickeringill on the *Rehearsal Transpros'd*

1673

Published sometime after May 1673 (see *Letters*, p. 328), *GREGORY, Father-Greybeard, with his Vizer off . . . in a Letter to Our Old Friend, R. L. from E. H.* refers to Marvell as 'the Headman Father Greybeard' but even more villainous. R. L. probably refers to Roger L'Estrange (see No. 17).

E[dmund] H[ickeringill] (1631–1708) was the rector of All Saints, Colchester, where his lively style of preaching endeared him to the public. In *RT II*, Marvell twice asserts that Hickeringill's work if not of Parker's own penning at least passed under his approval (pp. 175, 201).

Extracts from pp. 7, 12–13, 134–5.

It is a *marvel* (saith another) what you will make of this *New Author*, at the long run; for you have made him a *Ferret*, a *Tarrier*, and a *Jaccall* already; The Gentleman himself has reduc'd *thus many* Metaphors within the compass of one bare sentence, p. 49. [*I*, p. 23] fetching a *Conjurer*, a *Play house*, and a *Ferret* to make it up: sure his *Rhetorick* was born in a time when *Metaphors* were cheap; for though they be *far fetch'd*, yet sure they were not *dear bought*, he is so *prodigal* of them.

. . . then and even then, it is the *old cry* of the Rebells, who when they had got their will of the Earl of *Strafford*, and Arch-Bishop *Laud* and left the *King* no Councellors, nor Kingdomes, nor so much as liberty; then changed their note, and justified the *Evil Councellors*, more than the *King* himself; saying *he* himself was his *own* wicked Councellor, and a *Tyrant* and ought to *die*: And though their words (like these of this Authour) were devillish and malicious; yet they were *as good as their words*, and condemn'd him for a

Tyrant, and cut off his head. 'Tis indeed (answered another) all you say is infallibly true, and *undeniable* to a Tittle; but that which is *admirable*, and a greater *Marvel*, is the skill and cunning of the man:

He does the feat so cleaverly, as if he shot with *white Powder*; did *execution* indeed effectually, but makes no *noyse*, or evil *Report*; (like other unskilful and *bawling* Phanaticks;) for though you stare about, you shall not see the Executioner, nor know *whence* the shot comes; or if you do, he puts his vizard on presently, and looks, (like *Faux*) in disguise. Or, as the *Mountebank*, keeping a man, who is content to be slash'd and cut, that his master may thereby show his Dexterity and skill in the Cure; so this *Virtuoso* wounds and cuts (but indeed with design) mortally; and with matchless courage and boldness, (disdaining trivial force) fights neither with small nor great, (except they lye in his way and detard Royal assassination) but only the King of our *Israel*; against whom when he has spit his venome, and with bold and home thrusts assaulted his Innocence and honour;

Yet he has his *Playster* at hand, (though it be without vertue) and would seem to make all whole again, with crying, Oh Lord! Sir, *I beg your pardon*; and then; as you were: All is *well* again.

Was not this *Greg.* begot by some *Proteus* of a *Camælion*, an *Oedipus* cannot riddle him: he fights backward and forward, sometimes for the King, and sometimes for modern Orthodoxy; he slashes with a two edged Sword and cuts both ways; brandishes against the enemy, and then falls foul on his own party, and the *Good Old Cause*; but it is with pickeerings [skirmishes] and flourishes, rather than close fight, and good earnest; and therefore he gives the *Good Old Cause*, a good new name, and because the old one is odious, he calls it sometimes Primitive Simplicity, sometimes modern Orthodoxy, and p. 303. [*I*, p. 135] the Cause too good.

4. [? Joseph Glanvill] on the *Rehearsal Transpros'd*

1674

Publication of *RT II* in 1673 and again in 1674 elicited an anonymous twelve-page letter entitled *An Apology and Advice For some of the Clergy. ... Written on the Occasion of the Second Part Of the* Rehearsal Transpros'd. Having conceded that Marvell has had the better of the argument, the author offers a defense of Parker and advice as to his future conduct.

Jackson I. Cope (*Joseph Glanvill: Anglican Apologist*, St Louis, 1956) believes that it is the work of Glanvill, a friend of Parker's, and that it echoes his later publications. Some supporting evidence is afforded by the listing of this title among the books advertised by Glanvill in his *Essays*, 1676. Cope would also attribute to Glanvill the threat to cut the author's throat which was signed 'J. G.' and which Marvell reprinted on the title page to Part II.

Extracts from pp. 1–2, 4–5, 8–9.

SIR,

I have now read the second part of the *Rehearsal Transprosed*, which you so earnestly recommend to me in your last: And am very sorry to see that the difference between those ingenious men is inflamed to this height; and that the Controversie should be so far run out into matters of personal abuse. I shall not tell you at this time who I think hath the better in the argument; This is obvious, that M[aster] M[arvell] hath much the advantage in the *Reproaching* part. For though I confidently believe that his Adversary is clear, as to the foul things laid to his charge by this Author; Yet He is a Clergy man, and it is not enough for them to be innocent, while there are any who have the ill-will to accuse them; and such there will be, while there are *Sects*, and Jovial *Atheists* in the world. I have nothing to say in particular of the personal matters; only this I will adventure to observe; That I think you do amiss in conceiving so great a prejudice against the Authour of the E[*cclesiastical*] P[*olity*] from those *uncertain*, if not *untrue* things, which his heated Antagonist hath said of Him. You know it is a great piece of Injustice to entertain Reports hastily of any man, and especially of the Ministers of Religion, whom so many take pleasure to defame, either out of design to disgrace their profession, or to excuse, and extenuate their own vileness by it.

If this Church-man be wont to reprehend the pretended *Wits*, and *Wits* of the Age, with spirit and smartness, and endeavour to render the *Drollers* and Buffoons odious, and contemptible, as they deserve; If he be sharp, and frequent in reproving and exposing the concomitant *Atheism*, and vile humour of deriding Religion and things Sacred; He then draws the *Railers* and *Jesters* upon his back, who will put a thousand tricks upon him, and persecute him with their scoffs in all companies, and make him the constant mark of their malicious sport.

Now You know Sir, what a *taking* sort of people these are in our times, and how far this fooling will go with some to render those contemptible in their esteem, that deserve better thoughts of them. There is much malice in mankind, which this humour gratifyeth, when it exposeth any mans name to scorn and laughter; especially it is tickled when any of the Clergy are derided: So that no worth, no vertue, no Accomplishments are fence against this set of men: Yea the more eminent any of these are, the more subject to such wrongs, and the more the common Envy makes such abuses spread. For even the Sects that pretend to the greatest seriousness and gravity of humour are transported with the wit, that aims at making the *Sons* of the *Church* ridiculous, especially when it falls on those who have been so hardy as to declare against their dear follies, and fall on them it shall, while there are Buffoons to be hired for that service.

If the Minister useth to be close and pungent upon the great *Debauchees* of the Age, and endeavours by any more than ordinary earnestness, and power of reproof to make them despicable, and vile in the eyes and thoughts of all men:

If besides this in general, he chance to incurr the particular ill-will and displeasure of any one, or more of them, (though

43

innocently, and without giving just ground of offence) He must expect the utmost of their rage. They will toss his name about in every Ale-house and Tavern; and make Him their constant subject and their *Song*. They will inflame all their company, and acquaintance against him, and make it a great entertainment of their meetings to raise odious stories of him, which they will publish in all their neighbourhoods, and so blacken him, as if he were a *Devil*, though he be the most innocent person breathing. They will propagate and improve all the slanders that have been raised on him by his *Fanatick* Adversaries; And *they* again entertain and spread all those that are invented by *these debauched* ones; and so between the one and the other, they will make him appear as a very vile, and odious person, be he never so vertuous and unblameable in his conversation.

You would have the Author of the *E.P.* to refute and disprove those things of *Immorality* which his Adversary chargeth on him; and you think if he be guiltless, he owes himself and his Profession this right.

For my part I verily believe him *innocent*; But yet, if I were fit to be consulted, I should by no means advise his writing any particular vindication: The things are too foul to be touch't by his hands, and such spots are better worn out by time and patience, than wiped off by hasty Zeal of Reputation. Dirt while it is green will not be struck off clear, but the very *wiping* of it fastens some stain, and spreads it further: Industrious Apologies, in such cases, beget suspicions, and raise more scandal: And 'tis a scandalous thing to have so much *appearance* of *guilt*, as to *seem greatly concerned* to clear ones Innocence; such lewd Reproaches will dye of themselves when they are let alone, and despised; but they are revived, and kept alive by much ado of answering, and refuting.

5. An anonymous comment on the author of the *Rehearsal Transpros'd*

1674

A second anonymous pamphlet (of ten pages) appeared in 1674 in the guise of a burlesque letter. Calling his addressee 'Merry Andrew' (a popular term for a mountebank's assistant), its author signs himself 'Theophilus Thorowthistle' from his 'Mannor of *No-land* in the Isle of Silly.'

Extract from *Sober Reflections, or, A Solid Confutation of Mr. Andrew Marvel's Works, In a Letter ab Ignoto ad Ignotum*, pp. 1–4.

Marvel of *Marvels*, for that is the *Character* given you by a certain sort of Impertinent People who love mischief; Mischief your Minion Medium, which like a rich vein runs through the heart of all your Syllogismes, to the utter impoverishing of their Consequences; for, from a vicious medium (as unfledg'd a Logician as you are) you may Cock-sure, inferr, there must necessarily follow a vile consequence.

But, how defective soever you are in your *Syllogismes*, you make ample satisfaction; nay, you supererrogate in your *Dilemma's*, they are as surprizing as a *Welsh-hook*, with Pull her to her, push her from her; or like a Rope and Butter, if th'one slip, t'other will be sure to hold. Your Similitudes are most apposite and unparallel'd, *V[erbi] G[ratia]* even as a Wheel-barrow goes rumble-dee, rumble-dee, so my Lord Mayor owes me Five hundred pounds. Your Examples are without example; for Quibbles you are the very word-pecker of word-peckers, and for Rhetorical flourishes (like a *Whisler* before a Morris-dance) you carry it away from them all with flying-colours, your Workes being most artificially set forth and beautified with choice pieces of Poetry, like a Cow-turd stuck with Gilly flowers, most dexterously interwoven with Natural Experiments; most richly embroidered

45

with Theological Notions; most magnificently Tapestry'd with Reasons of State, hanging down in Clusters like bunches of Grapes; and most prodigiously stuff'd with Witty Conceits, thicker than Cloves in a Gammon of Bacon at *Easter*. Your Stile is for the most part smooth and insinuating, yet happily diversified here and there with Jirks and Short Girds, as if you had a spice of the Stringhalt [blind spavin, incident to horses]: although in your Clauses and Parentheses you are as unhoopable as if you stood with one leg at *Dover* and the other at *Calais*.

But, to make up more roundly to you, and to enumerate your Metaphysical parts, were not comparisons Odoriferous, I would play you off, for Cases of Conscience and Knotty points of Divinity, to *Hugh Peters*[1] himself: Yea, you have with the same Pharisaical Devotion, as liberally communicated your Spiritual Talent, yet I would not advise you to follow the Precedent too far, lest you fall again into the Clutches of Father *Gregory* [see No. 3], &c. *Mum's* the Word, you understand me. As for your Morality I am unwilling to harp too much on that string; thou Man of *Morals* seek severity elsewhere, I dare not be thy caution. I must confess it is enough to throw any man into a Fit of the Staggers to reflect upon your Confidence: that you who have been your self first Graduated at *Billingsgate*, and afterwards Civiliz'd in *Barbary* (your own Writings are sufficient Evidence) that you, to whom railing is as natural as habitual; a property belonging to you (*quarto modo*) should have so cauteriz'd a Conscience as to brand your Adversary without having the least regard to his Function, with Petulancy, want of Humanity, &c. and this you modestly term onely a competent stock of Ill-Nature, which you alwayes carry about you, as absolutely necessary to self-preservation, lest you should be found *felo de se; risum teneatis Amici?*[2] Is not this a pleasant companion?

How it tickles my fancy to think what a general Jubilee there would be, and how unmercifully it would edifie with your Party to see you set Doctor *Cathedraticus* in a Cucking-stool, Lording it over your Female-Auditory, the Water-*Nymphs* of *Wapping*,

[1] Chaplain to Cromwell, Hugh Peters (1598–1660) came to be travestied by opponents of the Puritans as the chief of English rogues.
[2] The author combines an Anglo-Latin legal phrase applied to one whose malicious act is the cause of his own death with one from Horace's *Ars Poetica*, 5: 'could you, friends, refrain from laughing?'

Magisterially maintaining your polemical Arguments and Debates, &c. *tanquam ex Tripode*,[1] pronouncing your Oracles concerning the Power of Princes; the Liberty of the Subject; the Authority of the Magistrate; the Obedience of the People; the Duty of the Prelates and Pastors unto their Flock; *cum multis aliis*: And, when you have tired your Auditors as well as your Readers, with your frequent Tautologies upon the same subject, 'tis but shifting your leg in your Gallop (lest you fall into a Dogtrot) and changing your Text, all will do well I'l warrant you.

6. Rochester on the Parker controversy

c. 1674–5

A leader of a group Marvell called the 'merry gang' (*Letters*, p. 355), John Wilmot, second Earl of Rochester (1647–80), includes a commendatory allusion to Marvell's exposure of Parker in his satire *Tunbridge Wells*, first published in the State Poems (1705). Marvell, for his part, according to John Aubrey (see No. 28), expressed high admiration for Rochester's satiric vein.

Extract from *The Works*, 1707: ll. 58–69.

List'ning I found the Cob [leading man] of all this Rabble,
Pert Bays [Parker], with his Importance comfortable [.] [2]
He being rais'd to an Arch-Deaconry,
By trampling on Religion, Liberty;
Was grown so great, and lookt too Fat and Jolly,
To be disturb'd with Care and Melancholy,

[1] Pronouncing 'as if from the Delphic oracle.'
[2] Importance comfortable: a phrase used by Parker, which Marvell mockingly derides as a reference to his mistress (*RT I*, p. 6); it was picked up by other writers, among them Bishop Burnet (see No. 9).

Though *Marvel* has enough expos'd his Folly.
He Drank to carry off some old Remains,
His Lazy dull Distemper[1] left in 's Brains;
Let him Drink on, but 'tis not a whole Flood
Can give sufficient sweetness to his Blood,
To make his Nature or his Manners good.

7.   Robert McWard comments on Parker and Marvell

1677

Robert McWard (?1633–87), a covenanting Scottish minister, was banished in 1661 and took up residence in Holland where he wrote prefaces to the works of his fellow exile, John Brown of Wamphrey.

Extract from 'To the Christian Reader' in John Brown's *Christ the Way, and the Truth, and the Life* (1677), from the 1740 reprint, p. xxxiv.

But I would recommend to you, who can neither purchase nor peruse what is more voluminous (how worthy soever) the serious perusal, as of the whole of that savoury and grace-breathing piece, *The Fulfilling of the Scriptures*;[2] so there in that short but sweet digression, against black-mouthed *Parker*, wherein the gracious author takes out his own soul, and sets before thine eye the image of God, impressed thereon: for while he deals with that *Desperado* by clear and convincing reason, flowing natively from the pure fountain of divine revelation, he hath the advantage

[1] Lazy dull Distemper: a phrase used by Parker in his *Reproof* to explain his delay in answering the *RT I*.

[2] By the Scots dissenter Robert Fleming (1630–94).

48

of most men, and writers too, in silencing that blasphemer of the good ways of God, with arguments taken from what he hath found acted upon his own soul. .... Nor can I here omit to observe, how when the devil raised up *Parker*, that monster, to bark and blaspheme, the Lord raised up a *Merveil* to fight him at his own weapon, who did so cudgel and quell that boasting *bravo*, as I know not if he be dead of his wound, but, for any thing I know, he hath laid his speech.

8. Thomas Long comments on the Transproser

1678

Prebendary of Exeter Cathedral and a staunch churchman and royalist, Thomas Long (1621–1707) published his *Mr. Hales's Treatise of Schism Examin'd and Censur'd* in 1678. Though he once refers to Marvell by name, elsewhere it is as the author of the *RT* or the *Transproser*.

Extract from the Preface, B7^v–B8^v, p. 13.

The *Author* of the *Rehearsal Transpros'd, speaks marvellously of Him*: I shall conclude (says he) with a Villainous Pamphlet,[1] of which a great Wit was the Author....

[Quotes Marvell, freely rendered, *I*, p. 79.]
(*And then he fills up near Eight Pages of his Book, out of* Mr. Hales *his Eight Leaves*.)

And necessary it is that such noxious and unsavory weeds should be rooted out, and not suffered to defile the grave of so Candid

---

[1] In the *RT I*, Marvell refers ironically to the 'villainous pamphlet' of the 'ever-memorable' John Hales as he was known to his contemporaries, and cites extensively from his treatise.

a person, or made use of as a shelter for unclean creatures to hide themselves and croak under them, as the *Transproser* doth, who having raked a heap of them together, from *p.* 175 to *p.* 183 [*I*, pp. 79–82] fancieth himself as secure on that dunghill, as if he were in some enchanted Castle.

9. Bishop Burnet on the Parker controversy

1678, before 1715

Chaplain to Charles II, a post from which he was dismissed, and later Bishop of Salisbury, Gilbert Burnet (1643–1715) is best remembered as a historian of the Reformation and of his own times. Obviously an admirer of Marvell's facility in demolishing Parker, he provides three evaluations of the controversy. The first, often cited, makes use of Marvell's terminology and was an answer to Parker's *Reasons for Abrogating the Test* (1678). The second, also often cited, appears in his *History of My Own Time*, published posthumously in 1724–34. The third derives from his manuscript papers.

(a) Extract from *An Enquiry into the Reasons for Abrogating the TEST, imposed on all Members of Parliament,* published in his *Collection of Eighteen Papers. Relating to the Affairs of Church and State,* 1689, pp. 201–3.

... so now the Price of the *Presidentship* [of Magdalen College, Oxford] is to be pay'd. ... and He [Parker] to preserve the Character of *Drawcansir* [*I*, p. 21; from *The Rehearsal*, IV. i], which is as due to Him as that of *Bays*, falls upon the *Articles* of the *Church*, and upon both *Houses* of *Parliament*. It is Reproach enough to the

House of Lords, that He is of it; but it is somewhat new, and a Character becoming *Sa. Oxon.* [Bishop of Oxford] to arraign that *House* with all the Insolence to which he can raise his wanton Pen. . . . And the Late *King* being so true a Judg of Wit, could not but be much taken with the best *Satyr* of our Time; and saw that *Bays's Wit*, when measured with another's, was of a piece with his Virtues, and therefore judged in favour of the *Rehearsal Transpros'd*: this went deep, and though it gave occasion to the single piece of Modesty, with which he can be charged, of withdrawing from the Town, and not importuning the Press more for some years, since even a Face of Brass must grow red, when it is so burnt as his was then; yet his Malice against the Elder *Brother* was never extinguished but with his Life: But now a strange Conjuncture has brought him again on the Stage, and *Bays* will be *Bays* still.

(b) Extract from the *History of My Own Time*, ed. Osmund Airy (1897), I, pp. 467–8.

But the most virulent of all that writ against the sects was Parker, afterwards made bishop of Oxford by king James, who was full of satirical vivacity, and was considerably learned; but was a man of no judgment, and of as little virtue, and as to religion he seemed rather to have become quite impious. After he had for some years entertained the nation with several virulent books, writ with much life, he was attacked by the liveliest droll of the age, who writ in a burlesque strain, but with so peculiar and so entertaining a conduct, that from the king down to the tradesman his book was read with great pleasure. That not only humbled Parker, but the whole party: for the author of the Rehearsal Transprosed had all the men of wit (or, as the French phrase it, all the *laughers*) on his side.

(c) Extract from Harl. MSS. 6584, *A Supplement to Burnet's History of My Own Time*, ed. H. C. Foxcroft (Oxford, 1902), pp. 215–16.

The other vacancy in Oxford was filled by Dr. Parker, who was at first an independent; but on the king's restoration he found his account in changing and striking up to the violentest form of the church of England. He is a man that has no regard either to religion or virtue, but will accommodate himself to everything that may gratify either his covetousness or his ambition. He has writ many books; there is a liveliness in his style that is more entertaining than either grave or correct. He has raised the king's authority in ecclesiastical matters and depressed it by turns, as he was pleased or displeased with the court; for though once he carried the king's power to that height of impiety as to say in so many plain words that the form of naming the king in our prayers as under God and Christ our supreme governor in all causes was a cursed and a profane expression (since he said that though the king was indeed under God, yet he was not under Christ, but above him), yet, not being preferred as he expected, he has writ many books to raise the power of the church to an independence on the civil authority. His extravagant way of writing gave occasion to the wittiest books that have appeared in this age, for Mr. Marvell undertook him and treated him in ridicule in the severest but pleasantest manner possible, and by this one character one may judge how pleasant these books were; for the last king, that was not a great reader of books, read them over and over again.

10. Anthony à Wood on the Parker controversy

1691–2

The antiquarian Anthony à Wood (1632–95) takes occasion to notice Marvell only in conjunction with his articles on Parker and John Denham.

Extract from *Athenae Oxonienses*, ed. P. Bliss (1813–20), IV, cols 230–2.

Whereupon our author Parker being esteemed by the non-conformists a forward, proud, ambitious and scornful person, was taken to task, purposely to clip his wings or take him shorter, by their buffooning champion Andrew Marvell sometime one of John Milton's companions. . . .

All, or most of which answers (which were to the first part of *The Rehearsal Transpos'd*) were wrote in a buffooning, burlesquing and ridiculing way and stile; in which fashion of writing, Marvell himself had led the way. . . . Before I go any farther, the reader is to note that this pen-combat exercised between our author and Marvell was briskly managed with as much smart, cutting and satyrical wit on both sides, as any other perhaps of late hath been, they endeavouring by all the methods imaginable, and the utmost forces they could by any means rally up, to blacken each others cause, and to set each other out in the most ugly dress: (their pieces in the mean while, wherein was represented a perfect trial of each others skill and parts in a jerking, flirting way of writing, entertaining the reader with a great variety of sport and mirth, in seeing two such right cocks of the game so keenly engaging with sharp and dangerous weapons). And it was generally thought, nay even by many of those who were otherwise favourers of Parker's cause, that he (Parker) thro' a too loose and unwary handling of the debate (tho' in a brave, flourishing and lofty stile) laid himself too open to the severe strokes of his snearing adversary, and that the odds and victory lay on Marvell's side: Howsoever it was, it wrought this good effect upon our author, that for ever after it took down somewhat of his high spirit, insomuch that tho' Marvell in a second part replied upon our author's reproof, yet he judged it more prudent rather to lay down the cudgels, than to enter the lists again with an untowardly combatant so hugely well vers'd and experienc'd in the then, but newly, refin'd art (tho' much in mode and fashion almost ever since) of sportive and jeering buffoonry. And moreover it put him upon a more serious, sober and moderate way of writing in other good treatises, which he since did set forth, and which have proved very useful and beneficial to the public. The reader may be pleased now to know by the way, for here I think it very proper to be brought in and no where else, that the said Andrew Marvell was son of Andrew Marvell the facetious, yet Calvinistical, minister of Kingston upon Hull in Yorkshire, that being very well educated in grammar learning was sent to Cambridge, particularly, as I conceive, to Trin. coll. where obtaining the mastership of the Latin tongue became assistant to Joh. Milton when he was Latin secretary to Oliver, and very intimate and conversant with that person. A little before his majesty's restoration the burghers of his native place of Kingston before mention'd did choose him their representative to sit in that parliament that began at Westminster the 25th of April 1660, and again after his majesty's restoration for that which began at the same place, 8 May 1661, and they loved him so well that they gave him an honourable pension to maintain him. From which time to his death, he was esteemed (tho' in his conversation very modest and of few words) a very celebrated wit among the fanatics, and the only one truly so, for many years after. ... This Andrew Marvell, who is supposed to have written other things, as I have told you in Joh. Denham, vol. iii, col. 827. died on the 18th of August 1678, and was buried under the pews in the south side of the church of S. Giles in the Fields, near London. Afterwards his widow published of his composition *Miscellaneous Poems*. Lond. 1681. fol. which were then taken into the hands of many persons of his persuasion, and by them cried up as excellent.

11. Dean Swift's allusion to the controversy

1710

Swift's *A Tale of a Tub* appeared in 1704, and in 1710 he added 'An Apology' to the fifth edition of the work which includes the often cited reference to Marvell.

Extract from 'An Apology,' A6^{v}–7.

This Apology being chiefly intended for the Satisfaction of future Readers, it may be thought unnecessary to take any notice of such Treatises as have been writ against this ensuing Discourse, which are already sunk into waste Paper and Oblivion; after the usual Fate of common Answerers to Books, which are allowed to have any Merit: They are indeed like Annuals that grow about a young Tree, and seem to vye with it for a Summer, but fall and die with the Leaves in Autumn, and are never heard of any more. When Dr. *Eachard* writ his Book about the Contempt of the Clergy,[1] numbers of those Answerers immediately started up, whose Memory if he had not kept alive by his Replies, it would now be utterly unknown that he were ever answered at all. There is indeed an Exception, when any great Genius thinks it worth his while to expose a foolish Piece; so we still read *Marvel*'s Answer to *Parker* with Pleasure, tho' the Book it answers be sunk long ago; so the Earl of *Orrery*'s Remarks[2] will be read with Delight, when the Dissertation he exposes will neither be sought nor found; but these are no Enterprises for common Hands, nor to be hoped for above once or twice in an Age. Men would be more cautious of losing their Time in such an Undertaking, if they did but consider, that to answer a Book effectually, requires more Pains and Skill, more Wit, Learning, and Judgment than were employ'd in the Writing it.

---

[1] This polemical work, published in 1670 by John Eachard, later master of St Catherine's Hall, Cambridge, elicited a number of replies.

[2] Charles Boyle, fourth Earl of Orrery, published as an undergraduate the letters of Phalaris which were declared spurious by the learned Richard Bentley. A witty response to Bentley was published in 1698 under Boyle's name, but it appears to have been largely the work of Francis Atterbury.

12. Isaac Disraeli on the Parker controversy

1814

Styled by Byron 'that most entertaining and researching writer,' Disraeli the elder (1766–1848) wrote a number of anecdotal works on literary matters. His essay on Marvell and Parker first appeared in 1814 in *Quarrels of Authors* and was then reprinted in 1859 under the title *The Calamities and Quarrels of Authors*. Although he was not, in fact, an altogether exact researcher and quite cavalier in his handling of quotations, frequently telescoping or juxtaposing disparate passages, his work was much pillaged by later writers.

Reprinted from *The Works*, ed. by his son (1880–1), IV, pp. 391–402, with one selection from the notes. There are minor textual variants from the first edition.

One of the legitimate ends of satire, and one of the proud triumphs of genius, is to unmask the false zealot; to beat back the haughty spirit that is treading down all; and if it cannot teach modesty, and raise a blush, at least to inflict terror and silence. It is then that the satirist does honour to the office of the executioner.

> As one whose whip of steel can with a lash
> Imprint the characters of shame so deep,
> Even in the brazen forehead of proud Sin,
> That not eternity shall wear it out.

[Randolph's *Muses' Looking-glass*, I. iv.]

The quarrel between PARKER and MARVELL is a striking example of the efficient powers of genius, in first humbling, and then annihilating, an unprincipled bravo, who had placed himself at the head of a faction.

Marvell, the under-secretary and the bosom-friend of Milton, whose fancy he has often caught in his verse, was one of the greatest wits of the luxuriant age of Charles II.; he was a master in all the arts of ridicule; and his inexhaustible spirit only required some permanent subject to have rivalled the causticity of Swift, whose style, in neatness and vivacity, seems to have been modelled on his. But Marvell placed the oblation of genius on a temporary altar, and the sacrifice sunk with it; he wrote to the times, and with the times his writings have passed away; yet something there is incorruptible in wit, and wherever its salt has fallen, that part is still preserved.

Such are the vigour and fertility of Marvell's writings, that our old Chronicler of Literary History, Anthony Wood, considers him as the founder of 'the then newly-refined art (though much in mode and fashion almost ever since) of sportive and jeering buffoonery;'* and the crabbed humorist describes 'this pen-combat as briskly managed on both sides; a jerking flirting way of writing entertaining the reader, by seeing two such right cocks of the game so keenly engaging with sharp and dangerous weapons.'—Burnett calls Marvell 'the liveliest droll of the age, who writ in a burlesque strain, but with so peculiar and entertaining a conduct, that from the king to the tradesman, his books were read with great pleasure.' Charles II. was a more polished judge than these uncouth critics; and, to the credit of his impartiality,— for that witty monarch and his dissolute court were never spared by Marvell, who remained inflexible to his seduction—he deemed Marvell the best prose satirist of the age. But Marvell had other qualities than the freest humour and the finest wit in this 'newly-refined art,' which seems to have escaped these grave critics—a vehemence of solemn reproof, and an eloquence of invective, that awes one with the spirit of the modern Junius, and may give some notion of that more ancient satirist, whose writings are said to have so completely answered their design, that, after perusal, their victim hanged himself on the first tree; and in the present case, though the delinquent did not lay violent hands on himself, he did what, for an author, may be considered as desperate a course, 'withdraw from the town, and cease writing for some years.'

* This is a curious remark of Wood's: How came raillery and satire to be considered as 'a newly-refined art?' Has it not, at all periods, been prevalent among every literary people? The remark is, however, more founded on truth than it appears, and arose from Wood's own feelings.

The celebrated work here to be noticed is Marvell's 'Rehearsal Transprosed;' a title facetiously adopted from Bayes in 'The Rehearsal Transposed' of the Duke of Buckingham. It was written against the works and the person of Dr. Samuel Parker, afterwards Bishop of Oxford, whom he designates under the character of Bayes, to denote the incoherence and ridiculousness of his character. Marvell had a peculiar knack of calling names,—it consisted in appropriating a ludicrous character in some popular comedy, and dubbing his adversaries with it. In the same spirit he ridiculed Dr. Turner, of Cambridge, a brother-genius to Parker, by nicknaming him 'Mr. Smirk, the Divine in Mode,' the name of the Chaplain in Etherege's 'Man of Mode,' and thus, by a stroke of the pen, conveyed an idea of 'a neat, starched, formal, and forward divine' [from A. Wood]. This application of a fictitious character to a real one, this christening a man with ridicule, though of no difficult invention, is not a little hazardous to inferior writers; for it requires not less wit than Marvell's to bring out of the real character the ludicrous features which mark the factitious prototype.

Parker himself must have his portrait, and if the likeness be justly hit off, some may be reminded of a resemblance. Mason [see No. 36] applies the epithet of 'Mitred Dullness' to him: but although he was at length reduced to railing and to menaces, and finally mortified into silence, this epithet does not suit so hardy and so active an adventurer.

The secret history of Parker may be collected in Marvell [*II*, p. 181], and his more public one in our honest chronicler, Anthony Wood. Parker was originally educated in strict sectarian principles; a starch Puritan, 'fasting and praying with the Presbyterian students weekly, and who, for their refection feeding only on thin broth made of oatmeal and water, were commonly called *Gruellers*.' Among these, says Marvell, 'it was observed that he was wont to put more graves [cracklings] than all the rest into his porridge, and was deemed one of the *preciousest* young men in the University.' It seems that these mortified saints, both the brotherhood and the sisterhood, held their chief meetings at the house of 'Bess Hampton, an old and crooked maid that drove the trade of laundry, who, being from her youth very much given to the godly party, as they call themselves, had frequent meetings, especially for those that were her customers.' Such is the dry humour of honest Anthony, who paints like the Ostade of literary history.[1]

But the age of sectarism and thin gruel was losing all its coldness in the sunshine of the Restoration; and this 'preciousest young man,' from praying and caballing against episcopacy, suddenly acquainted the world, in one of his dedications, that Dr. Ralph Bathurst had 'rescued him from the chains and fetters of an unhappy education' [*II*, p. 184], and, without any intermediate apology, from a sullen sectarian turned a flaming highflyer for the 'supreme dominion' of the Church.

It is the after-conduct of Parker that throws light on this rapid change. On speculative points any man may be suddenly converted; for these may depend on facts or arguments which might never have occurred to him before. But when we watch the weathercock chopping with the wind, so pliant to move, and so stiff when fixed—when we observe this 'preciousest grueller' clothed in purple, and equally hardy in the most opposite measures—become a favourite with James II., and a furious advocate for arbitrary power; when we see him railing at and menacing those, among whom he had committed as many extravagances as any of them; can we hesitate to decide that this bold, haughty, and ambitious man was one of those who, having neither religion nor morality for a casting weight, can easily fly off to opposite extremes? and whether a puritan or a bishop, we must place his zeal to the same side of his religious ledger—that of the profits of barter!

The quarrel between Parker and Marvell originated in a preface, written by Parker, in which he had poured down his contempt and abuse on his old companions, the Non-conformists. It was then Marvell clipped his wings with his 'Rehearsal Transprosed;' his wit and humour were finely contrasted with Parker's extravagances, set off in his declamatory style; of which Marvell wittily describes 'the volume and circumference of the periods, which, though he takes always to be his chiefest strength, yet, indeed, like too great a line, weakens the defence, and requires too many men to make it good' [*II*, p. 183]. The tilt was now opened, and certain masqued knights appeared in the course;

---

[1] Adrian Ostade (1610–85), a Dutch painter noted for realistic depiction of homely scenes and peasant folk.

they attempted to grasp the sharp and polished weapon of Marvell, to turn it on himself.[1] But Marvell, with malicious ingenuity, sees Parker in them all—they so much resembled their master! 'There were no less,' says the wit, 'than six scaramouches together on the stage, all of them of the same gravity and behaviour, the same tone, the same habit, that it was impossible to discern which was the true author of the "Ecclesiastical Polity." I believe he imitated the wisdom of some other princes, who have sometimes been persuaded by their servants to disguise several others in the regal garb, that the enemy might not know in the battle whom to single' [*II*, p. 174]. Parker, in fact, replied to Marvell anonymously, by 'A Reproof to the Rehearsal Transprosed,' with a mild exhortation to the magistrate to crush with the secular arm the pestilent wit, the servant of Cromwell, and the friend of Milton. But this was not all; something else, anonymous too, was despatched to Marvell: it was an extraordinary letter, short enough to have been an epigram, could Parker have written one; but short as it was, it was more in character, for it was only a threat of assassination! It concluded with these words: 'If thou darest to print any lie or libel against Dr. Parker, by the Eternal God I will cut thy throat.' Marvell replied to 'the Reproof,' which he calls a printed letter, by the second part of 'the Rehearsal Transprosed;' and to the unprinted letter, by publishing it on his own title-page.

Of two volumes of wit and broad humour, and of the most galling invective, one part flows so much into another, that the volatile spirit would be injured by an analytical process. But Marvell is now only read by the curious lovers of our literature, who find the strong, luxuriant, though not the delicate, wit of the wittiest age, never obsolete: the reader shall not, however, part from Marvell without some slight transplantations from a soil whose rich vegetation breaks out in every part.

Of the pleasantry and sarcasm, these may be considered as specimens. Parker was both author and licenser of his own work on 'Ecclesiastical Polity;' and it appears he got the licence for printing Marvell's first *Rehearsal* recalled.[2] The Church appeared in danger when the doctor discovered he was so furiously attacked. Marvell sarcastically rallies him on his dual capacity:

[1] After listing the titles of the answers to *RT I*, he adds, 'This was the very Bartlemy-fair of wit!'
[2] See Smith, pp. xx-xxv.

[Quotes *II*, p. 150.]

The satirist describes Parker's arrogance for those whom Parker calls the vulgar, and whom he defies as 'a rout of wolves and tigers, apes and buffoons;' yet his personal fears are oddly contrasted with his self-importance: 'If he chance but to sneeze, he prays that the *foundations of the earth* be not shaken.—Ever since he crept up to be but the *weathercock of a steeple*, he trembles and cracks at every puff of wind that blows about him, as if the *Church of England* were falling' [*ibid.*]. Parker boasted, in certain philosophical 'Tentamina,' or essays of his, that he had confuted the atheists: Marvell declares, 'If he had reduced any atheist by his book, he can only pretend to have converted them (as in the old Florentine wars) by mere tiring them out, and perfect weariness' [*II*, p. 183]. A pleasant allusion to those mock fights of the Italian mercenaries, who, after parading all day, rarely unhorsed a single cavalier.

Marvell blends with a ludicrous description of his answerers great fancy:

[Quotes *II*, pp. 171–3.]

Parker had accused Marvell with having served Cromwell, and being the friend of Milton, then living, at a moment when such an accusation not only rendered a man odious, but put his life in danger. Marvell, who now perceived that Milton, whom he never looked on but with the eyes of reverential awe, was likely to be drawn into his quarrel, touches on this subject with infinite delicacy and tenderness, but not with diminished energy against his malignant adversary, whom he shows to have been an impertinent intruder in Milton's house, where indeed he had first known him. He cautiously alludes to our English Homer by his initials: at that moment the very name of Milton would have tainted the page!

[Quotes *II*, pp. 312–13.]

Marvell, when he lays by his playful humour and fertile fancy for more solemn remonstrances, assumes a loftier tone, and a severity of invective, from which, indeed, Parker never recovered.

Accused by Parker of aiming to degrade the clerical character, Marvell declares his veneration for that holy vocation, and that he reflected even on the failings of the men, from whom so much is expected, with indulgent reverence:

[Quotes *II*, pp. 163, 165.]

And he frames an ingenious apology for the freedom of his humour, in this attack on the morals and person of his adversary:

[Quotes *II*, pp. 185–6.]

It was not only in these 'pen-combats' that this Literary Quarrel proceeded; it seems also to have broken out in the streets; for a tale has been preserved of a rencontre, which shows at once the brutal manners of Parker, and the exquisite wit of Marvell. Parker meeting Marvell in the streets, the bully attempted to shove him from the wall: but, even there, Marvell's agility contrived to lay him sprawling in the kennel; and looking on him pleasantly, told him to 'lie there for a son of a whore!' Parker complained to the Bishop of Rochester, who immediately sent for Marvell, to reprimand him; but he maintained that the doctor had so called himself, in one of his recent publications; and pointing to the preface, where Parker declares 'he is "a true son of his mother, the Church of England:" and if you read further on, my lord, you find he says: "The Church of England has spawned two bastards, the Presbyterians and the Congregationists;" ergo, my lord, he expressly declares that he is the *son of a whore!*'

Although Parker retreated from any further attack, after the second part of 'The Rehearsal Transprosed,' he in truth only suppressed passions to which he was giving vent in secrecy and silence. That, indeed, was not discovered till a posthumous work of his appeared, in which one of the most striking parts is a most disgusting caricature of his old antagonist [see No. 22]. Marvell was, indeed, a republican, the pupil of Milton, and adored his master: but his morals and his manners were Roman—he lived on the turnip of Curtius,[1] and he would have bled at Philippi. We do not sympathise with the fierce republican spirit of those unhappy times that scalped the head feebly protected by a mitre or a crown. But the private virtues and the rich genius of such a man are pure from the taint of party. We are now to see how far

---

[1] The substitution of Curtius for Curius Dentatus is in the first edition, and the error is continued by Dove (No. 50) and Coleridge (No. 52). Thompson (No. 38) seems to have been the first to make the allusion but without specifying the general's name.

private hatred can distort, in its hideous vengeance, the resemblance it affects to give after nature. Who could imagine that Parker is describing Marvell in these words?

[Quotes from No. 22.]

And elsewhere he calls him 'a drunken buffoon,' and asserts that 'he made his conscience more cheap than he had formerly made his reputation;' but the familiar anecdote of Marvell's political honesty, when, wanting a dinner, he declined the gold sent to him by the king, sufficiently replies to the calumniator. Parker, then in his retreat, seems not to have been taught anything like modesty by his silence, as Burnet conjectured; who says, 'That a face of brass must grow red when it is burnt as his was' [see No. 9]. It was even then that the recreant, in silence, was composing the libel, which his cowardice dared not publish, but which his invincible malice has sent down to posterity.

B *With Francis Turner*

In 1675 Herbert Croft, Bishop of Hereford, published four hundred copies of the *Naked Truth ... By an Humble Moderator*. Answering its sixty-six pages with a precise sixty-six pages the following year was the anonymously published *Animadversions ... upon the Naked Truth* by Francis Turner, master of St John's College, Cambridge, later bishop of Ely. This prompted Marvell's counter-attack: *Mr. Smirke: Or, the Divine in Mode ... Together with a Short Historical Essay ...* by Andreas Rivetus, Junior, Anagr[am] *Res Nuda Veritas*. (The French theologian and polemicist André Rivet had visited England in 1621, and his name happily allowed for an anagrammatic allusion to Croft's work.) Marvell again derived his titular character—in Wood's terms 'a neat, starcht, formal and forward divine'—from the minor character in a current dramatic production, Sir George Etherege's *The Man of Mode* (1676).

Marvell's authorship was apparently widely known. On 23 May 1676 Sir Christopher Hatton wrote: 'I hope Andrew Marvel will likewise be made an example for his insolence in calling Dr. Turner, Chaplain to His Royal Highnesse, Chaplaine to Sir Fobling Busy [for Fopling Flutter], as he terms him in his scurrilous satyrical answer to his Animadversions on Naked Truth' (*Correspondence of the Family of Hatton*, ed. E. M. Thompson, New York rept. 1965, I, p. 128). The printer had been imprisoned in early May for publishing without license after admitting that he had had the papers from Master Marvell (*CSP Dom.*, 1677-8, pp. 372-3).

13.   Bishop Croft's letter to Marvell

1676

The original of Bishop Croft's letter has disappeared. However, it is recorded in a copy, preserved at Lambeth Palace, of a letter of Marvell's sent to his nephew and dated 17 July 1676. In it he cited Croft's letter and his response. Both Thompson and Grosart printed the two as if they were individual items (*Letters*, p. 347).

Reprinted from Grosart II, pp. 489-90.

SIR,

I CHOOSE to run some hazard of this (haveing noe certaine information) rather than incurre the hateful censure of ingratitude to that person whoe hath set forth Mr. Smirk in soe trim and proper a dresse, unto whose hands I hope this will happily arrive to render him due thanks for the humane civility and Christian

charity shewed to the author of Naked Truth, soe bespotted with
the dirty language of foule mouthed beasts, whoe though he
feared much his owne weaknesse, yet by God's undeserved grace
is soe strengthened as not at all to be dejected or much concerned
with such snarling currs, though sett on by many spightefull
hands and hearts of a high stamp, but as base alloy. I cannot yet
get a sight of what the Bishop of Ely hath certainly printed,[1]
but keeps very close, to put forth, I suppose, the next approaching
session of parliament, when there cannot be time to make a reply;
for I have just cause to feare the session will be short. Sir, this
assures you that you have the zealous prayers and hearty service
(in voto, and would gladly be in actu)[2] of, Sir, the author of Naked
Truth, your humble servant [noe, I am wrong, 'tis your faithfull
servant.]

---

[1] In *Mr. Smirke* (Grosart IV, p 159), Marvell punningly refers to an attack on Croft by
Philip Fell and to an expected one by Peter Gunning, Bishop of Ely: 'But as to a new book
fresh come out, intitled "*The Author of the Naked Truth stripped naked*" (to the fell, or to the
skin) that hieroglyphical quibble of the "great gun" on the title page, will not excuse bishop
Gunning, for his sermon is still expected.'
[2] *in promise*, and ... *in deed*.

14. An anonymous poetic tribute to Marvell's character

c. 1689

This anonymous tribute, perhaps the work of Richard Graham whose elegiac poems were published in 1680, derives from a private manuscript. It was first printed in 1971 by L. A. Davies.

From *Yearbook of English Studies* 1 (1971), p. 101.

Mr Andrew Marvells character

Tho' faith in Oracles be long since ceas'd
And Truth in Miracles be much decreas'd
Yet all true wonders did not vanish quite
While Marvels tongue could speak or pen could write.
Marvell whose Name was for his Nature fitt,
Mirrour of Mirth, and Prodigie of Witt;
On whom the wondring Age did stare and gaze
As purblind People do when Comets blaze
And their presaging influence do spread
Upon the Crowned and the Mitred Head,   10
Perchance while he convers'd on earth with men
Poetick fury might misguide his Pen
Perhaps he might too daringly deride
A Princes Folly or a Prelats Pride;
Yet was his arm so farr from pulling down
A well-grac'd Mitre, or a right plac'd crown[1]
That Both when falling found from him support
Tho' neither were so kind as thank him for't:
Yet he ne'er envyed their auspicious Fate.
Who gain'd the Style of Poet Laureate   20

[1] Davies suggests that 'well-grac'd Mitre' may refer to Marvell's defense of Bishop Croft. 'A right plac'd crown' may equally well refer to the 'Horatian Ode'.

His Muse to greater Honour did aspire
She sings her Part in the celestiall Quire
Looks down with pity on the scribling crowd[1]
Whose witt is silent whilst their spite is proud.

15. W. P. Ker on the superiority of *Mr. Smirke*

1894

Academician and critic, W. P. Ker (1855–1923) published extensively on English literature. He contributed the essay on Marvell's prose to the multi-volume *English Prose Selections* edited by George Craik (see No. 58), appending the introductory section of *Mr. Smirke* (Grosart IV, 6–12) under the title (from Marvell) of 'Jocular Divinity.'

From *English Prose Selections*, III (1894), pp. 31–4.

The *Rehearsal Transprosed* and *Mr. Smirke* may still be read, but to come to them from *The Garden* and from *Appleton House*, is even a sorrier business than to pass from Milton's early poems into the thick of the warfare with Salmasius. Marvell can rail as well as Milton, but he has not Milton's dignity of anger at its highest. Both, in dealing with their adversaries, seem fully possessed by Dante's opinion that it is courtesy to spurn them in the face; and both seem to be pleased, as Dante is not, with the poor sport. Milton often makes some amends for this by the magnificence of his invective, but Marvell does not attempt to follow him. And even considered as invective, scolding, railing, 'flyting' (or whatever may be the right term for this, one of the

---

[1] Davies suggests ll. 19–22 perhaps recall 'Musicks Empire,' ll. 13–16.

oldest kinds of literature in the world), the *Rehearsal Transprosed* is apt to drag and grow wearisome. It is not as good as some things in Marvell's satiric couplets. The lines on *Holland* have more of the true Fescennine license in them; none of the jokes in prose are as good as the opening of *An Historical Poem*.

[Quotes ll. 1–4.]

The Proclamation of 'Bayes R.'—a *Declaration for the tolerating of Debauchery*—is the liveliest part of the *Rehearsal Transprosed*— a travesty of a solemn proclamation, bringing together all the fallacies picked out by Marvell from Parker's argument, especially, the theory that private vice is rather to be encouraged in the State than Nonconformity.

The serious part of the case against Parker is too much obscured and overlaid with railing accusations; but sometimes Marvell lets 'Bayes' alone, and argues more gravely than usual.

[Quotes *RT II*, p. 248.]

Here the fencing is good, the attack is not a noisy one. Marvell, in this and in some other places, by his close reasoning, and his self-command, makes his readers wish that Bayes and the Rehearsal had been out of the argument. It is thus, and not by anything like Milton's solemn denunciations, that Marvell shows his real strength.

The Divine in Mode is very much better than the *Rehearsal Transprosed*: there is more irony and less irrelevance. The comic invention is more effective: this passage on the author of the *Animadversions* is redeemed by one phrase from mere commonplace mockery:—

'And indeed the Animadverter hath many times in the day such fits take him, wherein he is lifted up in the air, that six men cannot hold him down; tears, raves, and foams at the mouth, casts up all kind of trash, *sometimes speaks Greek and Latin*, that no man but would swear he is bewitched' [Grosart IV, p. 32].

There is great comfort also in the allusion to 'the primitive times,' 'when the Defenders of the Faith were all heathens, and most of them persecutors of Christianity'—[Grosart IV, p. 14].

One of the best continuous passages of Marvell's prose is that which opens the description of *Mr. Smirke*. The 'voluntary humility' of it, the carefulness not to exact too much from the

other side, the irony, which one misses in the earlier book, may
be found in this one, at any rate in the beginning of it.

'For all are not of my mind, who could never see any elevated
to that dignity [of Bishop], but I presently conceived a greater
opinion of his wit than ever I had formerly' [Grosart IV, pp. 7–8].

'However it goes with excommunication, they should take
good heed to what manner of person they delegate the keys of
Laughter. It is not every man that is qualified to sustain the dignity
of the Church's jester' [Grosart IV, p. 9].

This same passage, in praising the original essay of the Bishop
of Hereford, rises to one of the few heights of serious eloquence
to be found in Marvell's prose, where for a moment he converses
again, in a sudden lull of the storm of controversy, with the Ideas
of Truth and Justice, and once again his mind, as in the Platonic
rapture of the *Garden*, 'withdraws into its happiness.' Passages of
this sort, however, are as uncommon in the prose essays as in the
satires of Marvell.

The *Account of the Growth of Arbitrary Government* is much less
emphatic, and at the same time a more elaborate piece of argument
and historical exposition, than the earlier treatises. Addressed as
it is 'to all English Protestants,' it escapes the temptation of the
more personal controversies, and can afford to be generous to
the old Cavaliers and the English Catholics, contrasting them with
'such as lie under no temptation of religion,' 'obliged by all the
most sacred ties of malice and ambition to advance the ruin of the
king and kingdom, and qualified much better than others, under
the name of good Protestants, to effect it' [Grosart IV, p. 263].

In the style of Marvell's prose, as in the style of his satiric
couplets, there are the marks of hesitation between two different
manners. He is sometimes clear, quick, and succinct, sometimes
he falls back into the heavier manner of the older writers. His
vocabulary is various. His practice on 'Bayes' involved a good
deal of slang; his satiric medley is dashed with a number of spices
from different languages, even from the Malay. He uses, without
distress, the heavier Latin armoury—'it is not wisdom in the
Church to pretend to, or however to exercise, that power of
angariating men further than their occasions or understandings
will permit' [Grosart IV, p. 24]. His reference in one place to 'the
musice and cadence of the period' is significant [R T I, p. 136].

C *With Roger L'Estrange*

The first edition of an *Account of the Growth of Popery and Arbitrary Government in England* appeared anonymously, with the title page dated 1677 and the place of publication given as Amsterdam. The following March the London *Gazette* printed an offer of a considerable reward to whoever could inform on the author or the printer. As Marvell himself makes clear in a letter of 10 June 1678 (*Letters*, p. 357), his authorship was known and, following his death in August, a second edition appeared with his name on the title page. In a series of virulent writings, Sir Roger L'Estrange (see No. 17) undertook to oppose Marvell both alive and dead.

16. An anonymous notice from *A Letter from Amsterdam*

1678

A Letter from Amsterdam, To A Friend in England, dated '18 April 1678, English stile' (p. 6) and printed in England, indicates that Marvell's authorship is known.

Extract from pp. 4–5.

Bring on *new Accounts of Growth of Popery and Arbitrary Government*: Charge them upon *evil Counsellers*: Be sure to lift 'em, at any hand lift 'em: Noyse may do it; ah, but Tumult is wanting! Then burn the Pope again, to fulfill the *Revelation*; that will draw together the Rabble; But forget not *Cakes and Ale for 'em*; Pot-valiant will do as much as *Press-money*, if you bid Defiance to a *Standing-army*, though it be but in the Clouds. . . .

The Pitcher hath two Ears: if you cannot lay hold on one side, take him by t'other, and dash him to the ground: Remember his name is not only *Lauderdail*, but *Guilford* too.[1] The honest *Covenanters* have been whetting their Pens at him these Five years; so have we our Spleens in *England*, we have spent the most part of our Gaul in Ink-pots; Try what the rest will do in a round Charge or two. Nevertheless, write on still: I am sorry we have lost the *Prime* Pen; therefore make sure of *Andrew*. Hee's a shrewd man against *Popery*, though for his Religion, you may place him, as *Pasquin* at *Rome* placed *Henry the Eighth*, betwixt *Moses*, the *Messiah*, and *Mahomet*, with this *Motto* in his Mouth, *quo me vertam nescio*.[2] 'Tis well he is now *Transprosed* into Politicks; they say he had much ado to live upon Poetry.

17. Sir Roger L'Estrange on the *Growth of Popery*

1678–1683/4

According to a mock-Rabelaisian sermon published in 1682, Roger L'Estrange (1616–1704) was acknowledged by common consent as the 'Yerker, Firker, Whipster, Scribler General of *Tory-Land*' (*Toryrorydammeeplotshamee*, p. 10). An ardent royalist, he was made a licenser of the press in 1633 (and subsequently forced to license *RT I*); he was also given the sole privilege of purveying the news but was driven from the field by the popularity of the *Gazette*. Taking the name Observator, he then published three series of generally bi- or tri-weekly comments on political matters from 1678 to 1686/7.

[1] Duke of Lauderdale and Earl of Guilford, John Maitland was active in suppressing Scots dissenters. (See *Letters*, pp. 313, 343.)
[2] I do not know whither I shall turn (from Cicero, *pro Cluent* 1.4).

Clearly recognizing its author, he first undertook to answer
the *Growth of Popery* under a parodic title in May 1678. With
the reprinting of the pamphlet after Marvell's death in August,
he then took the opportunity to reprint his own pamphlet
with a justifying address to the reader. Later, convinced that
the Popish Plot was 'only a *Fable*, accomodated to *Marvels*
Prediction,' he tirelessly and tiresomely repeated the connection in the dialogues—first between Tory and Whig, then
between Observator and Trimmer—that made up his
periodical.

(a)   Extract from *An Account of the Growth of Knavery, under the
Pretended Fears of Arbitrary Government and Popery* (1678), pp. 3–8.

SIR,
To give you my Opinion freely of the two Libels that you sent
me, me-thinks the Design of them lies too open to do much
Mischief; for I never saw so bare-fac'd an Araignment of the
Government, and all the Parts of it: *King, Lords, Commons, Judges,
Ministers of State*; they are all of them made *Conspirators*; against
the Sovereign Multitude, forsooth; and when the Libeller has
done with the *Body* of the *Commons*, he gives you a Defamatory
List of betwixt two and three hundred of their *Members*, provoking
and abusing all Sober Interests; Insomuch, that he has left himself
nothing to trust to, but the contemplation of a *General Tumult*,
which is the very Point he drives at in his *Appeal* to the *Rabble*.
   The Man, I confess, is a great Master of Words; but then his
Talent is that which the Lord *St. Albans* calls *Matter of Wonder
without Worthiness*; being rather the Suppleness and Address of
a Tumbler, than the Force and Vigor of a Man of Business. And
you cannot but observe too, that his Excursions, many of them,
are unmannerly and Vulgar, and fitter for the Stage of a *Merry-
Andrew*, or a *Jack-Pudding*,[1] than for a Paper of *State*.
   You would have me guess at the Author; and you might as
well bid me tell you the right Father of a Child by a common
Strumpet: But I think I may call him *Legion*; for they are *MANY*;
and there's a *Club* to his *Pen*, as well as to his *Pocket*. This I dare
assure you, that the Author of *A Letter from a Parliament-man*

[1] Synonym for Merryandrew.

72

to his Friend in the Country, concerning the Proceedings of the House of Commons, &c.[1] *in* 75. is very particularly acquainted with the Author of *An Accompt of the Growth of Popery, and Arbitrary Government, &c.* and the *Seasonable Argument*,[2] *&c.* that follow'd it, in 77.

The Pretence of the former Pamphlet is exhibited in the Title of it: *viz. An Account of the Growth of Popery, and Arbitrary Government in* England: And more particularly from *November* 1675, to *July* 1677. Upon these *Nineteen Months* the *Composer* has bestow'd precisely *Nineteen Sheets of Paper,* and laid himself out most wonderfully in his Politicks and Conceits, for the better Grace and Relish of the Discourse: But the Malignity of it is so rank, that there's scarce a Page where the Poyson has not eaten quite thorough the Vernish, and discover'd the Spring and Malice of the Design. View it narrowly, and you shall find the Pique to be as well Personal as Seditious, and the Work only of some Mercenary Pen to serve his principall's Animosity, as well as his Ambition. For a Man may see with half an Eye, how he *aggravates,* or *extenuates*; *disparages,* or *commends, reflects* upon, or *passes* over, as well *Actions,* as *Men,* according to the various Aspects of *Affections* or *Parties*; and without any regard to the Pulse or Truth of Publick Proceedings. By his Vein of improving the Invective Humour, it looks in some places as if he were *Transprosing* the *First Painter*,[3] only he has chang'd his Battery, which is a Property peculiar to his Party, constantly to hate those that are uppermost.

I was once a thinking to write a Just Reply upon the whole Relation, and to lay open the falshood of many Passages in it in matter of Fact; the Partiality of it in others; how perverted, and misapply'd it is throughout; and to shew what Gapps, and Maimes the Compiler of it has left in the Story, purposely to divert the *Reader* from minding the Coherence of Actions, and the reasonable Congruity of Counsels, and Affairs: What uncharitable and illogical Inferences he has drawn from matters as remote as *Tenterden* Steeple from being the cause of *Goodwin* Sands.[4] This was

1 This seven-page letter has been attributed to the Earl of Shaftesbury, whom Marvell admired (see *Letters,* p. 355) and whose spokesman he seems to have been to some extent. L'Estrange's statement has been interpreted as implying that Marvell was the author.

2 Purportedly also by Marvell and referred to above as the 'Defamatory List.'

3 An encomium of the Duke of York's victory (1655) over the Dutch by Edmund Waller (1666); other examples followed, though adapted to satiric intent.

4 A Kentish proverb (M. P. Tilley, *Dictionary of the Proverbs in England,* Ann Arbor: 1950, T91) signifying the use of a ridiculous cause to account for an important consequence.

the Method I had propounded to my self; but upon second Thoughts I quitted it, for these Reasons. First, It would have been too tedious; for I must in Honesty have printed the Libel as well as the Reply, which in Proportion would have amounted to near forty Sheets of Paper. Secondly, It would have been superfluous; for part of my Business being the Vindication of Truth from Calumny: I find the thing already done to my Hand, in the common Sentence is that pass'd upon it for a lew'd and shameless Imposture. And Thirdly, The Author himself, you see, has upon better consideration reduc'd his Pamphlet of 19 Sheets, into another of *Three*, as a more compendious Exposition of his Meaning: I speak of that Libel which you sent me, under the Name of *A Seasonable Argument to perswade all the Grand Juries in* England *to petition for a New Parliament; or a List of the Principal Labourers in the great Design of Popery, and Arbitary Power, &c.* So that my Task is only to make good in my Discourse the Parallel that I promis'd you in my Title, and then to pass some Remarks upon the Scope, and Venome of the Pamphlets themselves.

(b) 'The Address to the Reader' from *The Parallel or, An An* [*sic*] *Account of the Growth of Knavery* ... (1679).

There came forth about *two years since*, a *Couple* of *Seditious Pamphlets* in *quarto*; The *one*, just upon the heel of the *other*: The *former* was entitled, *An Account of the Growth of Popery and Arbitrary Government* in *England*, &c. which was followed by *A Seasonable Argument to perswade all the Grand Juries in England*, &c. the *latter* being only an *abstract* and *explication* of the *designe* of *the other*. This *Parallel* was in the *same Year* Printed and Published by way of reflection upon the aforesaid *Libles*, with references to the *Pages* of that *Edition*; and the *Controversy* should have rested there, if the *Authour* had not found himself honestly oblig'd to reprint the *Reply*; the *other side* having reviv'd the occasion of it, since the death of *Andrew Marvell*, by a *Posthumous Impression*, with his name at length to it.

There was at that time no mention or thought of the *PLOT*; and a man may see with half an eye that his *buzzing* so much about the matter of *Religion*, was only to make the *sedition* go down the better. For the main *drift* and *bent* of his *Discourse* is only *the paring of the Kings nails, clipping the wings of his Prerogative*, advancing a *pretended Soveraignty* in the *people*, and cutting his Majesty off from the most essential *privileges* of all *Government*, defaming his *Administration*, and furnishing the world with *Cases* and *Expedients* how a *Subject* may kill his *Prince* with a *good Conscience*.

Now if a body should speculate upon the *Reasons* of *Re-publishing* Mr. *Marvells Pamphlet* at *this time*, it would make the *Preface* longer then the *Book*, to recount them. First, there is *money* to be got by it, and that's five and fifty reasons in one. Secondly, the *Writing* or *Publishing* of a *Libell*, is lookt upon by some to be the high-way to preferment, as a *prickear'd Anabaptist* said t' other day, about the *Appeal from the Country to the City*; *'Tis a Nationall quarel* (says he) *and the Nation will stand by me in't*. Thirdly, as the *designe* gets ground, so it gathers *confidence;* and that which in 77. would have been worth two or three hundred pound to the *Discoverer*, may be worth twice as much now in 79. to the *Publisher* and *Printer*. There may be a fourth end in it, to *Canonize* Mr. *Marvell* (now in his grave) if not for a *Saint*, yet for a *Prophet*, in shewing how pat the *Popish Plot* falls out to his conjecture; and that he sees further into a millstone then another man: and why may not the *Replicant* as well be taken for a *Prophet*, that foretold the *Growth of Fanaticism*, as well as he did the *Growth of Popery*, and upon as good grounds too? *Dr. Don* in his *Ignatius's Conclave*, makes *Ignatius* to be so indu'd with the devil, that he was able to possess the very devil himself. Now whether the *Fanaticks* bring on the *Jesuits Plot*, or the *Jesuits* the *Fanaticks*, by counter-possessing one another, is not a farthing matter: But that the *devil* and his *dam* are now at work in the shape of *Angels of light*, to destroy our *Sacred Soveraign*, the *Church of England*, and the *Civil Government*, there is no more doubt to be made, then that if it were not for the hope of *another* world, a man had better be hang'd out of the way, then be Honest in *this*.

If the malevolent intent of the *Book* it self were not so *gross* and *manifest*, that a man may *run* and *reade* it, we could produce several other Instances of the same temper that fell from the *same pen*, and spake the *man* as much an *Enemy* to the *Monarchy* of *England* as to the *Ministers*: And it is no wonder, that the *Secretary* to a *Common-wealth* should write with the *Spirit* of a *Re-publican*: But we shall spare his *memory* in that particular, and only tell the *Reader* in one word more, that tho' the *many turns* of *State* that have hapned since Mr. *Marvells Account* of the *Growth of Popery* and

Arbitrary Government came first abroad; have laid the *book* open to further *confutation* and *censure;* we shall yet take no *advantage* of those *Events,* but leave this following *discourse* to shift for it self, *naked* and *unlick'd,* as it came *first* into the *world.*

(c)   Extract from the *Observator* 16 February 1683 (II, p. 16). L'Estrange's square brackets enclose quotations from Marvell.

To come now Close to the Matter; *Marvels Growth of Popery,* does not only *Suppose,* and *Presume,* but *Undertakes* to *Set forth* (even to the *Degree* of a *Demonstration*) The **Certainty** of a *Popish Plot:* Lays Open All the *Dreadfull Consequences* of *Slavery,* and *Damnation, that* are to *Attend* it; Tells ye(as it were *Prophetically*) that [*The Next Scene that Opens will be* Rome *or* Paris. fol. 54.] And All This, out of a *Pretended Zeal* for the *Preservation* of the *King,* the *Church,* and the *English Government.* Consider now, the *Seditious Doctrines* of the *Book;* The *Desperate Practices* and *Principles* of the *Greater Part* of the *True-Protestants,* and *Patriots,* that are *Celebrated* in it; Together with the *Condition* of the *Conspirators* that are to Carry on This *Popish* and *Arbitrary Design;* And you will see the *Cheat, Clearer* then the *Day;* and how the *Phanatical Conspiracy* puts it self forth, under the *Name* and *Colour* of a *Popish One.*

Trim. But do not you find *Marvels Conjecture,* and *Opinion* of the *Danger* of *Popery Confirm'd* by Mr *Otes'es Discovery,* the *Year Following?*

Obs. Yes Yes, as Jump, as if *Marvel* had Spit in the *Doctors Mouth;* And what the *One* **Foretold,** the *Other* **brought to pass**: (to **Light** I should say) *Marvel* **Dreamt** of a *Popish Plot,* and *Otes* **Expounded it.**

Trim. Will you have *Marvels Plot,* (as you call it) and *Otes'es,* to be all *One* then?

Obs. No No. How can *That* be; when the *One's* a *Romance,* and *T'other* a *History?* But yet let me tell ye, there are many that for want of looking **Very** *near* 'em, took 'em to be *Both* of a *Piece:* And 'tis a *Hard matter,* for a Body that has not some Skill in **Close Drawing,** to *Discern* the *Stitches* that *Tack* 'em together; for the *One* seems to *drop,* as naturally, into the *Other,* as a *River* does into the *Sea.*

Trim. Nay Nay. To give Every man his due; *Marvel* had the *Plot* in the *wind,* & Cry'd out **Treason**: But it was *Mr Otes* that found out the **Traytors.**

Obs. Or to give you it in a more *Familiar* Way: *Marvel* told the People that [**There was a thing to be done**] And then *Otes* told 'em [**who was to do it.** *The Next Scene will be* Rome] *says* Marvel *in Seaventy Seaven*; And then (to make **Him** *a Prophet*;) *Enter Guido Faux*, in *Seaventy Eight.* Now the *Foundation* of the *Main Cause*, Stands never the less *Firm*, for This *Wonderfull Connexion*, and *Resemblance*: That is to say, It does not at all *Impair* the *Credit* of *Otes'es Plot*, nor *Advance* the *Reputation* of *Marvels*, the *Transition* of the *One* into the *Other*; Though I find *many People* that are apt to think the *Better* of the *One*, and the *worse* of the *Other*, for *This appearance* of an *Intelligence* betwixt them; And no man has *Contributed* more to the *Scandal*, then *Otes Himself.*

18.   [? Marchamont Nedham] on the author of the *Growth of Popery*

c. 1678

In large part an ironic discourse in praise of the Earl of Shaftesbury's submission to his offences (25 February 1677/8), following on his imprisonment, *Honesty's Best Policy; or, Penitence the Sum of Prudence* was published without indication of author, place, or date. It has been ascribed to Marchamont Nedham (1620–78), the Cromwellian journalist whose political principles seem to have been persistently undercut by materialistic motives.

Extract from pp. 9–10, 14–15, 17–18.

It is for me only to give a few *Observations* about the Affairs which preceded his Lordships departure from Court, while he was a prime man in the Counsels of His Majesty, which have since been made the Subject of many a loud Clamor by the *Factious*

Party. Some *Observations* also I shall make of divers particulars, pointing out to you how, as soon as his Lordship went out, the World also it self was troubled, and began to grow out of Order. Perhaps it happened so, because his Lordship went out of Office, his great Wisdom and Conduct not being any longer at the Helm. A *Poet* of our own fancies the Frame of the World to be bolted together with a *small Pin* or two; if that be put out, all falls to pieces: therefore when he brings in *Catiline* in the *Third Act*, in a great chafe, because himself was rejected, and *Cicero* chosen *Consul*, he makes him thus vent himself in a *lofty Rant*,

> *Repulse upon Repulse?*
> *Oh that I could reach the Axel, where the Pins are,*
> *Which bolt this Frame, that I might pull them out,*
> *And pluck all into* Chaos *with my self!*

[Jonson's *Catiline*, III. i. 174–7 with variants.]

So that you see, if but a *Pin* or so be out, all falls into Confusion, if there be any Truth in *Poetry.* And it may be this was our Case, Who can tell? For, *Poets* have *unlucky Hits* many times, as well as *Polititians.* So have Historians too: For the *Record-keeper*, (or *Recorder*) of the *Faction*, I mean the Author of the *New Directory for Petty States-men*; that is to say, *The Account of the growth of Popery and Arbitrary Government*, &c. Reporteth to us, that the present *Lord Chancellor*,[1] another *Cicero*, came in his Lordships Place before the end of 1673. as the former *Cicero* came into that which was aim'd at by *Catiline.*

And then the *Golden times* before, and in 72. being gon, the *Iron Age* came on. But I must return where I left.

As to my Observations about the Affairs preceding his Lordships voidance from Court, I find the aforesaid *Recorder* hath been very punctual to record them; and one may well think he is not like to say any thing in prejudice of his Lordship, because I perceive in page 44 of his Pamphlet, he seems as if he would speak like a Friend of his: [quotes Grosart IV, pp. 291–2]....

What a lucky Defender and Advocate is this for his Lordship! I mean rather an unlucky; That he, who in a Treasonous Libellous Pamphlet, industriously now spread and dispersed into all hands

---

[1] Lord Heneage Finch, later Earl of Nottingham, replaced the Earl of Shaftesbury, dismissed 9 November 1673.

about the Kingdom, to rail down both *Houses of Parliament, his Royal Highness, all the high Officers of State,* the *Kings Privy Council,* the *Principal Secretaries,* all the *Judges,* all other *Officers of the Government,* and the *Court* it self, and then concludes all with a vile jeering Caress of His Majesty Himself; should in the same Book appear to be a Trumpeter of his Lordships Vindication and Praise. It looks ugly; but far be it from us, to think that there is any understanding betwixt him and the Author. 'Tis only his Lordships ill luck, that in divers other like Pamphlets the *Knaves* have been so bold as to commend him: and who can help it?

And I am sure the same Book [*A Letter from a Person of Quality to his Friend in the Country,* 1675], which condemned these [doctrines of the church], and vilified the *Bishops* too, bestows very high commendations of his Lordships Parts, Pains, and Labour about these matters: which, to the praise of his, and some other mens *Lungs,* took up the *House of Lords* with a debate of Sixteen or Seventeen whole days together, the House sitting many times till Eight or Nine a clock at night, and sometimes till midnight. However, they could not save the *Book* which makes report of this Noble Prize, from being, by order of the *Peers,* burnt by the hand of the *Hangman.* And indeed it well deserved so, because it charged the main stress of the Debate upon the shoulders of his Lordship; though the *Author* wrote as if he had been his Friend, by reason of the immoderate Praises that he loads him with in divers places. 'Tis an unhappy thing, and looks ill, that his Lordship should have such dangerous Friends as deserve Execution by the *Hangman*: for, what praise soever the fore-going *Author* may have fallen short in, another *Author* endeavors to make up, who seems a Friend too of his Lordships, by an excess of praising him for the opposing of that Oath; as may be seen in *pages* 57, 58, 59, 60, and 61, 62. [Grosart IV, pp. 305–10] of that *Author,* whom a little before we named the *Record-Keeper,* or *Recorder* of the *Faction*; that is more plainly, the Author of that most Villanous Book, Entituled, *An Account, &c.*

Nevertheless, the much long'd for 15*th* of *Feb.* 1676 being come, the King, as if He had forgotten all Faults, and Injuries of the former *Session,* (such is His marvailous Clemency and Patience) opened this with a Speech of a most obliging Nature, such a one

ANDREW MARVELL

as was a wonder, Considering what Provocations had been put
upon Him, and His Government in the Interval of the *Session*, by
the many most pernicious Books and Pamphlets which had been
spread by the *Faction* into all parts, to inflame and prepare the
People for new Commotions (if it might be) to disturb Him this
Session also, and Dissolve the Parliament.... But all this was but
Surdo canere;[1] what was to be done was before-hand resolved on;
the *Actors* entred in the House of Peers, and the *Tragy Comedy*
began thus, as the *Recorder of the Account of the growth of Popery*,
&c. *pages* 71 and 72. [Grosart IV, pp. 320–1] presents it (which
Book being now in the hands of the House of Peers, deserves
their most severe inquisition.) ...

What a virulent Scribe is this *Recorder*, that an ill Contest cannot
arise in Parliament, but he still brings in my Lord *Shaftsbury* as a
main man, a Beginner, or a Promoter of it! If he was so, the
greater then ought to be his Lordships Repentance all the days of
his Life; otherwise, though he hath done it at the *Lords Bar* there
is yet a Superior Bar hereafter which he must one day give an
Account to. In the meanwhile, both he and the *Duke* [of Buckingham, also sent to the Tower], being *Penitents Profest*, it sounds
not well that this *Recorder* should now be the Trumpet of their
Praises; for, we would fain believe they are real, and mean to give
him no more the like Occasion by *Parliament-pelting*; nor to
count him in the number of their Friends hereafter.

[1] To preach to the deaf.

19. An anonymous tribute
On his Excellent Friend

post 1678

This poem, consistently misdated 1677, was first published in *Poems of Affairs of State*, 1697, and ushers in the homage to Marvell as a patriot of renown. The single work alluded to (ll. 7–8) is the *Account of the Growth of Popery*.

From *Poems of Affairs of State*, pp. 131–2.

On his Excellent Friend Mr. Anth. Marvell

While lazy Prelates lean'd their Mitred-Heads
On downy Pillows, lull'd with Wealth and Pride,
(Pretending Prophesie, yet naught foresee.)
Marvell, this Islands watchful Centinel
Stood in the gap, and bravely kept his Post,
When Courtiers too in Wine and Riot slept:
Twas he th' approach of *Rome* did first explore,
And the grim Monster, Arbitrary Power.
The ugliest Giant ever trod the Earth,
Who like *Goliah* marcht before the Host: 10
Truth, Wit and Eloquence, his Constant Friends,
With swift dispatch he to the Main-Guard sends,
Th' Alarm strait their Courage did Excite,
Which check'd the Haughty Foes bold Enterprize,
And left them halting between Hope and Fear;
He like the Sacred *Hebrew* Leader stood.
The Peoples surest Guide, and Prophet too.
Athens may boast of Virtuous *Socrates*,
The Chief among the *Greeks* for Moral good.
Rome of her Orator, whose fam'd Harangues,   20
Foyl'd the Debauch'd *Antony*'s designs.
We him, and with deep Sorrows 'wail his loss;

81

But whether Fate or Art unturn'd his thread,
Remains in doubt, Fames lasting Register,
Shall leave his Name enroll'd as great as theirs,
Who in *Phillippi* for their Country fell.

20. Tell-Truth's comment on Marvell

c. 1680

This anonymous comment alludes both to Marvell's answers
to Parker ('the greatest Droll and Scribler') and to the *Growth
of Popery*.

Extract from *Tell-Truth's Answer to Tell-Troth's Letter* to
the Right Honourable the Earl of Shaftesbury, In Vindication
of his Lordship; By as down-right an ENGLISH-MAN as
himself, Without Scandalous REFLECTIONS, pp. 3–4.

And 'tis no wonder you should fling a stone at Mr. *Marvel's*
Grave, for any whiffling Cur will venture to beard a dead Lion:
'tis well known, that little *Andrew* (as you contemptibly call him)[1]
had Wit and Policy enough to silence the greatest Droll and
Scribler that ever troubled the Nation; and other Treatises that
are for the good of the Nation, cannot escape your Scurrilous
Reflections. And do not these Blisters on your Tongue betray the
venome of your heart, and plainly shew, you are no true friend to
the Church of *England*, but rather a Jesuite, or a favourer of
Popery, since you would hush us to sleep with apprehensions
that there is no fear of it till our throats are cut?

[1] In *A Letter to the Earl of Shaftesbury this* 9th *of July*, 1680, Tom Tell-Troth asserts that he
has read over an 'abundance of such ware as little Andrew Marvel's Unhoopable *Wit and
Polity*, and the Independent Comment amongst it, together with the *Growth of Popery*, &c...'
(p. 4).

21.   John Dryden's comments

1681, 1682

The sharp comments by the poet laureate and royal histori-
ographer John Dryden (1631–1700) can be accounted for in
part by his shifting political and religious allegiances and
in part by his personal and literary controversies. His elegy
on the death of Cromwell (in a volume that was to have
included Marvell's as well, entered in the Stationers' Register
20 January 1659) was later to be countered by his two celebra-
tions of the return of Charles II; his satire *Absalom and
Achitophel* (1681) was a vigorous attack on the Earl of
Shaftesbury, whose policies Marvell had favoured, as were
also *His Majesties Declaration Defended* (since 1935 accepted
as Dryden's) and *The Medal*; and in 1686 he was to become
a Roman Catholic.

For his share in inciting personal antagonism, Marvell had
given additional currency to the characterization of Dryden
as 'Bayes' in Buckingham's *Rehearsal* by derogatorily applying
the term to the high churchman Samuel Parker, and he had
mockingly alluded to Dryden as 'the *Town-Bays*' in his
commendatory poem on *Paradise Lost*.

(a)   Extract from *His Majesties Declaration Defended*, 1681 (in
answer to *A Letter from a Person of Quality to His Friend*, which
had attacked the Declaration), pp. 3–4, 13.

Accordingly, upon the first appearance of it in Print, five several
Pens of their *Cabal* were set to work; and the product of each
having been examin'd, a certain person of Quality appears to
have carried the majority of Votes, and to be chosen like a new
Matthias [Acts 1: 23–6], to succeed in the place of their deceas'd
Judas.[1] ...

---

[1] The allusion to the 'deceas'd *Judas*' is generally accepted as a reference to Marvell; cf.
Parker's earlier reference to him (No. 2) as *Judas*.

Popish and *Arbitrary*, are words that sound high amongst the multitude; and all men are branded by those names, who are not for setting up Fanaticism and a Common-wealth.

And when Papists are to be banished, I warrant you all Protestants in Masquerade must go for company; and when none but a pack of Sectaries and Commonwealths-men are left in *England*, where indeed will be the danger of a War, in a Nation unanimous? After this, why does not some resenting Friend of *Marvel's*, put up a Petition to the Soveraigns of his party, that his Pension of four hundred pounds *per annum*, may be transferred to some one amongst them, who will not so notoriously betray their cause by dullness and insufficiency?[1]

(b) Extract from 'Epistle to the Whigs' prefacing *The Medal*, 1682, A3ᵛ.

I have perus'd many of your Papers; and to show you that I have, the third part of your *No-protestant Plot*[2] is much of it stolen, from your dead Authour's Pamphlet call'd, the *Growth of Popery*; as manifestly as *Milton's* defense of the *English* people, is from Buchanan, *de jure regni apud Scotus.*

(c) Extract from the preface to *Religio Laici*, 1682, b1.

And *Martin Mar-Prelate* (the *Marvel* of those times) was the first Presbyterian Scribler, who sanctify'd Libels and Scurrility to the use of the Good Old Cause.

---

[1] There is no record of Marvell's having received a pension in addition to the standard pay of 6s.8d. as an MP for Hull (see No. 41).
[2] The third part of the *No-protestant Plot*, 1682, generally ascribed to 'the plotter' Robert Ferguson, is a vindication of the Earl of Shaftesbury.

22.   Bishop Parker on the *Growth of Popery* and the 'First Anniversary'

c. 1687

Many years after their flyting, Bishop Parker was still rankled by Marvell's attack. In commenting in general on the author of the *Growth of Popery* in his *De rebus sui temporis commentariorum* (pub. 1727), he also makes clear that Marvell was acknowledged as the author of the 'First Anniversary,' which had appeared anonymously in January 1655.

Extract from *Bishop Parker's History of His Own Time*, translated by Thomas Newlin (1727), pp. 332–7.

Amongst these lewd Revilers, the lewdest was one whose name was *Marvel*. As he had liv'd in all manner of wickedness from his youth, so being of a singular impudence and petulancy of nature, he exercised the province of a Satyrist, for the use of the Faction, being not so much a Satyrist thro' quickness of wit, as sowerness of temper; of but indifferent parts, except it were in the talent of railing and malignity. Being abandon'd by his father, and expell'd the University, he afterwards made his conscience more cheap than he had formerly made his reputation. A vagabond, ragged, hungry Poetaster, being beaten at every tavern, he daily receiv'd the rewards of his sawciness in kicks and blows. At length, by the interest of *Milton*, to whom he was somewhat agreeable for his ill-natur'd wit, he was made Under-secretary to *Cromwell's* Secretary. Pleas'd with which honour, he publish'd a congratulatory poem in praise of the Tyrant; but when he had a long time labour'd to squeeze out a panegyrick, he brought forth a satyr upon all rightful Kings; saying that *Cromwell* was the sun, but other Monarchs were slow bodies, slower than *Saturn* in their revolutions, and darting more hurtful rays upon the earth. That if each of their reigns were to be continued to the *Platonick* age, yet no King would ever do any good to the world: That it was the purpose of them all to bring their subjects into slavery: That they pursue no enemy but their own countrymen: That they wage war against foreigners unwillingly, and because they are forc'd to it, but voluntarily and freely against their own people; neither do they cease from it, till they can treat them as conquer'd slaves; nor do they fight against them only, but also against God: That they are all drunk with the enchantments of the Whore of *Babylon*: That they fight for Antichrist, against the Lamb: That they serve the *Roman* Whore: That they not only desert, but hinder the work of the Lord, begun in this age by his saints, under the auspicious conduct of *Cromwell*.

But the King being restor'd, this wretched man falling into his former poverty, did, for the sake of a livelihood, procure himself to be chosen Member of Parliament for a Borough, in which his father had exercis'd the office of a Presbyterian teacher, and done notable service in the Rebellion: For there was an ancient custom, that the expences of those that were elected into Parliament, should be born by the Borough for which they were chosen, at the rate of five shillings a day. This custom had a long time been antiquated and out of date, Gentlemen despising so vile a stipend, that was given like alms to the poor;[1] yet he requir'd it for the sake of a bare subsistence, altho' in this mean poverty he was nevertheless haughty and insolent. In all Parliaments he was an enemy to the King's affairs, being one of those Conspirators, who being sixty in number, of the remains of the Rebellion, had bound themselves by oath, from the beginning, to give all the trouble they could to the King, and especially never to vote for granting any taxes. But these men had little weight in that Assembly, being look'd upon with shame and disgrace; so that if they would do no good, they could do no hurt; for they were hardly ever suffer'd to speak without being hiss'd at; and our Poet could not speak without a sound basting: Wherefore, having frequently undergone this discipline, he learn'd at length to hold his tongue. But out of the House, when he could do it with impunity, he vented himself with the greater bitterness, and daily spewed infamous libels out of his filthy mouth against the King himself.

If at any time the Fanaticks had occasion for this libeller's help, he presently issued forth out of his cave, like a gladiator, or a wild beast. But this *Bustuarius*, or fencer, never fought with more fury,

[1] For this long-lived canard, see No. 41.

than near his own grave, in a book written a little before his death, to which he gave this title, *Commentaries concerning the Growth of Popery, and Tyrannical Government in* England [*sic*]. In which, after he had complain'd that the Papists had a long time laid in wait to subvert the Kingdom, and had accomplish'd their intended villany, unless *Shaftsbury*, with his associates, had interpos'd; he begun his scurrilous discourse with those seven deadly sins before-mentioned, by which he said it was almost to a miracle, that the Kingdom was not ruin'd. . . .

A shrewd man, and a lucky advocate for his friends! who blacken'd the King, the States of the Kingdom, the Privy-Council, and all the chief Ministers of State, that he might celebrate the merits of *Shaftsbury*'s party, who had deserved so well from their country, and therefore began with so evident and notorious a lie.

23. A further comment on the *Growth of Popery*

1689

In his eight-page pamphlet, the anonymous commentator prefaces a long citation from the *Growth of Popery* with an admiring comment.

Extract from *Mr. Andrew Marvell's Character of Popery*, 1689, pp. 3–4.

Now as no Government can subsist without Religion; we thought our selves the most happy People in the World, when once reform'd, not only to the Protestant Religion, which is that which comes nearest to the Rules of Sacred Institution, but to the most refined Exercise of the Protestant Religion, now practis'd in the World; Wherein there is neither Defect of Devotion, nor redundances of Superstition, a Decency with Gravity, a Decorum avoiding the Moroseness of a Clownish Behaviour to the Sovereign of Heaven. No Superstitious assuming to its self a Sanctity above others, but a Piety and Charity grounded upon and warranted by Scripture, without which all Religion is but a seeming, and no true Religion.

For this Reason it was, that the Author of this ensuing Paper, a Person of no less Piety and Learning then Sharpness of Wit and Soundness of Judgment, wrote with such an Abhorrence as he does of the Popish Religion, if it may deserve to be call'd a Religion, as the Gentleman well observes; and that he laboured to set it forth in its proper Colours, as if he had intended it as his last Legacy to this Nation, to shew how ruinous it would be to us, should we be again compell'd to imbrace it; and with the Dog be constrained to return to our former Vomit: And as it were prophetically to let us understand what a Deliverance God has bin pleased to bless us withal, in so lately freeing the Kingdom from that Inundation of Antichristian Pomp and Vanity, and Cheats of Romish Superstition, which was about to have overwhelmed it. 'Tis true, the touches are bold; but it is a Description to the Life: And bold Stroaks in Painting are many times more grateful to the Eye and Master-like, than the smooth Touches of an effeminate Pencil. For which Reason it was thought expedient to abstract these few Pages from the rest of the Treatise, and to hang them up in the Face of the Nation, as the most lively Picture of the Sensuality, Vanity and Treachery of the Romish Profession.

[Quotes Grosart IV, pp. 250–8]

24. Three eighteenth-century historians comment

post 1706, 1718, 1730

Roger North (1663–1734) wrote his *Examen* (pub. 1740) to vindicate Charles II and to answer a 'Cloaca of Libels,' that is, the third volume of the *Complete History of England* by White Kennet, politically a Whig. He describes Kennet's sources as 'scandalous Libels of the Time, wrote in dark Corners and sent out among the common People to delude the unthinking Part of Mankind.... Of this Sort are the *Growth of Popery*, first and second Parts [in reference to *The Second Part of the Growth of Popery*, 1682, by Philo-Veritas, that is Robert Ferguson, which was paginated to follow Marvell's work] ... whereof the Authors in their Time, as sometimes Thieves, by lying hid, escaped due Punishment' (p. vi).

Laurence Echard (?1670–1730), politically a Tory, published his three-volume history between 1707 and 1718.

John Oldmixon (1673–1742), a 'virulent Party-writer for hire,' according to Alexander Pope, published the first volume of his history in 1730.

(a)   Extract from North's *Examen: Or, an Enquiry Into the Credit and Veracity of a Pretended Complete History*, 1740, pp. 140, 141–2.

Now observe, in the Passage cited out of our Author, that he is so addicted to the Libels of that Time, that he has stole the Title of the worst of them, that is, *Growth of Popery*, to make good his Reflection here. And that very Libel was generally made Use of, by the Party, as Instructions, or a Repertory of Slanders and Misconstructions, to throw out against the Court, and, for that Purpose, was calculated proper for Use in Clubs and Coffee-houses; and therefore better deserves the old Title of *An Help to Discourse*, changing only the last Word for *Sedition*.

I shall not have a fairer Opportunity, than here, to take Notice of a stately Encomium the Author has dressed up, and bestowed upon *Andrew Marvel's Growth of Popery*, the Libel aforementioned.* He says, *The Dangers of Popery, and the Advances of the Popish Interest at Court, were freely represented in it, which was so offensive to the Ministry, that his Majesty caused an Order to be published*, for Rewards to the Discoverer of this and other Libels; which the Order terms 'seditious and scandalous—against the Proceedings of the two Houses of Parliament, and other his Majesty's Courts of Justice, to the Dishonour of his Majesty's Government, and the Hazzard of the public Peace.' The Author says, *freely represented*; that, in his *Lingua*, means *truly*; for Freedom, opposed to Restraint of Speech, hath no other Sense. And so he gives the Lye to a public Order of State that terms this a seditious and scandalous Libel. And, for his *Free*, we know how near akin his *Free-representers* are to his *Free-thinkers*, who use the Word in the Sense of *Dare-Devil*, which must needs run in his Mind; but I have no Business with them here. I do not condemn our Author of his singular Civility to this Libel; for he hath served himself, out of both the first and the second Parts, for the Loan of most of his considerable Abuses and Misrepresentations. . . .

The Author of that Libel was very well qualified for Mischief of that Kind; having been *Oliver Cromwell's* Secretary, and survived his Master to good Purpose.† Our Historian thinks he has shrewdly lampooned the Government, by an Eulogy on this vile Libel. I believe it is the first Time that a scandalous, infame State Libel was honoured with a direct Encomium in a solemn History, that titles itself *compleat*. And, for the Charm of his Word *Free*, if he himself had not been full of Freedoms, which good Men detest, and (for other than secular Reasons) dare not take, he had never wove in that Atheistical Term to commend Falseness and Undutifulness to lawful Superiors. But we do not wonder his Friend *Andrew* is so satyrical against the Authority of God's Vicegerent on Earth, when he wrote with no less Malice and Defiance against the Religion of *Christ*, and the Symbols of our Holy Faith; ridiculing the *Nicene* Fathers, and making an Idiot of *Constantine the Great*, and first Christian Emperor: As who will may see in a base

---

* The Author's Encomium on *A. Marvels* Libel, P. 361 [for 348].
† An account of *Andrew Marvel*, and his infamous Practices.

Pamphlet of his styled, *An History of Creeds and Councils*.[1] And yet this Free-thinker is set forth, with the Praises of a Free-representer, by the Reverend Author here. *O mores!*

(b) Extract from Echard's *History of England*, 1707–18, III, p. 501.

After all these, we shall mention two fam'd Writers that made much Noise in the World, *Andrew Marvel*, and *Marchamont Nedham*, both pestilent Wits, and noted Incendiaries. But Mr. *Marvel*, having an Appearance of more Honesty and Steadiness, is first mention'd. He was Son to *Andrew Marvel*, the facetious *Calvanistical* Minister of *Hull*, who gave him an Academical Education in *Cambridge*; where gaining the Mastership of the *Latin* Tongue, he became Assistant to *John Milton*, when he was *Latin* Secretary to *Cromwell*, and very intimate and conversant with him.... He was of a reserv'd Conversation, and a thoughtful keen Wit, which he employ'd with great Severity, not only against particular Persons, but against the Church and Crown; and he made himself very remarkable by his *Rehearsal transpros'd*, and his *Growth of Popery*, the latter of which brought him into Danger from the State; but Death put an end to all a little before the Discovery of the present [Titus Oates'] Plot.

(c) Extract from Jon Oldmixon's *History of England During the Reigns of the Royal House of Stuart* (1730), pp. 491, 607–8.

But when [Echard] comes to give an Account of the *Beaux Esprits*, the fine Wits of the Restoration Period, he omits telling us how *Waller*, *Sprat*, *Dryden*, *South*, had distinguish'd themselves by such Panegyricks upon *Cromwel*, that they out-did every thing which had till then been seen of *English* Poetry. Coke says, *The Poets strain'd their Wits to that Pitch to celebrate his Encomiums, that they cou'd never after arrive to it.* Dr. *Sprat*, Bishop of *Rochester*, and Dr. *South*, Canon of *Christ-church*, strain'd higher than even *Waller* and *Dryden* in praise of *Oliver*. To his List of polite Writers might have been added *Wilkins* and *Bates*; and as to *D'avenant* and *L'Estrange's* refining and improving our Tongue, he shew'd his Knowledge in Language to be as imperfect as in History. How came he to forget the immortal *Milton*, and the very witty *Marvel*?

---

[1] *A Short Historical Essay concerning General Councils, Creeds, and Impositions, in Matters of Religion* was appended to *Mr. Smirke* and then republished separately in 1680, 1687, 1703.

I suppose they were too *Republican* with him to have *Politeness* and *Taste*.

It must not be forgot, that *Echard* tells us, the King prepared for this Session of Parliament, by doing some terrible Things as well as popular, to shew his Authority as well as Clemency in suppressing Libels and seditious Discourses, particularly Mr. *Andrew Marvel's Growth of Popery*, which is as full of Truth as the Addresses publish'd by his Majesty's *Gazette* some Time after were full of Falshood.

D *With Thomas Danson*

In *Remarks Upon a Late Disingenuous Discourse, Writ by one T. D. ...* Marvell undertook to support a theological argument (on the absolute prescience of God and man's moral accountability) enunciated in 1677 by the dissenting minister John Howe against the attack of a fellow-dissenter and former fellow-student at Cambridge, Thomas Danson. Published anonymously in 1678 (the title page reads simply 'By a Protestant'), Marvell's castigating (and scarce) pamphlet seems to have evoked scant comment at the time and very little subsequently. In his *Memoirs of the Life of ... Howe* in 1724, Edmund Calamy, the grandson of one of the group of Presbyterian authors known as 'Smectymnuus,' contributed a single observation: 'I know not that Mr. *Howe* took any notice of him; tho the ingenious *Andrew Marvel* Esq; made a very witty and entertaining Reply to him' (p. 68).

Licensed 17 April 1678, scarcely four months before Marvell's death, the *Remarks* shows little of its author's characteristic humour. Since only the initials 'T.D.' appear on the title page of his opponent's treatise, Marvell mockingly assumes that they refer to 'The Discourse' and consequently derides his opponent throughout as 'it.'

---

25. Henry Rogers on Marvell's defense of Howe

1836

It was, interestingly enough, a reading of John Howe's *The Redeemer's Tears over Lost Souls* which diverted Henry Rogers (1806–77) from serving his apprenticeship as a surgeon to becoming a Congregationalist minister. In addition to his teaching, preaching, and editing, he was a steady contributor to the *Edinburgh Review* (see No. 57). His first important publication was *The Life and Character of John Howe* (1836, reprinted 1863, 1874, 1879), which was followed in 1862–63 by an edition in six volumes of Howe's works.

This extract, usefully summarizing the background of the controversy, is printed from the 1863 edition, pp. 157–76.

As the following chapter will probably contain little to interest the general reader, I may apprize him that it may be omitted without impairing the continuity of the narrative, since it is almost wholly parenthetical. . . . But to the curious in literary history, and to the admirers of Andrew Marvell's genius, I feel that no apology is necessary. They will probably think a chapter which has in it so much of Andrew Marvell, and so little of the author, by far the most interesting in the volume.

That I may not detain them, therefore, from matter which I know will be so much more grateful to them than any observations of mine, I shall simply beg their attention to a short detail of the circumstances which led to the curious publication from which the following extracts are made, and then dismiss them, to enjoy those extracts at their leisure. I would merely remark further, by way of whetting their appetite, that the tract in question is extremely rare; that it is not published in any edition of Marvell's works, and was evidently unknown to his biographers and editors. . . .

In 1677, Howe, at the request of the Hon. Robert Boyle, published his little treatise, entitled, 'The Reconcilableness of God's Prescience of the Sins of Men with the Wisdom and Sincerity of His Counsels and Exhortations, and whatever other means He used to prevent them.' ...

The views which this tract contains are so sober and chastened, that Anthony Wood—who, by the way, was about as competent a judge of such a question, as a mere antiquary would be of a question of science—proclaims the author 'a great and strict Arminian.'

It could hardly be expected, therefore, that it would satisfy those who held extreme opinions on the subject of the Divine *predetermination*, and it was, accordingly, attacked by no less than three writers. The first was Theophilus Gale, who inserted some animadversions in the fourth and last part of his celebrated work, 'The Court of the Gentiles.' To these animadversions Howe himself replied, in a postscript to his treatise, in which he exposes the false logic, and, what is worse, the glaring misstatements of his adversary. A second assailant was an ejected minister, named John Troughton. His initials only are prefixed to his piece, which professes to be a reply not only to Howe's original treatise, but to the postscript also. The third was Thomas Danson, also an ejected minister. He had been an intimate friend and fellow-collegiate of Howe's, for which reason he also affixed only his initials to the title-page.

To neither of these latter opponents did Howe publish any reply. As to Danson, his little book was not only most illogical, and full of misconception and misrepresentation, but displayed much arrogance and vanity; and these considerations alone would probably have deterred Howe from breaking silence. He would have been, in the last degree, unwilling to say anything in a case in which, if he had spoken at all, he must have spoken with an unwonted, and, to him, ungrateful severity.

But though Howe himself was silent, a very sufficient champion voluntarily undertook his defence. This was no less than Andrew Marvell.

If not distinguished by any extraordinary aptitude for metaphysical speculation, this great man at least possessed a clear, sound, healthy understanding; and, in more than ordinary measure, that practical sagacity, which admirably qualified him for appreciating the character and detecting the sophistry of an over-subtle and trifling disputant.

Much subtlety of reasoning was not what the case principally required. Marvell had what was much more effective in such a controversy; the wit and sarcasm which had so often chastised ignorance, insolence, and vanity.

It is highly honourable to Marvell that his extraordinary powers of satire, (powers which are so often employed to gratify malignity of feeling, or at the best an ostentatious vanity,) were in his case never employed except in the cause of truth or oppressed innocence. He reminds one of Spenser's Talus, the attendant of Arthegal, 'that yron man' whose terrible severities were meted out with the strictest justice, and never descended except on the head of flagrant crime.

His name was Talus, made of yron mould,
Immoveable, resistless, without end;
Who in his hand an yron flail did hold,
With which he threshed out falsehood and did truth unfold.
Spenser's Fairy Queen. Book V. canto i.

But though Marvell never employed his powers of wit and sarcasm for any selfish purpose, and seemed quite willing, as far as his own fame went, to let them slumber for ever in the cloud, any impudent assault on innocence and virtue, any extraordinary display of tyranny, meanness, fraud, or falsehood, never failed to provoke the bolts of this great avenger. All his principal productions owed their origin solely to his chivalrous love of truth, justice, and honour. It was thus with his greatest work, 'The Rehearsal Transprosed,' against Parker; with his 'Defence of the Naked Truth,' against the flippant and conceited Francis Turner; and with his present tract against Danson.

This tract is entitled, 'Remarks on a late disingenuous Discourse, written by one T. D., under the pretence "De Causa Dei," and of answering Mr. John Howe's letter and postscript of "God's Prescience," etc., affirming as the Protestant doctrine, "That God doth by efficacious influence universally move and determine men to all their actions, even to those that are most wicked." By a Protestant'* . . .

* Wood ('Athenae Oxonienses,' Edition Bliss, vol. iv) says, in the account of Thomas Danson, 'This Book,' speaking of the tract against Howe, 'hath only the initial letters

The tract opens with the following noble reflections on the unprofitable questions which often occupy speculative theology. To the sagacious and practical mind of Andrew Marvell, a man engaged all his life in public affairs, such questions were likely to appear in all their frivolity. He thus begins:

[Quotes Grosart IV, pp. 167–70.]

These observations are followed (for Marvell could not long maintain so grave a strain) by some good-humoured banter on Howe's apology for the *haste* with which his work had been written: after which, he suddenly drops his ironical vein, and breaks out into expressions of the most ardent admiration, both of Howe and his performance.

[Quotes IV, pp. 171, 172–5]

Such is the introduction to this tract. The author then proceeds to convict 'The Discourse' of several different kinds of misstatement, or fallacious reasoning;—as 'of its trifling and cavilling about words, when they affect not the cause; of its ignorance and confusion about the matter that is in controversy; of its falsifications and fictions of what its opponent hath *not* said; of its injurious perverting of what he *hath* said; of its odious insinuations; of its violent boasting and self-applause; of its gross absurdities, inconsistencies, self-contradictions, and unsafe expressions; and of the wrath and virulence of its spirit.'...[1]

T. D. set to it, because it was written against his intimate friend and fellow-collegiate. Afterwards came out a book entitled, "Remarks upon a late disingenuous Discourse, writ by one T. D., London, 1678," said to be by "A Protestant," but whether by John Howe, query.' This sage query shows that Wood could never have seen Marvell's Tract, or he would never have been at a loss for an answer to his own interrogatory. It is avowedly written by a *layman*, with the express purpose of inducing Howe *not to engage in the controversy*; it is full of his *praises* from beginning to end; and has just all those qualities, both of thought and style, of which he was most destitute.

But though it was certainly not written by Howe, this, it may be said, does not prove it to have been written by Marvell. I grant it: that is to be determined by other evidence. That the tract was, in Marvell's day, universally and undoubtingly ascribed to him, appears from Calamy. ... The point, however, would be sufficiently clear, even if this testimony were wanting. The internal evidence alone would decide it. None who are in the slightest degree acquainted with Andrew Marvell's peculiar vein of humour, can mistake any half-dozen pages as the composition of any other author.

[1] The author here telescopes Marvell's disparate 'articles' against Howe.

A few brief extracts will amuse the reader. The following is a ludicrous description of the manner in which his opponent manages to shift the terms of the question, as suited his convenience.

[Quotes IV, pp. 190–3, 198, 230.]

The conclusion is truly eloquent, and is all I can afford space to give. In the ludicrous remarks he makes on Howe's three opponents, the readers of Marvell cannot fail to recognise that felicitous readiness of repartee, and that sustained and apparently exhaustless humour, by which his wit is so especially characterized.

[Quotes IV, pp. 239–42.]

26. Dr John Brown on Marvell

1854

John Brown (1784–1858) of Edinburgh, DD, published a three-volume edition of scarce theological tracts, including Howe's discourse. His succinct comment indicates that even in theological circles an evaluation of Marvell's effort in matters of dogma was coloured by his general reputation as a wit.

Extract from the Prefatory Notice, *Theological Tracts* (Edinburgh, 1854), III, pp. 77–8.

Andrew Marvell, the friend of Milton, an incorruptible patriot, in most venal times, and perhaps the wittiest prose writer in the English language, was the son of a learned and pious Puritan minister of the same name, master of the Grammar school, and lecturer of Trinity church, in Kingston-upon-Hull. ... Besides the poems attributed to him, *some* of which are of high merit, he published a variety of tracts in prose, all of them occasional. His most celebrated work is, 'The Rehearsal Transposed' [*sic*], written in opposition to the infamous Samuel Parker, afterwards Bishop of Norwich [*sic*]. This little book, in two parts, with a profusion of witty sarcasm, contains much solid argument and eloquent writing, and may justly be reckoned one of the ablest exposures of the maxims of religious tyranny. It extorted high praise even from Swift, no friend to its principles. ...

The Tract that follows has never been included in any edition of Marvell's works, though its merits well entitle it to such a place, and its authenticity is indisputable.

SATIRIST, PATRIOT, AND EMERGENT POET

1652–1845

---

27. Milton's recommendation of Marvell

1652/3

In 1652–3 Milton recommended Marvell to the position of Assistant Latin Secretary to the council of State, an appointment he did not receive until 1657. Instead it was given to Sir Philip Meadows, whose English translation of some verses from the *Pharsalia* which Georges de Brebeuf had rendered into French and Marvell again into Latin is recorded in the Popple manuscript (Bod. MS. *Eng. poet. d.* 49) following Marvell's version.

Reprinted from the *Works of John Milton* (New York, 1936), XII, pp. 329–30.

My Lord,

But that it would be an interruption to the publick, wherein your studies are perpetually imploayd, I should now & then venture to supply this my enforced absence with a line or two, though it were my onely busines, & that would be noe slight one, to make my due acknowledgments of your many favours; which I both doe at this time & ever shall; & have this farder which I thought my parte to let you know of, that there will be with you to morrow upon some occasion of busines a Gentleman whose name is M^r. Marvile; a man whom both by report, & the converse I have had with him, of singular desert for the State to make use of; who alsoe offers himselfe, if there be any imployment for him. His father was the Minister of Hull & he hath spent foure yeares abroad in Holland, France, Italy, & Spaine, to very good purpose,

as I beleeve, & the gaineing of those 4 languages; besides he is a
scholler & well read in the latin & Greeke authors, & noe doubt
of an approved conversation; for he com's now lately out of the
house of the Lord Fairefax who was Generall, where he was in-
trusted to give some instructions in the Languages to the Lady
his Daughter. If upon the death of M^r. Wakerley the Councell
shall thinke that I shall need any assistant in the performance
of my place (though for my part I find noe encumberance of that
which belongs to me, except it be in point of attendance at Conferences with Ambassadors, which I must confesse, in my Condition I am not fit for) it would be hard for them to find a Man soe
fit every way for that purpose as this Gentleman, one who I beleeve
in a short time would be able to doe them as good service as
M^r. Ascan. This my Lord I write sincerely without any other end
than to performe my dutey to the Publick in helping them to an
able servant; laying aside those Jealosies & that æmulation which
mine owne condition might suggest to me by bringing in such a
coadjutor; & remaine,

My Lord your most obliged & faithfull servant } Feb: the 21:
              John Milton.   } 1652.

For the Honourable the Lord Bradshaw.

28.   John Aubrey's comments

post 1678

The lively antiquarian John Aubrey (1626–97) recorded
several comments on Marvell in his *Brief Lives* (first published
in 1813), which reappear in part in *Letters from the Bodleian*
and in Anthony à Wood's *Athenae Oxonienses* (see No. 10).

Extract from *Brief Lives*, ed. A. Clark (1898), II, pp. 53–4,
56, 304.

In the time of Oliver the Protector he was Latin Secretarie. He was a great master of the Latin tongue; an excellent poet in Latin or English: for Latin verses there was no man could come into competition with him. The verses called 'The Advice to the Painter' were of his making.

His native towne of Hull loved him so well that they elected him for their representative in Parliament, and gave him an honourable pension to maintaine him.

He was of a middling stature, pretty strong sett, roundish faced, cherry cheek't, hazell eie, browne haire. He was in his conversation very modest, and of very few words: and though he loved wine he would never drinke hard in company, and was wont to say that, *he would not play the good-fellow in any man's company in whose hands he would not trust his life.*

He kept bottles of wine at his lodgeing, and many times he would drinke liberally by himselfe to refresh his spirits, and exalt his muse.

As to Tom May, Mr. Edmund Wyld told me that he was acquainted with him when he was young, and then he was as other young men of this town are, scil. he said he was debaucht *ad omnia* : but doe not by any meanes take notice of it—for we have all been young. But Mr. Marvel in his poems upon Tom May's death falls very severe upon him.

Mr. Andrew Marvell, who was a good judge of witt, was wont to to say that [the Earl of Rochester] was the best English satyrist and had the right veine.

29.   James Yonge, from his *Journal*

c. 1681–2

Traveller, surgeon at Plymouth, and member of the Royal
Society, James Yonge (1647–1721) kept a journal recording
his experiences from his boyhood under Cromwell to his old
age under Queen Anne. Prefacing it is 'A List of Famous Men
and Women I have Seen in My Travels,' and his modern
editor places the reference to Marvell *c.* 1681–2.

Extract from the *Journal of James Yonge*, ed. F. N. L. Poynter
(1963), p. 23.

Mr. Andrew Marvell, Burgess for Hull, an ingenious man, author
of some poems, 'Advice to the Paynter,' *Miscellany* [*Poems*], *Re-
hersal transposed* [*sic*]; vindicated Mr. How, and the naked truthe,
a man not well affected to the Church or Government of England.

30.   Nahum Tate, an allusion

1694

The poet laureate Nahum Tate (1652–1715) is known for
his collaboration with Dryden in the second part of *Absalom
and Achitophel*, his libretto for Purcell's *Dido and Aeneas*, and
most of all for his version of *King Lear* with a happy ending.

Extract from *In MEMORY of Joseph Washington, Esq; Late of
the Middle Temple, an Elegy* (1694), ll. 69–80.

His Skill in Laws was less for private Gain
Employ'd, than publick Freedom to Maintain;   70
While Mercenaries with the Current steer'd,
His Country's constant Patron he appear'd.
With *Roman* Virtue at the needful Hour,
Oppos'd encroaching Tides of Lawless Pow'r.
His brandish'd Pen, in Liberty's Support,
Cou'd Lightning on th' astonish'd Foe retort.
Scarcely in *Marvel's* keen Remarks we find
Such Energy of Wit and Reason join'd.
Great *Milton's* Shade with pleasure oft look'd down,
A Genius to applaud so like his Own.   80

31.   Preface to *Poems on Affairs of State*

1697

Clearly designed as a puff in part since many of its attributions
are false, the 1697 edition of *Poems on Affairs of State* lists on
its title page ten of 'the greatest Wits of the Age,' including
'Andrew Marvell, Esq;' 'Mr. Milton,' and 'Mr. Dryden.'
Its unsigned Preface is of interest in defending both harsh
versification and the license of poets writing for political ends.

From the Preface, *Poems on Affairs of State* (1697), A3–A5^v.

The common Aim of Prefaces to prepossess the Reader in favour
of the Book, is here wholly useless; for what is now publish'd is
none of the trifling Performances of the Age, that are yet to make
their fortune, but a Collection of those Valuable Pieces, which
several great Men have produc'd, no less inspir'd by the injur'd
Genius of their Country, than by the Muses. They are of Establish'd Fame, and already receiv'd, and allow'd the best Patriots,
as well as Poets. I am sensible, that should we consult our super-

ficial Hypocriticks, they would often be apt to arraign the Numbers; for there are a sort of Men, who having little other merit, than a happy chime, would fain fix the Excellence of Poetry in the smoothness of the Versification, allowing but little to the more Essential Qualities of a Poet, great Images, good Sense, &c. Nay they have so blind a Passion for what they Excell in, that they will exclude all variety of Numbers from *English* Poetry, when they allow none but *Iambics*, which must by an identity of sound bring a very unpleasing satiety upon the Reader. I must own that I am of opinion that a great many rough Cadencies that are to be found in these Poems, and in the admirable *Paradise Lost*, are so far from Faults that they are Beauties, and contribute by their variety to the prolonging the pleasure of the Readers. But I have unawares faln into this Digression, which requires more time and room than I have here to allow to set it, in that just Light it requires. I shall return to the following Poems, writ by Mr. *Milton*, Mr. *Marvell*, &c. which will shew us, that there is no where a greater Spirit of Liberty to be found, than in those who are Poets; *Homer*, *Aristophanes*, and most of the inspired Tribe have shew'd it; and *Catullus* in the midst of *Caesar*'s Triumphs attack'd the Vices of that great Man, and expos'd 'em to lessen that Popularity and Power he was gaining among the *Roman* People, which he saw would be turn'd to the destruction of the Liberty of *Rome*.

> *Quis hoc potest videre, quis potest pati*, &c.

And

> *Pulchre convenit improbis cinædis*
> *Mamurræ, Pathicoque, Cæsarique.*

And again

> *Nil nimium studeo Cæsar tibi velle placere*, &c.[1]

But it would be endless to quote all the Liberties the Poets have of old taken with Ill men, whose Power had aw'd others to a servile Flattery; the succeeding Tyrants have not been able to suppress the numerous Instances we have yet of it. We have therefore reason to hope that no *Englishman* that is a true lover of his Countries Good, and Glory, can be displeased at the publishing a Collection, the Design of each of which was to remove those

---

[1] Catullus, 29. 1: Who can look on this, who can suffer this...; 57. 1–2: Well met are the impudent wantons, the effete Mamurra and Caesar...; 93.1: I have no great urge, Caesar, to please you....

pernicious Principles which lead us directly to Slavery; to promote a Publick and Generous Spirit, which was then almost a shame to the Prossessor, if not a certain Ruine. I believe were a man of equal Ability, and unbyass'd Temper to make a just Comparison, some of the following Authors might claim perhaps an equal share with many of the most celebrated of the *Romans* or *Greeks*. I know in a a Nation so factious as this, where the preposterous Principles of Slavery are run into a point of Conscience and Honour, and yet hold abundance in unseasonable and monstrous Divisions, it would be a task that must disoblige too many to undertake. But when all *Europe* is engag'd to destroy that Tyrannick Power, the mismanagement of those Times, and the selfish evil Designs of a corrupt Court had given Rise to, it cannot be thought unseasonable to publish so just an Account of the true sourse of all our present Mischiefs; which will be evidently found in the following Poems, for from them we may collect a just and secret History of the former Times.

> *And looking backward with a wise Affright,*
> *See Seams of Wounds dishonest to the Sight.*
> [Dryden, *Absalom and Achitophel*, ll. 71–2]

Oh that we cou'd yet learn, under this Auspicious Government founded on Liberty, the generous Principles of the Publik Good! Sure this Consort of Divine *Amphions* will charm the distracted pieces of the publik Building into one Noble and Regular Pile to be the wonder, as well as safeguard of *Europe*.[1] This being the Aim of this present Publication, it must be extreamly approv'd by all true Patriots, all lovers of the general Good of Mankind, and in that most certainly of their own particular.

> *Omnes profecto liberi libentius*
> *Sumus, quam servimus.*

Take off the gawdy veil of Slavery, and she will appear so frightfull and deform'd that all would abhor her: For all Mankind naturally prefer Liberty to Slavery.

'Tis true some few of these Poems were Printed before in loose Papers, but so mangled that the Persons that wrote them would hardly have known, much less have owned them, which put a Person on examining them by the Originals or best Copies, and

[1] Perhaps echoing Marvell's use of the image in the 'First Anniversary', ll. 49–56.

they are here published without any Castration, with many curious Miscellaneous Poems of the same great Men, which never before see the Light.

32. Defoe on satirical poetry

1703, 1711, 1713

Best known now for his novel *Robinson Crusoe*, Daniel Defoe (?1660–1731) was in his own day well known as a journalist, pamphleteer, and satiric poet. The burden of his remarks in the following passages is the decline of satire since the seventeenth century.

(a) Extract from *More Reformation. A Satyr upon Himself*, 16 July 1703, the precise date deriving from the Luttrell copy in the British Library. It was published again in 1705 in *A Second Volume of the Writings of the Author of the True-Born Englishman*. ll. 532–53.

Now, *Satyr*, all thy Grievances rehearse,
And so *retrieve* the Honour of thy Verse.
No more shalt thou old *Marvell*'s Ghost[1] lament,

[1] A reference to Marvell; but the phrase had apparently become generic, since there are at least two poems with the title 'Marvell's Ghost,' one written by his friend John Ayloff after 1678; the other, an anonymous piece, dated 1688/9, was published in 1707; both were reprinted in *Poems on Affairs of State*, Yale University Press, (1963; 1971) I, pp. 285–6; V, pp. 277–80.

Around 1712, Thomas Newcomb wrote a mock-heroic poem 'Biblioteca' in which the following lines appear with comments by the editor:

> Nay, to augment my last despair,
> Place Ayloffe's* self and Marvell† there
> (A fam'd dull pair, that purely wrote
> To raise our spleen, and die forgot).

* Captain Ayloffe, author of 'Marvell's Ghost.'
† The satire on Marvell is wonderfully misplaced.
(*A Select Collection of Poems*, ed. John Nichols, 1780–2, III, p. 50; IV, p. 355.)

106

Who always rally'd Kings and Government:
Thy Lines their awful Distance always knew,
And thought that Debt to Dignities was Due.
Crowns should be counted with the things Divine,
On which Burlesque is rudeness and profane;
The *Royal Banter*[1] cannot stand the Test,   540
But where we find the Wit, we lose the Jest.
Poets sometimes with Royal Praise appear,
And sometimes too much Flattery prepare,
Which wiser Princes hardly will Dispence,
Tho' 'tis a Crime of no great Consequence.
But Satyr has no business with the Crown,
No Wit can with good Manners there be shown.
He that the Royal Errors will Expose,
His Courage more than his Discretion shows.
Besides his Duty shou'd his Pen restrain,   550
And blame the Crime, but not describe the Man:
His proper Parallel of Vice may bring,
Expose the Error, not Expose the King.

(b)   Extract from *A Review of the State of the British Nation* (later
called *Review*), a periodical written almost solely by Defoe and
published in nine volumes, VIII (29 March 1711), pp. 6–7.

Yet Party Rage will break through, Lampoons, Pasquinades, and
Inveterate Satyrs will swarm more than before, and be dilligently
handed about by Parties all over the Kingdom, whose Darts will
be keener, and Poison stronger than any Thing Printed; and perhaps the more so, as they shall be receiv'd with more Gust by the
People on either Side—And I appeal to any Man that remembers
the Days of King *Charles* II. when the License Tyranny Reign'd
over the Press, whether that Age did not abound in Lampoons and
Satyrs, that Wounded; and at last went far in Ruining the Parties
they were pointed at, more than has ever been practis'd since the
Liberty of the Press—And he that does not know it, must be very
Ignorant of those Times, and has heard very little of *Andrew Marvel*,
Sir *John Denham*, *Rochester*, *Buckhurst*, and several others, whose Wit

[1] *Royal Banter* refers to Defoe's raillery directed at Charles II in his *True-Born Englishman*
(1701), ll. 289ff.

made the Court odious to the People, beyond what had been possible if the Press had been open.

(c) Extract from the *Review*, I. New Part [ix], 28 March 1713, pp. 151, 152.

The Fury of the Times being exerted most at this time by the *Pen* and *Ink*, it is not to be wonder'd at, that part of that *Salt* and *Fire* which People spit at one another, comes up to what we call Lampoon, Pasquinade, Ballad and Satyr: In all Reigns, and, *for ought I know*, in all Ages it has more or less been so.

But I cannot but make one Observation as I go, *viz*. That the Lampoons of this Age differ very much from those that we have seen in former Times; and tho', *at the same time*, we pretend much to have a degree of Polite Wit beyond those Days; yet nothing of that keenness of Satyr, the happy turns and brightness of Fancy appears in the Lampoons of this Age, that were seen in *Andr. Marvel*, Sir *John Denham*, *Rochester*, *Buckingham*, *Buckhurst*, *Sidley*, and others, *the Wits of that Day*; nay, give *Sing-Song D'Urfey* his due, even his Ballads *out did us* exceedingly: What wretched Stuff have we seen in our publick Prints on both sides, one as well as t'other, which pass for Satyr!...

I remember in the Days of King *Charles* the IId. some of the bitterest Invectives against him, when put into Lampoons, were cover'd with such a bewitching Fancy, and such a flood of Wit, that the King himself would laugh at them, and be pleased with them: And who can help, *tho' never so severely lash'd*, being pleas'd with the Wit of the incomparable *Hudibrass*?

The Dialogue between the two Horses[1] so pleas'd the King, that tho' it was the bitterest Satyr, *upon him and his Father*, that ever was made, the King would often repeat them with a great deal of Pleasure, and particularly these that follow:

[Quotes ll. 167–74.]

... it is my Opinion, that the Satyrs of this part of our Age are so mean, in comparison of the last that I believe the next will never

[1] The 'Dialogue between the Two Horses,' ascribed to Marvell only in the *Poems of Affairs of State*, 1689 and after, may be dated 1675–6 from its allusion to the closing of the coffee-houses (closed 29 December 1675; re-opened 10 January 1676). Its attribution is questionable.

think them worth Collecting, as the last were, into six Volumes of State Poems—And above all, I must needs say, I think I have not seen one yet that is worth an Authors marching from *Newgate* to *Aldgate* for; if any Author thinks otherwise, he is very welcome to make the Experiment.

If the great Men, whether *in* or *out*, must be Banter'd and Satyriz'd, I would fain perswade our Poets to go about it like Poets; that is, like Men of Sense and Men of Wit; and let it be done sharp and clever, suitable to the Quality of the Persons, and the Dignity of Satyr.

33. Thomas Cooke on the life and writings

1726

Thomas 'Hesiod' Cooke (1703–56) was the first to publish an edition of the poetry of Marvell subsequent to the 1681 Folio, with an anecdotal biographical account that was to be constantly pilfered by subsequent editors. His intent was political, his interest in the poetry scant: 'My Design in this is to draw a Pattern for all free-born *English-men*, in the Life of a worthy Patriot, whose every Action has truely merited to him, with *Aristides*, the Sirname of the *Just*.'

Extracts from his two-volume edition, 1726 (reprinted in 1772), I, pp. 14–15, 18–19, 20–1; II, Dedication to the Earl of Pembroke and Montgomery.

... he was often conversant, and to a great Degree of Intimacy, with the late Duke of *Devonshire*, and Mr. *Milton*; but more particularly with the latter. Their Friendship begun very early, which Nothing could end but Death. When *Paradise lost* was first published, to the Shame of those Times be it told, it was valued, but by few, no more than a lifeless Piece, till Mr. *Marvell* and Dr. *Barrow* publickly espoused it, each in a judicious Poem. . . .

NOW, Sir [William Cavendish, Duke of Devonshire], we must view him in a different, but not less advantageous Light: I mean in his Writings. In all which the same Love, and Hatred, of Right, and Wrong, are as apparent, and the same publick Spirit exerted, as in his other Proceedings. No private Favours could ever bribe him to Flattery, nor personal Resentments provoke him to Revenge. He regarded all Men as the Instruments of good or bad Actions. I shall give one great Instance of this from the first Part of *the Rehearsal transprosed.* Tho he was as free, at other Times, in censuring the Vices of his Sovereign, as of his fellow Subjects, yet he knew to praise him, when the Author of a laudable Action.

[Quotes *RT I*, pp. 43–4.]

BUT first we must consider him as a Poet, which, Sir, I believe you will imagine, gives him no small Claim to my Favour, independent of his other Virtues. There are few of his Poems which have not Something pleasing in them, and some he must be allowed to have excelled in. Most of them seem to be the Effect of a lively Genius, and manly Sense, but at the same Time seem to want that Correctness he was capable of making. If we have any which may be properly said to come finished from his Hands, they are these, *On Milton's Paradise lost, On Blood's stealing the Crown*, and *A Dialogue between two Horses.*

He has several Poems in *Latin*, some of which he translated into *English*, and one in *Greek.* They have each their proper Merit. He discovers a great Facility of writing in the *Latin* Tongue.

We have some few small Pieces of his, in Prose, which must not escape our Observations. . . . By his familiar Letters we may easyly judge, what Parts of his greater Works are laboured, and what not.

If, in some Parts of his Satires, he seems too severe; that is owed to a Detestation of the Vices with which those Persons, the Subjects of his Satire, were branded, and which he then thought they deserved, and to no Partiality of thinking. The Crimes, therefore, not the Persons, he hated.

34. James Parsons on 'Eyes and Tears'

1747

In 1747 Dr. James Parsons (1705–70) delivered a series of lectures, entitled *Human Physiognomy*, to the Royal Society. Notably in one, he quoted seven of the fourteen stanzas of the lyric 'Eyes and Tears' with specific attribution to Marvell, reflecting an early if *post*-seventeenth-century interest in a poem that was to stir comment up to the end of the nineteenth century. The following year Parsons's remarks on Marvell, together with the seven stanzas, were given wider circulation in the *Gentleman's Magazine*, 18 (1748), p. 555.

Extract from *Human Physiognomy* (1747), p. 79.

But, besides these [Juvenal, Vergil], I find an *English* Poet singing their other Uses in the most pathetic and engaging Manner; whose charming Song it would be unpardonable to conceal, since no Language can boast of one more expressive upon the Subject, and wherein he has shewn, that Tears are a Blessing peculiar only to human Nature.

[Omits stt. 3, 4, 7, 10, 11, 13 and the Latin version of st. 8.]

35. Voltaire on *In eandem* [*Effigiem*] *Reginae Sueciae transmissam*

1748

Voltaire's comments on a variety of topics appeared in articles contributed to the *Encyclopédie* and in his *Dictionnaire philosophique* (1764) and *Questions sur l'Encyclopédie* (1770–2). After his death these articles were combined into one alphabetical order and given the omnibus title *Dictionnaire philosophique* (see the edition of R. Naves and J. Benda, Paris, 1935). M. Beuchot gives the provenance of Voltaire's remarks on Cromwell as deriving from the 1748 Dresden edition, vol. IV.

Extract from *Oeuvres de Voltaire*, ed. M. Beuchot (Paris, 1829), XXVIII, pp. 265–6.

When [Cromwell] had insulted all monarchs in causing the head of his legitimate king to be cut off and when he himself began to rule, he sent his portrait to a crowned head: Christina, Queen of Sweden. Marvell, a famous English poet, who wrote excellent Latin poetry, prepared six verses to accompany the portrait where he makes Cromwell himself speak. In the last two lines Cromwell makes amends as follows [quotes the Latin]:

> But this image submits his brow to you most reverently
> Nor are these looks always harsh to kings.

The *bold* sense of these verses may perhaps be rendered thus [in French]:

> With sword in hand I have defended the laws;
> I have avenged the cause of a bold people.
> Look without trembling on this faithful image:
> My brow is not always the terror of kings.

This queen was the first to acknowledge him Protector of three realms.

112

36.   William Mason, from the ode 'To Independency'

1756

By his own boast, a compère, as well as the literary executor, of Thomas Gray, William Mason (1724–97) is largely remembered as his first (and worst) editor—*The Life and Letters of Gray* (1774).

His *Odes* were published in 1756 in Cambridge and Dublin. The second, which includes three strophes on Marvell, was addressed to Robert D'Arcy, fourth Earl of Holdernesse (see st. 6).

Extract from the Cambridge edition (1756).

III

As now o'er this lone beach I stray;
Thy fav'rite Swain* oft stole along,
And artless wove his Doric lay,
Far from the busy throng.
Thou heard'st him, Goddess, strike the tender string,
And badst his soul with bolder passions move:
Strait these responsive shores forgot to ring,
With Beauty's praise, or plaint of slighted Love;
To loftier flights his daring Genius rose,
And led the war, 'gainst thine, and Freedom's foes.

IV

Pointed with Satire's keenest steel,
The shafts of Wit he darts around;
Ev'n mitred Dulness† learns to feel,

* Andrew Marvell, born at Kingston upon Hull in the year 1620.
† Parker, Bishop of Oxford.

And shrinks beneath the wound.
In awful poverty his honest Muse
Walks forth vindictive thro' a venal land:
In vain Corruption sheds her golden dews,
In vain Oppression lifts her iron hand;
He scorns them both, and, arm'd with truth alone,
Bids Lust and Folly tremble on the throne.

VI

'Fond Youth! to MARVELL's patriot fame,
Thy humble breast must ne'er aspire.
Yet nourish still the lambent flame;
Still strike thy blameless Lyre:
Led by the moral Muse securely rove;
And all the vernal sweets thy vacant Youth
Can cull from busy Fancy's fairy grove,
O hang their foliage round the fane of Truth:
To arts like these devote thy tuneful toil,
And meet its fair reward in D'ARCY's smile.'

37. Charles Churchill on satiric poetry

c. 1763

A writer of social and political satire, Charles Churchill (1731–64) crammed all of his poetic career into four years. Directing his fierce invective at contemporaries, he is most famous for his *Rosciad,* a satire on London stage personalities, and *The Prophecy of Famine,* a satire on Lord Bute and the Scots.

The Author, which was directed against Tobias Smollett, novelist turned controversialist, was not published until

1765, though excerpts had appeared in issues of the *London Chronicle* for 1763. The two extracts printed here include a defense of satiric verse with the allusion to the 'hardy Poet' and his 'honest rimes' (ll. 87–92), an implicit homage to Marvell.

(a)   Extract from *The Author* (1765), ll. 1–4, 39–106.

Accurs'd the man, whom fate ordains, in spite,
And cruel parents teach, to Read and Write!
What need of letters? Wherefore should we spell?
Why write our names? A mark will do as well.[1]

When with much pains this boasted Learning's got,
'Tis an affront to those who have it not.   40
In some it causes hate, in others fear,
Instructs our Foes to rail, our Friends to sneer.
With prudent haste the worldly-minded fool,
Forgets the little which he learn'd at School;
The Elder Brother, to vast fortunes born,
Looks on all Science with an Eye of Scorn;
Dependent Breth'ren the same features wear,
And younger Sons are stupid as the Heir.
In Senates, at the Bar, in Church and State,
Genius is vile, and Learning out of date.   50
Is this—O Death to think! is this the Land
Where Merit and Reward went hand in hand,
Where Heroes, Parent-like, the Poet view'd?—
By whom they saw their glorious deeds renew'd;
Where Poets, true to Honour, tun'd their lays,
And by their Patrons sanctify'd their praise?
Is this the Land, where, on our SPENCER's tongue,
Enamour'd of his voice, Description hung;
Where JOHNSON rigid gravity beguil'd,
Whilst Reason thro' her Critic sences smil'd;   60
Where NATURE list'ning stood, whilst SHAKESPEAR play'd,
And wonder'd at the Work herself had made?
Is this the Land, where, mindful of her charge

---

[1] Perhaps echoing Marvell's witty denunciation of printing in *RT I*, pp. 4–5.

And Office high, fair Freedom walk'd at large;
Where, finding in our Laws a sure defence,
She mock'd at all restraints, but those of Sense;
Where, health and honour trooping by her side,
She spread her sacred empire far and wide;
Pointed the Way, Affliction to beguile,
And bade the Face of Sorrow wear a smile,   70
Bade those, who dare obey the gen'rous call,
Enjoy her blessings, which GOD meant for all?
Is this the Land, where, in some Tyrant's reign,
When a *weak, wicked Ministerial* train,
The tools of pow'r, the slaves of int'rest, plann'd
Their Country's ruin, and with bribes unman'd
Those wretches, who, ordain'd in Freedom's cause,
Gave up our liberties, and sold our laws;[1]
When Pow'r was taught by Meanness where to go,
Nor dar'd to love the Virtue of a foe;   80
When, like a lep'rous plague, from the foul head
To the foul heart her sores Corruption spread,
Her iron arm when stern Oppression rear'd,
And Virtue, from her broad base shaken, fear'd
The scourge of Vice; when impotent and vain,
Poor Freedom bow'd the neck to Slav'ry's chain;
Is this the Land, where, in those worst of times,
The hardy Poet rais'd his honest rimes
To dread rebuke, and bade controulment speak
In guilty blushes on the villain's cheek,   90
Bade Pow'r turn pale, kept mighty rogues in awe,
And made them fear the Muse, who fear'd not Law?

How do I laugh, when men of narrow souls,
Whom folly guides, and prejudice controuls;
Who, one dull drowsy track of business trod,
Worship their Mammon, and neglect their God;
Who, breathing by one musty set of rules,
Dote from the birth, and are by system fools;
Who, form'd to dullness from their very youth,
Lies of the day prefer to Gospel truth,   100

---

[1] Referring to the debate in the House of Commons on whether or not privilege of Parliament covered the writing and publishing of seditious libels.

Pick up their little knowledge from Reviews,
And lay out all their stock of faith in news:
How do I laugh, when Creatures, form'd like these,
Whom Reason scorns, and I should blush to please,
Rail at all lib'ral arts, deem verse a crime,
And hold not Truth, as Truth, if told in rime?

(b) These lines, though omitted from Churchill's collected
works, were attributed to him by his contemporary Captain
Edward Thompson, who preserved the text in his edition of
Marvell, III, pp. 487–8.

Tho' Sparta, Athens, and immortal Rome,
Adorn'd with laurels ev'ry patriot's tomb;
Tho' to their fames the sweetest poets sung,
And Brutus' virtue lives on Plutarch's tongue;
Tho' both the classick chissel and the pen
Engrav'd the noblest acts of noblest men;
Yet shall our Marvell's spotless virtues rise,
And shine a constellation of the skies:
Shall shine the foremost of the patriot band,
A guiding beacon to his native land;
And teach succeeding children of the north
To imitate his manners and his worth;
Inspire his kinsmen with his patriot flame,
And raise his *Hull* above the Roman name.

38. Captain Edward Thompson on Marvell's works

1776

Captain Edward Thompson (?1738–86) was the first to publish the complete works of Marvell in poetry and prose and
the first to make generally available the three major poems
on Cromwell which had been cancelled in most copies of the
1681 Folio. (He also included much that was spurious in his
three-volume edition.) Like Cooke (No. 33), his main motive
was political: 'One of my first and strongest reasons for
publishing the works of Marvell, was the pleasing hopes of
adding a number of strenuous and sincere friends to our
Constitution; but alas! what is to be expected in this degenerate age, when virtue does not even nominally exist
amongst us, when arbitrary power, by her baneful engines
of venality and corruption, is daily putting a check to every
notion of rational and manly liberty!' (I, p. lvi). Although
he acknowledges the excellence of the lyrical poetry, it is
clearly the 'witty and intrepid' character of Marvell that he
most admires.

Extract from *The Works* III, pp. 466–72.

The compositions of our author are of various sorts, and not less
excellent in verse than prose; especially any of those pieces with
which he has taken pains: but in general they appear to be the
warm effusions of a lively fancy, and are very often thrown off in
the *extempore* moment of their conception and birth, whether
begotten in satire or humour. The poem of *Paradise Lost*, that
literary ornament of dignity to our most copious language, which
a bookseller bought for fifteen pounds, (and which booksellers
hitherto, in virtue of *true and just copy-right*, have made fortunes
by) had lain in lifeless rust and obscurity longer, but for Mr. Marvell
and Dr. Barrow, who wrote two complimental poems in English

and Latin on its publication, which unveiled its beauties to the undiscerning eyes of the heedless world, which dim suffusion veiled.[1] The poem to his *coy mistress* is sweet, natural and easy, and bespeaks his heart to be high in love; and perhaps his not being married, might arise from her coldness, and want of the compleat composition of love-enraptured and cœlestial mutuality; without which the partial passion on one side, produces every evil which attends on marriage. There is no sublime rapture without reciprocation; and when the flame is mutual and general, it is above all earthly blisses, and only inferior to heavenly. His little poem of the *Gallery* loosely and pleasingly depicts this beloved fair one, whom he follows through all his pastoral dialogues, and in a most pleasing and epigrammatical manner in that of *Thyrsis and Dorinda*. But for a true relish of his poetry, we must drink of his Helicon, and not sip at the side of the stream; and indeed, were I to recommend further, it would be taking in a high measure from the right of each individual reader, who is entitled to chuse and judge for himself.

The satires and state poems are not more severe than humourous; and indeed, when satire is conveyed in risible terms, so as to raise the laugh against the object, it is the most poignant of any; of this sort is *Nostrodamus' Prophecy, Clarendon's House-warming, Royal Resolutions, Dialogue between two Horses, Tom May's Death*, &c. The graver and severer satires are upon *Blood's stealing the Crown, Oceana and Britannia*,[2] &c. His panegyric carries with it that apparent truth and honesty, that no one can read it without a conviction of its sincerity; and though he frequently wrote bitterly against the Scots, as foes to his country only; so when merit appeared, he could praise in the smoothest strain the gallant *Douglas*, who was burned in his ship at Chatham:

[Quotes 'Loyal Scot,' ll. 67–8, with variants, and ll. 691–6 of 'The Last Instructions' with no indication of ellipsis.]

Mr. Marvell dates all the feuds, jealousies, and animosities since the Union, in this poem, to have arisen from the disputes of the clergy:

---

[1] Compare Cooke (No. 33).
[2] Except for 'Tom May's Death' and probably 'Blood's stealing the crown,' these titles are of uncertain attribution.

[Quotes 'Loyal Scot,' ll. 98–9, 102–3, 234–5, 260–1, with no ellipses.]

There is much truth in this observation of Mr. Marvell's; though I am at a loss to determine, whether the animosity which subsists between the two people arises from the pride of the Scot, or from the prejudice of the English. Be it both: the prejudice in one is unnatural and ungenerous, and the pride of the other is unbecoming and contemptible. The simile of the powdered bees, by the way of obtaining a useful and general reconciliation, is happily introduced, and musically versed:

[Quotes 'Loyal Scot,' ll. 266–73.]

His compositions in Latin are written with elegance and facility, and the specimen which he gives us of the Greek, sufficiently proves that he was a proficient in both the languages. His epistolary stile is nervous and plain, though the periods are often too long, which sometimes make him difficult to be understood; but his judgement makes ample amends for such deficiency.

His controversial writings were the most voluminous of his works, and he had very furious partisans to contend with, for all his political compositions were written against popery and arbitrary power; and so well did he maintain his fight, that none took the field against him but repented of the battle: of these, the most furious, virulent, and violent, was Dr. Parker, afterwards made Bishop of Oxford, by King James II. The Dissenters at this time were harassed and hunted with an uncommon barbarity; and authors of the most inflammatory dispositions were encouraged to attack them. The most sanguine hound of this clerical pack, was Dr. Parker, who seemed to have a mitre in his eye; and to gain it by acts violent, unjust and cruel, nature seemed to have formed him. He was a man without virtue or honour, and a divine without religion. . . .

This monster of the earth, Marvell, like another Hercules, undertook to slay; and in his *Rehearsal Transprosed*, he gave him the first attack; though Parker had every defence on his side, and the court for his stalking-horse. In this reply he was abundantly fortunate; he did not coldly argue with the prelate, but shamed him by the dint of true wit and humour; and made such music, that the priest

even danced to it with rage.... Mr. Marvell did not confine himself to Dr. Parker's principles, but he also exposed and confuted
several other things advanced in his compositions, and those
likewise of smaller authors, which he only glanced at as he went
along, reserving his heavy artillery for the well garrisoned doctor;
and so excellently did he apply his ammunition, that Dr. Parker
never replied again. Some things followed in his defence, but they
met with no applause, for they were believed to be his own compositions in his own praise.[1]

Note: Extract from Ralph Griffiths's unsigned review in the
Monthly Review 55 (November 1776), pp. 354, 358.

We are very glad to see so handsome an edition of the works of so
respectable a WRITER, and so excellent a MAN, as Andrew
Marvell; the affectionate friend of Milton, the ardent lover of his
country, and the undaunted champion of the common rights of
mankind.

[The] '*Addenda*,' containing some original poems, now first
published, from *manuscript* book, and not inserted in the preface.
These consist of several spirited, noble panegyrics on Cromwell:
such as might be expected from Marvell's powerful, masculine,
genius, exerting itself on a favourite subject.

---

[1] A point also made by Marvell, *RT II*, pp. 175, 201.

39. John Aikin on Marvell

1799–1815

Dr John Aikin (1744–1822) retired from medical practice in 1798 to devote himself to various literary pursuits, including the editing of the *Monthly Magazine* and the *Athenaeum*. His *General Biography; or Lives of the Most Eminent Persons* was published in ten volumes, 1799–1815. Although largely biographical, the account of Marvell was much pillaged, particularly the concluding succinct evaluation of his poetic style.

Extract from the grangerized version in twenty-two volumes (1818) with the assistance of William Enfield and others, XIV, pp. 607–9.

MARVELL, ANDREW, a witty writer and incorruptible patriot, was born in 1620, at Kingston-upon-Hull. ... From the records of Trinity college, it appears, that in 1641, Marvell with some others was excluded from its benefits on account of non-attendance. Possibly he might then have begun the course of travels which we find he pursued through Holland, France, and Italy, and which doubtless contributed to that enlargement of mind which distinguished him from the mere party writers of the time. His propensity to ridicule was displayed by a humorous though carelessly-written satire upon one Flecknoe, an English priest and poetaster at Rome; and in a burlesque poem addressed to an abbot de Maniban at Paris, a pretender to fortune-telling. Of his residence and employment for many subsequent years, we have very little information. From a letter of his to Oliver Cromwell, dated in 1653, it appears that he was engaged by the protector to superintend the education of a Mr. Dutton, who was lodged with Mr. Oxenbridge at Eton. ... If some of the poems attributed to him in the last edition of his works be genuine, he was a greater panegyrist of that usurper than might be wished; but the vigour with which Cromwell ruled contending factions, and the honour acquired by the nation under his government, seem to have dazzled men of undoubted patriotism. . . . It was not till the parliament of October 1665 that, from his letters to his constituents, his attendance seems to have been constant and uninterrupted. From that period to 1674 he made a regular report of the proceedings of both houses to the mayor and corporation of Hull. The corruptions of the court, and the tendency to arbitrary measures, which marked the unprincipled reign of Charles II. necessarily threw a man of Marvell's character into opposition; and his whole efforts in and out of parliament were directed to the preservation of civil and religious liberty. He rarely spoke in the house, but his influence over the members of both houses was considerable. The patriotic earl of Devonshire was on terms of intimacy with him; and prince Rupert often privately visited him and took his advice; insomuch that when he gave a vote on the popular side, it was commonly said by the courtiers 'that he had been with his tutor.'

By his writings Marvell obtained the character of the wittiest man of his time, and doubtless was of great service to the cause he espoused, which had in general been defended rather by serious argument than by ridicule. He occasionally threw out a number of poetical effusions of the humorous and satirical kind, in which he did not spare majesty itself. These are careless and loose in their composition, and frequently pass the bounds of decorum; but they were well calculated for effect as party pieces, and became very popular. He exercised his wit still more copiously in prose. In 1672, Dr. Sam. Parker, afterwards bishop of Oxford, a flaming and intolerant high churchman, published a work of bishop Bramhall's, to which he added a preface of his own, maintaining the most extravagant positions concerning the rights of sovereigns over the consciences of their subjects. This piece Marvell attacked in the same year in a work which he entitled 'The Rehearsal Transprosed.' With a profusion of witty sarcasm, it contains much solid argument, and may be reckoned one of the ablest exposures of the maxims of religious tyranny. Parker wrote an answer, to which Marvell replied; and the reverend champion did not choose to carry the controversy further. . . .

Notwithstanding the acrimony with which Marvell opposed the court and its plans, his character as a man of wit ingratiated him with the mirth-loving monarch, and his powers as a writer made the ministry extremely desirous of silencing or gaining him over. . . .

Marvell was a dark-complexioned man, with an expressive countenance, silent and reserved among strangers, but lively and facetious in the company of his intimates. His early poems express a fondness for the charms of rural nature, and much delicacy of sentiment; they are ingenious and full of fancy, after the manner of Cowley and his contemporaries.

40. William Wordsworth's sonnet

c. 1802

Political events in the early years of the nineteenth century stimulated Wordsworth (1770–1850) to many expressions of patriotic fervor. In 1802 he copied the 'Horatian Ode' into his notebook W and composed some of his political sonnets as well. The one printed below, while commenting on the current scene, looks back with admiration to seventeenth-century Republican leaders and writers. Three years later he was to suggest to Sir Walter Scott, at work on an edition of Dryden, that he might 'peep with advantage' into Marvell's poems, adding, somewhat disingenuously, 'which I have not seen these many many years' (*Early Letters of William and Dorothy Wordsworth*, ed. E. de Selincourt, 1935, p. 541).

From *Poems*, 2 vols, 1807, I, Sonnet XV (*c.* 1802)

Great Men have been among us; hands that penn'd
And tongues that utter'd wisdom; better none:
The later Sydney, Marvel, Harrington,
Young Vane, and others who call'd Milton Friend.[1]

[1] Algernon Sidney (1622–83) was beheaded for supposed complicity in the Rye House Plot; James Harrington (1611–77), author of *Oceana*, was imprisoned after the Restoration; Sir Henry Vane (1612–92) was a Puritan statesman; 'and others' included Cyriac Skinner, according to a manuscript note.

These Moralists could act and comprehend:
They knew how genuine glory was put on;
Taught us how rightfully a nation shone
In splendour: what strength was, that would not bend
But in magnanimous meekness. France, 'tis strange,
Hath brought forth no such souls as we had then.
Perpetual emptiness! unceasing change!
No single Volume paramount, no code,
No master spirit, no determined road;
But equally a want of Books and Men!

41. Three political comparisons

1735–1845

In December 1726, Caleb D'Anvers (Nicholas Amhurst) started the *Craftsman*, a periodical designed to oppose Sir Robert Walpole as a 'man of craft.' Bolingbroke was its most distinguished contributor. The article 'Mr. Bayes modernized' first appeared in the *Craftsman*, 8 February 1735, signed 'D,' with citations from *RT I* in order to point up the political analogies. It was almost immediately reprinted, with minor variants, in the *Gentleman's Magazine*.

In the summer of 1794, Henry Wansey (1751–1827), a noncon-formist entrepreneur, made an excursion to the United States and recorded his experiences in a journal which was to be published two years later. A second edition appeared in 1796 and an edition by D. J. Jeremy (Philadelphia: *American Philosophical Society*), 1970.

In a letter written in 1845, the American writer and statesman James Russell Lowell comments on Marvell, including a reference to the hoary legend that he was the last to receive the parliamentary stipend of 6s.8d. (See R. C. Latham, 'Parliamentary Wages—The Last Phase,' *English Historical Review*, January 1951.) For his brief but penetrating remarks on the poetry in general, see No. 64; for those on two of the Cromwell poems, see No. 72.

(a) Extract from the *Gentleman's Magazine*, 5 (February 1735), pp. 69, 71.

The Resemblance between Dr *Parker*, that implement of arbitrary Power in the Reign of K. *Charles* II. and our *present ministerial Advocates* upon reading the *Rehearsal transpros'd*, written by *Andrew Marvel*, Esq; appears so exact, that I cannot give my Readers a more lively Portrait of the *Walsinghams* and *Osbornes* of these Days, than in the Words of *that excellent Writer*.

First, it appears that Mr *Bays*, as the *Doctor* is there styled, had acquir'd a Perfection in *railing*, was a great Enemy to the *trading Part of the Nation*, and abused Them 'as a Sort of People who are more inclinable than any other to *seditious Practices*,' *i.e.* according to our modern Court Writers in their *Billingsgate* Language, a Crew of *fraudulent perjur'd Rascals* and *sturdy Beggars*.

Again, as *our Adversaries* are always trumping up the *last four Years of Queen* Anne's *Reign*, for Want of Arguments to defend some late Transactions, so Mr *Bays* made the same Use of the Year 1641, and the subsequent Misfortunes, as appears by the following Passage: 'But as to That, Mr *Bays*, which you still inculcate of the *late War*, and its horrid Catastrophe, 'tis 24 *Years ago*, and after an *Act of Oblivion*, it had been as seasonable to have shewn *Caesar's* bloody Coat, or *Thomas a Becket's* bloody Rochet' [*RT I*, p. 112].

But his Ruffian-like *Scurrility* suits exactly the Case of *that egregious Blockhead*, who raves and foams and throws about his Venom in the *Courant*.

Mr *Marvel* having made an Observation, *that the King of* Poland *is obliged to wear that Country Habit*, He was menaced for it, by his *insolent Adversary*, in the following Terms—'This is an impudent Intrenchment upon *his Majesty's Crown* and *Prerogative*; for the *Polish Kingdom* being *elective*, and not *hereditary*, the *Parliament* deals with *their Kings* as &c.—Friend, by your politick Lectures, you endanger your Head' [Parker, *Reproof*, p. 498].

Just in the same Manner was I attack'd for calling our Government *a Sort of Regal Commonwealth, or a Republick with a King at the Head of it*; which was candidly represented as an Attempt to change our Government into an *elective Kingdom*. (See V. III, *p.* 364.)

Mr *Marvel* complains, that his *Antagonist* was troubled with a Faculty of denying his *own Assertions*, and their natural Import, after the Wickedness, or Absurdity of them had been exposed— 'What have *my Readers* and *I* to do, *says He*, but to pity one another? *I* must quote all over again, and *They* read it all; and *you* will affirm and deny; deny and affirm, without any Regard to *Truth*, or *Honesty*; and yet all This and more We must endure, out of Love to *Justice*' [*RT II*, p. 207].

Again, 'his Book is *in Print*, and I have also *in Print* charg'd This upon Him, and nevertheless by this *last Book* He puts me again upon this double Drudgery: to prove first *that He said* it, and then to prove *that He meant what he said*' [*RT II*, p. 215].

I leave the Publick to judge whether This is not exactly the Case of our *present ministerial Advocates*, with Regard to *Corruption* and *Dependency*.

I shall conclude with another Passage from *Andrew Marvel*, only desiring my Readers to remember that Mr *Marvel* was engaged with an Advocate for *ecclesiastical Tyranny*, which is not our Case at present; but the Satire will hold equally strong, *mutatis mutandis*, against all Contenders for *civil Oppression*. [Quotes *RT I*, pp. 4–5].

(b)   Extract from Henry Wansey's *Journal* (1796), pp. 169–70.

Commend me, however, to honest Andrew Marvel, dining on his cold shoulder of mutton, sweetened with the enjoyment of an independent mind, rather than to honest Edmund Burke, ruminating (but not in trope and figure) over *one thousand two hundred pounds per annum, out of the civil list, with two thousand five hundred pounds per annum more, out of the four and a half per cents, accepted by him, in defiance of a law (passed at his own particular instigation)* against such enormous pensions being ever granted without the previous consent of parliament, and for procuring which, his country once honored, respected, and loved him;[1]

---

[1] Burke retired from parliament in 1794.

ANDREW MARVELL

Heu quantum mutatus ab illo! [Alas, how changed from that one: Vergil, *Aeneid* II, 274.]

(c) Extract from James Russell Lowell's letter to Charles F. Briggs, 8 August 1845, from the *Letters*, ed. C. E. Norton (New York, 1894), I, p. 94.

The paying of popular representatives had its origin in a good principle, and has been perverted no more than other good principles by the license of the times. The last English member of the Commons house who took pay was Andrew Marvell, the worthy friend of Milton and possessing even a purer mind than that of the great poet. I would not compare [John Quincy] Adams with Marvell, for I think that there is a vast deal of humbug in the reputation of the former. He is not well seen in the very A B C of Freedom. It is a good trait in us Americans that we are so fond of plastering together an image of greatness to fall down before and worship—we shall be all the more ready to worship the reality when we are fortunate enough to get it.

128

42.   William Lisle Bowles, a note on two poems

1806

The Reverend William Lisle Bowles (1762–1850), who anticipated the revival of the sonnet form with his publication
of *Fourteen Sonnets* in 1789, showed to better advantage in his
ten-volume edition of Pope. Stressing a romantic esthetic
(nature over art), his edition, not surprisingly, stirred up a
lively reaction—the 'Pope and Bowles' controversy—with
Lord Byron and Thomas Campbell, among others, championing the tenets of neo-classicism.

Bowles's comments on two of Marvell's poems, representing
a distinctly new approach to his poetry, derive from the notes
to *Windsor Forest*. By 1871, they had been incorporated into
the introductory essay to the poem in the edition by Elwin
and Courthope.

From the *Works of Alexander Pope* (1806), I, pp. 122–4.

Johnson remarks, that this Poem was written after the model of
Denham's Cooper's Hill, with perhaps an eye on Waller's Poem of
The Park. Marvel has also written a Poem on Local Scenery,
'upon the Hill and Grove at Billborow;' and another, 'on Appleton
House,' (now Nunappleton in Yorkshire).

Marvel abounds with conceits and false thoughts, but some of
the descriptive touches are picturesque and beautiful. His description of a gently rising eminence is more picturesque, although not
so elegantly and justly expressed, as the same subject is in Denham.
I transcribe the following, as the Poem is but little read.

[Quotes 'Upon the Hill and Grove at Bill-borow,' ll. 17–20, 25–34.]

Sometimes Marvel observes little circumstances of rural nature with the eye and feeling of a true Poet.

[Quotes 'Appleton House,' ll. 529–32.]

The last circumstance is new, highly poetical, and could only have been described by one who was a real lover of nature, and a witness of her beauties in her most solitary retirements. It is the observation of such *circumstances*, which can alone form an accurate descriptive rural Poet. In this province of his art, Pope therefore must evidently fail, as he could not describe what his physical infirmities prevented his observing. For the same reason, Johnson, as a critic, was not a proper judge of this sort of Poetry.

43. Thomas Campbell on Marvell

1819

Also sharing in the 'Pope and Bowles' controversy, the Scottish poet Thomas Campbell (1777–1844) published his *Specimens of the British Poets* in 1819, an anthology with critical and biographical notices of the writers. He included three lyrics of Marvell's, only one of which he printed in its entirety ('Young Love').

Extract from *Specimens of the British Poets*, extra-illustrated (1819), IV, p. 193.

A better edition of Marvell's work than any that has been given, is due to his literary and patriotic character. He was the champion of Milton's living reputation, and the victorious supporter of free principles against Bishop Parker, when that venal Apostate to bigotry promulgated, in his Ecclesiastical Polity, 'that it was more necessary to set a severe government over men's consciences and religious persuasions, than over their vices and immoralities.' The humor and eloquence of Marvell's prose tracts were admired and probably imitated by Swift. In playful exuberance of figure he sometimes resembles Burke. For consistency of principles it is not so easy to find his parallel. His few poetical pieces betray some adherence to the school of conceit, but there is much in it that comes from the heart warm, pure, and affectionate.

Note: Francis Jeffrey in an unsigned review of Campbell's anthology in the *Edinburgh Review* for March 1819 (31, 482), prefaces a quotation of Campbell's remarks on Marvell with this comment:

The following brief account of Andrew Marvell is worth extracting, for the spirit with which it is written—though, we think, Mr. Campbell does not do justice to the sweetness and tenderness which characterize the poetry, as it did the private life, of this inflexible patriot.

44. Charles Lamb's comments

1800, 1821

On the basis of the descriptive phrase 'witty delicacy,' repeatedly echoed, the essayist Charles Lamb (1775–1834) later received considerable, if undue, acclaim for having rediscovered Marvell as a poet, particularly a 'garden-loving poet,' as he referred to him in 1824 in the *London Magazine*.

(a)   Extract from a letter to William Godwin (14 December 1800) in *The Works of Charles and Mary Lamb*, ed. E. V. Lucas (1903–5), VI, p. 202.

I remember two honest lines by Marvel (whose poems by the way
I am just going to possess)

> Where every Mower's wholesome heat
> Smells like an Alexander's Sweat.
> ['Appleton House,' ll. 427–8]

(b) Extract from 'The Old Benchers of the Inner Temple,'
London Magazine, September, 1821; reprinted from *The Works*,
II, pp. 83–4.

It was a pretty device of the gardener, recorded by Marvell, who,
in the days of artificial gardening, made a dial out of herbs and
flowers. I must quote his verses a little higher up, for they are full,
as all his serious poetry was, of a witty delicacy. They will not come
in awkwardly, I hope, in a talk of fountains and sun-dials. He is
speaking of sweet garden scenes:

[Quotes in telescoped fashion, stt. 5, 6, 7, then 9 of 'The Garden'.]

45. William Hazlitt on the poetry

1818–1824

An acute critic, William Hazlitt (1778–1830) made several,
if brief, mentions of Marvell's poetry in his lectures and in
his anthology of British poetry which did much to make
the poet's name familiar to the public.

The extracts are from the *Complete Works*, ed. P. P. Howe
(1931): (a) V, p. 83; (b) VI, p. 54; (c) VI, pp. 311, 314.

(a) From *Lectures on the English Poets* (1818; with *errata*, 1819).

Marvel is a writer of nearly the same period and worthy of a better
age. Some of his verses are harsh, as the words of Mercury; others

musical, as is Apollo's lute. Of the latter kind are his boat-song, his description of a fawn, and his lines to Lady Vere. His lines prefixed to Paradise Lost are by no means the most favourable specimen of his powers.

(b)   From *Lectures on the English Comic Writers* (1819).

Marvel (on whom I have already bestowed such praise as I could, for elegance and tenderness in his descriptive poems) in his satires and witty pieces was addicted to the affected and involved style here reprobated, as in his Flecknoe (the origin of Dryden's Macflecknoe) and in his satire on the Dutch. As an instance of this forced, far-fetched method of treating his subject,[1] he says, in ridicule of the Hollanders, that when their dykes overflowed, the fish used to come to table with them,

> And sat not as a meat, but as a guest. [l. 30]

There is a poem of Marvel's on the death of King Charles I. which I have not seen, but which I have heard praised by one whose praise is never high but of the highest things, for the beauty and pathos, as well as generous frankness of the sentiments, coming, as they did, from a determined and incorruptible political foe.

(c)   From *Lectures on the Dramatic Literature of the Age of Elizabeth* (1820).

Marvell deserves to be remembered as a true poet as well as a patriot, not in the best of times.

Of Marvell I have spoken with such praise, as appears to me his due, on another occasion: but the public are deaf, except to proof or to their own prejudices, and I will therefore give an example of the sweetness and power of his verse.

[Quotes 'To His Coy Mistress.']

(d)   From *Select British Poets* (1824; this edition was withdrawn and then reprinted in 1825 as *Select Poets of Great Britain*). He

---

[1] Hazlitt's view of Marvell's style as 'forced' and 'far-fetched' should be contrasted with that of Leigh Hunt (see No. 46e).

includes eight lyrics; notice from the prefectory 'Critical List of Authors.'

MARVELL is a writer almost forgotten: but undeservedly so. His poetical reputation seems to have sunk with his political party. His satires were coarse, quaint, and virulent; but his other productions are full of a lively, tender, and elegant fancy. His verses leave an echo on the ear, and find one in the heart. See those entitled BERMUDAS, TO HIS COY MISTRESS, ON THE DEATH OF A FAWN, &c.

46. Leigh Hunt's multiple comments

1819–1846

A liberal journalist and writer, Leigh Hunt (1784–1859) did much to popularize Marvell's writings, both non-political and political, in his various publications.

(a) Extract from the *Indicator*, 24 November 1819, no. 7 (repr. 1822), pp. 51–2.

We do not know, and perhaps it would be impossible to discover, whether Butler wrote his minor pieces before those of the great patriot Andrew Marvell, who rivalled him in wit and excelled him in poetry. Marvell, though born later, seems to have been known earlier as an author. He was certainly known publicly before him. But in the political poems of Marvell there is a ludicrous Character of Holland, which might be pronounced to be either the copy or the original of Butler's, if in those anti-Batavian times the Hollander had not been baited by all the wits; and were it not probable, that the unwieldy monotony of his character gave rise to much the same ludicrous imagery in many of their fancies. Marvell's wit has the advantage of Butler's, not in learning or multiplicity of contrasts (for nobody ever beat him there), but in a greater variety of them, and in being able, from the more poetical turn of his mind, to bring graver and more imaginative things to wait upon his levity.

He thus opens the battery upon our amphibious neighbour: [quotes ll. 1–6, 9–16]. He goes on in a strain of exquisite hyperbole: [quotes ll. 17–48].

We can never read these or some other ludicrous verses of Marvell, even when by ourselves, without laughter; but we must curtail our self-indulgence for the present.

(b) Extract from the *Indicator*, 27 September 1820, no. 51 (repr. 1822), p. 406.

The verses of Andrew Marvell prefixed to Paradise Lost, beginning

When I behold the poet, blind yet bold,

are well known to every reader of Milton, and justly admired by all who know what they read. We remember how delighted we were to find who Andrew Marvell was, and that he could be so pleasant and lively as well as grave. Spirited and worthy as this panegyric is, the reader who is not thoroughly acquainted with Marvell's history does not know all their spirit and worth. That true friend and excellent patriot stuck to his old acquaintance, at a period when all canters and timeservers turned their backs upon him, and would have made the very knowledge of him, which they themselves had had the honour of sharing, the ruin of those that put their desertion to the blush. There is a noble burst of indignation on this subject, in one of Marvell's prose works, against one Parker, who succeeded in getting made a bishop. Parker seems to have thought that Marvell would have been afraid of acknowledging his old acquaintance; but so far from resembling the bishop in that or any other particular, he not only publicly proclaimed and gloried in the friendship of the overshadowed poet, but reminded Master Parker that he had once done the same.

(c) Extract from the *Literary Examiner*, 6 September 1823, no. 83, pp. 148–9.

On the Latin Poems of Milton

Epigram the 13th and last is very noble. It is addressed, in the name of Cromwell, to Christina, Queen of Sweden; and accompanied a present which he made her of his portrait. A doubt has been raised whether it was written by Milton or Andrew Marvell, a man quite capable of the performance; but as Marvell was not then associated with Milton in the office of secretary, the chance appears in favour of the latter. However, the verses were published in the posthumous collection of Marvell's poems, which were 'printed,' says his nominal wife Mary (who appears to have been married to him after some fashion of his own) 'according to the exact copies of my late dear husband, under his own hand-writing.' Marvell, besides being the inventor of our modern prose style in wit, and an inflexible patriot, had a strong and grave talent for poetry, as the reader may see (and ought to see) in his song about the Bermudas boat, his lines on a Wounded Fawn, the verses in which he mentions 'Fairfax and the starry Vere,' and those others where he speaks of

> Tearing our pleasures with rough strife
> Thorough the iron gates of life.

His satire is sometimes coarse, and must be excused by the age he lived in; but it was witty and formidable. His spirit, at once light and powerful, hung admirably between the two parties of Dissenters and Cavaliers; was the startling shield of the one, and a sword still more perplexing to the other: for it could dip and fashion its sturdy metal in the levity of their own fires. His talent at exaggeration, at running a joke down, is exquisite. He was Milton's admiring and inflexible friend.—But I forget the verses before us.

> Ad Christinam Suecorum Reginam,
> Nomine Cromwelli.

[Quotes the Latin.]

The following translation, which it would be difficult to excell, appeared in Toland's Life of Milton:—

> Bright martial Maid, Queen of the Frozen Zone!
> The northern pole supports thy shining throne:
> Behold what furrows age and steel can plow;
> The helmet's weight oppressed this wrinkled brow.
> Through fate's untrodden paths I move; my hands
> Still act my freeborn people's bold commands:
> Yet this stern shade to you submits his frowns,

Nor are these looks always severe to crowns.

['Englished' by Sir F. S.]

Mr. Todd ingeniously conjectures, that the appellations of Martial Maid and Lucid Star (for that also is given her in the original) might allude 'to a gold coin of the Queen, on one side of which she is represented with a helmet as *Minerva*; the other side exhibiting the *sun*.' Perhaps she sent it to Cromwell when it was struck, and his portrait was a return for it. —'These lines,' says Warton, speaking of the original, 'are simple and sinewy. They present Cromwell in a new and pleasing light, and throw an air of amiable dignity on his rough and obstinate character. The uncrowned Cromwell,' he continues, 'had no reason to approach a princess with so much reverence who had renounced her crown.' (Perhaps this however was what particularly excited the reverence of the poet.)

(d)   Extract from the *Monthly Repository*, NS 1 (July 1837–April 1838), pp. 413–14.

But we now come to the great wit and partizan, Andrew Marvell, whose honesty baffled the arts of the Stuarts, and whose pamphlets and verses had no mean hand in putting an end to their dynasty. He unites wit with earnestness and depth of sentiment, beyond any miscellaneous writer in the language. Glorious Andrew's partizanship did not hinder his being of the party of all mankind, and doing justice to what was good in the most opposite characters. In a panegyric on Cromwell he has taken high gentlemanly occasion to record the dignity of the end of Charles the First [quotes ll. 9–16, 21–36].

The emphatic cadence of this couplet,

—Bow'd his comely head
Down, as upon a bed,

is in the best taste of his friend Milton, with greater simplicity than the latter usually evinced.

(e)   Extract from 'An Illustrative Essay' in *Wit and Humour Selected from the English Poets* (1846), reprinted from the 1876 edition, pp. 33–5.

The two best pieces of comic exaggeration I am acquainted with
(next to whole poems like *Hudibras*) are the *Descriptions of Holland*
by the author of that poem, and Andrew Marvel. The reader will
find passages of them in the present volume. Holland and England
happened to be great enemies in the time of Charles the Second,
and the wits were always girding at the Dutchmen and their 'ditch.'
Butler calls them a people

> That feed, like cannibals, on other fishes,
> *And serve their cousins-german up in dishes:*—[ll. 13–14]

and Marvel, in the same strain, says,

> The fish oft-times the burgher dispossess'd,
> *And sat, not as a meat, but as a guest,* [ll. 29–30]

Hazlitt, in his observations on Marvel (*Lectures* ut sup., Tem-
pleman's edition, p. 105), cannot see the jest in this line. He thinks
it 'forced' and 'far-fetched.' I remember he made the same observation once to Charles Lamb and myself, and was entering into a
very acute discourse to prove that we ought not to laugh at such
exaggerations, when we were forced to interrupt him by a fit of
laughter uncontrollable. The exaggerations, no doubt, are extremely far-fetched, but they are not forced; Marvel could have
talked such by the hundred *ad libitum*; and it is this easiness and
flow of extravagance, as well as the relative truth lurking within
it, that renders it delightful to those who have animal spirits enough
to join the merriment; which Hazlitt had not. His sense of humour,
strong as it was, did not carry him so far as that. Had it done so, I
doubt whether, on the very principle of extremes meeting, he
would have enumerated among his provocatives to laughter 'a
funeral,' 'a wedding,' or even 'a damned author, *though* he may be
our friend.' What he says about the difficulty of bearing demands on
our gravity is very true. I would not answer for my own upon
occasions of common formal solemnity, or even at 'a sermon,'
if the preacher were very bad. But the same liability to sympathy
with the extremest present emotion, which would have made him
laugh heartily with Marvel, would probably have absorbed him
in the troubles and griefs of the other occasions, and so prevented
his having a thought of laughter: for he was a very goodnatured
man at heart. But the risibilities of the serious are not always to be
accounted for.

138

(f)   Extract from 'Andrew Marvell' in *Wit and Humour*, reprinted from the 1876 edition, pp. 214–21.

ANDREW MARVEL, a thoughtful and graceful poet, a masterly prose-writer and controversialist, a wit of the first water, and above all, an incorruptible patriot, is thought to have had no mean hand in putting an end to the dynasty of the Stuarts. His wit helped to render them ridiculous, and his integrity added weight to the sting. The enmity, indeed, of such a man was in itself a reproach to them; for Marvel, though bred on the Puritan side, was no Puritan himself, nor a foe to any kind of reasonable and respectable government. He had served Cromwell with his friend Milton, as Latin Secretary, but would have aided Charles the Second as willingly, in his place in Parliament, had the king been an honest man instead of a pensioner of France. The story of his refusing a *carte blanche* from the king's treasurer, and then sending out to borrow a guinea, would be too well known to need allusion to it in a book like the present, if it did not contain a specimen of a sort of practical wit.

Marvel being pressed by the royal emissary to state what would satisfy his expectations, and finding that there was no other mode of persuading him that he had none, called in his servant to testify to his dining three days in succession upon one piece of mutton.

Even the wise and refined Marvel, however, was not free from the coarseness of his age; and hence I find the same provoking difficulty as in the case of his predecessors, with regard to extracts from the poetical portion of his satire. With the prose I should not have been at a loss. But the moment these wits of old time began rhyming, they seem to have thought themselves bound to give the same after-dinner licence to their fancy, as when they were called upon for a song. To read the noble ode on *Cromwell*, in which such a generous compliment is paid to Charles the First,—the devout and beautiful one entitled *Bermuda*, and the sweet overflowing fancies put into the mouth of the *Nymph lamenting the loss of her Faun*,—and then to follow up their perusal with some, nay most of the lampoons that were so formidable to Charles and his brother, you would hardly think it possible for the same man to have written both, if examples were not too numerous to the contrary. Fortunately for the reputation of Marvel's wit, those who choose to become acquainted with it, he wrote a great deal better in prose than verse, and the prose does not take the licence of the verse. Hence, as Swift for another reason observes, we can still read with pleasure his answer to his now forgotten antagonist Parker. Of his witty poems, I can only give a single one entire, which is the following. The reader knows the impudent Colonel Blood, who, in the disguise of a clergyman, attempted to steal the crown, in payment (as he said) of dues withheld from him in Ireland. Marvel had not forgotten the days of Laud, and he saw people still on the bench of bishops who were for renewing the old persecutions. Hence the bitterness of the implication made against prelates.

[Quotes 'On Blood's Stealing the Crown.']
[Quotes 'Description of Holland,' ll. 1–6; 9–48, with the following note:]

The jest of this effusion lies in the intentional and excessive exaggeration. To enjoy it thoroughly, it is necessary perhaps that the reader should be capable, in some degree, of the like sort of jesting, or at least have animal spirits enough to run willing riot with the extravagance. Mr. Hazlitt, for defect of these, could see no kind of joke in it, notwithstanding his admiration of Marvel. He once began an argument with Charles Lamb and myself, to prove to us that we ought not to laugh at such things. Somebody meanwhile was reading the verse; and the only answer which they left us the power to make to our critical friend was by laughing immeasurably. But I have mentioned this in the Introductory Essay.

[Quotes 'Flecknoe,' ll. 1–14, 19–36, 45–94, with the following note:]

Poor Flecnoe was the poetaster, after whom Dryden christened Shadwell 'MacFlecnoe.' See passages from the satire thus entitled in the present volume. The verses before us, which are written in the same spirit of exaggeration as the preceding, exhibit that strange ruggedness in the versification, which was intentional in the satirists of those days when they used the heroic measure, and which they took to be the representative of the satirical numbers of Horace or his predecessors. Flecnoe luckily appears to have rendered the most good-natured poets callous, by a corresponding insensibility to the hardest attacks.

47. A two-part anonymous account of Marvell

1824, 1825

Although in large part biographical, this two-part account appearing in the *Retrospective Review*, a periodical founded in 1820 by Henry Southern, was to be enormously influential: parts of it were to be incorporated in the first separately published life, that of John Dove, in 1832 (see No. 50), which, in turn, became the basis for Hartley Coleridge's two derivative accounts of Marvell in his multiply issued biography of the worthy from Yorkshire (see No. 52).

In 1844, Henry Rogers (see No. 57) published an unsigned review of Dove's *Life* (which was itself to become very influential, see No. 64), and he took occasion to note that it represented a 'pillage' from these two articles. Acknowledging that Dove (who had provided him with 'friendly communications' on some points in his memoir of John Howe, see No. 25) could have been their author, he wondered if that were so why he had not acknowledged them.

The 'copious' quoting from both the poetry and prose is a practice followed by Dove and, to a lesser extent, by Coleridge. From this date on, Marvell's poetry is frequently anthologized both in England and America.

Extract from *Retrospective Review*, 10.2 (1824), pp. 328–30, 332–41; 11.1 (1825), pp. 174–85, 193, 195.

It cannot be a matter of surprise, when the literary character of Milton was so long in struggling into public admiration, from beneath the mass of political and polemical prejudice,* that the

* The following remarkable proof, earlier than Johnson's day, may not be known to all of our readers—'JOHN MILTON was one whose natural parts might deservedly give him a

poetical fame of Andrew Marvell (his assistant Latin secretary to
the Protector) should experience a similar fate, and his works a
temporary neglect. If the humiliating and sturdy prejudices of
Johnson were so far overcome or overawed, as charitably to admit
the biography (and such a biography!) of Milton among 'The Lives
of the most eminent English Poets,' he could, however, hardly be
expected to chronicle the stern patriotism or fugitive poetry of
Marvell; nor, indeed, could it be very desirable, for the memory
of our poet, that Johnson should have shewn him such a distinction, if the price of it had been injustice, proportionate to that so
liberally lavished on Marvell's illustrious friend and co-adjutor
in office. Dr. Johnson could not but have known of the merit and
beauties of Marvell's poems; probably he did not wish to assist in
perpetuating the *fame* of the author, and perhaps the absence of
his commemoration will assist it in now assuming its deserved rank
in the estimation of those who do not consider our great moralist
and lexicographer the absolute dictator of English poetry.

It is the province of time, and the grateful duty of posterity, to
smelt the mixed ore of former ages, and to separate the gold dust
of literature from the dross and incrustations of party and ephemeral writing: as the stream of time rolls rapidly from former to
present ages, desultory writing is lost in the ocean of oblivion;
the personal failings of the individual are 'buried deep in the
obscurity of time,' and mankind are only anxious to preserve the
valuable intellectual legacies left them by their ancestors.

These remarks are not intended to extenuate aught in the *private*
character of Marvell: the 'British Aristides' [see No. 33] has been
long the great exemplar of public and private integrity; and the
mildew of defamation has singularly avoided his irreproachable
reputation. Nor can we justly say that the works of Andrew
Marvell have been altogether neglected: the long list of publications, at different periods, which front this article, is a proof of the
contrary;[1] but, in this reading and reprinting age his *poems*, little

place amongst the principal of our English poets, having written two heroic poems and
a tragedy,—viz. *Paradise Lost, Paradise Regained,* and *Sampson Angonista*; but his fame is
gone out like a candle in a snuff, and his memory will always stink, which might have ever
lived in honourable repute, had not he been a notorious traitor, and most impiously and
villainously belied that blessed martyr, King Charles the First!'—*The Lives of the most
famous English Poets, &c.*1687, *by William Winstanley. Licensed, June* 16, 1686. *Robert Midgley.*
[1] Lists the two parts of *RT,* the 1681 edition of the poems, 'A Short Historical Essay'
(originally appended to *Mr. Smirke*), *Poems on Affairs of State* (1689), and the editions of
Cooke (misdated) and Thompson.

read, are by no means so generally known or so critically admired as they richly deserve to be. The enquiry naturally arises, why? He left behind him no epic or poem of any considerable length; and although his satirical poetry is fraught with sparkling and poignant wit, yet the subjects were chiefly personal and temporary, and not like the more elaborate work of Butler, identified with the national history, manners, and opinions.

We shall give some short biographical account of this accomplished man and English senator, but we shall be as brief as possible—the most impartial and honourable history of his mind will be best perused in his own works, from which we shall make as copious extracts as our limits will allow.

He who has left behind so perfect a mirror of his own mind in his admirable writings, and so irreproachable a character, cannot be further illustrated by the dull pages of pedigree. Poetical genius is not hereditary, it is no heir-loom in family property.

His poem of *Flecknoe*, a humourous satire on an English priest at Rome, Richard Flecknoe, an incorrigible poetaster, is the first recorded instance of his satirical writing; when, or whether at all, published, at the period of its composition, is unknown. It is not worth extracting, to the exclusion of other superior poems; and, though possessing considerable humour, is composed in slovenly metre. It has, however, the merit of originating one of the best satirical poems in the language, *Dryden's M'Flecknoe, against the 'lambent dulness' of Thomas Shadwell.* . . .

We have no room here to particularise, or quote the various prose works in which he boldly advocated the public cause. He was proof against every assault on his invincible public integrity. The personal compliment of the king himself, who delighted in the wit of his society; the golden offers of Charles's treasurer, Danby, who with difficulty found him in his 'elevated retreat, in the second floor of a court in the Strand,' the very day he borrowed a guinea; nothing could daunt his courage, or stay his opposition to the government, much less tempt him to prostitute his pen in its behalf. His personal satire against the king himself, his tracts against popery and the ministry, his desperate literary battles with Parker and others, repeatedly endangered his life: it was all to no purpose on the part of his enemies; he was a rock amidst the foaming ocean; his Roman virtue was incorruptible. . . .

The most interesting poetical piece in the whole miscellaneous collection, is his address to *The Nymph complaining for the Death of her Fawn*. [Quoted.]

The following address of the 'Lover to the Glow-worms' is pretty and fanciful, and more in the taste of the times than Marvell's verses in general. [Quoted.]

Among Marvell's miscellaneous poems, there are several Latin ones. We select some very beautiful verses on a 'Dew Drop,' which are as beautifully translated.

[Quotes Latin and English.]

The following is a very pleasing little poem on the Bermudas, supposed to be sung by the English exiles who had taken refuge there: [Quoted.]

The Poem on *Paradise Lost*, which, though it is frequently prefixed to the editions of Milton, still must not be omitted here. [Quoted.]

We regret that our limits in this number prevent us from doing justice to the remains of Marvel in this article.

We resume our notice of the works of Marvell, to which we could not do justice in the limits of one number.

As a poet, Marvel was certainly unequal; and some of his most beautiful passages are alloyed with vulgarism and common-place similes. His poem of the Nymph lamenting the Death of her Fawn, is, perhaps, the most finished, and, on the whole, the best of the collection. All the poems, however, contain more or less of poetic beauty; some, great tenderness of feeling and expression; and others, successful descriptions of nature and pastoral scenes. Before we proceed to an account of his prose works, we shall give some further extracts from the poetical ones.

The following passages are selected from a poem of considerable length, entitled 'Appleton House,' a residence of Lord Fairfax's, in Yorkshire, now called Nun Appleton, and addressed to that nobleman.

[Quotes ll. 497–512, 561–776.]

The next extract we make is descriptive of those two destructive engines, 'eyes and tears,' which the society for the abolition of war will, we fear, never get the better of.

[Quotes 'Eyes and Tears.']

The following fanciful and ingenious 'Dialogue between Soul and Body' is well known as the original of several quaint and witty imitations. [Quoted.]

Johnson says that Milton was the first Englishman who wrote Latin verses with facility and purity. Marvell may justly claim the secondary honour of latinity, for he is little inferior in this accomplishment to Milton. The Carmina on the Dew Drop in our last, may be given in proof with the following:—

[Quotes 'Hortus' and 'The Garden.']

We have not extracted any other specimens of Marvell's burlesque or facetious poetry, that we might have space for the more interesting and superior extracts from the foregoing poems, and from his prose writings. His political facetiae, although extremely witty and caustic, are generally interwoven with references to persons and public occurrences, now gone to the 'tomb of the Capulets.'

One of the pleasantest of Marvell's poems, is his character of Holland, with which we shall conclude our poetical extracts. It is pregnant with wit, and deserves to be quoted entire. We can only afford room for the first half of it.

[Quotes ll. 1–76.]

The friendship between Milton and Marvell is one of the most interesting subjects in the biography of two of the most noble characters this country has produced.

The encomiastic verses, by Marvell, extracted in our last number [pp. 341–2], which were prefixed to the *second* edition of 'Paradise Lost,' are extremely interesting and prove not only the admiration of Marvell for the 'mighty Poet,' but that, long before the Earl of Dorset and Dryden, Marvell discovered and appreciated the incomparable Epic. Barrow, the physician, also shares in the glory of contributing, according to the custom of the times, 'an introductory Ode, to the author,' in the same edition.

We must now reluctantly close our extracts from Marvell. His volumes, like the prose works of Milton's, will one day attract the attention which, as part of the standard literature and history of our country, they so justly merit; and that day is not very far distant.

In our preceding article we gave a brief biographical memoir of Marvell, the Roman virtues of whose public and private character were alike distinguished; and it was one of his great maxims, that a man dishonest in private life would not honestly serve his country as a public servant.

The following imitation, by Marvell, from Seneca, (Traged. ex Thyeste, Chor. 2,) is highly characteristic of his own mind and private virtues: [quoted.]

48.   Ralph Waldo Emerson's comments

1828, 1875

Lecturer and man of letters, Ralph Waldo Emerson (1803–82) is best remembered for his transcendental philosophy.

(a)   Extract from his *Journal* (1828), reprinted from the *Journals*, ed. E. W. Emerson and W. Emerson Forbes (Boston-New York, 1909), II, pp. 253–4.

Is it not true, what we so reluctantly hear, that men are but the mouthpiece of a great progressive Destiny, in as much as regards literature? I had rather asked, is not the age gone by of the great splendour of English poetry, and will it not be impossible for any age soon to vie with the pervading etherial poesy of Herbert, Shakespeare, Marvell, Herrick, Milton, Ben Jonson; at least to represent anything like their peculiar form of ravishing verse? It is the head of human poetry. Homer and Virgil and Dante and Tasso and Byron and Wordsworth have powerful genius whose amplest claims I cheerfully acknowledge. But 't is a pale ineffectual fire when theirs shines. They would lie on my shelf in undisturbed honour for years, if these Saxon lays stole on my ear. I have for them an affectionate admiration I have for nothing else. They set me on speculations. They move my wonder at myself. They suggest the great endowment of the spiritual man. They open glimpses of the heaven that is in the intellect. When I am caught by a magic word and drop the book to explore the infinite charm— to run along the line of that ray—I feel the longevity of the mind; I admit the evidence of the immortality of the soul. Well, as I said, I am afraid the season of this rare fruit is irrecoverably past; that the earth has made such a nutation of its nodes, that the heat will never reach again that Hesperian garden in which alone these apricots and pomegranates grew.

(b) Extract from the Preface, p. viii, to *Parnassus* (Boston, 1875), a collection of poems from his commonplace book.

Many of [Wordsworth's] poems, as, for example, 'The Rylstone Doe,' might be all improved: nothing of Milton, nothing of Marvell, of Herbert, of Dryden, could be.

[Quotes *in toto* or in part under the rubrics 'Nature,' 'Heroic,' and 'Dirges and Pathetic Poems' the following poems: 'A Drop of Dew,' 'The Garden,' 'Horatian Ode' (entitled 'Cromwell and King Charles'), 'The Nymph.']

49. John Clare, from a letter to H.F. Cary

1829

Successively a shepherd, pot-boy, gardener, vagrant, and, ultimately, a madman, John Clare (1793–1864) enjoyed a few short years as a poet of some esteem.

Having successfully pawned off a composition of his own in 1825 as a poem of Marvell's, he admitted both the fabrication and his rationale in a letter to H. F. Cary, the translator of Dante.

Extract from *The Letters of John Clare*, ed. J. W. and A. Tibble (1951), pp. 223–5.

Helpstone Jany 1829

MY DEAR SIR

... I write to beg your opinion of the enclosed Poem as one of those I intended to pass off as the writings of others—this I sent to the '*Everyday book*'[1] as the production of Andrew Marvel, & the Editor took it for granted that it was so & paid me a compliment in praising it which he would not have done had it passed under my own name & as I still have thoughts of going on with the deception I have sent it to request your opinion of it. I know nothing of the writing of the old Poets further then the '*Specimens of Ellis*' & the '*Songs of Ritson*'[2] but the idea of their manner is all I want to be acquainted with—I had read that Marvel was a great advocate for liberty & as death is a great leveller I thought it would add to the disguise to father upon him that subject. I have written several others for Sir Walter Raleigh, Sir Henry Wooton &c &c; the old manner is all that I attempt with sprinkling a few old words [h]ere

---

[1] Edited by William Hone, 1825.

[2] The first edition (1790) of *Specimens of the Early English Poets*, edited by George Ellis, did not, in fact, include any Marvell; the second (1801) included two poems, both abridged: 'Daphnis and Chloe' and 'Young Love.' Joseph Ritson's *Ancient Songs* (1792) and *Ancient Songs and Ballads* (1829) also did not include any Marvell, though 'The Nymph' is one he did include in his three-volume English *Anthology* (1793–4).

and there—but Taylor wished me not to disguise them under the names of others but publish them under the Title of '*Visits of the Earlier Muses*' but I thought if I could succeed well I should like to have published them as old things found in imaginary Books & M.S.S. There would be no harm in it I think, would there?

50.   John Dove, from
The Life of Andrew Marvell

1832

John Dove (fl. 1830) of Leeds, a 'Whig and a Dissenter—terms all but synonymous with conceit, ignorance, presumption, and vulgarity' in Hartley Coleridge's disdainful words, published the first single biography of the poet. By his own admission he had collected his material from a variety of sources, particularly from Cooke, Thompson, Aikin, Disraeli, and the anonymous writer in the *Retrospective Review*, and his biography in turn was to provide Hartley Coleridge with the materials for two versions of his multiply–issued life of Marvell. More importantly, Dove printed seventeen poems. His only other publication was a history of the Wesley family (1840).

Extract from *The Life of Andrew Marvell, the Celebrated Patriot* (1832), pp. 1–2, 42, 48–9, 57–8, 67–8, 85.

It is the privilege of posterity to adjust the characters of illustrious persons:—ANDREW MARVELL has therefore become a celebrated name, and is now known as one of the most incorruptible patriots that England, or any other country, ever produced. The 'British Aristides' [see No. 33] has been long the great exemplar of public and private integrity. A character so exalted and pure astonished a corrupt age, and overawed even majesty itself. His manners were Roman: he lived on the turnip of Curtius, and would have bled at Philippi [see No. 12].

As a *Poet*, too, Marvell possesses considerable merit, and as a *Satirist* he was one of the keenest in the luxuriant age of Charles II. It is not matter of surprise, when the literary character of MILTON was so long in struggling into public admiration, that the poetical fame of Marvell should experience a similar fate [Cites note from No. 47.] If the humiliating and sturdy prejudices of Dr. JOHNSON were so far overcome, or overawed, as charitably to admit the biography of Milton among his 'Lives of the Poets,' he could hardly be expected to chronicle the stern patriotism, or fugitive poetry, of Marvell; nor, indeed, would it have been desirable that Johnson should have shown him such a distinction, if the price of it had been injustice proportionate to that lavished on Marvell's illustrious friend and coadjutor in office.

The controversy between Marvell and Parker is a striking example of the efficient powers of genius, in first humbling, and then annihilating, an unprincipled bravo, who has placed himself at the head of a faction. Marvell was a master in all the arts of ridicule; and his inexhaustible spirit only required some *permanent* subject, to rival the causticity of SWIFT, whose style, in neatness and vivacity, seems to have been modelled from it; for, in his '*Tale of a Tub*,' he says, 'we still read Marvell's answer to Parker with pleasure, though the book it answers be sunk long ago.' But Marvell placed the oblation of genius on a *temporary* altar, and the sacrifice sunk with it; he wrote to the times, and with the times his writings have, in some measure, passed away [see No. 12]. He left behind him no Poem of permanent interest; and although his satirical poetry is fraught with sparkling and poignant wit, yet the subjects were chiefly personal and temporary, and not like the more elaborate work of BUTLER, identified with the national history, manners, and opinions [see No. 47].

Parker had accused Marvell with having served CROMWELL, and being the friend of MILTON, then living, at a moment when such an accusation, not only rendered a man odious, but put his life in danger. Marvell, who now perceived that Milton, whom he never looked on but with reverential awe, was likely to be drawn into his quarrel, touches on this subject with great delicacy and tenderness, but not with diminished energy against his malignant adversary, whom he shows to have been an impertinent intruder into Milton's house, where he had first seen him. He cautiously alluded to our English Homer by his initials; at *that* time the very name of Milton would have *tainted* the page!*

[Quotes *RT II*, p. 312.]

Marvell, when he lays by his playful humour, and fertile fancy, for more *solemn* remonstrances, assumes a loftier tone, and a severity of invective, from which, indeed, Parker never recovered. Accused by Parker of aiming to degrade the *clerical* character, Marvell declares his veneration for that holy vocation, and would reflect even on the failings of the men, from whom so much is expected, with indulgent reverence.

[Freely paraphrases *RT II*, pp. 163–5.]

Marvell was also the author of several valuable political tracts, advocating frequent Parliaments as the spirit of the English Constitution, and of many admirable pamphlets on religious liberty. His political *facetiae*, although extremely witty and caustic, are generally interwoven with references to persons and public occurrences, now gone to 'the tomb of the Capulets' [see No. 47].

Thus have we collected, from a variety of sources, and reduced into narrative, all that we can find authentically recorded of ANDREW MARVELL, a man who united, in an eminent degree, the wit, the scholar, the disinterested and incorruptible patriot. The modern political maxim, that 'every man has his price,' did not apply to Marvell. It is surprising that an individual, so highly gifted, and who made so considerable a figure in his day, found no contemporary biographer to record the memorials of his life; and this is

* The friendship between Milton and Marvell is an interesting fact in the history of two of the noblest characters this country has produced. The encomiastic verses prefixed to 'Paradise Lost,' prove not only the admiration of Marvell for the 'mighty poet,' but that, long before the EARL OF DORSET or DRYDEN, Marvell had discovered and fully appreciated the incomparable Epic. EDWARD PHILLIPS, the nephew of Milton states, that 'Marvell, with other friends, frequently visited the Poet when secreted on account of the threats of Government.' It is not improbable that the humour of Marvell contrived the premature and mock funeral of Milton, which is reported, for a time, to have duped his enemies into a belief of his real death; and to Marvell's friendship the world is probably indebted for the great poems which were afterwards published.

the more to be regretted, as it would have furnished many interesting anecdotes which are now buried in oblivion. It must, however, be remembered, that Marvell lived at a very critical period, and being prominently placed in office, and possessing considerable influence, during the *Commonwealth*; this may be a reason why we hear so little of him afterwards. Besides, he seems to have been, from the united testimony of his contemporaries, a man of retired habits, and reserved conversation, except amongst his most intimate friends, with whom he was lively, facetious, and instructive.

The following imitation, by Marvell, from SENECA, *(Traged. ex Thyeste, Chorus 2.)* is highly characteristic of his own mind, and shows the absence of ambition, and love of retirement.

[Quotes; see No. 47.]

As a *Poet*, MARVELL was certainly unequal, and some of his most beautiful passages are alloyed with vulgarism and common-place similes [see No. 47]. His early poems express a fondness for the charms of rural and pastoral scenes, with much delicacy of sentiment; and are full of fancy, after the manner of COWLEY and his contemporaries [see No. 39]. Marvell's *wit* was debased, indeed, by the coarseness of the time, and his *imagination* by its conceits; but he had a true vein of poetry.

51. Three anonymous reviews of Dove's *Life*

1832, 1833

(a) Extract from the *Eclectic Review*, 8 (November, 1832), pp. 416–17, 420–5.

ANDREW MARVELL is a name that has come down to us associated with traditional veneration, as that of an incorruptible patriot, an accomplished scholar, a wit, polemic, and poet, the friend of

Milton, himself eulogized by Sheffield (Duke of Buckingham), by Churchill, and by Mason, most fortunate and honoured in his life, and bewailed, at his death, as a public loss: and yet, of this extraordinary person, no satisfactory biographical memorial exists; and his name survives in history, rather than in our literature. His works consist, for the most part, of fugitive pieces and tracts of temporary interest, never collected during his life-time, and now almost unknown. In fact, his name has preserved his writings, rather than his writings his name. He wrote for his age, rather than for posterity; but the high example he has bequeathed, is a more valuable legacy than half the works of Johnson's Poets. In a venal age, he was proof against corruptions; though poor, he maintained his independence, and, what was more, while so many were changing sides around him, his consistency; and his wit and humour, which might have rendered him the favourite of the court, were zealously dedicated to the cause of patriotism and civil freedom. Bp. Burnet, who knew, or affects to have known, every body, and whose amusing history is a gallery of living characters, speaks of Marvell slightingly, yet bears testimony to the cleverness and effectiveness of his writings.... Dean Swift, who devoted similar powers of caustic wit to a worse purpose, remarks of this work: 'We still read Marvell's answer to Parker with pleasure, though the book it answers be sunk long ago.' But it is read no longer. Wit loses its flavour when it is not drunk new. Some curiosity, however, may be felt, to know, from a few specimens, what was the style of 'refined buffoonery' which so delighted the age, and by which Marvell drove out of the field the bitter and unprincipled renegade, who, writhing under the lash he had provoked, appealed to the Government to 'crush with the secular arm, the pestilent wit, the servant of Cromwell and the friend of Milton.' The few specimens in this little volume will therefore prove acceptable; and will probably excite in most readers a desire to see more. Marvell's entire works, however, are not worth republishing—any more than Swift's, who has been more fortunate, or less so, in having all his rubbish collected in evidence of the criminal abuse he made of his talents;—or than Defoe's, a man of greater genius, perhaps, than either, though with less of the old Roman in his character than Marvell, and to whom has at length been rendered the tardy justice of a biographical monument. The Author of Robinson Crusoe could never indeed have been forgotten; yet, but for that exquisite romance, the name of one of the most voluminous and powerful writers of his age would by this time have survived only in the Dunciad. A well edited selection of Marvell's writings, with a memoir by a competent biographer, might even now be worth publishing. In the meantime, Mr. Dove's modest performance may serve the purpose of making the reader better acquainted with the life and character of this not too celebrated Patriot.

The first edition of Marvell's Poems is posthumous, and was published in folio, in 1681, by a bookseller who bought his manuscripts from the woman in whose house Marvell lodged, and who is made to certify their authenticity in the advertisement prefixed to them, in the assumed character of his widow. Marvell was never married; and 'the cheat was soon detected.' As these poems were not left by Marvell for publication, but merely found among his papers, it is impossible to determine whether he was the actual author of all the compositions ascribed to him. That he was a poet of no contemptible talents, his Lines on Paradise Lost evince; but nothing is more likely than that he should have copied into his common-place book, many productions which pleased him, by different authors. ... As undoubted specimens of Marvell's poetry, Mr. Montgomery has inserted in his 'Christian Poet' [Glasgow, 1827], 'The Emigrants,' and 'Eyes and Tears,' both of which will be found in the present volume. We regret that, as to several others, we cannot help having strong doubts whether they are justly ascribed to him. It must surely have been in his juvenile days, if the poem be really his, that Marvell addressed 'to his coy mistress,' the quaint and unequal lines, not quite unworthy of Cowley, in which we are surprised with the following striking thought:

[Quotes ll. 21–4.]

'The Character of Holland' is more likely to have proceeded from Marvell's satirical pen:—

> Holland, that scarce deserves the name of land,
> As but th'off-scouring of the British sand.

The allusions indicate that it was written during the Protectorate. We wish that we had sufficient authority for assigning to our Author the 'Dialogue between the Resolved Soul and created

Pleasure'; but the versification seems much too polished, the turns of thought too delicate, and the whole is in too pure a taste for Marvell's day: it must, we think, be of later date. It is given in Thompson's editions of the Works, but, we presume, does not appear in the folio edition of the Poems. It is by far the most beautiful of all the specimens selected by Mr. Dove; and, as it may be new to many of our readers, we shall indulge ourselves in extracting it [quoted] . . . .

Marvell might occasionally trifle in poetry; but, in his prose writings, he appears in his native vigour of character as the indignant satirist and the intrepid advocate of freedom. In the 'Rehearsal Transprosed,' appears the following ironical lament on the 'doleful evils' of the press, which must serve as a sufficient specimen.

[Quotes *RT I*, pp. 4–5.]

(b) Extract from the *Monthly Review*, 3 (September—December 1832), pp. 193, 200–6.

Andrew Marvell is known to all the readers of English history, as one of the few true patriots whose names adorn its pages.

Marvell's [*RT*] is certainly written with great ability and bitter sarcasm; it may even still be read with interest, for the pungent quality of its style, and its well-turned classical allusions. The following paragraph will give the reader some notion of its merits. All books were at that time licensed before they were published, and as Parker held the office of licenser, he issued the imprimatur for his own works, and recalled the license that had been granted for Marvell's.

[Quotes *RT II*, p. 150.]

Junius must have formed his style, in a great measure, upon that of Marvell. . . .
We shall add a few extracts from Marvell's letters and poems, in order to show the versatility of his talents. The following letter, though exhibiting rather too much of artifice and study on such a subject, is, however, highly creditable to Marvell's heart; it was addressed to Sir John Trott, on the death of his son.

[Quotes *Letters*, pp. 311–13.]

Marvell's poetry is more unequal than his prose, to which we think it much inferior. There is something of the delicacy of Cowley in his earlier effusions, and rather too much, in all of them, of those conceits which were then found in poetry of every description. The following lines frequently exhibit this blemish, but in other respects they are not destitute of merit.

[Quotes 'Eyes and Tears.']

The 'Mower's Address to the Glow-worm' is not in better taste: we give it as a sample of the fashion of the day in such trifles [quoted].

Marvell's character of Holland shews that his true forte, even in poetry, was the satirical. It is full of his powerful wit, and displays some fancy.

[Quotes ll. 1–92, 135–52.]

Marvell would very probably have been more successful in poetry had he been less engaged in politics, and in religious controversy. If he had given up his genius to literature, he must, we think, have become one of its brightest ornaments. He may, therefore, be set down as one amongst the many men of genius, whom the temporary charms of public life have seduced, in this country, from the path that might otherwise have led them to a more permanent and a more enviable fame. We look back with a degree of pity upon those men of talent, who, though they may have achieved some good in parliamentary contests, yet seem to have had a fretful existence, and have left little behind them that posterity cares to become acquainted with. But Milton, Dryden, Addison, Pope,—what a luminous and unfading glory is theirs, as compared with the constantly decaying names of even the most eminent among their political contemporaries!

(c) Extract from the *Westminster Review*, 18 (January 1833), pp. 85, 101.

The poem entitled 'Appleton House,' (a seat of Lord Fairfax), which contains the preceding lines [721–4], displays an intense feeling for the beauties of nature, expressed with a felicity which not infrequently recalls 'L'Allegro' and 'Il Penseroso' of Milton, written in the same sort of verse, the octosyllabic of 'fatal facility.' The following beautiful picture has not been given by any modern poet:

[Quotes ll. 529–32.]

But a great blemish in most of Marvell's poems is the occasional coarseness, surprising in the friend and contemporary of Milton; a perfect freedom from which is one of the many ennobling characteristics of that great writer.

The admiration of Marvell is to be based, not on his intellectual, but his moral qualities. Neither as a philosopher nor as a poet does Marvell belong to the first order of great minds. His intellectual merits are those of a wit and satirist; and though distinguished in that capacity, he could claim no particular notice beyond the crowds of wits and satirists who have blazed out their little hour and passed away. But Andrew Marvell possesses other claims to attention, other and higher demands on respectful and affectionate remembrance; and his name will not pass away. There is no man who worships political virtue, but must adore the memory of Marvell.

52.   Hartley Coleridge from *The Worthies of Yorkshire and Lancashire*

1832

In the summer of 1832, Hartley Coleridge (1796–1849) moved to Leeds to continue work on the series of biographies of notable figures from Yorkshire and Lancashire that had been started by John Dove (No. 50). Based on Dove and his sources, one version of his life of Marvell appeared in 1832 in the collection entitled *The Worthies of Yorkshire and Lancashire*; it was to be re-issued a number of times under different titles and imprints. A second version of his *Life* of Marvell, so closely based upon its predecessor's that the *British Museum Catalogue* describes it as Dove's, appeared twice in 1835, but, despite its date, it must have preceded the revised version published in 1832.

Extract from *The Worthies of Yorkshire and Lancashire*, 1832, pp. 61–4.

Of his poetic merits, we would gladly speak at large, but our limits allow not of immoderate quotation, and his works are too little known, and in general too inaccessible, to be referred to with confidence. It is disgraceful to English booksellers, (we say not to the English nation,) that they find not a place in our popular collections. The writer of this notice can truly say that he met with them only by accident, and was astonished that they were not familiar as household words. But probably the same causes which retarded the poetic fame of Milton, went nigh to extinguish that of Andrew Marvell. The classical Republicans were few and inefficient. The Puritans would not read poetry. The High-Church Bigots would read nothing but what emanated from their own party. The common-place roystering Royalists were seldom sober enough to read, and the mob-fanatics did not know their letters.

Moreover, the mere celebrity of a man, in one respect, sometimes throws a temporary shade over his accomplishments in a different line. Milton had produced Poems in his youth, that alone would place him high among Poets, yet no one remembered that the author of the 'Defensio populi Anglicani' had ever written Comus; and [William] Roscoe was perhaps the first to remind the people of England, that Lorenzo di Medici ranks high among the bards of Italy. It is not without effort that we remember that Cæsar's Commentaries were written by the same man who conquered at Pharsalia. And what reader of Childe Harold thinks of Lord Byron's speech about the Nottingham Framebreakers? Lord John Russell's Tragedies are obscured by the lustre of his Reform Bill, and should Paganini produce another Iliad, it would only be read as the preposterous adventure of a fiddler. Hence we may fairly conclude that Marvell's fame would have been greater, had it been less; that had he been as insignificant a being as [John] Pomfret [see No. 90], or [Thomas] Yalden [see No. 71], Dr. Johnson might have condescended to rank him among the Poets of Great Britain.

We took occasion[1] to allude to Marvell's sentiments on the death of Charles the First, expressed in his Horatian Ode to Oliver Cromwell. The lines are noble:—

[Quotes ll. 37–70.]

The poems of Marvell are, for the most part, productions of his early youth. They have much of that over-activity of fancy, that remoteness of allusion, which distinguishes the school of Cowley; but they have also a heartfelt tenderness, a childish simplicity of feeling, among all their complication of thought, which would atone for all their conceits, if conceit were indeed as great an offence against poetic nature as Addison and other critics of the French school pretend. But though there are cold conceits, a conceit is not necessarily cold. The mind, in certain states of passion, finds comfort in playing with occult or casual resemblances, and dallies with the echo of a sound.

We confine our praise to the poems which he wrote for himself. As for those he made to order, for Fairfax or Cromwell, they are as dull as every true son of the muse would wish these things to be. Captain Edward Thomson, who collected and published Marvell's works in 1776, has, with mischievous industry, scraped together, out of the state poems, and other common sewers, a quantity of obscene and scurrilous trash, which we are convinced Marvell did not write, and which, by whomsover written, ought to be delivered over to condign oblivion.

With less injury to Marvell's reputation, but equal disregard of probability, Captain Thompson ascribes to him the hymns or paraphrases, 'When all thy mercies, Oh my God,' 'The spacious firmament on high,' which were published in the Spectator, and afterwards in the works of Addison, to whom they undoubtedly belong. He was not the man to claim what was not his own. As to their being Marvell's, it is just as probable that they are Chaucer's. They present neither his language, his versification, nor his cast of thought.

---

[1] On p. 18, Coleridge comments on Marvell's expression not merely of pity but of admiration for King Charles 'but so worded, that it may pass either for a satire or an eulogy on the Protector.'

We cannot better conclude, than with the following beautiful extract from a letter to a friend in affliction, which is novel on a trite subject,—that of consolation:—

[Quotes freely from *Letters*, p. 311.]

53.   Samuel Carter Hall on the poetry

1836

Journalist and editor, Samuel Carter Hall (1800–89) collected and published 'the most perfect specimens of the Poets' up to Prior in his first *Book of Gems*. Interestingly, he included one example from Spenser, three from Milton, four from Marvell, and ten from Donne. In the biographical portion, he adds to the romantic legends: Marvell 'was flattered and threatened, watched by spies, waylaid by ruffians, tempted by women and by gold. In vain!'

For Edgar Allan Poe's review of the volume in 1836, see No. 54.

Extract from the *Book of Gems* (1836), p. 264.

His genius was as varied as it was remarkable. In this volume he occupies a loved and respected place as an exquisite and tender poet—elsewhere he may stand in the first and very highest rank, *facile princeps*,[1] as an incorruptible patriot, the best of controversialists, and the leading prose wit of England. His are the 'first sprightly runnings' [Dryden, *Aureng-zebe* IV.i] of that glorious stream of wit, which will bear upon it down to the latest posterity the names of Swift, Steele, and Addison. Before the time of Marvell,

---

[1] From Edmund Waller's epitaph: *inter poetas sui temporis facile princeps*: among poets easily the foremost of his time (*The Poems*, ed. G. Thorn Drury [1904], I, p. lxix).

to be witty was to be forced, strained, and conceited. From him wit first came sparkling forth untouched with baser matter. It was like his personal character. Its main feature was an open clearness. Mean detraction or sordid jealousy never for an instant stained it. He turned aside in the midst of an exalted panegyric to Oliver Cromwell, to say the finest things that have ever been said of Charles I.—he left for a while his own wit in the Rehearsal Transposed [sic], to praise the wit of [Samuel] Butler, his rival and political enemy [RT I, p. 22]. As a poet Andrew Marvell was true, and this is the grand point in poetry. He was not of the highest order, not perhaps in even a high order, but what he did was genuine. It is sweetness speaking out in sweetness. In the language there is nothing more exquisitely tender than the 'Nymph complaining for the loss of her Fawn.' Such poems as this and 'the Bermudas' may live, and deserve to live, as long as the longest and the mightiest. Of as real a quality are the majority of the poems of Marvell. In a playful and fantastic expression of tender and voluptuous beauty, they are well nigh unrivalled. His fancy indeed some times overmasters him, but it is always a sweet and pleasant mastery. His strong love of the actual at times bursts forth, but his poetry still survives it, and will not be fairly clogged and over-laden with the body corporate.

54.   Edgar Allan Poe comments

1836

Poet, short-story writer, critic, and editor, Edgar Allan Poe (1809–49) first reviewed S.C. Hall's *Book of Gems* (see No. 53) for the *Southern Literary Messenger*, August 1836; the review was then slightly modified for the *Broadway Journal*, 17 May, 1845.

Reprinted from the *Complete Works*, ed. J.A. Harrison (1902), XII, pp. 139–46.

It should not be doubted that at least one-third of the affection with which we regarded the elder poets of Great Britain, should be attributed to what is, in itself, a thing apart from poetry—we mean to the simple love of the antique—and that, again, a third of even the proper poetic sentiment inspired by their writings, should be ascribed to a fact which, while it has strict connexion with poetry in the abstract, and with the old British poems themselves, should not be looked upon as a merit appertaining to the authors of the poems. Almost every devout admirer of the old bards, if demanded his opinion of their productions, would mention vaguely, yet with perfect sincerity, a sense of dreamy, wild, indefinite, and he would perhaps say, indefinable delight; on being required to point out the source of this so shadowy pleasure, he would be apt to speak of the quaint in phraseology, and in general handling. This quaintness is, in fact, a very powerful adjunct to ideality, but in the case in question, it arises independently of the author's will, and is altogether apart from his intention. Words and their rhythm have varied. Verses which affect us today with a vivid delight, and which delight, in many instances, may be traced to the one source, quaintness, must have worn, in the days of their construction, a very common-place air. This is, of course, no argument against the poems *now*—we mean it only as against the poets *then*. There is a growing desire to over-rate them. The old English muse was frank, guileless, sincere, and although very learned, still learned without Art. No general error evinces a more thorough confusion of ideas than the error of supposing Donne and Cowley metaphysical in the sense wherein Wordsworth and Coleridge are so. With the two former ethics were the end—with the two latter the means. The poet of the 'Creation' wished, by highly artificial verse, to inculcate what he supposed to be moral truth—the poet of the 'Ancient Mariner' to infuse the Poetic Sentiment through channels suggested by analysis. The one finished by complete failure what he commenced in the grossest misconception; the other, by a path which could not possibly lead him astray, arrived at a triumph which is not the less glorious because hidden from the profane eyes of the multitude. But in this view even the 'metaphysical verse' of Cowley is but evidence of the simplicity and single-

heartedness of the man. And he was in this but a type of his *school*—
for we may as well designate in this way the entire class of writers
whose poems are bound up in the volume before us, and throughout all of whom there runs a very perceptible general character.
They used little art in composition. Their writings sprang immediately from the soul—and partook intensely of that soul's nature.
Nor is it difficult to perceive the tendency of this *abandon*—to
elevate immeasurably all the energies of mind—but, again, so to
mingle the greatest possible fire, force, delicacy, and all good
things, with the lowest possible bathos, baldness, and imbecility,
as to render it not a matter of doubt that the average results of
mind in such a school will be found inferior to those results in
one (*ceteris paribus*) more artificial.

We cannot bring ourselves to believe, that the selections of the
'Book of Gems' are such as will impart to a poetical reader the
clearest possible idea of the beauty of the *school*—but if the intention had been merely to show the school's character, the attempt
might have been considered successful in the highest degree.
There are long passages now before us, of the most despicable
trash, with no merit whatever, beyond that of their antiquity.
The criticisms of the Editor do not particularly please us. His
enthusiasm is too general and too vivid not to be false. His opinion,
for example, of Sir Henry Wotton's 'Verses on the Queen of
Bohemia'—that 'There are few finer things in our language' is
untenable and absurd. [Quotation.]

In such lines we can perceive not one of those higher attributes
of Poesy which belong to her under all circumstances and throughout all time. Here everything is art-naked or but awkwardly
concealed. No prepossession for the mere antique (and in this
case we can imagine no other prepossession) should induce us
to dignify with the sacred name of Poetry, a series, such as this,
of elaborate and threadbare compliments, stitched, apparently,
together, without fancy, without plausibility, and without even
an attempt at adaptation.

In common with all the world, we have been much delighted
with 'The Shepherd's Hunting,' by Wither—a poem partaking,
in a remarkable degree, of the peculiarities of *Il Penseroso*. Speaking
of Poesy, the author says:

[Quotes Wither, *Ecl*. 4, pp. 371–96.]

But these lines, however good, do not bear with them much of the general character of the English antique. Something more of this will be found in [Richard] Corbet's 'Farewell Rewards and Fairies!' We copy a portion of Marvell's 'Maiden lamenting for her Fawn'—which we prefer not only as a specimen of the elder poets, but in itself as a beautiful poem abounding in pathos, exquisitely delicate imagination and truthfulness, to anything of its species.

[Quotes ll. 63–92.]

How truthful an air of lamentation hangs here upon every syllable! It pervades all. It comes over the sweet melody of the words—over the gentleness and grace which we fancy in the little maiden herself—even over the half-playful, half-petulant air with which she lingers on the beauties and good qualities of her favorite—like the cool shadow of a summer cloud over a bed of lilies and violets, 'and all sweet flowers.' The whole is redolent with poetry of a very lofty order.[1] Every line is an idea—conveying either the beauty and playfulness of the fawn, or the artlessness of the maiden, or her love, or her admiration, or her grief, or the fragrance and warmth and *appropriateness* of the little nest-like bed of lilies and roses which the fawn devoured as it lay upon them, and could scarcely be distinguished from them by the once happy little damsel who went to seek her pet with an arch and rosy smile on her face. Consider the great variety of truthful and delicate thought in the few lines we have quoted—the *wonder* of the maiden at the fleetness of her favorite—the 'little silver feet'—the fawn challenging his mistress to a race with 'a pretty skipping grace,' running on before, and then, with head turned back, awaiting her approach only to fly from it again—can we not distinctly perceive all these things? How exceedingly vigorous, too, is the line,

And trod as if [*sic*, from Tonson] on the four winds!—

a vigor fully apparent only when we keep in mind the artless character of the speaker and the four feet of the favorite—one for each wind. Then consider the garden of 'my own,' so over grown—entangled—with roses and lilies, as to be 'a little wilderness'—the fawn, loving to be there, and there 'only'—the maiden seeking it 'where it *should* lie'—and not being able to distinguish it from the

[1] 1836 version reads '*of the very loftiest order.*'

flowers until 'itself would rise'—the lying among the lilies 'like a bank of lilies'—the loving to 'fill itself with roses,'

> And its pure virgin limbs to fold
> In whitest sheets of lilies cold,

and these things being its 'chief' delights—and then the pre-eminent beauty and naturalness of the concluding lines—whose very hyperbole only renders them more true to nature when we consider the innocence, the artlessness, the enthusiasm, the passionate grief, and more passionate admiration of the bereaved child—

> Had it lived long, it would have been
> Lilies without—roses within.

55. Robert Chambers on Marvell

1835, 1844

Robert Chambers (1802–71), together with his brother William, compiled the *History of the English Language and Literature* (Edinburgh, 1835), which was described as the only history of English literature yet given to the world. It was to be twice reprinted in 1836, and again in the following year, this time in Hartford, Conn., with the addition of American authors, its editor conjecturing that there were more than two thousand eminent living writers and he knew not how many deceased.

Recognizing a change in public taste, in 1844 Chambers, together with his friend Robert Carruthers, then compiled his two-volume *Cyclopaedia*, this time including four poems of Marvell but only one—'Bermudas'—in its entirety.

ANDREW MARVELL

(a)   Extract from the *History of the English Language and Literature*
(London-Edinburgh, n.d.), p. 80.

After having for upwards of a century been excluded from the
ranks of the English poets, ANDREW MARVELL (1620–1678) has
recently begun once more to attract attention. He was the friend
of Milton, and, like him, zealously devoted to the popular cause
in politics. It is related of him, that, while he represented the town
of Hull in Parliament, and was without any other resources than
a small allowance, which he received for that duty, a courtier was
sent with a thousand pounds in gold to buy him over to the
opposite side; he placidly refused the bribe, pointing to a blade-
bone of mutton which was to serve for his dinner on the ensuing
day, as a proof that he was above necessity. The works of Marvell,
amidst much sorry writing, contain a few passages of exquisite
beauty; one of which is here presented under the title of

THE NYMPH'S DESCRIPTION OF HER FAWN

[Quotes ll. 55–92.]

(b)   Extract from the *Cyclopaedia of English Literature* (1844), I,
pp. 342–3.

ANDREW MARVELL (1620–1678) is better known as a prose writer
than a poet, and is still more celebrated as a patriotic member of
parliament. He was associated with Milton in friendship and in
public service. . . .
    Marvell's prose writings were exceedingly popular in their day,
but being written for temporary purposes, they have mostly gone
out of mind with the circumstances that produced them. In 1672
he attacked Doctor, afterwards Bishop, Parker, in a piece entitled
The Rehearsal Transposed [*sic*]. In this production he vindicates the
fair fame of Milton, who, he says, 'was and is a man of as great
learning and sharpness of wit as any man [*RT II*, p. 312]'. One of
Marvell's treatises, *An Account of the Growth of Popery and Arbitrary
Government in England*, was considered so formidable, that a reward
was offered for the discovery of the author and printer. Among
the first, if not the very first, traces of that vein of sportive humour
and raillery on national manners and absurdities, which was
afterward carried to perfection by Addison, Steele, and others,

166

may be found in Marvell. He wrote with great liveliness, point, and vigour, though often coarse and personal. His poetry is elegant rather than forcible: it was an embellishment to his character of patriot and controversialist, but not a substantive ground of honour and distinction. 'There is at least one advantage in the poetical inclination,' says Henry Mackenzie, in his Man of Feeling, 'that it is an incentive to philanthropy. There is a certain poetic ground on which a man cannot tread without feelings that enlarge the heart. The causes of human depravity vanish before the enthusiasm he professes; and many who are not able to reach the Parnassian heights, may yet approach so near as to be bettered by the air of the climate.' This appears to have been the case with Andrew Marvell. Only a good and amiable man could have written his verses on *The Emigrants in the Bermudas*, so full of tenderness and pathos. His poem on *The Nymph Complaining for the Death of her Fawn*, is also finely conceived and expressed.

[Then quotes 'The Emigrants in the Bermudas;'* from 'The Nymph Complaining for the Death of her Fawn;' from 'Thoughts in a Garden;' from 'A Whimsical Satire on Holland'† —compilers' titles.]

* This piece of Marvell's, particularly the last verse, seems to have been in the mind of a distinguished poet of our own day, Mr Thomas Moore, when he composed his fine lyric, 'The Canadian Boat Song.' [See also No. 60.]
† Holland was the enemy of the commonwealth, and protector of the exiled king; therefore odious to Marvell.

56.   From the *Penny Cyclopaedia*

1839

The *Penny Cyclopaedia*, issued in twenty-seven volumes in 1833–43 with three supplements, was published by the Society for the Diffusion of Useful Knowledge, founded in 1825–6. As the title of the Society indicates, its intention was to provide useful historical information to a wide range of readers. Its superintendent of publications was Charles Knight (1791–1873).

Extract from the *Penny Cyclopaedia* (1839).

Marvell's powers as a poet were not sufficient to ensure him lasting fame. Few or none of his poetical compositions, any more than his prose, obtained a lasting popularity. Many of his verses, particularly the satirical, are defaced by the coarseness of his time, from which his contemporary Milton is so remarkably free. Others display a degree of feeling and a perception of the beauties of nature, expressed with a harmony of versification and felicity of language which not unfrequently recall the 'L'Allegro' and 'Il Penseroso' of Milton. But Marvell's verse did not possess sufficient vitality to secure its continued existence.…

Upon the whole Andrew Marvell's claim to be honourably remembered is founded rather on his moral than his intellectual qualities. His intellectual merits are those of a wit and satirist [see No. 51c]; and though in these departments considerably above mediocrity, and even famous in his day, he could scarcely have hoped for a different fate from that of other wits and satirists who are now forgotten. But the degree in which Andrew Marvell possessed that very rare quality, political integrity, gives him a claim to the remembrance and even the reverence of after-ages, still greater than is due to him as the friend and associate of Milton.

57. Henry Rogers's observations on Marvell
1844

Twelve years after the appearance of John Dove's *Life of Andrew Marvell*, the first biography of the poet separately published, Henry Rogers printed an unsigned review essay in the *Edinburgh Review* (1844). Such tardiness is perhaps to be explained by a developing interest in Marvell, the result of his first important work on John Howe (see No. 25). His comments on Dove's reliance on the two anonymous articles in the *Retrospective Review* (see No. 47)* points up the reliance of critics on earlier accounts. Curiously, he does not seem to know of the tangled connection of the Dove-Coleridge biographies.

Rogers's own account was to be utilized, in turn, in the first American edition of Marvell's poetry (Boston, 1854), on this occasion, it happens, with due acknowledgment. Terming it 'on the whole, the best in print,' James Russell Lowell, the editor of the volume on Marvell in the British Poets Series, none the less thought it proper to omit some passages and to make some additions (see No. 64).

* We gladly admit that Mr. Dove's little volume is a tolerably full and accurate compilation of what is known to us of Andrew Marvell's history, and contains some pleasant extracts from his writings. But we must express our regret that he has been, in a trifling degree, misled, by adhering too literally to the etymology of the word 'compilation.' It is true that 'compilation' comes from *compilatio*, and equally true that *compilatio* means 'pillage;' but it does not follow that 'compilation' is to be literally 'pillage.' A considerable number of his sentences, sometimes whole paragraphs, are transferred from Mr D'Israeli's Miscellanies, and from two articles on Andrew Marvell which appeared in the *Retrospective Review* some twenty years ago, without alteration and without any sort of acknowledgement. Had they been printed between inverted commas, and the sources specified, we should have call it 'compilation,' but no 'pillage'—as it is, we must call it pillage, and not compilation. Mr Dove may, it is true, have been the author of the articles in question. If so, there was no conceivable reason why he should not have owned them, and we can only regret that he has omitted to do it. If not, we cannot justify the use he has made of them (p. 70, n.). [In his Preface to *The Life of ... Howe*, Rogers had acknowledged Dove's 'friendly communications on some minute points in the memoir.']

Rogers was to reprint the review in his *Essays*, consisting of selected contributions to the *Edinburgh Review* (1850, 1855).

Extract from the *Edinburgh Review*, 79 (January 1844), pp. 70–2, 81, 88–90, 92–104.

Soon after this, probably at the commencement of 1642, Marvell seems to have set out on his travels, in the course of which he visited a great part of Europe. At Rome he stayed a considerable time, where Milton was then residing, and where, in all probability, their lifelong friendship commenced. With an intrepidity, characteristic of both, it is said they openly argued against the superstitions of Rome within the precincts of the Vatican. It was here, also, that Marvell made the first essay of his satirical powers in a lampoon on Richard Flecknoe. It is now remembered only as having suggested the terrible satire of Dryden on the laureate Shadwell. At Paris he made another attempt at satire in Latin, of about the same order of merit. The subject of it was an Abbé named Lancelot Joseph de Maniban, who professed to interpret the characters and prognosticate the fortunes of strangers by an inspection of their handwriting....

On the publication of Milton's second 'Defence,' Marvell was commissioned to present it to the Protector. After doing so, he addressed a letter of compliment to Milton, the terms of which evince the strong admiration with which his illustrious friend had inspired him. His eulogy of the 'Defence' is as emphatic as that of the Paradise Lost, in the well known recommendatory lines prefixed to most editions of that poem....

During his long parliamentary career, Marvell maintained a close correspondence with his constituents—regularly sending to them, almost every post night during the sittings of Parliament, an account of its proceedings. These letters were first made public by Captain Thompson, and occupy about four hundred pages of the first volume of his edition of Marvell's works. They are written with great plainness, and with a business-like brevity, which must have satisfied, we should think, even the most laconic of his merchant constituents. They are chiefly valuable now, as affording proofs of the ability and fidelity with which their author discharged his public duties; and as throwing light on some curious points of parliamentary usage and history. Some few sentences, interesting on these accounts, may be worth extracting. Of his diligence, the copiousness and punctuality of the correspondence itself are themselves the best proofs; but many of the letters incidentally disclose others not less significant.

In 1672 commenced Marvell's memorable controversy with Samuel Parker, afterwards Bishop of Oxford, of which we shall give a somewhat copious account. To this it is entitled from the important influence which it had on Marvell's reputation and fortunes; and as having led to the composition of that work, on which his literary fame, so far as he has any, principally depends— we mean the *Rehearsal Transprosed*.

Of this greatest work of Marvell's singular genius it is difficult, even if we had space for it, to present the reader with any consider- able extracts. The allusions are often so obscure—the wit of one page is so dependent on that of another—the humour and pleasan- try are so continous—and the character of the work, from its very nature, is so excursive, that its merits can be fully appreciated only on a regular perusal. We regret to say, also, that there are other reasons which render any very lengthened citations undesirable. The work has faults which would, in innumerable cases, disguise its real merit from modern readers, or rather deter them from giving it a reading altogether. It is characterized by much of the coarseness which was so prevalent in that age, and from which Marvell was by no means free; though, as we shall endeavour hereafter to show, his spirit was far from partaking of the male- volence of ordinary satirists. Some few instances of felicitous repartee, or ludicrous imagery, which we have noted in a reperusal of the work, will be found further on.

Yet the reader must not infer that the only, or even the chief, merit of the *Rehearsal Transprosed* consists in wit and banter. Not only is there, amidst all its ludicrous levities, 'a vehemence of solemn reproof, and an eloquence of invective, that awes one with the spirit of the modern Junius' [see No. 12]; but there are many passages of very powerful reasoning, in advocacy of truths then but ill understood, and of rights which had been shamefully violated.

Perhaps the most interesting passages of the work are those in which Marvell refers to his great friend, John Milton. Parker, with his customary malignity, had insinuated that the poet, who was then living in cautious retirement, might have been the author of the *Rehearsal*—apparently with the view of turning the indignation of Government upon the illustrious recluse. Marvell had always entertained towards Milton a feeling of reverence akin to idolatry, and this stroke of deliberate malice was more than he could bear. He generously hastened to throw his shield over his aged and prostrate patron.

About three years after the publication of the second part of the *Rehearsal*, Marvell's chivalrous love of justice impelled him again to draw the sword. In 1675, Dr Croft, Bishop of Hereford, had published a work entitled, 'The Naked Truth, or the true state of the Primitive Church, by a humble Moderator.' ... It was petulantly attacked by Dr Francis Turner, Master of St John's College, Cambridge, in a pamphlet entitled, 'Animadversions on the Naked Truth.' This provoked our satirist, who replied in a pamphlet entitled, 'Mr Smirke, or the Divine in Mode.' He here fits his antagonist with a character out of Etherege's 'Man of Mode'—as he had before fitted Parker with one from Buckingham's Rehearsal.' The merits and defects of this pamphlet are of much the same order as those of his former work—it is perhaps less disfigured by coarseness and vehemence. Of Dr Croft's pamphlet, he beautifully expresses a feeling, of which we imagine few of us can have been unconscious when perusing any work which strongly appeals to our reason and conscience, and in which, as we proceed, we seem to recognize what we have often thought, but never uttered. 'It is a book of that kind, that no Christian can peruse it without wishing himself to have been the author, and almost imagining that he is so: the conceptions therein being of so eternal an idea, that every man finds it to be but a copy of the original in his own mind' [Grosart IV, pp. 9–10].

To this little *brochure* was attached, 'A Short Historical Essay concerning general Councils, Creeds, and Impositions in matters of Religion.' It is characterized by the same strong sense and untiring vivacity as his other writings, and evinces a creditable acquaintance with ecclesiastical history; but it is neither copious nor profound enough for the subject.

In 1677 [1678], Marvell published his last controversial piece, elicited like the rest by his disinterested love of fair play. It was a defence of the celebrated divine, John Howe, whose conciliatory tract on the 'Divine Prescience' had been rudely assailed by three several antagonists. This little volume, which is throughout in Marvell's vein, is now extremely scarce, is not included in any edition of his works, and was evidently unknown to any of his biographers.[1]

His last work of any extent was entitled, 'An Account of the growth of Popery and Arbitrary Government in England.' It first appeared in 1678 [1677]. It is written with much vigour—boldly vindicates the great principles of the constitution—and discusses the limits of the royal prerogative. The gloomy anticipations expressed by the author were but too well justified by the public events which transpired subsequently to his death. But the fatal consequences of the principles and policy he denounced, were happily averted by the Revolution of 1688.

The characteristic attribute of Marvell's genius was unquestionably wit, in all the varieties of which—brief sententious sarcasm, fierce invective, light raillery, grave irony, and broad laughing humour—he seems to have been by nature almost equally fitted to excel. To say that he *has* equally excelled in all would be untrue, though striking examples of each might easily be selected from his writings. The activity with which his mind suggests ludicrous images and analogies is astonishing; he often absolutely startles us by the remoteness and oddity of the sources from which they are supplied, and by the unexpected ingenuity and felicity of his repartees.

His *forte*, however, appears to be a grave ironical banter, which he often pursues at such a length that there seems no limit to his fertility of invention. In his endless accumulation of ludicrous images and allusions, the untiring exhaustive ridicule with which he will play upon the same topics, he is unique; yet this peculiarity not seldom leads him to drain the generous wine even to the dregs—to spoil a series of felicitous railleries by some far-fetched conceit or unpardonable extravagance.

But though Marvell was so great a master of wit, and especially of that caustic species which is appropriate to satirists, we will venture to say that he was singularly free from many of the faults which distinguish that irritable brotherhood. Unsparing and

[1] In 1863 Rogers recorded its reprinting by John Brown (see No. 26).

merciless as his ridicule is, contemptuous and ludicrous as are the lights in which he exhibits his opponent; nay, further, though his invectives are not only often terribly severe, but (in compliance with the spirit of the age) often grossly coarse and personal, it is still impossible to detect a single particle of malignity. His general tone is that of broad laughing banter, or of the most cutting invective; but he appears equally devoid of malevolence in both. In the one, he seems amusing himself with opponents too contemptible to move his anger; in the other, to lay on with the stern imperturbable gravity of one who is performing the unpleasant but necessary functions of a public executioner. This freedom from the usual faults of satirists may be traced to several causes; partly to the *bonhommie* which, with all his talents for satire, was a peculiar characteristic of the man, and which rendered him as little disposed to take offence, and as placable when it was offered, as any man of his time; partly to the integrity of his nature, which, while it prompted him to champion any cause in which justice had been outraged or innocence wronged, effectually preserved him from the wanton exercise of his wit for the gratification of malevolence; partly, perhaps principally, to the fact, that both the above qualities restricted him to encounters in which he had personally no concern. If he carried a keen sword, it was a most peaceable and gentlemanly weapon; it never left the scabbard except on the highest provocation, and even then, only on behalf of others. His magnanimity, self-control, and good temper, restrained him from avenging any insult offered to himself;—his chivalrous love of justice instantly roused all the lion within him on behalf of the injured and oppressed. It is perhaps well for Marvell's fame that his quarrels were not personal: had they been so, it is hardly probable that such powers of sarcasm and irony should have been so little associated with bitterness of temper.

This freedom from malignity is highly honourable to him. In too many cases it must be confessed that wit has been sadly dissociated from amiability and generosity. It is true, indeed, that there is no necessary connexion between that quality of mind and the malevolent passions, as numberless illustrious examples sufficiently prove. But where wit is conjoined with malevolence, the latter more effectually displays itself; and even where there is originally no such conjunction, wit is almost always combined with that constitutional irritability of genius which it so readily gratifies, and which, by gratifying, it transforms into something worse. Half the tendencies of our nature pass into habits only from the facilities which encourage their development. We will venture to say, that there is not a tithe of the quarrels in the world that there used to be when all men were accustomed to wear arms; and we may rest assured, that many a waspish temper has become so, principally from being in possession of the weapon of satire. Not seldom, too, it must with sorrow be admitted, the most exquisite sense of the ridiculous has been strangely combined with a morbid, gloomy, saturnine temperament, which looks on all things with a jaundiced imagination, and surveys human infirmities and foibles with feelings not more remote from those of compassionate benevolence than of good-humoured mirth. Happy when, as in the case of Cowper, the influence of a benign heart and unfeigned humility, prevents this tendency from degenerating into universal malevolence. There are few things more shockingly incongruous than the ghastly union of wit and misanthropy. Wit should be ever of open brow, joyous, and frank-hearted. Even the severest satire may be delicious reading, when penned with the *bonhommie* of Horace, or of Addison, or the equanimity of Plato, or of Pascal. Without pretending that Marvell had aught of the elegance or the delicacy of any of these immortal writers, we firmly believe he had as much kindly feeling as any of them. Unhappily the two by no means go together; there may be the utmost refinement without a particle of good-nature; and a great deal of good-nature without any refinement. It were easy to name writers, who with the most exquisite grace of diction can as little disguise the malice of their nature, as Marvell, with all his coarseness, can make us doubt his benevolence. Through the veil of their language (of beautiful texture, but too transparent) we see chagrin poorly simulating mirth; anger struggling to appear contempt, and failing; scorn writhing itself into an aspect of ironical courtesy, but with grim distortion in the attempt; and sarcasms urged by the impulses which, under different circumstances, and in another country, would have prompted to the use of the stiletto.

It is impossible, indeed, not to regret the coarseness, often amounting to buffoonery, of Marvell's wit; though, from the consideration just urged, we regard it with the more forbearance. Other palliations have been adverted to, derived from the character of his adversaries, the haste with which he wrote, and the spirit of the age. The last is the strongest. The tomahawk and the scalping-knife were not yet discreditable weapons, or thrown aside as fit only for savage warfare; and it is even probable, that many of the things which we should regard as gross insults would then pass as pardonable jests. It is difficult for us, of course, to imagine that callousness which scarcely regards any thing as an insult but what is enforced by the *arguementum baculinum* [flogging argument]. Between the feelings of our forefathers and our own, there seems to have been as great a difference as between those of the farmer and the clergyman, so ludicrously described by Cowper, in his 'Yearly Distress:'—

> O, why are farmers made so coarse,
>   Or clergy made so fine?
> A kick that scarce would move a horse,
>   May kill a sound divine.

The haste with which Marvell wrote must also be pleaded as an excuse for the inequalities of his works. It was not the age in which authors elaborated and polished with care, or submitted with a good grace to the *limae labor* [Horace, *Ars Poetica*, l. 291]; and if it had been, Marvell allowed himself no leisure for the task. The second part of the 'Rehearsal,' for example, was published in the same year in which Parker's 'Reproof' appeared.—We must profess our belief, that no small portion of his writings stand in great need of this apology. Exhibiting, as they do, amazing vigour and fertility, the wit is by no means always of the first order.

We must not quit the subject of his wit, without presenting the reader with some few of his pleasantries; premising that they form but a very small part of those which we had marked in the perusal of his works; and that, whatever their merit, it were easy to find others far superior to them, if we could afford space for long citations.

Ironically bewailing the calamitous effects of printing, our author exclaims—'O Printing! how hast thou disturbed the peace of mankind? Lead, when moulded into bullets, is not so mortal as when founded into letters. There was a mistake, sure, in the story of Cadmus; and the serpents' teeth which he sowed, were nothing else but the letters which he invented.' Parker having declared, in relation to some object of his scurrility, that he had written, 'not to impair his esteem,' but 'to correct his scribbling humour;'

Marvell says—'Our author is as courteous as lightning; and can melt the sword without ever hurting the scabbard.' After alleging that his opponent often has a byplay of malignity even when bestowing commendations, he remarks—'The author's end was only railing. He could never have induced himself to praise one man but in order to rail on another. He never oils his hone but that he may whet his razor, and that not to shave but to cut men's throats.' On Parker's absurd and bombastic exaggeration of the merits and achievements of Bishop Bramhall, Marvell wittily says—'Any worthy man may pass through the world unquestioned and safe, with a moderate recommendation; but when he is thus set off and bedaubed with rhetoric, and embroidered so thick that you cannot discern the ground, it awakens naturally (and not altogether unjustly) interest, curiosity, and envy. For all men pretend a share in reputation, and love not to see it engrossed and monopolized; and are subject to enquire (as of great estates suddenly got) whether he came by all this honestly, or *of what credit the person is that tells the story*? And the same hath happened as to this bishop. .... Men seeing him furbished up in so martial accoutrements, like another Odo, Bishop of Baieux, and having never before heard of his prowess, begin to reflect what giants he defeated, and what damsels he rescued. .... After all our author's bombast, when we have searched all over, we find ourselves bilked in our expectation; and he hath created the Bishop, like a St Christopher in the Popish churches, as big as ten porters, and yet only employed to sweat under the burden of an infant.' Of the paroxysms of rage with which Parker refers to one of his adversaries, whom he distinguishes by his initials, Marvell says— 'As oft as he does but name those two first letters, he is, like the island of Fayal, on fire in threescore and ten places;' and affirms, 'that if he were of that fellow's diet here about town, that epicurizes on burning coals, drinks healths in scalding brimstone, scranches the glasses for his dessert, and draws his breath through glowing tobacco-pipes, he could not show more flame than he always does upon that subject.' Parker, in a passage of unequalled absurdity, having represented Geneva as on the south side of the lake Leman, Marvell ingeniously represents the blunder as the subject of discussion in a private company, where various droll solutions are proposed, and where he, with exquisite irony, pretends to take Parker's part. 'I,' says Marvell, 'that was still on the doubtful and

177

excusing part, said, that to give the right situation of a town, it was necessary first to know in what position the gentleman's head then was when he made his observation, and that might cause a great diversity—as much as this came to.' Having charged his adversary with needlessly obtruding upon the world some petty matters which concerned only himself, from an exaggerated idea of his own importance, Marvell drolly says—'When a man is once possessed with this fanatic kind of spirit, he imagines if a shoulder do but itch that the world has galled it with leaning on it so long, and therefore he wisely shrugs to remove the globe to the other. If he chance but to sneeze, he salutes himself, and courteously prays that the foundations of the earth be not shaken. And even so the author of the *Ecclesiastical Polity*, ever since he crept up to be but the weathercock of a steeple, trembles and creaks at every puff of wind that blows him about, as if the Church of England were falling, and the state tottered.' After ludicrously describing the effect of the first part of the 'Rehearsal' in exacerbating all his opponent's evil passions, he remarks—'He seems not so fit at present for the archdeacon's seat, as to take his place below in the church amongst the *energumeni*.' Parker had charged him with a sort of plagiarism for having quoted so many passages out of his book. On this Marvell observes—'It has, I believe, indeed angered him, as it has been no small trouble to me; but how can I help it? I wish he would be pleased to teach me an art (for, if any man in the world, he hath it) to answer a book without turning over the leaves, or without citing passages. In the mean time, if to transcribe so much out of him must render a man, as he therefore styles me, a "scandalous plagiary," I must plead guilty; but by the same law, whoever shall either be witness or prosecutor in behalf of the King, for treasonable words, may be indicted for a highwayman.' Parker having viewed some extravaganza of Marvell's riotous wit as if worthy of serious comment, the latter says—'Whereas I only threw it out like an empty cask to amuse him, knowing that I had a whale to deal with, and lest he should overset me;—he runs away with it as a very serious business, and so moyles himself with tumbling and tossing it, that he is in danger of melting his spermaceti. A cork, I see, will serve without a hook; and, instead of a harping-iron, this grave and ponderous creature may, like eels, be taken and pulled up only with bobbing.' After exposing in a strain of uncommon eloquence the wickedness and folly of suspending the peace of the nation on so frivolous a matter as 'ceremonial,' he says—'For a prince to adventure all upon such a cause, is like Duke Charles of Burgundy, who fought three battles for an imposition upon sheep-skins;' and 'for a clergyman to offer at persecution upon this ceremonial account, is (as is related of one of the Popes) to justify his indignation for his peacock, by the example of God's anger for eating the forbidden fruit.' He justifies his severity towards Parker in a very ludicrous way—'No man needs letters of marque against one that is an open pirate of other men's credit. I remember within our own time one Simons, who robbed always on the bricolle—that is to say, never interrupted the *passengers*, but still set upon the *thieves themselves*, after, like Sir John Falstaff, they were gorged with a booty; and by this way—so ingenious that it was scarce criminal—he lived secure and unmolested all his days, with the reputation of a judge rather than of a highwayman.' The sentences we have cited are all taken from the 'Rehearsal.' We had marked many more from his 'Divine in Mode,' and other writings, but have no space for them.

But he who supposes Marvell to have been nothing but a wit, simply on account of the predominance of that quality, will do him injustice. It is the common lot of such men, in whom some one faculty is found on a great scale, to fail of part of the admiration due to other endowments; possessed in more moderate degree, indeed, but still in a degree far from ordinary. We are subject to the same illusion in gazing on mountain scenery. Fixing our eye on some solitary peak, which towers far above the rest, the groups of surrounding hills look positively diminutive, though they may, in fact, be all of great magnitude.

This illusion is further fostered by another circumstance in the case of great wits. As the object of wit is to amuse, the owl-like gravity of thousands of common readers, would decide that wit and wisdom must dwell apart, and that the humorous writer must necessarily be a trifling one. For similar reasons, they look with sage suspicion on every signal display, either of fancy or passion; think a splendid illustration nothing but the ambuscade of a fallacy, and strong emotion as tantamount to a confession of unsound judgment. As Archbishop [Richard] Whately [1787–1863] has well remarked, such men having been warned that 'ridicule is not the test of truth,' and that 'wisdom and wit are not the same thing, distrust every thing that can possibly be regarded as

witty; not having judgment to perceive the combination, when
it occurs, of wit and sound reasoning. The ivy wreath completely
conceals from their view the point of the *thyrsus*.'

The fact is, that all Marvell's endowments were on a large scale,
though his wit greatly predominated. His judgment was remarkably clear and sound, his logic by no means contemptible, his
sagacity in practical matters great, his talents for business apparently of the first order, and his industry indefatigable. His
imagination, though principally employed in ministering to his
wit, would, if sufficiently cultivated, have made him a poet considerably above mediocrity: though chiefly alive to the ludicrous,
he was by no means insensible to the beautiful. We cannot, indeed,
bestow all the praise on his Poems which some of his critics have
assigned them. They are very plentifully disfigured by the conceits
and quaintnesses of the age, and as frequently want grace of
expression and harmony of numbers. Of the compositions which
Captain Thompson's indiscriminate admiration would fain have
affiliated to his Muse, the two best are proved—one not to be his,
and the other of doubtful origin. The former, beginning—

When Israel, freed from Pharaoh's hand,

is a well-known composition of Dr Watts; the other, the ballad
of 'William and Margaret,' is of dubious authorship. Though
probably of earlier date than the age of Mallet, its reputed author—
the reasons which Captain Thompson gives for assigning it to
Marvell, are altogether unsatisfactory.[1] Still, there are unquestionably many of his genuine poems which indicate a rich, though ill-
cultivated fancy; and in some few stanzas there is no little grace
of expression. The little piece on the Pilgrim Fathers, entitled the
'Emigrants,' the fanciful 'Dialogue between Body and Soul,' the
'Dialogue between the Resolved Soul and Created Pleasure,' and
the 'Coronet,' all contain lines of much elegance and sweetness.
It is in his satirical poems, that, as might be expected from the
character of his mind, his fancy appears most vigorous; though
these are largely disfigured by the characteristic defects of the age,
and many, it must be confessed, are entirely without merit. With
two or three lines from his ludicrous satire on Holland, we cannot

[1] Thompson's indiscriminate attributions led to a spirited controversy in the *Gentleman's
Magazine* during 1776 and 1777.

refrain from amusing the reader. Some of the strokes of humour are irresistibly ridiculous:

[Quotes ll. 1–14, 39–46, without ellipses.]

His Latin poems are amongst his best. The composition often shows no contemptible skill in that language; and here and there the diction and versification are such as would not have absolutely disgraced his great coadjutor, Milton. In all the higher poetic qualities, there can of course be no comparison between them.

With such a mind as we have ascribed to him—and we think his works fully justify what we have said—with such aptitudes for business, soundness of judgment, powers of reasoning, and readiness of sarcasm, one might have anticipated that he would have taken some rank as an orator. Nature, it is certain, had bestowed upon him some of the most important intellectual endowments of one. It is true, indeed, that with his principles and opinions he would have found himself strangely embarrassed in addressing any parliament in the days of Charles II., and stood but a moderate chance of obtaining a candid hearing. But we have no proof that he ever made the trial. His parliamentary career in this respect resembled that of a much greater man—Addison, who, with wit even superior to his own, and with much more elegance, if not more strength of mind, failed signally as a speaker.

Marvell's learning must have been very extensive. His education was superior; and, as we have seen from the testimony of Milton, his industry had made him master, during his long sojourn on the Continent, of several continental languages. It is certain also, that he continued to be a student all his days: his works bear ample evidence of his wide and miscellaneous reading. He appears to have been well versed in most branches of literature, though he makes no pedantic display of erudition, and in this respect is favourably distinguished from many of his contemporaries; yet he cites his authors with the familiarity of a thorough scholar. In the department of history he appears to have been particularly well read; and derives his witty illustrations from such remote and obscure sources, that Parker did not hesitate to avow his belief that he had sometimes drawn on his invention for them. In his Reply, Marvell justifies himself in all the alleged instances, and takes occasion to show that his opponent's learning is as hollow as all his other pretensions.

ANDREW MARVELL

The style of Marvell is very unequal. Though often rude and
unpolished, it abounds in negligent felicities, presents us with
frequent specimens of vigorous idiomatic English, and now and
then attains no mean degree of elegance. It bears the stamp of the
revolution which was then passing on the language; it is a medium
between the involved and periodic structure so common during
the former half of the century, and which is ill adapted to a language
possessing so few inflections as ours, and that simplicity and
harmony which were not fully attained till the age of Addison.
There is a very large infusion of short sentences, and the structure
in general is as unlike that of his great colleague's prose as can be
imagined. Many of Marvell's pages flow with so much ease and
grace, as to be not unworthy of a later period. To that great
revolution in style to which we have just alluded, he must in no
slight degree have contributed; for, little as his works are known
or read now, the most noted of them were once universally popular,
and perused with pleasure, as Burnet testifies, by every body, 'from
the king to the tradesman.'

Numerous examples show, that it is almost impossible for even
the rarest talents to confer permanent popularity on books which
turn on topics of temporary interest, however absorbing at the
time. If Pascal's transcendant genius has been unable to rescue
even the *Letters Provinciales* from partial oblivion, it is not to be
expected that Marvell should have done more for the *Rehearsal
Transprosed*. Swift, it is true, about half a century later, has been
pleased, while expressing this opinion, to make an exception in
favour of Marvell. 'There is indeed,' says he, 'an exception, when
any great genius thinks it worth his while to expose a foolish
piece; so we still read Marvell's answer to Parker with pleasure,
though the book it answers be sunk long ago.' But this statement
is scarcely applicable now. It is true that the 'Rehearsal' is
occasionally read by the curious; but it is by the resolutely curious
alone.

Yet assuredly he has not lived in vain who has successfully
endeavoured to abate the nuisances of his own time, or to put
down some insolent abettor of vice and corruption. Nor is it
possible in a world like this, in which there is such continuity of
causes and effects—where one generation transmits its good and
its evil to the next, and the consequences of each revolution in
principles, opinions, or tastes, are propagated along the whole

182

line of humanity—to estimate either the degree or perpetuity of the benefits conferred by the complete success of works even of transient interest. By modifying the age in which he lives, a man may indirectly modify the character of many generations to come. His works may be forgotten while their effects survive.

Marvell's history affords a signal instance of the benefits which may be derived from well-directed satire. There are cases in which it may be a valuable auxiliary to decency, virtue, and religion, where argument and persuasion both fail. Many, indeed, doubt both the legitimacy of the weapon itself, and the success with which it can be employed. But facts are against them. To hope that it can ever supply the place of religion as a radical cure for vice or immorality, would be chimerical; but there are many pernicious customs, violations of propriety, ridiculous, yet tolerated, follies, which religion can scarcely touch without endangering her dignity. To assail them is one of the most legitimate offices of satire; nor have we the slightest doubt that the 'Spectator' did more to abate many of the prevailing follies and pernicious customs of the age, than a thousand homilies. This, however, may be admitted, and yet it may be said that it does not reach the case of Marvell and Parker. Society, it may be argued, will bear the exposure of its own evils with great equanimity, and perhaps profit by it—no individual being pointed at, and each being left to digest his own lesson, under the pleasant conviction that it was designed principally for his neighbours. As corporations will perpetrate actions of which each individual member would be ashamed; so corporations will listen to charges which every individual member would regard as insults. But no man, it is said, is likely to be reclaimed from error or vice by being made the object of merciless ridicule. All this we believe most true. But then it is not to be forgotten, that it may not be the satirist's object to reclaim the individual—he may have little hope of that; it may be for the sake of those whom he maligns and injures. When the exorcist takes Satan in hand, it is not because he is an Origenist, and 'believes in the conversion of the devil,' but in pity to the supposed victims of his malignity. It is much the same when a man like Marvell undertakes to satirize a man like Parker. Even such a man may be abashed and confounded, though he cannot be reclaimed; and if so, the satirist gains his object, and society gets the benefit. Experience fully shows us that there are many men who will be restrained by ridicule long after they are lost to virtue, and that they are accessible to shame when they are utterly inaccessible to argument.

This was just the good that Marvell effected. He made Parker, it is true, more furious; but he diverted, if he could not turn the tide of popular feeling, and thus prevented mischief. Parker, and others like him, were doing all they could to inflame angry passions, to revive the most extravagant pretensions of tyranny, and to preach up another crusade against the Nonconformists. Marvell's books were a conductor to the dangerous fluid; if there was any explosion at all, it was an explosion of merriment. 'He had all the laughers on his side,' says Burnet. In Charles II.'s reign, there were few who belonged to any other class; and then, as now, men found it impossible to laugh and be angry at the same time. It is our firm belief, that Marvell did more to humble Parker, and neutralize the influence of his party, by the 'Rehearsal Trans-prosed,' then he could have done by writing half a dozen folios of polemical divinity; just as Pascal did more to unmask the Jesuits and damage their cause by his 'Provincial Letters,' than had been effected by all the efforts of all their other opponents put together.

But admirable as were Marvell's intellectual endowments, it is his moral worth, after all, which constitutes his principal claim on the admiration of posterity, and which sheds a redeeming lustre on one of the darkest pages of the English annals. Inflexible integrity was the basis of it—integrity by which he has not un-worthily earned the glorious name of the 'British Aristides' [see No. 33]. With talents and acquirements which might have justified him in aspiring to almost any office, if he could have disburdened himself of his conscience; with wit which, in that frivolous age, was a surer passport to fame than any amount either of intellect or virtue, and which, as we have seen, mollified even the monarch himself in spite of his prejudices; Marvell preferred poverty and independence to riches and servility. He had learned the lesson, practised by few in that age, of being content with little—so that he preserved his conscience. He could be poor, but he could not be mean; could starve, but could not cringe. By economizing in the articles of pride and ambition, he could afford to keep what their votaries were compelled to retrench, the necessaries, or rather the luxuries, of integrity and a good conscience. Neither menaces, nor caresses, nor bribes, nor poverty, nor distress, could induce him to abandon his integrity; or even to take an office in which it might be tempted or endangered. He only who has arrived at this pitch of magnanimity, has an adequate security for his public virtue. He who cannot subsist upon a little; who has not learned to be content with such things as he has, and even to be content with almost nothing; who has not learned to familiarize his thoughts to poverty, much more readily than he can familiarize them to dishonour, is not yet free from peril. Andrew Marvell, as his whole course proves, had done this. But we shall not do full justice to his public integrity, if we do not bear in mind the corruption of the age in which he lived; the manifold apostasies amidst which he retained his conscience; and the effect which such wide-spread profligacy must have had in making thousands almost sceptical as to whether there were such a thing as public virtue at all. Such a relaxation in the code of speculative morals, is one of the worst results of general profligacy in practice. But Andrew Marvell was not to be deluded; and amidst corruption perfectly unparalleled, he still continued untainted. We are accustomed to hear of his virtue as a truly Roman virtue, and so it was; but it was something more. Only the best pages of Roman history can supply a parallel: there was no Cincinnatus in those ages of her shame which alone can be compared with those of Charles II. It were easier to find a Cincinnatus during the era of the English Commonwealth, than an Andrew Marvell in the age of Commodus.

The integrity and patriotism which distinguished him in his relations to the Court, also marked all his public conduct. He was evidently most scrupulously honest and faithful in the discharge of his duty to his consituents; and, as we have seen, almost punctilious in guarding against any thing which could tarnish his fair fame, or defile his conscience. On reviewing the whole of his public conduct, we may well say that he attained his wish, expressed in the lines which he has written in imitation of a chorus in the Thyestes of Seneca [quoted].

He seems to have been as amiable in his private as he was estimable in his public character. So far as any documents throw light upon the subject, the same integrity appears to have belonged to both. He is described as of a very reserved and quiet temper; but, like Addison, (whom in this respect as in some few others he resembled,) exceedingly facetious and lively amongst his intimate friends. His disinterested championship of others, is no less a proof of his sympathy with the oppressed than of his abhorrence of oppression; and many pleasing traits of amiability occur in his private correspondence, as well as in his writings. On the whole, we think that Marvell's epitaph, strong as the terms of panegyric are, records little more than the truth; and that it was not in the vain spirit of boasting, but in the honest consciousness of virtue and integrity, that he himself concludes a letter to one of his correspondents in the words—

> Disce, puer, virtutem ex me, verumque laborem;
> Fortunam ex aliis.[1]

58.   George L. Craik's observations on Marvell

1844–5

Devoting himself early on to the study of literature, George L. Craik (1798–1866) published under the auspices of the Society for the Diffusion of Useful Knowledge (see No. 56). In 1844–5, his six-volume *Sketches of the History of Literature and Learning in England* appeared. It was to be reprinted many times, with revisions, additions, and abridgments.

Extract from *Sketches of the History of Literature and Learning* (1844–5), IV, pp. 119–26.

The chief writer of verse on the popular side after the Restoration was Andrew Marvel, the noble-minded member for Hull, the friend of Milton, and, in that age of brilliant profligacy, renowned alike as the first of patriots and of wits. Marvel, the son of the Rev. Andrew Marvel, master of the grammar school of Hull, was born there in 1620, and died in 1678. His poetical genius has

[1] From a letter to his nephew William Popple (*Letters*, pp. 313–16), dated 21 March 1670: 'Learn, my boy, courage and true labour from me/Fortune from others' (*Aeneid* XII, 435–6).

scarcely had justice done to it. He is the author of a number of satires in verse, in which a rich vein of vigorous, though often coarse, humour runs through a careless, extemporaneous style, and which did prodigious execution in the party warfare of the day; but some of his other poetry, mostly perhaps written in the earlier part of his life, is eminent both for the delicate bloom of the sentiment and for grace of form. His Song of the Exiles, beginning 'Where the remote Bermudas ride,' is a gem of melody, picturesqueness, and sentiment, nearly without a flaw, and is familiar to every lover of poetry. Not of such purity of execution throughout are the lines entitled 'To his Coy Mistress,' but still there are few short poems in the language so remarkable for the union of grace and force,[1] and the easy and flowing transition from a light and playful tone to solemnity, passion, and grandeur. How elegant, and even deferential, is the gay extravagance of the commencement:

[Quotes ll. 1–20.]

And then how skilfully managed is the rise from this badinage of courtesy and compliment to the strain almost of the ode or the hymn; and how harmonious, notwithstanding its suddenness, is the contrast between the sparkling levity of the prelude and the solemn pathos that follows:

[Quotes ll. 21–7.]

Till, at the end, the pent-up accumulation of passion bursts its floodgates in the noble lines:

[Quotes ll. 41–4.]

The following verses, which are less known, are exquisitely elegant and tuneful. They are entitled 'The Picture of T. C. in a Prospect of Flowers' [quoted].[2]

---

[1] For the congruence of this phrase with those used by A. C. Benson (No. 79) and T. S. Eliot (No. 103), see Introduction.

[2] Craik compares ll. 35–40 ('Gather the Flow'rs, but spare the Buds ...') with Wordsworth's lines

> Here are Daisies, take your fill;
> Pansies, and the Cuckow-flower:
> Of the lofty Daffodil
> Make your bed, and make your bower;
> Fill your lap, and fill your bosom;
> Only spare the Strawberry-blossom.   ('Foresight,' ll. 11–16)

Certainly neither Carew, nor Waller, nor any other court poet of that day, has produced anything in the same style finer than these lines. But Marvel's more elaborate poetry is not confined to love songs and other such light exercises of an ingenious and elegant fancy. Witness his verses on Milton's Paradise Lost—'When I behold the poet blind, yet bold'—which have throughout almost the dignity, and in parts more than the strength, of Waller. But, instead of transcribing these, which are printed in most editions of Milton, we will give as a specimen of his more serious vein a portion of his longer poems on the Death of the Lord Protector.

[Quotes ll. 1–6, 21–30, 73–8, 135–64, 171–88, 227–72, 277–86.]

This poem was written very soon after Cromwell's death, in the brief reign of Richard, and most probably at its commencement; for all good and high things are anticipated of that worthy successor of his great father.

[Quotes ll. 309–14.]

59. A portrait of the poet and prose writer

1847

Old English Worthies: A Gallery of Portraits is attributed by the British Library to the Utilitarian Lord Henry Brougham (1778–1868) and others. Largely biographical, the long article on Marvell shows the influence of Hartley Coleridge (see No. 52), who is called 'Marvell's best biographer,' even though the anonymous author was aware of Dove's earlier effort (see No. 50) which, in turn, had been based on previous accounts. As such, the portrait may be correctly said to represent a diffusion both of true and specious facts about Marvell.

Extract from *Old English Worthies: A Gallery of Portraits*
(1847), pp. 150–4.

A few beautiful verses, an acquaintanceship with the immortal
Milton, and a traditional reputation for great political honesty
in a most corrupt age, have given Marvell a permanent and honourable place among the worthies of his country. His public life was
never illustrated by any great or very conspicuous deed, and of
his private life very little, with any certainty, is known. Yet is his
name familiar to every Englishman that loves his country and his
country's literature, and that reveres the associations of genius. . . .

In the summer of the following year, 1653, Marvell, who had
taught languages to my Lord General Fairfax's daughter, was
appointed by Cromwell to take charge of the education of his
nephew, a young Mr. Dutton. It has been said of a letter which
honest Andrew wrote to the 'magnanimous usurper,' shortly after
getting this appointment, that it is 'rather more respectful than
would please either a Royalist or a determined Republican'
[Coleridge]; but Marvell was never either a decided Royalist or
a determined Republican; he, apparently, never indulged in abstract political speculation; his mind, on that side, being wholly
of a practical, ready-working kind; he would have loved a free
constitutional monarchy if any such could have been established,
and if *Church* had been separated from *State*; but, as matters stood,
after the terrible intestine war, he, in common with some of the
honestest hearts and brightest intellects that ever did honour to
this land, rallied round the almost kingly Protector as the only
barrier to mad, intolerant fanaticism, anarchy, and dead-levelling,
on the one side; and to the unconditional restoration of a vicious
and faithless prince, and of a tyrannical church supremacy, on the
other. Marvell's sober nature could not be intoxicated by the
effusions of an orator and enthusiastic Republican like Sir Harry
Vane; still less could his eyes be dazzled by the visions of ordinary
Fifth-monarchy men, who would have no king or ruler but King
Jesus, and who would divide the whole world and the fulness
thereof, in mathematically-equal portions, among the saints—*i.e.*
among themselves. He knew that the English people were not—
and were not likely soon to become—fit for Republican institutions; of war and its horrors he had seen enough; he dreaded a re-

newal of the war, he dreaded anarchy, he dreaded an unconditional restoration; and therefore he clung to the Protector, whose entire ecclesiastical polity, however unseemly and odious to others, conciliated his respect and admiration; and this son of the Low-Church lecturer of Hull seems always to have dreaded the 'Prelates' rage' more than the tyranny of kings or of any other lay-rulers. But a greater man than Andrew Marvell, and one quite as honest, might, without any moral abasement or sacrifice of principle, have written the respectful letter he wrote to the great Cromwell. If the pupil was such as the tutor describes him,—and we have no good reason to doubt that he was not, as, generally, the kith and kin of Oliver were eminent for their virtues if not for their acquirements —there is not a word of flattery in it. We will quote the epistle, which is otherwise interesting, and the reader will judge for himself:—

[Quotes *Letters*, pp. 304–5.]

Early in 1660 he was elected by his native town of Hull to that Parliament which voted the restoration of Royalty. The Houses met on the 25th of April, and then Marvell made his first public appearance as a statesman. But for the patriotism and forethought of a few men like himself, and the jealousies and fears of the Presbyterian leaders, this parliament, which gave far too much, would have denied absolutely nothing that the king or his courtiers could have asked. We have no reports of Marvell's parliamentary speeches; but when he had been a few months in the House he began to correspond regularly with his constituents; and from these letters may be gathered what was his conduct, and what were his opinions on the great state questions of that most critical time, when the vast majority of the nation seemed anxious to make a renunciation of liberty. Marvell's parliamentary conduct was cautious, circumspect, calm, and persevering. For a long time his aim and hope was rather to prevent or diminish evil than to do good. He always considered things practically, never theoretically or speculatively, or angrily, except, perhaps, the one question of church government, with the re-establishment of episcopacy. The great Protector being gone, Marvell could be no Cromwellite; and so far was he from being a disappointed, soured, and intolerant Republican, that in the earlier of his letters to his Hull friends, he spoke respectfully, and even favourably, of Charles II. and the rest of the restored royal family. Of the execution of the king's unhappy father he had sung in the Cromwellian days, and in an ode addressed to Cromwell himself:

[Quotes ll. 55–64.]

Marvell, too, is said to have written a most pathetic letter, in prose, on the execution of King Charles. It seems, therefore, quite certain that he did not sympathise with the anti-monarchical prejudices of Milton, and that he could have lived not only tranquilly but happily under the government of Charles II. if he had not found it rapidly degenerating into a despotism, and a source and centre of national demoralization. For some few years, though unable to give it his full approbation and confidence, Marvell did live happily under this government, and found pleasure in serving it. And this, his moderation of political temper being well known, enabled him to serve his friend Milton at the hour of need. The fanatic Royalists would have excepted the great poet out of the Bill of Indemnity, but Andrew Marvell, uniting with Sir William Davenant, Sir Thomas Clarges, Mr. Secretary Morrice, and other friends of literature prevented this useless piece of vengeance and barbarity. True, Marvell had held office under Cromwell as well as Milton; but it was not for his having been Latin secretary to the Protector, but for his having written the Eiconoclastes and the two Defences of the trial and execution of Charles I., that Milton was so obnoxious to the Royalists. Marvell, on the contrary, though he had been tutor to Cromwell's nephew, and under-secretary to Milton, had shed tears over the Whitehall tragedy, and had given in a few verses the most graceful, pathetic, yet noble picture of that royal execution: Marvell, therefore, may very well be supposed to have possessed some influence at court at the time when the Bill of Indemnity was being voted; and he certainly enjoyed favour and influence at court about three years after this period when he was appointed to accompany an embassy. . . .

Busy as he was in parliament he found time to devote to friendship and to poetry. In the year 1667, 'a great epoch in the history of the human mind' [Coleridge], because Milton then first gave to the world his 'Paradise Lost,' Marvell took up his pen to serve his friend, writing some English couplets, which were inserted among the commendatory verses prefixed, as usual, to the epic. To a lover of literary history these commendatory verses, which come thick upon us in most old books, are very interesting, even though the quality of the rhyme should not be first-rate. But Andrew Marvell's couplets on the first [second] appearance of 'Paradise Lost' offer many good lines. He thus judiciously calls the public attention to Milton's blindness, and to the sublimity and awfulness of his subject:—

[Quotes ll. 1–10.]

He thus defends the great poet's preference of blank verse to rhyme:—

[Quotes ll. 45–54.]

About five years after the appearance of 'Paradise Lost,' Marvell again stood forth as the champion of Milton. One Doctor Samuel Parker, who had gone through most of the changes in politics and religion, having been royalist, republican, fifth-monarchy man, conventicler, and now royalist and high-churchman over again, published, in 1670, in a book called 'Ecclesiastical Polity,' the most violent invectives against Nonconformists and Commonwealth-men like Milton, against all who favoured and protected them, and against every approach to liberty of conscience. ... Marvell instantly took up the pen; and soon there came forth, to the amusement of court and town, his first brilliant prose satire, entitled '*The Rehearsal Transprosed*; ... ' This production overran with wit and irony; while here and there the writer's wrath was as majestic as that of Juvenal. Of the invention of printing he writes with this finished irony:—

[Quotes *RT I*, pp. 4–5.]

Besides much more wit of the same kind, there is in the 'Rehearsal Transprosed' much solemn and most energetic writing—Marvell pleads for toleration in language which seems inspired. Parker, as deficient in modesty as in wit, attempted a reply, under the title of 'A Reproof of the "Rehearsal Transprosed," with a mild Exhortation to the Magistrate, to crush with the Secular Arm, the pestilent Wit, the Servant of Cromwell, and the Friend of Milton.' But this turn-coat politician and unmannerly polemic, who very probably knew that Charles II., whose keen relish for wit of all kinds has passed into a proverb, had declared Marvell to be the best prose satirist of the age, much doubted whether the vengeance of the secular arm could be made to fall upon his adversary, and therefore had recourse to other threats. An anonymous epistle, 'short as a blunderbuss,' was pitched into honest Andrew's very humble lodging. No doubt it was written by or for the Doctor, and thus was it worded:—'*If thou darest to print any lie or libel against Dr. Parker, by the eternal God I will cut thy throat.*' The pestilent wit, Marvell, adopted the words as a motto, and printed them on the title-page of his 'Second Part of the Rehearsal Transprosed,' which was published in 1673. However dull and obtuse he may have been to the sense of shame, this second pamphlet must have brought some blushes to the cheek of Parker. Milton, though blind, poor, and otherwise afflicted, was still alive, and it was easy for his witty friend to expose the monstrosity of attempting to make still more wretched the last hours of such a man. Marvell also exposed, in his happiest manner, the baseness and interested changeableness of the poet's assailant, telling the world how Parker, in former times, used to pride himself on the friendship of Milton, much frequenting his house in Moorfields, and there predicting to Marvell himself the speedy death of Charles II. and the consequent restoration of the Commonwealth and the Cromwellian order of things.

[Quotes *RT II*, p. 312.]

Marvell's generous and tender care of the author of 'Paradise Lost,' began with his troubles at the Restoration, and never ceased until the poet's death. Edward Phillips, the nephew of Milton, states that 'Marvell, with other friends, frequently visited the poet when secreted on account of the threats of Government.'

In the tyrannous temper of the times it was necessary to use caution, not only in writings destined for the press, but even in private letters, the privacy of which was but too often invaded. Before this time, however, Marvell had given up the good hopes he once entertained of the restored monarch; and the vices of the court and the corruption of nearly all public men had converted him into an habitual political satirist. He frequently used the medium of verse, but prose was more natural to him. His first prose satire [*sic*], 'Letter to a Friend in Persia,' appears to have been written in 1671, though not published until some years after. The following extract from it, which contains not a word that is not more than borne out by other historical evidence, may convince the reader that there was enough of guilt, and shame, and national dishonour, to sour the temper of any amiable man who loved his country:—

[Quotes *Letters*, pp. 324–5.]

It was seldom that Andrew Marvell could make common cause with a bishop: he had imbibed from his father, a decided low-church man, a dislike of the hierarchy; and the general conduct of the restored king's bench of bishops was certainly not calculated to conciliate him: yet, on one occasion, he found a prelate into whose views he could heartily enter. In 1675, Dr. Herbert Croft, bishop of Hereford, published a short treatise, entitled 'The naked Truth, or the true State of the Primitive Church. By an humble Moderator'. .... The whole was written with great plainness and piety, as well as with much force of argument and learning. It was assailed with fury by several of the high-church party; but no one was so vituperative as Dr. Francis Turner, Master of St. John's College, Cambridge, a very fashionable but very shallow and affected divine. To Turner's pamphlet, called 'Animadversions on the naked Truth,' Marvell replied with great vivacity in a brochure, entitled 'Mr. Smirke, or the Divine in Mode.' A part of honest Andrew's wit lay in a peculiarly happy knack of calling names, or in appropriating a ludicrous character in some popular comedy, and dubbing his adversary with it. In this spirit, he ridiculed Dr. Turner, by giving him the name of a chaplain in Etherege's comedy of 'The Man of Mode,' and thus, by the mere application of a name, conveyed the idea which he wished to convey of 'a neat, starched, formal, and forward divine' [from A. Wood]. In the same way, he had taken the name or character of Bayes out of Buckingham's 'Rehearsal,' and had applied it to his older adversary, Dr. Parker. But in combating for the wisely tolerant bishop of Hereford, Marvell did a good deal more than bestow a nick-name. He dwelt eloquently upon the great principles which that prelate had ventured to promulgate in his modest essay.

[Quotes Grosart IV, pp. 9–10.]

The last work of Marvell's, published before his death, was, 'An Account of the Growth of Popery and arbitrary Government in England.' It was printed in 1678, the year made memorable in history by the production of the so-called Popish Plot; and it was reprinted in the State Trials soon after the Revolution of 1688. In this work the principles of our constitution, or rather what ought to be its principles (for our constitution was not practically established until after the expulsion of the Stuarts), are clearly laid down; the legal authority of the kings of England is nicely ascertained and defined; and the glory of the monarch, and the happiness of the people, are proved equally to depend upon a veneration of the laws, and a strict observance of their respective obligations. He gives the consoling proof that the constitutional monarch of a free country may, and indeed must be, more glorious and far more happy than the absolute monarch of an enslaved people. He says, in his happiest manner:—

[Quotes Grosart IV, p. 250.]

He likewise drew a striking contrast of the miseries of a nation living under a degrading Popish administration, and the blessings enjoyed under a liberal Protestant government. . . .

Although his poetry is inferior to his prose, and only a few of his verses are of transcendant grace and beauty, Marvell can have been excluded from an honourable post among our minor poets only by political prejudice and a want of taste and feeling. Nearly all the poems which can be proved to be his were juvenile productions. We quote one of them which, though well known, has not been so universally read as it deserves to be.

[Quotes 'Bermudas' entitled 'The Emigrants.']

Among the satirical poems attributed to him, there are some so flat and dull and so offensively coarse, that we cannot for our lives believe that they were ever written by the friend and bosom companion of Milton. Marvell, as we have said, put forth a good many of his productions anonymously. On the title-page of other pieces he placed some fictitious fanciful name, which other writers of the day, according to a prevalent practice, may have assumed after him for their frouzy trash. . . .

As a senator honest Andrew's character does indeed appear to have been unimpeachable. He was above corruption when nearly all were corrupt: his untiring attention to the interests of his constituents, and to parliamentary business in general, might make him a model for parliamentary men, now that gross and direct corruption at least has ceased.

60. John Greenleaf Whittier on Marvell

1848

As a popular American poet and ardent liberal, John Green-leaf Whittier (1807–92) was attracted to Marvell by the dual appeal of poetry and politics, as his essay, first published in the *National Era* for 18 May 1848, indicates.

Extract from *Old Portraits and Modern Sketches* in the collected works (Cambridge, Mass., 1888–9), VI, pp. 87–8, 92–103. In his citations, Whittier 'improves' the texts at will.

Among the great names which adorned the Protectorate,—that period of intense mental activity, when political and religious rights and duties were thoroughly discussed by strong and earnest statesmen and theologians,—that of Andrew Marvell, the friend of Milton, and Latin Secretary of Cromwell, deserves honorable mention. The magnificent prose of Milton, long neglected, is now perhaps as frequently read as his great epic; but the writings of his friend and fellow secretary, devoted like his own to the cause of freedom and the rights of the people, are scarcely known to the present generation. It is true that Marvell's political pamphlets were less elaborate and profound than those of the author of the glorious *Defence of Unlicensed Printing*. He was light, playful, witty, and sarcastic; he lacked the stern dignity, the terrible invective, the bitter scorn, the crushing, annihilating retort, the grand and solemn eloquence, and the devout appeals, which render immortal

the controversial works of Milton. But he, too, has left his foot-
prints on his age; he, too, has written for posterity that which they
'will not willingly let die.' As one of the inflexible defenders of
English liberty, sowers of the seed, the fruits of which we are now
reaping, he has a higher claim on the kind regards of this generation
than his merits as a poet, by no means inconsiderable, would
warrant.

The friendship between Marvell and Milton remained firm and
unbroken to the last. The former exerted himself to save his
illustrious friend from persecution, and omitted no opportunity
to defend him as a politician and to eulogize him as a poet. In 1654
he presented to Cromwell Milton's noble tract in *Defence of the
People of England*, and, in writing to the author, says of the work,
'When I consider how equally it teems and rises with so many
figures, it seems to me a Trajan's column, in whose winding ascent
we see embossed the several monuments of your learned victories'
[*Letters*, p. 306]. He was one of the first to appreciate *Paradise
Lost*, and to commend it in some admirable lines. One couplet is
exceedingly beautiful, in its reference to the author's blindness:—

> Just Heaven, thee like Tiresias to requite,
> Rewards with prophecy thy loss of sight.

His poems, written in the 'snatched leisure' of an active political
life, bear marks of haste, and are very unequal. In the midst of
passages of pastoral description worthy of Milton himself, feeble
lines and hackneyed phrases occur. His *Nymph lamenting the Death
of her Fawn* is a finished and elaborate piece, full of grace and tenderness. *Thoughts in a Garden* will be remembered by the quotations
of that exquisite critic, Charles Lamb. How pleasant is this picture!

[Quotes stt. 5, 7, 9, without ellipses.]

One of his longer poems, *Appleton House*, contains passages of
admirable description, and many not unpleasing conceits. Witness
the following:

[Quotes ll. 561–72, 575–8, 581–2, 591–602, without ellipses.]

Here is a picture of a piscatorial idler and his trout stream, worthy
of the pencil of Izaak Walton:

[Quotes ll. 633–4, 637–48, without ellipses.]

A little poem of Marvell's, which he calls *Eyes and Tears*, has the following passages:

[Quotes ll. 1–8, 25–32, 37–48, without ellipses.]

The *Bermuda Emigrants* has some happy lines, as the following:—

> He hangs in shade the orange bright,
> Like golden lamps in a green night.

Or this, which doubtless suggested a couplet in [Thomas] Moore's *Canadian Boat Song*:—

> And all the way, to guide the chime,
> With falling oars they kept the time.[1]

His facetious and burlesque poetry was much admired in his day; but a great portion of it referred to persons and events no longer of general interest. The satire on Holland is an exception. There is nothing in its way superior to it in our language. Many of his best pieces were originally written in Latin, and afterwards translated by himself. There is a splendid Ode to Cromwell—a worthy companion of Milton's glorious sonnet—which is not generally known, and which we transfer entire to our pages. Its simple dignity and the melodious flow of its versification commend themselves more to our feelings than its eulogy of war. It is energetic and impassioned, and probably affords a better idea of the author, as an actor in the stirring drama of his time, than the 'soft Lydian airs' of the poems that we have quoted.

[Quotes 'Horatian Ode' with variants.]

Marvell was never married. The modern critic, who affirms that bachelors have done the most to exalt women into a divinity, might have quoted his extravagant panegyric of Maria Fairfax as an apt illustration.

---

[1] Moore's opening lines:

> Faintly as tolls the evening chime,
> Our voices keep tune and our oars keep time.

Cf. No. 55 n.

[Quotes 'Appleton House,' ll. 689–712.]

It has been the fashion of a class of shallow Church and State defenders to ridicule the great men of the Commonwealth, the sturdy republicans of England, as sour-featured, hard-hearted ascetics, enemies of the fine arts and polite literature. The works of Milton and Marvell, the prose-poem of Harrington, and the admirable discourses of Algernon Sydney are a sufficient answer to this accusation. To none has it less application than to the subject of our sketch. He was a genial, warmhearted man, an elegant scholar, a finished gentleman at home, and the life of every circle which he entered, whether that of the gay court of Charles II., amidst such men as Rochester and L'Estrange, or that of the republican philosophers who assembled at Miles's Coffee House, where he discussed plans of a free representative government with the author of *Oceana*, and Cyriack Skinner, that friend of Milton, whom the bard has immortalized in the sonnet which so pathetically, yet heroically, alludes to his own blindness. Men of all parties enjoyed his wit and graceful conversation. His personal appearance was altogether in his favor. A clear, dark, Spanish complexion, long hair of jetty blackness falling in graceful wreaths to his shoulders, dark eyes, full of expression and fire, a finely chiselled chin, and a mouth whose soft voluptuousness scarcely gave token of the steady purpose and firm will of the inflexible statesman: these, added to the *prestige* of his genius, and the respect which a lofty, self-sacrificing patriotism extorts even from those who would fain corrupt and bribe it, gave him a ready passport to the fashionable society of the metropolis. He was one of the few who mingled in that society, and escaped its contamination, and who,

> Amidst the wavering days of sin,
> Kept himself icy chaste and pure.

The tone and temper of his mind may be most fitly expressed in his own paraphrase of Horace:

[Quotes 'Climb at *Court*,' from Seneca's *Thyestes*]. . . .

Thus lived and died Andrew Marvell. His memory is the inheritance of Americans as well as Englishmen. His example commends itself in an especial manner to the legislators of our Republic. Integrity and fidelity to principle are as greatly needed at this time in our halls of Congress as in the Parliaments of the Restoration; men are required who can feel, with Milton, that 'it is high honor done them from God, and a special mark of His favor, to have been selected to stand upright and steadfast in His cause, dignified with the defence of Truth and public liberty.'[1]

61.   Mrs S.C. Hall on Marvell

1851, 1852

Anna Marie Fielding (1800–81) became well known as Mrs S. C. Hall (see No. 53). Although familiar with Marvell's poetry, she clearly was most charmed by the image of the incorruptible patriot and wrote two highly romanticized sketches of the poet that were several times reprinted. The first appeared in 1850 in *Pilgrimages to English Shrines*, and was then reprinted in two American journals: the *International Magazine* (1851) and the *National Magazine* (1853). In addition to its biographical embroidery, the essay is notable for its terming the *RT* 'a witty and sarcastic poem,' though she recognized that Marvell's 'last reply' to Parker was a pamphlet.

The second sketch, which first appeared in 1852 in *Sharpe's Magazine*, is also largely concerned with Marvell's life, but by this date she had had the benefit of Henry Rogers's essay (see No. 57) from which she quotes extensively. It was also to be reprinted—in the *Eclectic Magazine* (New York), 1852.

---

[1] Adapted from *Eikonoklastes*, Columbia edition of the *Works* (New York, 1932), V, p. 74.

(a)   Extract from the *International Magazine*, 2 (1851), p. 439.

This, then, was the garden [at Highgate] the poet loved so well, and to which he alludes so charmingly in his poem, where the nymph complains of the death of her fawn:

[Quotes ll. 71–4.]

The garden seems in nothing changed; in fact, the entire appearance of the place is what it was in those glorious days when inhabited by the truest genius and the most unflinching patriot that ever sprang from the sterling stuff that Englishmen were made of in those wonder-working times. The genius of Andrew Marvel was as varied as it was remarkable;—not only was he a tender and exquisite poet, but entitled to stand *facile princeps* as an incorruptible patriot, the best of controversialists, and the leading prose wit of England. We have always considered his as the first of the 'sprightly runnings' of that brilliant stream of wit, which will carry with it to the latest posterity the names of Swift, Steele, and Addison [see No. 53]. Before Marvel's time, to be witty was to be strained, forced, and conceited; from him—whose memory consecrates that cottage—wit came sparkling forth, untouched by baser matter. It was worthy of him; its main feature was an open clearness. Detraction or jealousy cast no stain upon it; he turned aside, in the midst of an exalted panegyric to Oliver Cromwell, to say the finest things that ever were said of Charles I.

(b)   Extract from the *Eclectic Magazine*, New York, 5 (February 1852), pp. 278–9.

'The characteristic attribute of Marvell's genius,' says the Edinburgh critic [see No. 57] already quoted, 'was unquestionably *wit*, in all the attributes of which—brief sententious sarcasm, fierce invective, light raillery, grave irony, and broad laughing humor— he seems to have been by nature almost equally fitted to excel. ....'

But whoever supposes Marvell to have been *nothing* but a wit, simply on account of the predominance of that quality, will do him great injustice. ... Though wit was his most predominating endowment, the rest of Marvell's talents were all of a high order of development. His judgment was remarkably clear and sound, his logic ingenious and adroit, his sagacity in practical affairs admir-

able, his talents for business apparently of the first order, and
his industry in whatever he undertook steady and indefatigable.
He had all the qualities which would have enabled him to succeed
in almost any department of exertion; while in regard to candor,
strict integrity, and all the solid merits which render a man honorable and worthy, he was not surpassed by any man of his
generation.

Marvell has some, though not very considerable reputation as a
poet. His poems are, for the most part, quaint, fantastic, uncouth
in rhythm; but there are a few pieces which display both beauty of
thought and no indifferent elegance of expression. The 'Emigrants
in Bermudas,' a 'Dialogue between Body and Soul,' 'The Nymph
complaining for the Death of her Fawn,' and a 'Dialogue between
the Resolved Soul and Created Pleasure,' though all more or less
unequal, contain nevertheless many sweet and pleasant lines.
Besides these, there are some satirical pieces which, though
largely disfigured by the characteristic defects of the age, are upon
the whole highly felicitous and amusing. A few lines from a
whimsical Satire on Holland may not be unacceptable, by way of
enlivening the growing dulness of the present paper.

[Quotes ll. 1–14, 39–44.]

Though Marvell's works are now but little read and are not
unlikely to be by-and-by forgotten, there can be no question that
they considerably modified the character of his own generation.
With his keen weapons of satire, he did manful service in the cause
of virtue, by assailing, and to some extent subduing various
principalities and powers of despicability and corruption. By
exposing and rendering contemptible the False, he vindicated and
did honor to the True. Thus, he did not live his life in vain; nor
did the influence of his activity or of his example cease when his
own existence terminated. Though dead, and imperfectly remembered, he nevertheless speaketh through that transmitted and
ever-present power which belongs inseparably to goodness. The
uttered word may cease to be repeated, but the spirit of truth,
whose manifestation and embodiment it was, departs not out of
the world, but like an invisible electric current, circulates with
an enduring efficacy throughout the whole development of
humanity.

Personally, Marvell is memorable mainly for his high integrity and moral worth. It is this which attracts, and will continue to attract the admiration of posterity, more than anything which he actually accomplished by means of his particular endowments. His steadfast and inflexible abidance by an individual uprightness and sincerity, when all the rewards and enticements of life thronged round him like syren shapes to beguile him into apostasy, is a grand and striking spectacle, the rarity and the beauty whereof will never fail to command the earnest homage of mankind. Admiring men have called him the 'British Aristides' [see No. 33], and certainly no other man connected with our history can be mentioned who has more honestly deserved the honor thus attributed.

62. Mary Russell Mitford, from *Recollections of a Literary Life*

1852

Minor literary writer and perennial gossip, Mary Russell Mitford (1787–1855) compiled her *Recollections of a Literary Life* in 1852. Despite its misleading title, the work is an anthology dressed with comments. She includes 'Bermudas,' 'The Garden,' 'The Nymph' with omissions, and excerpts from the 'Horatian Ode'.

Extract from the chapter entitled 'Old Poets,' reprinted from the six-volume extra-illustrated edition, III, pp. 251–2.

As a poet, he is little known, except to the professed and unwearied reader of old folios. And yet his poems possess many of the finest elements of popularity: a rich profusion of fancy which almost dazzles the mind as bright colours dazzle the eye; an earnestness and heartiness which do not always, do not often belong to these flowery fancies, but which when found in their company add to them inexpressible vitality and savour; and a frequent felicity of phrase, which when once read, fixes itself in the memory and *will* not be forgotten.

Mixed with these dazzling qualities is much carelessness and a prodigality of conceits which the stern Roundhead ought to have left with other frippery to his old enemies, the Cavaliers. But it was the vice of the age—all ages have their favourite literary sins—and we must not blame Marvell too severely for falling into an error to which the very exuberance of his nature rendered him peculiarly prone. His mind was a bright garden, such a garden as he has described so finely, and that a few gaudy weeds should mingle with the healthier plants does but serve to prove the fertility of the soil.

63. An anonymous notice on the 'Horatian Ode' and 'Eyes and Tears'

1853

This anonymous notice first appeared in the *Biographical Magazine* (reprinted as *Lives of the Illustrious*, 1852–5, III, pp. 271–7). In focusing on Marvell's life and career, the writer draws on the 'Horatian Ode' to interpret the character of the poet and the historical context. He then selects stanzas from 'Eyes and Tears' for comment on Marvell as poet.

Extract from the reprint in *Eclectic Magazine*, New York, 29 (May-August 1853), pp. 507–12.

It has been said that great men make great times. Invert the sentence and it is still true—great times make great men. Those who recognize the providential government of the world, note its workings in this, that a crisis brings the men fitted to meet it; close upon the heels of the danger ever follows the means of safety. If it were our task to trace the progress of humanity, we might show how, with the spirit of inquiry which marked the era of the Reformation, came intellectual power from which rose Shakespeare and his contemporaries, and how the two blended to produce the pure, earnest, unwavering, stern faith of the puritans. But that is not our purpose. We may only so far touch history as to observe the general circumstances which preceded and accompanied a particular life—only so far indulge in speculation as to trace the connection of the wide-spread cause with the one effect which forms our subject. . . .

It has been observed by a satirist, that if the testimony of tombstones is to be taken, the living have sadly degenerated from the virtues of the dead. Monuments are so infected with the vice of flattery, that monumental inscriptions are not often to be depended upon; but this tombstone is as much a verity as the man whom it commemorates. Andrew Marvell was one of the worthiest of the old English worthies. The friend of Oliver Cromwell and of John Milton, he shared the firm adherence to a settled purpose of the one, and the stern truthfulness of the other, to which he added those lighter qualities which make men as loveable in private life as high virtue makes them estimable in public.

It is worth while to try to look into the heart of such a man; to know what he thought and how he lived—to distinguish from the broad stream of life the current of his existence, and to trace in the great web of history the threads which he wove into it. . . .

His college course ended, young Marvell went upon the Continent to enlarge his knowledge of men and manners. It is believed that it was in Italy he first met Milton, and began that friendship which lasted throughout his life. The first literary event of Marvell's life took place in Rome, and it serves to show that he had become more than indifferent to the Jesuits; that he was inimical to them. His first effort was a satire upon Richard Flecknoe, an English Jesuit of some notoriety. It is a critique full of pungent humor and biting sarcasm, and at once gained for him the undying enmity of those from whose toils he had escaped. This satire was followed by another, also upon an ecclesiastic. The pursuits of the graphiologists of our day only illustrate the adage, that, 'there is nothing new under the sun.' The Abbot de Mani[b]an of Paris, like the gentlemen and ladies of today, who discover firmness in a down-stroke, instability in an up-stroke, and levity in a long-tailed letter, pretended to prognosticate people's dispositions from their hand-writings, and Marvell lashed him much as the satirical writers of *Punch* do the imposters of our own day. . . .

The body was, as it often is, the correct indicator of the nature of the mind it enshrined. He gained much of the harder portions of his character from the circumstances in which he was placed. His was no hand to lift itself first against a monarchy. His was a mind which sought for gradual reform rather than violent revolution. He looked to gentle means rather than to force, and had it not been that there was at the bottom of his kindly nature a fixed regard for right, he would have been more likely to have clung to the fallen fortunes of the monarchy, than the rising hopes of the republic. That which stronger men regarded as capable of being prevented, he sometimes regarded with the eye of the fatalist as inevitable, and thought, to quote his own words,—

> 'Tis madness to resist or blame
> The face of angry Heaven's flame. [ll. 25–6]

But though he could not have emulated Cromwell's deeds, and would not have imitated them if he could, he looked with that admiration which most men accord to the powerful, as one who

> Could by industrious valor climb
> To ruin the great work of time,
> And cast the kingdoms old
> Into another mould. [ll. 33–6]

He evidently views strength as the arbiter, when he says,

> Though justice against fate complain,
> And plead the ancient rights in vain;
> But those do hold or break
> As men are strong or weak. [ll. 37–40]

And looks upon its successes as a consequence of incurring natural law—

> Nature, that hateth emptiness,
> Allows of penetration less,
> And therefore must make room
> Where greater spirits come. [ll. 41–4]

206

Apart from this, however, he regarded the triumph of Republican principles as the triumph of right, and while he looked upon
the death of the First Charles as necessary, accorded to the fallen
monarch his pity and respect.

[Quotes ll. 57–64.]

If we may take Marvell's ode on Cromwell's return from Ireland,
from which we have quoted, as an authority, we may presume that
in some minds there was an expectation that Cromwell would carry
'the sword of the Lord and of Gideon' into other countries, in
defence of the persecuted Protestants.

[Quotes ll. 101–4.]

And there are some other lines which seem to settle a disputed
point in history, about which rival writers are even now contending. When Charles escaped to Carisbrooke Castle, and these fell
into the hands of an adherent of the Protector's, it is asserted on
one hand that Cromwell so intrigued as to give the King an opportunity of apparently escaping, and so planned as that he should be
led to direct his flight to Carisbrooke, where preparations were
already made for his capture. The motive assigned is that he wished
to irritate the army and the nation against Charles. On the other
side the tale is regarded as a fabrication, not to be charged against
Cromwell's memory. Whichever may be true, Marvell, who was in
the secret of the time, gives ground for inferring the truth of the
accusation. In the same poem (referring to Cromwell) he says—

> And Hampton shows what part
> He had of wiser art;
>
> Where twining subtle fears with hope,
> He *wove a net* of such a scope,
>   That Charles himself might chase
>   To Carisbrooke's narrow case.
>
> That hence the royal actor borne,
> The *tragic scaffold might adorn*,
>   While round the armed bands
>   Did clap their bloody-hands. [ll. 47–56]

Here then we have an avowal, in poetry it is true—but still an
express avowal by a republican, who was at once Cromwell's Latin

Secretary, admirer, and friend, that he prompted Charles to escape
so that he might come to the block. That one would think would
almost suffice to settle the controversy. The admirers of Cromwell
will regret to see this dark stain of treachery fixed upon his character, but regard for historic truth is of more consequence than
partiality for an individual, however great he may be. . . .

As a controversialist, Marvell was perhaps in his day held in
higher estimation than Milton himself. It is possible that, while he
never neglected principle, he dealt in a spirit of biting satire with
the men he opposed. The satirist seldom lives much beyond his
own age, because the persons whom he satirizes are forgotten,
and his gibes lose the application which gives them point. The
game of the controversialist is often equally short lived, but the
pamphlets of Milton have, apart from their immediate objects, so
much dignity of style and depth of argument, bearing upon the
highest principles, that the world is not likely to let them die. One
of Marvell's works of that kind is still, however, much admired.
Dr. Parker, the high churchman, who led the persecution of the
non-conformists, supported the power of Government to stereo-
type a faith, and impose it upon a people on the ground that
'princes may with less hazard give liberty to men's vices and
debaucheries than to their consciences.' Marvell answered this
with a cutting satire. The Dr. replied, and the reply drew forth a
rejoinder in which, while the argument was completely disposed
of, the poor Doctor was handled with such savage wit, that he was
glad to retire from town to escape the ridicule which was showered
upon him from all sides. This brought upon Marvell a threat of
assassination from one of Dr. Parker's adherents. So great was
the rage of the party that there is little doubt Marvell's life was in
danger; but he heeded the threat as little as he had the blandish-
ments of the Court. He was as much above fear, as he was above
prudence. He went on his way ever ready to defend the right, and
as his monument tells us—'beloved by good men, feared by
bad' . . . .

We have omitted to touch upon the character of Marvell as a
poet. His poems were rather an amusement than an occupation,
and written in hurried moments snatched from the bustle of his
busy political life. Nevertheless some of them have considerable
merit, and are full of beautiful thoughts and quaint images enough
to set up a whole tribe of small modern poetasters. From a poem

entitled 'Eyes and Tears' we take the following stanzas, which are characteristic of the tender, thoughtful nature of the man:

[Quotes ll. 1–8, 25–32, 37–48.]

Such were the works of Andrew Marvell—such was his life—such was his sudden, early death, before the prime of manhood was passed. Fearless of danger—not to be tempted or bought—keen of perception, and strong in argument, pure in life, and ever ready to stand nobly for the right, he is one of England's noblest worthies—a man whose works and acts are wedded,

> Like perfect music unto noblest words. [variant of Tennyson's
> *The Princess*, VII, 270]

If there have been greater men, there have not been many better; and he does what few do—he justifies the eulogy which his tombstone records.

64. James Russell Lowell's observations on Marvell's poetry

1854

The first American edition of Marvell's poetry, edited by the poet and Harvard academician James Russell Lowell, was published in Boston in the British Poets Series under the general editorship of F. J. Child. Although the earliest copy I have seen is that of 1857, a later limited edition records the copyright notice for 1854 and his letters show that he was at work on it in that year. (See J. C. Chamberlain and Luther S. Livingston, *A Bibliography of the First Editions in Book Form of the Writings of James Russell Lowell*, pr. pr., 1914, pp. 48–9; they, however, had not found an edition with a copyright notice.) Described by John Ormsby (No. 71) as 'very elegant,' it was to go through a dozen printings in the United States and

England, sometimes in conjunction with Milton's poetry and
Masson's life of Milton. As noted above (No. 57), Lowell used
the biographical account of Henry Rogers, shortened in some
respects but also extended by additional citations from the
prose. To this he added his brief but pointed observations
on the poetry. (For his other comments on Marvell, see Nos
41, 72.)

Extract from *Andrew Marvell* (Boston, 1857), pp. lii-liii.

There has been no edition of Marvell's poems since 1776, and that
seems to have retained the blunders of the three previous editions,
beside adding a few of its own. ... The poems were never published, or at any rate, collected by the author himself.

The intellect of Marvell was a remarkably compact and sincere
one, and his habitual character was that of prudence and uprightness. But whenever he surrendered himself to his temperament,
his mind sought relief in wit, so sportful and airy, yet at the same
time so recondite, that it is hard to find anywhere an instance in
which the Court, the Tavern, and the Scholar's Study are blended
with such Corinthian justness of measure. Nowhere is there so
happy an example of the truth that wit and fancy are different
operations of the same principle. The wit is so spontaneous and
so interfused with feeling that we can scarce distinguish it from
fancy; and the fancy brings together analogies so remote that
they give us the pleasurable shock of wit. Now and then, in his
poems, he touches a deeper vein, but shuns instinctively the
labour of laying it open, and escapes gleefully into the more congenial sunshine. His mind presents the rare combination of wit
with the moral sense, by which the one is rescued from scepticism
and the other from prosing. His poems form the synthesis of
Donne and Butler.

65. George Dawson, from
Biographical Lectures

1859

A nonconformist minister, George Dawson (1821–76) lectured on literary subjects and helped to found the Shakespeare Memorial Library at Birmingham. The lecture on Marvell, stressing his personal integrity to the almost total exclusion of his poetry, was delivered in 1859 at Birmingham.

Extract from *Biographical Lectures* (1887), pp. 89, 95–7.

Amongst English worthies of a second rank, one of the most noble is Andrew Marvell. He was not one of the greatest men of his time, but was the honestest and best of the second class men. He lives by virtue of one anecdote and one characteristic: the anecdote I shall hereafter refer to,[1] and the characteristic you will see running through the whole of his life. He was one of the most incorruptible Englishmen that ever lived; he lived in days the most corrupt and thoroughly despicable that England ever knew—in the reign of the weakest, and at the same time the vilest monarch that ever disgraced the English throne, Charles the Second. Charles was, as a king, as vile as he was as a man, and nothing but the subservience we shall have to look into by-and-bye, backed by the Church, and therefore followed by the State, could ever have induced a man to believe the king worthy of his support, or have led great men to grovel at his feet. All the great trees in England were cut down, except two or three, and amongst these, the tallest and most noble was Andrew Marvell.

The shoulder of mutton of Marvell ranks with the wine tub of Diogenes, the Roman general's dish of turnips, the leather coat and continuations of George Fox, and the sawdust dumplings of

---

[1] It is that of Lord Danby's bribe elaborated.

Benjamin Franklin. They should all be borne in mind, as proving
the true secret of independence to be having few wants.

Then came the contest between Marvell and Parker, Bishop of
Oxford, a man with the morals of a publican and the bigotry of a
Pharisee, who called Dissenters vipers, and heresy a greater sin
than adultery. Marvell put down that prelate by the publication of
his satire *The Rehearsal* [*sic*]; and a reward of £50 was offered
for the discovery of the printer, and of £100 for the author.[1]
Marvell, however, escaped prosecution. This man maintained his
position in the senate for twenty years; but by-and-bye his enemies
began to thicken and multiply. You cannot have a sharp pen
without having many enemies. He was waylaid more than once;
but it never put him out, he said. . . . He had a most biting satirical
talent, and he used it as few men do. He used it lawfully, because
only against base curs; for satire is always lawful and laudable
against bad and mean things, though it should never be used
against good ones. Some people doubt whether it is right to be
satirical. Now, I would say, never doubt whether it is right to be
satirical, so long as there are any vermin in the world. I am certain
that almost any instrument is lawful against them. If a thing be an
imposture, lash it as hard and as fast as you can. Satire is abominable
only when it is directed against anything that is weak or gentle.
Marvell wrote a droll satire on the Dutch, in which he depicted
them as manufacturing their country with handfuls of earth
dragged out of the sea, and alleged that their king should be the
man amongst them who could drain best.

Marvell also wrote several poems. Some of them are beautiful
enough, and they show a rather extensive knowledge of the classic
languages, and a rare culture. Nature had bestowed upon this
man some of her most admirable gifts, and cultivation had done
everything that was possible to perfect him. He began life a poor
man, and he died a poor man. So long as there are left in this nation
just ten righteous men—enough to save us—so long will Andrew
Marvell's name be remembered among us.

---

[1] A confusion of the publication history of *An Account of the Growth of Popery and Arbitrary Government*.

66. George Gilfillan comments on Marvell

1860

Editor and critic George Gilfillan (1813–78) included Marvell in his three-volume anthology, but, not untypically, he omits lines from the poems he includes—'Bermudas,' 'The Nymph' (where, in accord with other anthologists like William Cullen Bryant, he alters the rhyme in ll. 53–4), 'On Mr Milton's Paradise Lost,' 'The Garden,' and 'The Character of Holland.' In his biographical account, he calls Marvell the 'noble-minded patriot and poet, the friend of Milton, [and] the Abdiel of a dark and corrupt age.'

Extract from *Specimens with Memoirs of the Less-Known British Poets*. (Edinburgh, 1860), II, pp. 176–7.

Although a silent senator, Marvell was a copious and popular writer. He attacked Bishop Parker for his slavish principles, in a piece entitled 'The Rehearsal Transposed' [*sic*], in which he takes occasion to vindicate and panegyrise his old colleague Milton. His anonymous 'Account of the Growth of Arbitrary Power and Popery in England' [*sic*] excited a sensation, and a reward was offered for the apprehension of the author and printer. Marvell had many of the elements of a first-rate political pamphleteer. He had wit of a most pungent kind, great though coarse fertility of fancy, and a spirit of independence that nothing could subdue or damp. He was the undoubted ancestor of the Defoes, Swifts, Steeles, Juniuses, and Burkes, in whom this kind of authorship reached its perfection, ceased to be fugitive, and assumed classical rank. . . .

'Out of the strong came forth sweetness,' saith the Hebrew record. And so from the sturdy Andrew Marvell have proceeded such soft and lovely strains as 'The Emigrants,' 'The Nymph complaining for the Death of her Fawn,' 'Young Love,' &c. The statue of Memnon became musical at the dawn; and the stern patriot, whom no bribe could buy and no flattery melt, is found

sympathising in song with a boatful of banished Englishmen in
the remote Bermudas, and inditing 'Thoughts in a Garden,'
from which you might suppose that he had spent his life more
with melons than with men, and was better acquainted with the
motions of a bee-hive than with the contests of Parliament, and
the distractions of a most distracted age. It was said (not without
truth) of Milton, that he could cut out a Colossus from a rock,
but could not carve heads upon cherry-stones [Johnson, in
Boswell's *Life*, 13 June 1784]—a task which his assistant may be
said to have performed in his stead, in his small but delectable
copies of verse.

67. Matthew Arnold on the 'Horatian Ode'

1861

Eminent alike as poet and critic, Matthew Arnold (1822–88)
sent off a copy of Palgrave's *Golden Treasury of English Songs
and Lyrical Poems* to the noted French critic C. A. Sainte Beuve
(see No. 69) inscribed as a 'loving token of remembrance.'
The following letter (in French) commending the 'Horatian
Ode' was preserved in the covers of the book.

Reprinted by T. B. Smart in the *Athenaeum*, 3 September 1898,
p. 325.

2, Chester Square, London
31 December, 1861

Dear Sir,
    I pay my respects with a very modest gift: *parvum sed bonum*:
it is a collection of the best English lyric poetry made by one of my
friends. This small volume is an astonishing success; it has already

sold nearly 10,000 copies. That which is so difficult to do in a
volume of this kind my friend has done; he has saved the wheat
and rejected the chaff. He has also unearthed some real treasures
which have remained buried and unknown to nearly all the world.
Above all, note the [Horatian] Ode by Andrew Marvell on page
50. All the world has ignored it in spite of the fact that it is beautiful
and vigorous. More—and, in my opinion, it is the great merit of
this little volume—there exists a continuity, a logicality—I do
not know how to say it—a *teneur fondamentale* as you would say,
which allows one to read it from one end to the other with no
jarring of feeling by too violent transitions, too abrupt changes
of subject. In brief, my dear Sir, I believe you will take pleasure in
reading this little work. For myself, I read it with more than
pleasure, with astonishment. How has it happened that our nation,
in general so little happy in the other arts, has known how to
produce in poetry things so admirable? Because, in short, though
little inclined, I hope, to boasting out of national vanity, I found
myself saying in closing the book, 'After all, when it comes to
poetry, only Greece equals us.'

68. Herman Merivale's comments on the political poetry

1861

Herman Merivale (1839–1906) was a poet, novelist, and successful playwright. In an unsigned review of William Walker
Wilkins' *Political Ballads of the Seventeenth and Eighteenth
Centuries* (1860) which included several post-Restoration
satires attributed to Marvell, he introduced comments on the
political poetry.

Extract from the *Edinburgh Review*, 113 (January 1861),
pp. 97–9.

ANDREW MARVELL

But a far nobler specimen [than Buckingham's epitaph on his
father-in-law] exists in that magnificent ode of Andrew Marvell's,
if his it be, of which the evidence seems slight, on the Protector:
stanzas, in which the poet so daringly combined a tribute to the
conqueror and the victim, and, all Republican as he was, paid a
homage to what there was of greatness in the martyred King far
more choice, and more dignified, than ever was tendered by
Royalist versifier.

[Quotes the 'Horatian Ode,' ll. 27–36, 45–64.]

This style of political poetry, manly and forcible in a high degree,
but often hard, and deficient in natural flow as well as in polish,
with a strong tendency to the epigrammatic, continued in fashion
while men were much in earnest; but it lost its power when political
life became itself commonplace; political verse then became
stilted whenever it endeavoured the heroic. . . .

It costs something to descend from the rugged elevation of the
political ode of the Seventeenth Century, to rake the kennels for
its political ballads, or lampoons, generally pointless when not
gross, almost always poor in laguage and limping in metre. . . .
There are few men of similar date whose memory lives so fresh,
and whose name, when mentioned among us, still calls up so
much of almost affectionate feeling, as Andrew Marvell. And no
doubt deservedly. He had much of the qualities which Englishmen
prize most, and fancy distinctive of their nation; bravery, honesty,
independence, love of country, plain and practical sense; and he
combined them with no ordinary poetical powers. Nevertheless
it must be confessed, that we habitually shut our eyes to the unat-
tractive side of his character. This same Andrew Marvell was one
of the most unsparing, reckless, nay, malignant of libellers. It is
impossible to exaggerate the grossness, as well as virulence, of the
ordinary run of his lampoons, in verse; at least if a tithe of those
ascribed to him in the 'State Poems,' and similar collections, were
really by his hand.

69. Sainte Beuve on the 'Horatian Ode'

1864

One of the first among French critics to break out of the straitjacket of neo-classical theories, Charles Augustin Sainte Beuve (1804–69) contributed many critical essays to various papers and periodicals. In commenting (6 June 1864) on Hippolyte Taine's four-volume *History of English Literature*, which does not mention Marvell, he introduces remarks on the 'Horatian Ode,' to which he had been introduced by Matthew Arnold's 'loving token of remembrance' (see No. 67).

Extract from the reprinted collection of his essays entitled *Nouveaux Lundis* (3rd edn, Paris, 1879), VIII, pp. 100–1.

There exists an ode of Andrew Marvell's[1] which belonged to that same movement of the Christian and patriotic Renaissance [as did Milton's works]. It is in the form, and approaches the rhythms, of the odes of Horace where he celebrates the return of the victorious Augustus: it has for subject and theme the return of Cromwell from his expedition to Ireland in that memorable year 1649 (which was the '93 of England). It predicts the exploits of the following year and shows us Cromwell hurrying to accomplish his destiny, although still obedient to the laws. Never has the fire of enthusiasm for public matters, never have the grandeur and terror which inspired those great revolutionary deliverers—men of the sword and rapier—found more vibrant and truer accents breaking forth from a candid breast in such a compressed stream: [paraphrases ll. 25–36]. Here one feels that English reality and freedom of tone is with difficulty held in by

[1] Echoing Arnold, Sainte Beuve notes: 'It has long remained unknown to the English themselves; it is to be found on p. 50 of a charming small volume—*The Golden Treasury* . . . collected by Francis Turner Palgrave, published in 1861 at Cambridge. This small collection is indeed a treasure of vigorous and mellifluous poetry.'

the classical model since in some sort they puncture and break out of the wrappings of Horace.

The poet compares Cromwell still modest, according to him, glorying only in obeying the Republic and the Commons, to the noble bird of prey who, docile with the falconer, has only bloodied the atmosphere for him. 'Thus when the falcon has descended heavily from the loftiness of the sky, once the prey has been put to death, it thinks only of perching on a nearby green branch where at the first call, the falconer is sure to find him' [ll. 91–6]. Thus the Republic is sure of its Cromwell.

70. Archbishop Trench's comments on 'Eyes and Tears,' 'Horatian Ode,' and 'On a Drop of Dew'

1868, 1870

R. C. Trench (1807–86), who became Archbishop of Dublin, conceived of his anthology as supplementary to that of Palgrave. Although he included only three of Marvell's lyrics, they were indeed to become 'household' examples. The first edition omits any comment on 'On a Drop of Dew.'

(a) Extract from *A Household Book of English Poetry* (1868), pp. 394, 398–9.

I have obtained room for these lines ['Eyes and Tears'] by excluding another very beautiful poem by the same author, his 'Song of the Emigrants in Bermuda.' To this I was moved in part by the fact that the 'Song' has found its way into many modern collections; these lines, so far as I know, into none; in part by my conviction that we have here a poem which, though less popular than the 'Song,' is of a still higher mood. If after this praise, these lines should, at the first perusal, disappoint a thoughtful reader, I would ask him to read them a second time, and, if needful, a third. Sooner or later they will reveal the depth and riches of meaning which under their unpretending forms lie concealed.

Marvell showed how well he understood what he was giving to the world in this ode, one of the least known but among the grandest which the English language possesses, when he called it 'Horatian.' In its whole treatment it reminds us of the highest to which the greatest Latin Artist in lyrical poetry did, when at his best, attain. To one unacquainted with Horace, this ode, not perhaps so perfect as his are in form, and with occasional obscurities of expression which Horace would not have left, will give a truer notion of the kind of greatness which he achieved than, so far as I know, could from any other poem in the language be obtained.

(b) Extract from the second revised edition (1870), pp. 402–3, 411–12. To the above note on the 'Horatian Ode' Trench added the following statement:

We can fix very accurately the time of its composition, namely, after Cromwell's return from the campaign in Ireland, after, too, he had been designated for the expedition to Scotland, but while as yet the 'laureate wreath' of Dunbar Field was unwon,—the summer, therefore of the year 1650. A little later the assurances of Cromwell's moderation could scarcely have been uttered. To understand this poem as at all its deserves to be understood, the reader must be fairly acquainted with the chief persons and events of our great Civil War; and the more familiar he is with these, the greater his admiration will be. It is worth while to compare it with Milton's panegyric of Cromwell at the close of his second *Defensio Populi Anglicani.*—l. 53–64: Lines which in the noble justice they do to a fallen enemy, and to the courage with which he met the worst extremities of fortune, are worthy to stand side by side with that immortal passage in which Horace celebrates the heroic fashion with which Cleopatra accepted the same (*Carm.* i. 37, 21–32).—l. 67–72: At the digging of the foundations of the Capitol at Rome a human head is reported to have been found, which was at once accepted as an augury that Rome should be the *head* of the world, and gave a name to the temple (Capitolium from caput) which was being reared (*Livy*, i. 55).

If the poem which has just gone before [Vaughan's 'Retreat'] contains, at least in part, the undeveloped germ of Wordsworth's greatest Ode, this exquisite poem ['On a Drop of Dew'] has also some prophecy of the same. Here too, as there, the poet dwells with a thankful gladness on those recollections of former heights which prompt the soul to an earnest effort to make those heights its own once more.

71. John Ormsby's essay from the *Cornhill Magazine*

1869

This long and judicious essay appeared anonymously, though a later editor (Leonard Huxley) was to identify the author as John Ormsby (see Pierre Legouis, *Andrew Marvell*, 1965, p. 478). A specialist in Spanish literature, Ormsby (1829–95) is best known for his translation of *Le Cid* (1879).

Extract from the *Cornhill Magazine*, 20 (July 1869), pp. 21, 25–40.

When Marvell's name occurs in any work on English literature or any collection of old English poetry, the mention is generally followed by the remark that as a poet he has not received full justice. In his lifetime he does not appear to have ranked as a poet at all, but that was because he himself laid no claim to the rank. The only productions of his in verse that appeared in print during his life were three or four commendatory pieces prefixed to works of friends after the friendly fashion of the time, and some political satires which were necessarily anonymous and unacknowledged. If with posterity he has not held his due place among the minor poets of his time, one cause, undoubtedly, is that he already occupies, in another character, a higher position in the eyes of the world. The 'mind's eye' is so far like that of the body, that it finds a difficulty in seeing at once more than one side of any object, and having settled itself to one point of view, it is slow to take up any other. It was Marvell's fate to stand out before the eyes of succeeding generations as an example of purity and integrity in a corrupt age, and the brightness of his virtues has in some degree outshone the lustre of his genius. Had he been less brilliant as a patriot, he would have been more conspicuous as a poet.

It would be unjust, however, to represent Marvell as an altogether neglected poet. Up to the present time five editions of his poems have appeared, a number which implies a greater posthumous popularity than any of his contemporaries obtained,—Milton, Butler, and Dryden excepted.

To Captain Thompson, however, we owe the addition of three pieces undoubtedly Marvell's, which were probably considered too eulogistic of Cromwell and the Commonwealth to be inserted in the edition of 1681: the poem on Cromwell's Government—the genuineness of which is vouched for by Marvell's old enemy, Bishop Parker,—that on the *Death of His late Highness the Protector*, and the *Horatian Ode upon Cromwell's Return from Ireland*, in which occur those noble lines on the death of Charles I. so often quoted. Upon these, and the collection of Marvell's prose tracts and letters, the merits of this edition rest, for the editor took no pains to correct the errors or supply the deficiencies of his predecessors, and merely flung together, without any attempt at order, method, or examination, all the materials he could lay his hands upon. ...

It will be seen, from this statement of the case, that Marvell has not been treated with that utter neglect which the expressions made use of by some of his admirers would seem to imply. None of his contemporaries except those we have named,—neither Cowley nor Waller nor Denham, so famous in their own day, and still so conspicuous on the roll of English poets,—have in modern times received so much attention from editors or publishers. They, however, in a manner discounted their fame. They secured great popularity while they lived, and left extant a sufficient number of editions of their works to supply the demands of posterity for a considerable period. Still, though not overlooked, Marvell cannot be said to have been generally recognized as one of the poets until the present century. That Dr. Johnson should have not thought him worthy of a place beside men whose lives and works are so ardently desired as those of [George] Stepney, [William] King, [Richard] Duke, [Thomas] Yalden, [Thomas] Sprat, and [Edmund] Smith, is not indeed surprising. Marvell's earlier poetry is not of a kind at all likely to find favour in the eyes of a critic of Johnson's mould, and in manner as well as in matter, his political pieces are not well calculated to conciliate a Jacobite, high churchman, and strict moralist. He who could not forgive Milton could scarcely be expected to acknowledge Marvell. But it is not a little strange that his poetry should have been so generally excluded from the various collections and miscellanies of the last century, and his name so seldom mentioned by any of its writers. When Churchill alludes to him, it is of his 'spotless virtue' he speaks [see No. 37]; and Mason,—as far as we remember, the only one who seems aware of the fact that he was a poet,—commends him for deserting poetry for politics [see No. 36].

Another impediment to Marvell's fame as a poet is the undeniable coarseness of some of his political satires. His works come to us weighted with matter in the highest degree offensive to modern taste. This, however, was not the fault of the man but of the age he lived in, and it is one from which few of the writers of his time are free. . . .

But the poems on which Marvell's reputation as a poet must rest belong, with scarcely an exception, to a different period, and have really as little connection with the satires written in the service of his side as if they had been written by a different hand. A slight sketch of his life will suffice to show under what circumstances and influences it was that he wrote; and it is the more necessary as there are sundry errors in the accounts given by his biographers.

. . . we must presume that, having attained his majority, succeeded to the property left him by his father, and finding himself his own master, he felt a craving for that other 'part of education' which, according to Bacon, lies in foreign travel; for at the close of 1641, or the beginning of 1642, he left England, and remained abroad four years, travelling in Holland, France, Spain, and Italy. All the notices of his life agree in stating that it was during this period he made the acquaintance of Milton; and the more imaginative of his biographers say that Milton and he were in the habit of openly denouncing the superstitions of the Romish Church even under the shadow of the Vatican. Unfortunately for the accuracy of this picture, Milton had returned from the Continent about a year and a half before Marvell could have set out. Besides which, we can fix the date of Marvell's visit to Rome. It was there he encountered Richard Flecknoe the poet, or poetaster as Leigh Hunt calls him, and Flecknoe's *Relation of Ten Years' Travels* shows that it was not until 1645 that he was in Rome; at which time Milton was married, though not exactly settled, for he was then employed on his *Tetrachordon* and *Doctrine of Divorce*. Another story, if possible more inconsistent with possibility, is that of his having served as Secretary to the Embassy at Constantinople. For two or three years after his return from abroad we have no trace of him; but in 1649 we find him among the friends writing commendatory verses to Lovelace's *Lucasta*, and also to Brome's *Lachrymæ Musarun*. ...

He was at his post again when Parliament met at Oxford in 1665, the Plague year, and resumed his correspondence with his constituents. At the Restoration, a resolution was passed forbidding any publication of the proceedings of the House without special leave. The represented were, therefore, left wholly in the dark as to these matters, unless they happened to have a conscientious representative like Marvell, who, besides his duties as a legislator, was willing to undertake also those of a reporter. It is said that, during the session, he rarely missed a post, in which case the mass of his letters in the possession of the corporation of Hull probably form a collection as valuable, from an historical and political point of view, as any in the kingdom, and scarcely inferior in general interest to the Pepys and Evelyn diaries. It was apparently no trifling addition to the labours of a seat. On one occasion he says, 'The business of the House hath been of late so earnest, daily and so long, that I have not had the time, and scarce the vigour, left me by night to write to you; and to-day, because I would not omit any longer, I lose my dinner to make sure of this letter [*Letters*, p. 59];' and on another, apologizing for a hurriedly-written letter, 'Really I have, by ill-chance, neither eat nor drank from yesterday at noon till six o'clock to-night, when the House rose [*Letters*, p. 189].' But, during this time, his pen was equally

active in another direction. In rapid succession he threw off
vigorous trenchant attacks, in verse and in prose, on the abuses
against which he and those who acted with him were contending.
Proofs are not wanting that these were widely read and deeply
felt. ... The greatest effect he produced, however, was in his
encounter with Samuel Parker, afterwards Bishop of Oxford. ...
Parker's pompousness, self-conceit, prolixity, and incoherence,
suggested a certain affinity to Buckingham's caricature of Dryden
under the name of 'Bayes:' so Marvell at once invested Parker
with the character, and came out with his *Rehearsal Transpros'd*,
the second word being borrowed from a chance remark of Johnson
to Bayes in the farce. The effect produced was that of stirring a
wasp's nest. A swarm of books, booklets, and pamphlets buzzed
out of the press in reply: *Rosemary and Bayes; S'too him, Bayes;
Gregory Father Greybeard; The Transproser Rehearsed*, and others;
and at length Parker's own reply, the *Reproof to the Rehearsal
Transpros'd*. In style these are very much alike, and all make an
attempt at answering Marvell in his own manner. This was an
irresistible temptation; but what seems to have stimulated him
most was that some of the writers, including Parker himself,
endeavoured to drag Milton's name into the controversy, and
by innuendo to fix him with a share in the authorship of Marvell's
tract. This, as Milton was then living secluded, and carefully
keeping aloof from politics and polemics, could not but be distasteful, and might have been even dangerous to him as one who
was to some extent a suspect. Marvell, therefore, as soon as his
antagonists had had their say, produced his second part of the
Rehearsal. ... In wit, drollery, and sarcasm, the second part is
quite equal to the first. It does not, it is true, contain any one
passage comparable to that inimitable page in the first part on the
mischiefs of printing, a piece of grave irony that Swift
might have been proud to have written. All through these
volumes, indeed, we are constantly reminded of Swift, with whom,
as we know, Marvell's *Rehearsal* was a favourite book; and also
not a little of Sydney Smith, whose peculiar style of ridicule more
closely resembles Marvell's than that of any other English humour-
ist. But Marvell, in his prose, as well as in his verse, had a way of
raising himself suddenly above the tone of banter and sarcasm he
usually adopted, and passing into higher regions; and of this we
have many examples in the second part, especially in those passages

where, becoming eloquent with indignation, he reproaches Parker with the meanness and treachery of his conduct towards Milton.

Never had a hastily written controversial pamphlet a more brilliant or triumphant success. ... Indeed, we have now before us a proof of the popularity of Marvell's *Rehearsal*, in the shape of a copy of the first part as well thumbed from beginning to end as ever was *Robinson Crusoe* or *Pilgrim's Progress*. In Marvell's lifetime, neither 'Bayes' nor any of the 'scaramuccios,' or 'ecclesiastical droles,' ventured to renew the attack; but soon after his death Parker took a characteristic revenge in his *History of his own Time*, written about 1680, which he made the vehicle for his accumulated spite and venom [see No. 22]. ... Parker also describes Marvell as belonging to the old Roundhead faction in the House, a party with which Marvell, judged by the evidence of his own writings, certainly did not act. Among the 'State Tracts,' privately printed in the reign of Charles II., and collected in 1689, there is a 'Letter from a Parliament man to his Friend,' which, at the time, was attributed to Marvell, and, judging by its style and sentiments, with good reason. It describes the House in 1675 as 'a pied Parliament,' composed of four parties, 'Old Cavaliers, Old Roundheads, Indigent Courtiers, and True Country Gentlemen:' the two last pretty nearly matched, the two first comparatively small in numbers, but inspired with such a bitter hatred of each other that by dexterous management of their animosities, the court-party was able generally to secure a majority. ... It was with this country party that Marvell's sympathies clearly lay. This is that section of the House which he describes in the *Advice to a Painter*.

[Quotes 'Last Instructions to a Painter,' ll. 287–92.]

Some of his bitterest lines were drawn from him by the desertions from these ranks, when men like Howard, Lee, Temple, Garroway, and Seymour, went over to the enemy, decoyed by Danby and court patronage. It was this party he appealed to in prose and verse, and it was this party he again and again implored the King to rally round him, discarding those who—

> —to improve themselves by false pretence,
> About the common prince would raise a fence;
> The kingdom from the crown distinct would see,
> And peel the bark to burn at last the tree. [ll. 969–72]

ANDREW MARVELL

He would have had the King shake off 'the scratching courtiers,'
as he calls them, that 'undermine a realm,' and lean upon the
country and its best and truest representatives:

[Quotes ll. 983–90.]

Nor is there much of Roundhead sympathy or sentiment in
Marvell's works. He certainly admired Cromwell, because when
anarchy threatened he put down disorder with the strong hand,
and because, even though his rule—

> did a tyrant's resemble,
> He made England great, and her enemies tremble.[1]

But even in his eulogy of Cromwell he could not withhold his
sympathy from the victim.

[Quotes 'Horatian Ode,' ll. 57–64.]

Marvell's life, therefore, divides itself into two very distinct
portions, the Restoration being the point at which the division
occurs. The Restoration, in effect, imposed upon him a task, to the
conscientious fulfilment of which he devoted all his energies and
all his faculties, the poetic faculty included. From that time forth
his pen seems to have been employed only in the service of the
country, and in the cause to which he felt himself bound; except
on the one occasion when his friendship for Milton turned it aside
from politics. ... The last time his name is found in connection
with Milton's is when it appears in the second edition of *Paradise
Lost*, appended to the well-known lines—

> When I beheld the poet, blind yet bold,
> In slender book his vast design unfold, &c.

The verses are not, indeed, among the best specimens of Marvell's
poetry. These friendly, commendatory pieces have seldom any
greater merit than that of serving to link together the names of the
past in a chain of sympathy stretching from age to age and across
the barriers of party and politics. Thus, through Marvell we have
Milton connected with his brother-poet Richard Lovelace, a
Royalist of Royalists; and Marvell, again, through Milton with
Wotton, and so with Donne, Ben Jonson, and Shakspeare.
There is, however, dignity as well as vigour in Marvell's lines,

[1] 'A Dialogue between the Two Horses,' l. 139, a dubious attribution.

226

and they are worth notice as pointing out the first difficulty that Milton's poem had to contend with, the popular prejudice in favour of rhyme, to ridicule which in the person of its staunchest advocate Dryden, 'the town Bayes' as Marvell calls him, was one of the objects of the Duke of Buckingham's *Rehearsal*. With the exception of these lines there is scarcely one of Marvell's poems, as distinguished from his political satires, which does not bear internal evidence of having been written before the Restoration. As a poet he is generally classed among the poets of Charles the Second's reign; but in reality he belongs to an earlier age, and has nothing whatever in common with Waller, Sedley, Dorset, or Rochester. He is, in fact, no more one of the Restoration poets than Milton. His true place is with the men of the preceding period,— with Herrick, Habingdon, Suckling, Lovelace, and Wither, to each of whom occasional resemblances may be traced in his poetry. But the poet that influenced him most, probably, was Donne. When Marvell was a student at Cambridge the influence of Donne's poetry was at its height, and it acted in the same way as the influence of Spenser in the preceding generation, of Cowley some thirty years later, and of Byron and Tennyson in modern times. Donne was the accepted poet with the young men, the orchestra-leader from whom they took their time and tone, and whose style, consciously or unconsciously, they assimilated. Marvell's earliest poem is an illustration of this. His satire on *Flecknoe, an English Priest at Rome*, might easily pass for one of Donne's, so thoroughly has he caught not only the manner and rugged vigorous versification of Donne's satires, but also his very turns of thought, and the passion for elaborate conceits, recondite analogies, and out-of-the-way similitudes with which his poetry is so strongly imbued.

Few of the poets of the time of Charles I, and the Commonwealth escaped the infection of this, the metaphysical school of poetry, as Dryden somewhat awkwardly called it, which Donne is generally accused of having founded. In truth, neither he in England, nor Marini in Italy, nor Gongora in Spain, can be properly said to have founded a school. They were simply the most prominent masters of a certain style or method of writing, which came into fashion from causes independent of the example or teaching of any man, and affected prose as well as poetry. Its essential characteristic may be described as wit run to seed, or rather, perhaps, an unnatural growth of wit produced by the very

richness and high cultivation of the literature of the period; for
in each case the phenomenon made its appearance in, or immediately after, a period eminently rich in literature, that of Shakspeare, of Tasso, or of Cervantes and Lope de Vega. Metaphysical
poets, Marinisti, or Conceptistas, all wrote under the same inspiration—a desire of being distinguished for wit and fancy at a time
when wit and fancy were especially held in honour; a nervous
dread of being thought trite, unoriginal, and commonplace, if
they should be found treading in the footsteps of others; and a
sort of suspicion that the legitimate fields of imagination were
already worked out, and that now nothing was left to the poet but
to fall back upon ingenuity. Traces of the prevailing fashion are to
be met with frequently in Marvell's poems; and that they are not
more abundant is probably owing to the fact that he wrote simply
to please himself, 'for his own hand,' and not with any ambition
of one day claiming a place among the poets. But in this respect
there is a difference between his earlier and later verses. For
instance, his 'Nymph complaining for the Death of her Fawn,'
written, it would seem, before the close of the civil war, graceful,
simple, and tender as the lines are, is not free from those *tours de
force* of fancy which disfigure so much of the poetry of that day.
Even the lowest, the mere verbal form of this forced wit, breaks
out, *e.g.*

> But Sylvio soon had me beguiled.
> This waxéd tame; while he grew wild,
> And, quite regardless of my smart,
> Left me his *fawn*, but took his *heart*. [ll. 33–6]

On the other hand, the poem on the *Bermudas*, produced, we may
fairly presume, several years later, when Marvell was in daily
communication with John Oxenbridge,—one of those very exiles
to the Bermudas whose feelings the poem is supposed to express,—
is as direct, natural, and unaffected as a poem of Wordsworth's
could be. Both of these pieces have been of late frequently printed
in collections of old poetry and works on English literature,
especially the last, which a critic whose taste and judgment no one
will dispute, has called 'a gem of melody, picturesqueness, and
sentiment, nearly without a flaw' [see No. 58]. They are therefore
probably, too familiar already to the majority of our readers to
justify quotation here, however tempting they may be as specimens

of Marvell at his best; and we shall take, instead, a few illustrations from less-known poems. In the verses addressed *To his Coy Mistress*, the extravagant fancy, that in the graver sort of poetry is a blemish, becomes an ornament, employed as it is to push a kind of *argumentum ad absurdum* to the farthest possible limits, and its effect is heightened by the exquisite assumption of gravity in the opening lines:

[Quotes ll. 1–24.]

The conclusion, therefore, is to the same effect as Herrick's advice, 'Then be not coy, but use your time:'

[Quotes ll. 33–46.]

The little poem of which we have here quoted the greater part is characteristic of Marvell in many ways, but more especially of that peculiarity of his which has been before alluded to, his trick—if anything so obviously natural and spontaneous can be called a trick—of passing suddenly from a light, bantering, trivial tone, to one of deep feeling, and even as in the instance just quoted, of solemnity. Nothing in Suckling, or Carew, or any other of the poets to whom love-making in verse was a pastime, is more gay, folâtre, careless, and at the same time, profoundly obsequious, than the first part; but lightly and playfully as the subject is treated, it suggests thoughts that lead to a graver and more impassioned strain. A few pages further on we find a poem which is in truth only a conceit expanded into a poem, but which in its very flimsiness shows a rare lightness of hand, and neatness of execution. It is a sort of miniature idyll cast in the amœbean form, and entitled *Ametas and Thestylis making Hay-ropes*. [Quoted.]

Nothing could be more designedly trifling than this, and yet what a finished elegance there is about it. It is not the highest art, perhaps, but there is a certain antique grace in the workmanship that reminds one, somehow, of a cameo or an old engraved gem. Charles Lamb, with his own peculiar felicity of expression, has hit off the precise phrase when he speaks of 'a witty delicacy,' as the prevailing quality in Marvell's poetry. If he did sin, as it must be confessed he did occasionally, in forcing wit beyond its legitimate bounds, he made amends for the offence by the graceful turn he gave to a conceit. To take an instance from the lines *To a Fair Singer*: poets have again and again tasked their ingenuity to compliment ladies who are fortunate enough to add skill in music to their other charms, but we doubt if it has been ever done with greater elegance than here:

[Quotes ll. 7–12.]

The taste for subtleties, ingenuities, and prettinesses, which here and there breaks out in Marvell's verse, is, however, his only artificiality. He had, what was very rare among his contemporaries, a genuine love and reverence for nature. Most of the poets of his day seem to treat nature in a somewhat patronizing spirit, as a good sort of institution, deserving of support, especially from poets, as being useful for supplying illustrations, comparisons, and descriptions available for poetic purposes. They, we suspect, regarded it very much as the cook does the shrubbery, from which he gets the holly and laurel leaves to garnish his dishes. Marvell is one of the few men of that time who appear to have delighted in nature for its own sake, and not merely for its capabilities in the way of furnishing ideas. He enjoyed it thoroughly and thankfully, and in the poems written during his residence with Lord Fairfax at Nun-Appleton, he shows a keen sense of pleasure in natural beauty and scenery, and, what was even rarer in those days, close observation and study of nature. The longest, that upon Appleton House, for an adequate specimen of which we have not sufficient space, is an ample proof of this, and from beginning to end 'breathes'—to use a phrase of Washington Irving's—'the very soul of a rural voluptuary.' One of his most graceful little poems, evidently belonging to this time, is a protest against the artificial gardening then coming into fashion, of which he says:

[Quotes 'The Mower Against Gardens,' ll. 31-40.]

The specimens we have quoted are rather one-sided, exhibiting Marvell's poetry only in its lighter and more elegant phase. In justice to his powers, we must give a few lines as an example of his graver and loftier verse. The following passage is from the conclusion of his poem *Upon the Death of his late Highness the Lord Protector*:

[Quotes ll. 261–76.]

There is one more point to be considered in connection with Marvell's place among the minor poets of the seventeenth century.

To Butler is generally given the credit of having turned the extravagance of idea peculiar to the so-called metaphysical school of poetry to good purpose, by enlisting it in the service of burlesque, as he did in *Hudibras*. But Marvell has a certain claim to a share of the credit, such as it is. His delightful vagary in verse called *A Character of Holland* was written, as the latter portion clearly shows, at the time of the great burst of national exultation at the victory obtained by Blake, supported by Dean and Monk, over the Dutch under Van Tromp, off Portland, in February, 1653, and, therefore, probably some time before *Hudibras*, the first part of which did not appear till 1663. But to whichever the merit of priority may belong, Marvell certainly struck the same note as Butler, and if not with the same success, at least with sufficient success to give him a high place among the poets of wit and humour. To take for example, his description of the genesis of Holland:

[Quotes ll. 9–22.]

Here, as in Butler's happiest passages, we have the ludicrous exaggerations chasing each other like waves, and each as it rises seeming to overtop the absurdity of its predcessor.

Marvell's poetry cannot rank with the very highest in our language, but it unquestionably has high and varied qualities. It makes little pretension to depth or sublimity, but it abounds in wit and humour, true feeling, melody, and a certain scholarly elegance and delicate fancy. The late Mr. Tupling, the most erudite of London bibliopoles, used to add to the description of a copy of Marvell's poems in one of his quaint annotated catalogues of old books, 'Few know how great the poetry here is.' 'Great' is not exactly the word; but it is at least genuine.

72. James Russell Lowell on two of the Cromwell poems

1870

Lowell again (see Nos 41 and 64) recalls Marvell by introducing comments on two of the Cromwell poems in his essay on Dryden, written in 1870.

Extract from the *Complete Writings* (Cambridge, Mass., 1904), III, pp. 27–8.

If it be true that 'every conqueror creates a Muse,' Cromwell was unfortunate. Even Milton's Sonnet, though dignified, is reserved if not distrustful. Marvell's 'Horatian Ode,' the most truly classic in our language, is worthy of its theme. The same poet's 'Elegy' in parts noble, and everywhere humanly tender is worth more than all Carlyle's biography as a witness to the gentler qualities of the hero, and of the deep affection that stalwart nature could inspire in hearts of truly masculine temper. As it is little known, a few verses of it may be quoted to show the difference between grief that thinks of its object and grief that thinks of its rhymes.[1]

[Quotes ll. 227–32; no ellipses, 237–40; ellipses, 247–60.]

Such verses might not satisfy Lindley Murray,[2] but they are of that higher mood which satisfies the heart. These couplets, too, have an energy worthy of Milton's friend:

[Quotes ll. 145–6, 277–8.]

---

[1] Alluding to Dryden's hunt after rhymes.
[2] Called 'the father of English grammar,' Murray (1745–1826) published a number of school texts.

73. Charles Cowden Clarke on Marvell

1871

Friend of Keats, the schoolmaster Charles Cowden Clarke is best remembered for his *Recollection of Writers* (1878), written in collaboration with his wife Mary. In 1871 he contributed a series of articles 'On the Comic Writers of England' to the *Gentleman's Magazine*.

Extract from No. VIII, 'English Satirists,' *Gentleman's Magazine*, 231 (November 1871), pp. 691, 695–7.

Satirical writing is a class of composition attractive to the million, because its object is to expose the weaknesses, follies, or vices of our species; upon the same principle as Drawcansir criticism[1] is always more popular than dispassionate judgment; for the majority would rather read a rough and detracting article upon the production of a popular author than a well-digested analytical treatise on its merits; in the former case, the egotism and self-love (not to say the envy) of mankind are gratified by the thought that great mental structures have their assailable points for attack; and common minds believe that their own position rises in proportion as the higher natures suffer from detraction. Rochefoucauld says, 'There is a something in the misfortunes of our friends that is not wholly displeasing to us.' This 'something' is the vital principle and the aliment of satire. The well-known aphorism upon slanderers is applicable to the satirist: 'Like flies, they pass over the healthy parts of a beast, and fix upon its sores.'

No class of composition is so uninteresting, and even worthless, as mediocre satire. Indeed, it has no medium; it is like an olive—if not palatable, it is disgusting. Flabby satire is a satire upon satire; a scorpion that turns its sting upon itself. It commits suicide in

[1] Draw-Can-Sir, a character in Buckingham's *Rehearsal*, is a fierce hero, who frights his mistress, snubs up kings, baffles armies, and does what he will without regard to good manners, justice, or numbers (IV. i). Marvell terms Parker 'the Ecclesiastical *Draw-Can-Sir*' (*RT I*, p. 21).

endeavouring to wound another. When, however, the satirist is a
true knight-errant—a redresser of wrongs, a reformer of abuses—
and his weapons are polished and keen and tempered and true as his
own nature—then his calling becomes an important one, and his
mission is sure; for nothing but truth can stand the test of ridicule.
Where truth—moral, intellectual, and artistical—is concerned, a
compromising satirist is a traitor.

In alluding to the great and glorious Andrew Marvell as a wit and
satirist, it is almost impossible to separate his political from his
literary career; for almost the whole of his compositions—civil,
epistolary, and poetic—bear upon the one paramount and engros-
sing object of his pursuit—that of serving his country and advancing her liberties with zeal, efficiency, and integrity. The prevailing
characteristic of Marvell's mind (after his firmness and consistency
of purpose) was his well-ordered balance of judgment with
placability of nature. Marvell seems to have been the most reasonable of mortals, and, therefore, he was the object of hatred to the
fanatics of the two extreme parties in the State. He inherited his
humour from his father, who was an eminent Calvinistic minister
in Hull; the town which the son afterwards represented in Parliament for twenty years with such lustrous ability and rectitude.
From his father, too, he imbibed his steady, cheerful piety, many
of his little poems being embellished with some apt moral, or
sweet and serene reflection. No one possessed more fully, and yet
maintained more distinctly, the two qualities of a gentle gravity
with an unmitigated freedom of satire and ridicule. . . .

Marvell's Satires possess but little modern interest. . . . His
severer satires are upon Flecknoe, the poetaster—the man whom
Dryden so ruthlessly mauled; and upon Colonel Blood, who
attempted to steal the Crown jewels. His remonstrance with his
'Coy Mistress,' protesting against her tardy recognisance of his
passion, is an agreeable specimen of his playful and well-bred
humour.

The event of the Dutch war supplied the English wits of that
age with a fertile theme for passing their jokes upon their amphibious neighbours. Marvell's is not so epigrammatic and condensed
as Butler's, the illustrious author of 'Hudibras;' it is more dis-
cursive and classical in character; but it is quite as witty, and even,
perhaps, more imaginative—mounting to its climax with a delight-

ful flourish of the mock-heroic. The reader cannot fail to notice
the felicitous choice of some of his terms, and, above all, his
qualifying epithets. In two words, it is a great composition of the
satire class.

[Quotes 'The Character of Holland,' ll. 1–48.]

74. Edward FitzGerald's comments on two poems

1872

Friend of the Tennysons, father and son, Edward FitzGerald
(1809–83) is best known for his verse translation of the
Rubáiyát of Omar Khayyám. In a letter to W. A. Wright,
dated 20 January 1872, he comments on two of Marvell's
poems. His puzzlement over the misreading 'Holtseltster'
for 'holtfelster' points up the waywardness with texts in the
period; his reference to Alfred Lord Tennyson's admiration
for 'To His Coy Mistress' is again endorsed by the recollection
of F. T. Palgrave (see No. 79).

Extract from *Letters and Literary Remains of Edward Fitz-
Gerald*, ed. W. A. Wright (1889), I, p. 337.

By way of flourishing my Eyes, I have been looking into Andrew
Marvell, an old favourite of mine, who led the way for Dryden
in Verse, and Swift in Prose, and was a much better fellow than
the last, at any rate.

Two of his lines in the Poem on 'Appleton House,' with its
Gardens, Grounds, &c. run:

> But most the *Hewel's* wonders are,
> Who here has the Holtselt-ster's care. [ll. 537–8]

The 'Hewel' being evidently the Woodpecker, who, by tapping the Trees &c. does the work of one who measures and gauges Timber; here, rightly or wrongly, called 'Holtseltster.' 'Holt' one knows: but what is 'seltster'? I do not find either this word or 'Hewel' in Bailey or Halliwell.[1] But 'Hewel' may be a form of 'Yaffil,' which I read in some Paper that Tennyson had used for the Woodpecker in his Last Tournament.[2]

This reminded me that Tennyson once said to me, some thirty years ago, or more, in talking of Marvell's 'Coy Mistress,' where it breaks in—

> But at my back I always hear
> Time's winged chariot hurrying near.

'That strikes me as sublime, I can hardly tell why.' Of course, this partly depends on its place in the Poem.

75. W.D. Christie's reviews of Grosart's edition

1873

The biographer W. D. Christie (1816–74) published not one but two unsigned reviews of the first volume (verse) of A. B. Grosart's edition, which stirred its editor to a rebuttal (and identification of the reviewer) in his second volume (1875, pp. xvi–xxvii).

(a) Extract from the *Spectator*, 46 (15 February 1873), p. 210.

Drollery was Marvell's chief reputation while he lived; his prose was greatly thought of, and his poetry little. Dryden, before he

---

[1] For *holtfelster*, woodcutters; this is the sole example cited in the *OED*. Nathan (or Nathaniel) Bailey compiled a popular English dictionary (1721); James Orchard Halliwell (later Halliwell-Phillipps) a *Dictionary of Archaic and Provincial Words* (1847).
[2] Line 695, where there is an allusion to the 'garnet-headed yaffingale.'

became a Roman Catholic, when he would naturally have been bitter against Marvell, twice mentions him only as a political writer and controversialist, and without respect; of his poetry he says nothing, and seems to know nothing. ... Now, and it has been so for many years past, the 'Rehearsal Transprosed' and the rest of Marvell's prose pieces are little read, but his poetry has found its way to men's hearts, and on his poetry his very considerable present reputation mainly rests. This is the secret of Mr. Grosart's enthusiasm, which has produced this handsome and laboriously prepared edition. Marvell and his poetry come recommended to us by his intimate friendship with Milton, and by his stout political honesty in a dark time of general corruption. The sensational story of his interview with Danby, who went himself to bribe the honest, plain-spoken Member for Hull, is probably apocryphal; but it is valuable as bespeaking Marvell's reputation. The genuine sweetness and beauty of much of Marvell's serious poetry are enhanced by contrast with the exceeding grossness of language in which his political satires abound, and which must have served as obstacles to the diffusion of his chaste poems. The best thing that an enthusiast for Marvell's memory like Mr. Grosart could do, after the completion of this very handsome edition, would be to publish a little volume of his poetry from which his obscene satires should be excluded. It is a wonder to see this luxuriance of filth in men like Marvell and Oldham, whose lives, there is every reason to believe, were virtuous, and who have succeeded, and evidently found delight, in sacred themes. That Marvell was of an amatory nature he himself confesses; he confesses both to love and to bitter hate, the latter abundantly displayed in his satires. Says the Body to the Soul in one of his serious poems:

[Quotes ll. 31–44.]

But no scandal of profligacy attaches to Marvell's name, and his amatory poems are innocent.

Mr. Grosart has been right to put in the front Archbishop Trench's and George Macdonald's testimonies of high admiration of Marvell's poetry. 'The Eyes and Tears,' singled out by the Archbishop for his highest praise, seems to us more than usually (for Marvell) infected with the conceits of the Donne and Cowley school, and to be an overstretched development of a flimsy fancy.

But we most cordially join in the Archbishop's eulogies of Marvell's Horatian ode on the return of Cromwell from Ireland,— 'among the greatest,' he says, 'which the English language possesses;' and similar praise may be given to Marvell's poem on the death of Cromwell. How superior is this, proceeding from the depth of Marvell's heart, for he had been the friend and hearty admirer of Cromwell, to the artificial poetry on the same subject of Waller, and even of Dryden!

[Quotes ll. 261–86.]

(b) Extract from the *Saturday Review*, 35 (26 April, 1873), pp. 553–4.

It would be better for Marvell's fame if it could be proved that he had written none of the political satires ascribed to him. None of them were printed in the widow's edition of his poetry in 1681, three years after his death. But his political satires and lampoons were necessarily anonymous, and it would have been then too soon to disclose the secret of his authorship. As it is, the fact of any poem being published among the 'Poems on Affairs of State,' with Marvell's name attached to it, is no sufficient proof of his authorship. But, without being able generally to be positive as to any one particular poem, common fame and general contemporary belief amply justify us in assuming that many, if not most, of the political satires ascribed to him are his. His rabid enemy, Bishop Parker, describes him as the lewdest of lewd revilers, a 'satirist for the faction,' a 'vagabond, ragged, hungry poetaster' [see No. 22]. Bishop Parker's language and tone about his witty antagonist who conquered him are unseemly enough; but there must exist underneath the fact that Marvell, the member of Parliament for Hull, was an habitual pamphleteer and satirist; and the truth must be added that he who was Milton's friend and a sweet poet of nature and of sentiment has been the accredited author of many satires full of loathsome obscenity and virulent malice. The anonymous is full of danger for men of warm feelings and strong antipathies, as Marvell's were. He was the author of a remarkable political tract, anonymously published, on the growth of Popery and arbitrary government, which incensed the courtier majority of the House of Commons; and the following passage of a letter of his to Mr. William Ramsden of Hull shows how he was careful to avoid acknowledgement of authorship to an intimate friend, while he also abstained from denial.

[Quotes from *Letters*, p. 357.][1]

The letter was written June 10, 1678. About two months after he suddenly died. The widow may well have been afraid to avow his political satires, full of scurrilous personality, in 1681. We do not quarrel with Mr. Grosart for publishing all Marvell's poems, or all believed to be his, whether disfigured or not by indecencies, for Marvell is an English classic and celebrity, and posterity, to judge him truly, must have all before them. 'I will not castrate John Dryden' was Sir Walter Scott's defiant announcement when he undertook his edition of Dryden's works. But it is well to warn fathers of families that the political poems imputed to Marvell contain extreme grossness and unmitigated filth. The virulent personality of these poems is another great blot in Marvell's character. His political animosity against the Duke of York carried him to unmanly and loathsome war against the Duchess. Anne Hyde, who in youthful weakness had yielded to the Duke's dishonourable overtures, and whom he had married by compulsion wholesomely exercised on him, was by general testimony an amiable, and, ever after her early fault, a virtuous woman, much to be pitied for her husband's indiscriminate and unconcealed amours, and bearing her unhappiness with calm dignity. The sinning Duke aggravated against his poor wife the innocent attentions of two gentlemen of their household—Henry Sydney and Henry Jermyn—who probably pitied the Duchess, and in whose sympathetic courtesies she might be excused for finding some solace of her woes. Marvell, with the utmost unmanliness, rips up her early history, charges her over and over again with profligacy, and over and over again accuses her, against authority and against probability, of poisoning one of her husband's mistresses, Lady Denham. No well-conditioned man can do less than grieve over this style of anonymous satire. One of the most likely of these political poems to be really Marvell's is 'The Last Instructions to a Painter,' written in 1667. It contains a description of the Duchess of York, of which the two following lines, bad enough, are a tame sample; most of the rest it is not possible for us to print:—

[1] This letter was, in fact, addressed to his nephew William Popple.

Paint her with oyster lip, and breath of fame,
Wide mouth that 'sparagus may well proclaim. [ll. 61–2]

Marvell then charges her with the foulest vices. Crimes, mis-
demeanours, and vices are constantly charged in the coarsest
language against high officials and members of Parliament; this
could only be done anonymously. There is a prose tract, always
ascribed to Marvell, being a list of the members of the House of
Commons who supported the Court, published at Amsterdam in
1677, which is rampant with personal scurrility.[1] Here is a mild
specimen:—Sir Solomon Swale, member for Aldborough, 'one
whose word will not pass for threepence where he is known, an
old Papist, if not priest, but his bald pate excuses his tonsure; a
forger of wills.' Sir Robert Carr, member for Lincolnshire, brother-
in-law of Earl of Arlington, is said to have 'two wives living at this
hour, one Arlington's sister.' We are forced to assume that Marvell
was the author of these scurrilous libels. We have no sympathy
with Bishop Parker, his vindictive and virulent enemy, but there
is some justice in his foul languages. The Bishop calls Marvell also
a 'drunken buffoon'; there is truth here also. His admiring friend
Aubrey [No. 28] says of him that 'he kept bottles of wine at his
lodging, and many times he would drink liberally by himself to
refresh his spirits and exalt his muse.' It is idle and worse to ignore
the truth; Marvell's faults must not be denied or cloaked. The
biographer who sees nothing to blame, everything indeed apparently to worship, in the filth and scurrility of his satires, and will
admit no truth in Bishop Parker's invective, is afflicted with the
lues Boswelliana in a very aggravated form. Mr. Grosart describes
the satires and political poems as 'noble, profound, prescient, wise
as witty and witty as wise, penetrating and burning.' We cannot
go with him here. We refer for our justification to the accounts of
Lady Castlemaine (lines 80–104), and of Colonel Birch (142–6),
to a passage on Clarendon (473), and another on the Speaker
Turner (831–6), in 'The Last Instructions to a Painter,' besides the
abominable description of the Duchess of York, already
noticed. . . .

Allow Marvell his faults, that he wrote anonymous libels, and
drank intemperately in secret; still he was a brilliant scholar, and

[1] This is *A Seasonable Argument* . . . which Grosart, in fact, rejected as Marvell's.

had great attainments, and was in poverty an honest, incorruptible man. Was not the Bishop [Parker] a furious bigot and unchristianly implacable foe? What were not the demerits of the fine courtiers and personages who huffed and hooted Marvell? The few notices on record of Marvell in the House of Commons show that he was not in his element there, and was not a favourite. . . .

We have not loved to dwell on Marvell's faults and short-comings. He is associated in general memory with Milton, who has reflected light on him; but it cannot be said that his soul was, as his illustrious friend's, like 'a star and dwelt apart.' Words-worth's praise of Marvell may be turned to exaggerated use, and results only from remembrance of him as Milton's friend. . . . We gladly believe that it must have been an ineffable relief to him to exchange malicious satire and debasing thoughts for the study of his loved classics and the composition of that sweet poetry which has made him famous in after-time. His scholarship was of the first order. Many Latin poems of his are before the world. . . . We are spared the need of large quotation from Marvell's sweet and serious poetry. There is a recent cheap edition of his poems. Gems of his poetry are encased in favourite collections, in Pal-grave's *Golden Treasury*, and in the *Household Book of English Poetry* of Archbishop Trench, a poet of merit who has set the stamp of his high authority on Marvell's poetry. We make an exception by quoting some lines, of dignity suitable to the subject, from Marvell's 'Poem on Paradise Lost' which has done much to unite his name with Milton's:

[Quotes ll. 1–10, 31–50.]. . . .

Let us now contrast the poet Marvell, with all his faults, with the great Bishop Parker, his vindictive and railing enemy. Two centuries after both have disappeared from the earth, what are the relative fames of the names of the haughty Bishop and the poor poet and scholar and low-born faithful member of Parlia-ment? Who cares for the Bishop's memory, and who does not value Marvell's? It would be well if transitory worldly greatness would take a lesson from such an instance. When Marvell re-monstrated in the House of Commons against heavy fees imposed on Milton by the Sergeant-at-arms who had had him in custody, Sir Heneage Finch, the Solicitor-General, pronounced his opinion that Milton deserved hanging. Some years before a future Primate of Ireland, Bramhall, wrote that Milton had deserved to be turned, not only out of the University of Cambridge, but out of the society of men; and that if Salmasius knew as much of Milton as he did, he would make him go near to hang himself (*Rawdon Papers*, p. 109). Locke, whom all now revere as a philosopher, was ignominiously expelled by a truckling Bishop from a Christ Church studentship at Oxford, in obedience to the arbitrary mandate of a profligate Secretary of State, for alleged 'factious and disloyal behaviour,' which the Bishop disbelieved. Who would now care to exchange the place of Locke, Milton, and Marvell in the gallery of fame for those of Bishop Fell, Earl of Sunderland, Archbishop Bramhall, Sir Heneage Finch, afterwards Earl of Nottingham, and Bishop Parker?

76. An American divine comments

1877

In 1877 the Reverend R. Weiser of Georgetown, Colorado, wrote an article on Marvell ('The Incorruptible Member from Hull') for the *Lutheran Quarterly*, published in Gettysburg, Pennsylvania. Totally lacking in critical value, it is none the less illustrative of the way in which the derivative image of the incorruptible statesman was kept current. As the essayist acknowledges, his immediate impetus was provided by 'an old musty volume'—E. P. Hood's biographical and critical study, *Andrew Marvell, the Wit, Statesman, and Poet*, published in 1853. As Hood himself acknowledged, he too had had recourse to the lives of Marvell by Dove (No. 50) and Hartley Coleridge (No. 52), though since they seemed 'so precisely alike, and appeared so simultaneously' he could not ascertain who was, in fact, the original author. These two lives, in turn, were derived from a two-part anonymous article in the *Retrospective Review* for 1824–5 (No. 47), from

Cooke (No. 33), from Captain Thompson (No. 38), and from
Disraeli (No. 12), while Hood had also availed himself of
Mrs Hall's romantic accounts (No. 61). These earlier writers
stressed the poet's political integrity.

Extract from the *Lutheran Quarterly* (Gettysburg, Pa.), July
1877, pp. 371–3, 377–8.

In looking over my library, I found an old musty volume entitled,
'*The Life and Writings of Andrew Marvell, the Statesman, the Wit, and
the Poet.*' I looked it through, and found it interesting and instructive, and so came to the conclusion to furnish an epitome of this
rare book for the readers of the REVIEW. Although Marvell was
not exactly a theologian, yet he figured quite conspicuously in the
religious discussions during the latter part of the seventeenth
century in England. These discussions throw a good deal of light
upon the religious spirit of the age in which he lived—an age of
fierce contests among giants in church and state.

The age of Charles II., immediately succeeding the Commonwealth, was perhaps the most venal and corrupt in the annals of
England. Here we can see how a pure minded man can keep
himself unspotted in the midst of the greatest venality and corruption. Marvell was one of that noble band of Christian statesmen,
who stood up with Cromwell, Bradshawe, Milton, Sidney,
Hampden, and others, for the defence of civil, and religious liberty.
Hull was his native city, where he was born in 1620, and died in
1678; and those fifty-eight years of his life cover one of the most
eventful periods in the history of England. ...

Soon after leaving the University, as was then the custom, he
made a tour of the continent. During his travels he acquired a
good knowledge of the French, Italian, and Spanish languages,
and when he returned, was one of the most accomplished young
men in England. It was during his visit to Italy that Marvell and
John Milton met each other for the first, in the city of Rome.
They were both gentlemen and scholars, congenial in their tastes,
and a warm friendship sprang up between them, which continued
through life. Marvell read the manuscript of '*Paradise Lost,*' and
seems with Dr. Barrow to have been among the first who could
appreciate that immortal Epic. Marvell and Barrow recommended
its immediate publication, but it was not published until 1667.

It is said that Marvell wrote an introduction to the first edition of Paradise Lost, but I have not been able to find it. . . .

The Puritans had had a short triumph during the Protectorate, but on the Restoration, the Cavaliers got the ascendency, and they seem to have been determined to make up for the self-denial they had to undergo when under the iron rod of Cromwell. Marvell sided with the Puritans, and nobly defended their cause. And no man of his age wielded a more caustic and powerful pen, and perhaps no man was more feared. The king was corrupt, and his court was no better, the men that hung around him were the Chesterfields, the Clarendons, the Churchills and the Halifaxes, polite, and polished charlatans, and hollow-hearted hypocrites. The king and all his court were governed by pimps and lewd women. Yet these unprincipled and vile men undertook to legislate for the Church, and tell the people of England how they were to worship God! Marvell published severe strictures on the corruptions of the court—he spared neither court nor king. And nothing that was published, not even Milton's powerful defences, were half as much feared as Marvell's home thrusts.

In 1662, Butler published his Hudibras, a satire on the Puritan[s], this was a godsend to Charles, and his corrupted courtiers. The king made Butler a present of fifteen hundred dollars, and the poem was quoted with great zest by all the cavaliers. But Marvell who was the acknowledged satirist on the Puritan side, though not quite as grotesque as Butler, was quite as keen in his wit and humor, and more poetical, and more classical. Butler might well venture to ridicule the Puritans when they were crushed under the heel of a cruel despotism, and when the abusing of religious men was the quickest way to honor and fame, But Marvell in the face of power, and fashion, scourged the corrupted king and court. This required moral courage, such as Butler never possessed. Take all the circumstances into account, there is no satire in the English language more pungent and fearless than Marvell's.

77. Sir Edmund Gosse on the garden poetry

1885

Critic and academician, Edmund Gosse (1849–1928) included comments on Marvell in his inaugural course at Cambridge, which was then delivered at various locales in the United States. He was later to contribute an article on Marvell to the *Sunday Times*, 27 March 1921 (reprinted in the *Tercentenary Tributes* ed. W. H. Bagguley, Oxford, 1921), that added little of value to the earlier notice.

Extract from *Shakespeare to Pope* (New York, 1885), pp. 219–20.

In the long Nunappleton poem, then, and in that celebrated piece which is printed now in most collections of English poetry, *The Garden*, we find a personal sympathy with nature, and particularly with vegetation, which was quite a novel thing, and which found no second exponent until Wordsworth came forward with his still wider and more philosophical commerce with the inanimate world. For flowers, trees, and grasses, Marvell expresses a sort of personal passion. ... His style, when he can put his conceits behind him, is extremely sharp and delicate, with a distinction of phrase that is quite unknown to most of his contemporaries.

78. Alfred Lord Tennyson's comments

1887–8, 1849–92

The comments of the poet laureate Alfred Lord Tennyson (1809–92) on Marvell are recorded by his son Hallam and his close friend F. T. Palgrave, well known for his anthology *The Golden Treasury of English Songs and Lyrical Poems* (see Nos 67, 69).

Extracts from *Alfred Lord Tennyson, A Memoir*, compiled by his son (1897), II, pp. 335, 500–1.

(a) 1887–8: He would now quote long pieces from Andrew Marvell to us, 'The Bermudas,' 'The Garden,' and he told us that he had made Carlyle laugh for half-an-hour at the following line from 'The Character of Holland'—

> They, with mad labour, fish'd the land to shore.

'And,' he continued, 'about poetry or art Carlyle knew nothing. I would never have taken his word about either, but as an honest man, yes—on any subject in the world.'

(b) *Personal Recollections* by F. T. Palgrave, 1849–92: With most by far of the pieces submitted [to the *Golden Treasury*] he was already acquainted: but I seem to remember more or less special praise of Lodge's 'Rosaline,' of 'My Love in her attire ...' and the 'Emigrants' Song' by Marvell. For some poems by that writer then with difficulty accessible, he had a special admiration: delighting to read, with a voice hardly yet to me silent, and dwelling more than once, on the magnificent hyperbole, the powerful union of pathos and humour in the lines 'To his Coy Mistress' where Marvell says

> Had we but world enough, and time,
> This coyness, lady, were no crime ...

[Quotes ll. 7–10; 21–4.]

Youth, therefore, Marvell proceeds, is the time for love;

> Let us roll all our strength, and all
> Our sweetness up into one ball,
> And tear our pleasures with rough strife
> Through the iron gates of life:

on this line remarking that he could fancy *grates* would have intensified Marvell's image.

POETIC REASSESSMENT

1892–1921

79. A.C. Benson on Marvell

1892

Man of letters and Master of Magdalene College, Cambridge,
A. C. Benson (1862–1925) was a prolific critic and essayist.
The essay on Marvell first appeared anonymously in
Macmillan's Magazine and was later reprinted in his *Essays*
(1896).

Extract from *Macmillan's Magazine*, 65 (January, 1892),
pp. 194–203.

Few poets are of sufficiently tough and impenetrable fibre as to
be able with impunity to mix with public affairs. Even though the
spring of their inspiration be like the fountain in the garden of
grace 'drawn from the brain of the purple mountain that stands
in the distance yonder,' that stream is apt to become sullied at the
very source by the envious contact of the world. Poets conscious
of their vocation have generally striven sedulously, by sequestering
their lives somewhat austerely from the current of affairs, to
cultivate the tranquillity and freshness on which the purity of
their utterance depends. If it be hard to hear sermons and remain
a Christian, it is harder to mix much with men and remain an
idealist. And if this be true of commerce in its various forms, law,
medicine, and even education, it seems to be still more fatally
true of politics. Of course the temptation of politics to a philosophical mind is very great. To be at the centre of the machine; to
be able perhaps to translate a high thought into a practical measure;
to be able to make some closer reconciliation between law and
morality, as the vertical sun draws the shadow nearer to the feet,—
all this to a generous mind has an attraction almost supreme.

248

And yet the strain is so great that few survive it. David,—the inspired bandit, as M. Renan with such fatal infelicity calls him—was law-giver, general, king, and poet in one. Sophocles was more than once elected general, and is reported to have kept his colleagues in good humour by the charm of his conversation through a short but disagreeable campaign. Dante was an ardent and uncompromising revolutionary. Goethe was a kind of statesman. Among our own poets Spenser might perhaps be quoted as a fairly successful compromise; but of poets of the first rank Milton is the only one who deliberately took a considerable and active part in public life.

It is perhaps to Milton's example, and probably to his advice, that we owe the loss of a great English poet. It seems to have been if not at Milton's instigation, at any rate by his direct aid that Andrew Marvell was introduced to public life. The acquaintance began at Rome; but Marvell was introduced into Milton's intimate society, as his assistant secretary, at a most impressionable age. He had written poetry, dealing like *L'Allegro* and *Il Penseroso* mainly with country subjects, and was inclined no doubt to hang on the words of the older poet as on an oracle of light and truth. We can imagine him piecing out his aspirations and day-dreams, while the poet of sterner stuff, yet of all men least insensible to the delights of congenial society, points out to him the more excellent way, bidding him to abjure Amaryllis for a time. He has style, despatches will give it precision; knowledge of men and life will confirm and mature his mind; the true poet must win a stubborn virility if he is to gain the world. The younger and more delicate mind complies; and we lose a great poet, Milton gains an assistant secretary, and the age a somewhat gross satirist.

At a time like this, when with a sense of sadness we can point to more than one indifferent politician who might have been a capable writer, and so very many indifferent writers who could well have been spared to swell the ranks of politicians, we may well take the lesson of Andrew Marvell to heart.

The passion for the country which breathes through the earlier poems, the free air which ruffles the page, the summer languors, the formal garden seen through the casements of the cool house, the close scrutiny of woodland sounds, such as the harsh laughter of the woodpecker, the shrill insistence of the grasshopper's dry note, the luscious content of the drowsy, croaking frogs, the musical sweep of the scythe through the falling swathe; all these are the work of no town-bred scholar like Milton, whose country poems are rather visions seen through the eyes of other poets, or written as a man might transcribe the vague and inaccurate emotions of a landscape drawn by some old uncertain hand and dimmed by smoke and time. Of course Milton's *Il Penseroso* and *L'Allegro* have far more value even as country poems than hundreds of more literal transcripts. From a literary point of view indeed the juxtapositions of half-a-dozen epithets alone would prove the genius of the writer. But there are no sharp outlines; the scholar pauses in his walk to peer across the watered flat, or raises his eyes from his book to see the quiver of leaves upon the sunlit wall; he notes an effect it may be; but they do not come like treasures lavished from a secret storehouse of memory.

With Andrew Marvell it is different, though we will show by instances that his observation was sometimes at fault. Where or when this passion came to him we cannot tell. ... Wherever it was,—and such tastes are rarely formed in later years—the delicate observation of the minute philosopher side by side with the art of intimate expression grew and bloomed. ...

Such an escapade [as joining the Jesuits] belongs to a mind that must have been ardent and daring beyond its fellows; but it also shows a somewhat shifting foundation, an imagination easily dazzled and a pliability of will that cost us, we may believe, a poet. After Cambridge came some years of travel, which afforded material for some of his poems, such as the satire on Holland, of which the cleverness is still apparent, though its elaborate coarseness and pedantic humour make it poor pasture to feed the mind upon.

But the period to which we owe almost all the true gold among his poems, is the two years which he spent at Nunappleton House, 1650–1652, as tutor to the daughter of the great Lord Fairfax, the little Lady Mary Fairfax, then twelve years old. Marvell was at this time twenty-nine; and that exquisite relation which may exist between a grown man, pure in heart, and a young girl, when disparity of fortune and circumstance forbids all thought of marriage, seems to have been the mainspring of his song. Such a relation is half tenderness which dissembles its passion, and half worship which laughs itself away in easy phrases. The lyric *Young Love*, which indubitably though not confessedly refers to

Mary Fairfax, is one of the sweetest poems of pure feeling in the language: [quotes ll. 9–20].

It is delightful in this connection to think of the signet-ring with the device of a fawn, which he used in early life and may still be seen on his papers, as a gift of his little pupil, earned doubtless by his poem on the Dying Fawn, which is certainly an episode of Lady Mary's childhood.

In the group of early poems, which are worth all the rest of Marvell's work put together, several strains predominate. In the first place there is a close observation of Nature, even a grotesque transcription, with which we are too often accustomed only to credit later writers. For instance, in *Damon the Mower* he writes:

> The grasshopper its pipe gives o'er,
> And hamstringed frogs can dance no more;
> But in the brook the green frog wades,
> And grasshoppers seek out the shades. [ll. 11–14]

The second line of this we take to refer to the condition to which frogs are sometimes reduced in a season of extreme drought, when the pools are dry. Marvell must have seen a frog with his thighs drawn and contracted from lack of moisture making his way slowly through the grass in search of a refreshing swamp; this is certainly minute observation, as the phenomenon is a rare one. Again, such a delicate couplet as,

> And through the hazels thick espy
> The hatching throstle's shining eye,
> ['Appleton House,' ll. 531–2]

is not the work of a scholar who walks a country road, but of a man who will push his way into the copses in early spring, and has watched with delight the timorous eye and the upturned beak of the thrush sunk in her nest. Or again, speaking of the dwindled summer stream running so perilously clear after weeks of drought that the fish are languid:

> The stupid fishes hang, as plain
> As flies in crystal overta'en
> ['Appleton House,' ll. 677–8]

Or of the hayfield roughly mown, into which the herd has been turned to graze:

251

And what below the scythe increast,
Is pinched yet nearer by the beast. ['Appleton House,' ll. 453–4]

The mower's work begun and ended with the dews, in all its
charming monotony, seems to have had a peculiar attraction for
Marvell: he recurs to it in more than one poem: [quotes 'Damon
the Mower,' ll. 1–4].
And again of the mowers:

[Quotes 'Appleton House,' ll. 389–92.]

The aspects of the country on which he dwells with deepest
pleasure—and here lies the charm—are not those of Nature in
her sublimer or more elated moods, but the gentler and more
pastoral elements, that are apt to pass unnoticed at the time by all
but the true lovers of the quiet country side, and crowd in upon
the mind when surfeited by the wilder glories of peak and preci-
pice, or where tropical luxuriance side by side with tropical
aridity blinds and depresses the sense, with the feeling that made
Browning cry from Florence,

Oh, to be in England, now that April's there!
['Home-Thoughts, from Abroad,' l. 1]

Marvell's lines, *On the Hill and Grove at Billborow*, are an instance
of this; there is a certain fantastic craving after antithesis and
strangeness, it is true, but the spirit underlies the lines. The poem
however must be read in its entirety to gain the exact impression.
Again, for simple felicity, what could be more airily drawn than
the following from *The Garden*?

[Quotes ll. 49–54.]

Or this, from the Song to celebrate the marriage of Lord
Fauconberg and the Lady Mary Cromwell, of the undisturbed
dead of night?

[Quotes 'First Song,' ll. 1–6.]

Other poems such as the *Ode on the Drop of Dew* and the *Nymph
Complaining for the Death of her Fawn*, too long to quote, are
penetrated with the same essence.
At the same time it must be confessed that his imagery is
sometimes at fault,—it would be strange if it were not so; he falls

now and then, the wonder is how rarely, to a mere literary conceit. Thus the mower Damon sees himself reflected in his scythe; the fawn feeds on roses till its lip 'seems to bleed,' not with a possibly lurking thorn, but with the hue of its pasturage. With Hobbinol and Tomalin for the names of swain and nymph unreality is apt to grow. When the garden is compared to a fortress and its scents to a salvo of artillery,—

> Well shot, ye firemen! O how sweet
> And round your equal fires do meet, ['Appleton House,' ll. 305–6]

and,

> Then in some flower's beloved hut
> Each bee as sentinel is shut,
> And sleeps so too,—but if once stirred,
> She runs you through, nor asks the word, ['Appleton House,'
> ll.317–20]

here we are in the region of false tradition and mere literary hearsay. The poem of *Eyes and Tears*, again (so strangely admired by Archbishop Trench [see No. 70]) is little more than a string of conceits; and when in *Mourning* we hear that

> She courts herself in amorous rain,
> Herself both Danae and the shower; [ll. 19–20]

when we are introduced to Indian divers who plunge in the tears and can find no bottom, we think of Macaulay's *Tears of Sensibility*, and Crashaw's fearful lines on the Magdalene's tears,—

> Two walking baths, two weeping motions,
> Portable and compendious oceans. [*Saint Mary Magdalene*,
> st. 19]

At the same time Marvell's poems are singularly free as a rule from this strain of affectation. He has none of the morbidity that often passes for refinement. The free air, the wood-paths, the full heat of the summer sun,—this is his scenery; we are not brought into contact with the bones beneath the rose-bush, the splintered sun-dial, and the stagnant pool. His pulses throb with ardent life and have none of the 'inexplicable faintness' of a deathlier school. What would not Crashaw have had to say of the *Nuns of Appleton* if he had been so unfortunate as to have lighted on them? But Marvell writes:

> Our orient breaths perfumed are
> With incense of incessant prayer,
> And holy water of our tears
> Most strangely our complexion clears,
> Not tears of Grief, but such as those
> With which calm Pleasure overflows. [ll. 109–14]

And passing by a sweet and natural transition to his little pupil, the young Recluse of Nunappleton,—

> I see the angels in a crown
> On you the lilies showering down,
> And round about you glory breaks
> That something more than human speaks. [ll. 141–4][1]

The poems contain within themselves the germ of the later growth of satire in the shape of caustic touches of humour, as well as a certain austere philosophy that is apt to peer behind the superficial veil of circumstance, yet without dreary introspection. There is a Dialogue between Soul and Body which deals with the duality of human nature which has been the despair of all philosophers and the painful axiom of all religious teachers. Marvell makes the Soul say:

> Constrained not only to endure
> Diseases, but what's worse, the cure,
> And ready oft the port to gain,
> Am shipwrecked into health again. [ll. 27–30]

In the same connection in *The Coronet*, an allegory of the Ideal and the Real, he says:

> Alas! I find the serpent old,
> Twining in his speckled breast
> About the flowers disguised doth fold,
> With wreaths of fame and interest. [ll. 13–16]

Much of his philosophy however has not the same vitality, born of personal struggle and discomfiture, but is a mere echo of stoical and pagan views of life and its vanities drawn from Horace and Seneca, who seem to have been favourite authors. Such a sentiment as the following, from *Appleton House*—

---

[1] The lines do not refer to Mary Fairfax.

> But he superfluously spread,
> Demands more room alive than dead;
> What need of all this marble crust
> To impart the wanton mole [*sic*] of dust? [ll. 17–18; 21–2][1]

and from *The Coy Mistress*,—

> The grave's a fine and private place,
> But none, methinks, do there embrace [ll. 31–2]

are mere pagan commonplaces, however daintily expressed.

But there is a poem, an idyll in the form of a dialogue between Clorinda and Damon, which seems to contain a distinct philosophical motive. Idylls in the strict sense of the word are not remarkable for having a moral; or if they have one it may be said that it is generally bad, and is apt to defend the enjoyment of an hour against the conscience of centuries; but in *Clorinda and Damon*, the woman is the tempter and Damon is obdurate. She invites him to her cave, and describes its pleasures.

[Quotes ll. 13–16, 18–17 (*sic*); 19–21.]

This poem seems to us a distinct attempt to make of the sickly furniture of the idyll a vehicle for the teaching of religious truth. Is it fanciful to read in it a poetical rendering of the doctrine of conversion, the change that may come to a careless and sensuous nature by being suddenly brought face to face with the Divine light? It might even refer to some religious experience of Marvell's own: Milton's 'mighty Pan,' typifying the Redeemer, is in all probability the original.[2]

The work then on which Marvell's fame chiefly subsists,— with the exception of one poem which belongs to a different class, and will be discussed later, the Horatian Ode—may be said to belong to the regions of nature and feeling and to have anticipated in a remarkable degree the minute observation of natural phenomena characteristic of a modern school, even to a certain straining after unusual, almost bizarre effects. The writers of that date,

---

[1] Though the reading 'mole' for 'mote' here and in No. 86 represents a Cooke-Thompson emendation, it was also to appear in George A. Aitken's edition (1892). Note that though the Folio reading is a misprint, it is correct in Bod. MS. *Eng. poet. d.* 49.

[2] 'On the Morning of Christ's Nativity,' l. 89, but cf. E. K.'s gloss to the May eclogue in Spenser's *Shepheardes Calender*.

indeed, as Green points out, seem to have become suddenly and unaccountably modern,[1] a fact which we are apt to overlook owing to the frigid reaction of the school of Pope. Whatever the faults of Marvell's poems may be, and they are patent to all, they have a strain of originality. He does not seem to imitate, he does not even follow the lines of other poets; never,—except in a scattered instance or two, where there is a faint echo of Milton,— does he recall or suggest that he has a master. At the same time the poems are so short and slight that any criticism upon them is apt to take the form of a wish that the same hand had written more, and grown old in his art. There is a monotony for instance about their subjects, like the song of a bird recurring again and again to the same phrase; there is an uncertainty, an incompleteness not so much of expression as of arrangement, a tendency to diverge and digress in an unconcerned and vagabond fashion. There are stanzas, even long passages, which a lover of proportion such as Gray (who excised one of the most beautiful stanzas of the Elegy because it made too long a parenthesis) would never have spared. It is the work of a young man trying his wings, and though perhaps not flying quite so directly and professionally to his end, revelling in the new-found powers with a delicious ecstasy which excuses what is vague and prolix; especially when over all is shed that subtle precious quality which makes a sketch from one hand so unutterably more interesting than a finished picture from another,—which will arrest with a few commonplace phrases, lightly touched by certain players, the attention which has wandered throughout a whole sonata. The strength of his style lies in its unexpectedness. You are arrested by what has been well called a 'predestined' epithet, not a mere otiose addition, but a word which turns a noun into a picture; the 'hook-shouldered' hill 'to abrupter greatness thrust,' 'the sugar's uncorrupting oil,' 'the vigilant patrol of stars,' 'the squatted thorns,' 'the oranges like golden lamps in a green night,' 'the garden's fragrant innocence,'—these are but a few random instances of a tendency that meets you in every poem. Marvell had in fact the qualities of a consummate artist, and only needed to repress his luxuriance and to confine his expansiveness. In his own words,

[1] J. R. Green, *Short History of the English People*, 1874, ch. 9.

Height with a certain grace doth bend,
But low things clownishly ascend. ['Appleton House,' ll. 59–60]

Before we pass on to discuss the satires we may be allowed to say a few words on a class of poems largely represented in Marvell's works, which may be generally called Panegyric.

Quite alone among these,—indeed, it can be classed with no other poem in the language—stands the Horatian Ode on Cromwell's return from Ireland. Mr. Lowell said of it that as a testimony to Cromwell's character it was worth more than all Carlyle's biographies [see No. 72]; he might without exaggeration have said the same of its literary qualities. It has force with grace [see No. 58], originality with charm, in every stanza. Perhaps almost the first quality that would strike a reader of it for the first time is its quaintness; but further study creates no reaction against this in the mind,—the usual sequel to poems which depend on quaintness for effect. But when Mr. Lowell goes on to say that the poem shows the difference between grief that thinks of its object and grief that thinks of its rhymes (referring to Dryden), he is not so happy. The pre-eminent quality of the poem is its art; and its singular charm is the fact that it succeeds, in spite of being artificial, in moving and touching the springs of feeling in an extraordinary degree. It is a unique piece in the collection, the one instance where Marvell's undoubted genius burned steadily through a whole poem. Here he flies *penna metuente solvi*.[1] It is in completeness more than in quality that it is superior to all his other work, but in quality too it has that lurking divinity that cannot be analysed or imitated.

[Quotes ll. 25–36, l. 31 emended.]

This is the apotheosis of tyrants; it is the bloom of republicanism just flowering into despotism. But the Ode is no party utterance; the often quoted lines on the death of Charles, in their grave yet passionate dignity, might have been written by the most ardent of Royalists, and have often done service on their side. But indeed the whole Ode is above party, and looks clearly into the heart and motives of man. It moves from end to end with the solemn beat of its singular metre, its majestic cadences, without self-consciousness or sentiment, austere but not frigid. His other panegyrics

---

[1] Adapted from Horace, *Odes* 2.2.7: with unflagging pen.

are but little known, though the awkward and ugly lines on Milton
have passed into anthologies, owing to their magnificent exordium,
'When I beheld the poet blind yet old' [*sic*]. But no one can pretend
that such lines as these are anything but prosaic and ridiculous to
the last degree—

> Thou hast not missed one thought that could be fit,
> And all that was improper dost omit,
> At once delight and horror on us seize,
> Thou sing'st with so much gravity and ease—[ll. 27–8; 35–6]

though the unfortunate alteration in the meaning of the word
improper makes them even more ridiculous than they are. The
poems on the *First Anniversary of the Government of the Lord Protector*, on the *Death of the Lord Protector*, and on *Richard Cromwell*
are melancholy reading though they have some sonorous lines.

> And as the angel of our Commonweal
> Troubling the waters, yearly mak'st them heal,
> ['On the Death of O. C.,' ll. 401–2]

may pass as an epigram. But that a man of penetrating judgment
and independence of opinion should descend to a vein of odious
genealogical compliment, and speak of the succeeding of

> Rainbow to storm, Richard to Oliver [l. 322, misquoted],

and add that

> A Cromwell in an hour a prince will grow [l. 312],

by way of apology for the obvious deficiencies of his new Protector, makes us very melancholy indeed. Flattery is of course
a slough in which many poets have wallowed; and a little grovelling
was held to be even more commendable in poets in that earlier
age; but we see the pinion beginning to droop, and the bright eye
growing sickly and dull. Milton's poisonous advice is already at
work.

But we must pass through a more humiliating epoch still. The
poet of spicy gardens and sequestered fields seen through the
haze of dawn is gone, not like the Scholar Gipsy to the high lonely
wood or the deserted lasher, but is stepped down to jostle with
the foulest and most venal of mankind. He becomes a satirist, and
a satirist of the coarsest kind. His pages are crowded with filthy

pictures and revolting images; the leaves cannot be turned over so quickly but some lewd epithet or vile realism prints itself on the eye. His apologists have said that it is nothing but the overflowing indignation of a noble mind when confronted with the hideous vices of a corrupt court and nation; that this deep-seated wrath is but an indication of the fervid idealistic nature of the man; that the generous fire that warmed in the poems, consumed in the satires; that the true moralist does not condone but condemn. To this we would answer that it is just conceivable a satirist being primarily occupied by an immense moral indignation, and no doubt that indignation must bear a certain part in all satires; but it is not the attitude of a hopeful or generous soul. The satirist is after all only destructive; he has not learned the lesson that the only cure for old vices is new enthusiasms. Nor if a satirist is betrayed into the grossest and most unnecessary realism can we acquit him entirely of all enjoyment of his subject. It is impossible to treat of vice in the intimate and detailed manner in which Marvell treats of it without having, if no practical acquaintance with your subject, at least a considerable conventional acquaintance with it, and a large literary knowledge of the handling of similar topics; and when Dr. Grosart goes so far as to call Marvell an essentially pure-minded man, or words to that effect, we think he would find a contradiction on almost every page of the satires.

They were undoubtedly popular. Charles II. was greatly amused by them; and their reputation lasted as late as Swift, who spoke of Marvell's genius as preeminently indicated by the fact that though the controversies were forgotten, the satires still held the mind. He started with a natural equipment. That he was humorous his earlier poems show, as when for instance he makes Daphne say to Chloe:

> Rather I away will pine,
>   In a manly stubbornness,
>   Than be fatted up express,
> For the cannibal to dine. [ll. 69–72]

And he shows, too, in his earlier poems, much of the weightier and more dignified art of statement that makes the true satirist's work often read better in quotations than entire; as for instance—

> Wilt thou all the glory have,
>   That war or peace commend?

> Half the world shall be thy slave,
> The other half thy friend.
> ['Resolved Soul and Created
> Pleasure,' ll. 63–6]

But belonging as they do to the period of melancholy decadence of Marvell's art, we are not inclined to go at any length into the question of the satires. We see genius struggling like Laocoon in the grasp of a power whose virulence he did not measure, and to whom sooner or later the increasing languor must yield. Of course there are notable passages scattered throughout them. In *Last Instructions to a Painter*, the passage beginning, 'Paint last the king, and a dead shade of night,' where Charles II. sees in a vision the shape of Charles I. and Henry VIII. threatening him with the consequences of unsympathetic despotism and the pursuit of sensual passion, has a tragic horror and dignity of a peculiar kind; and the following specimen from *The Character of Holland* gives on the whole a good specimen of the strength and weakness of the author:

[Quotes ll. 1–8.]

Clever beyond question; every couplet is an undeniable epigram, lucid, well-digested, elaborate; pointed, yet finikin withal,—it is easy to find a string of epithets for it. But to what purpose is this waste? To see this felicity spent on such slight and intemperate work is bitterness itself; such writing has, it must be confessed, every qualification for pleasing except the power to please.

Of the remainder of Marvell's life, there is little more to be said. He was private tutor at Eton to a Master Dutton, a relative of Cromwell's, and wrote a delightful letter about him to the Protector; but the serious business of his later life was Parliament. Of his political consistency we cannot form a high idea. He seems as we should expect him to have been, a Royalist at heart and by sympathy all along; ''Tis God-like good,' he wrote, 'to save a falling king.'[1] Yet he was not ashamed to accept Cromwell as the angel of the Commonweal, and to write in fulsome praise of Protector Richard; and his bond of union with the extreme Puritans was his intense hatred of prelacy and bishops which is constantly coming up. In *The Loyal Scot* he writes:

[1] *Britannia and Rawleigh*, l 140, ascribed to Marvell's friend John Ayloffe in Bod. MS. *Eng. poet. d.* 49.

The friendly loadstone has not more combined,
Than Bishops cramped the commerce of mankind. [ll. 102–3]

And in *The Bermudas* he classes the fury of the elements with
'Prelates' rage' as the natural enemies of the human race. Such
was not the intermeddling in affairs that Milton had recommended.
To fiddle, while Rome burnt, upon the almost divine attributes of
her successive rulers, this was not the austere storage of song which
Milton himself practised.

Andrew Marvell was for many years member for Hull, with
his expenses paid by the Corporation. His immense, minute, and
elaborate correspondence with his constituents, in which he gave
an exact account of the progress of public business, remains to
do him credit as a sagacious and conscientious man. . . .

Of his Prose Works we have no intention of speaking; they
may be characterised as prose satires for the most part, or political
pamphlets. *The Rehearsal Transprosed* and *The Divine in Mode* are
peculiarly distasteful examples of a kind of controversy then much
in vogue. They are answers to publications, and to the ordinary
reader contrive to be elaborate without being artistic, personal
without being humorous, and digressive without being entertaining; in short, they combine the characteristics of tedium, dulness,
and scurrility to a perfectly phenomenal degree. Of course this is
a matter of taste. No one but a clever man could have written
them, and no one but an intelligent man could have edited them;
but we confess to thinking that a conspiracy of silence would
have done more credit both to editor and author. As compared with
the poems themselves, the prose works fill many volumes; and
any reader of ordinary perseverance has ample opportunities of
convincing himself of Andrew Marvell's powers of expression,
his high-spirited beginning, the delicate ideals, the sequestered
ambitions of his youth, and their lamentable decline.

It is a perilous investment to aspire to be a poet,—*periculosae
plenum opus aleæ*.[1] If you succeed, to have the world present and to
come at your feet, to win the reluctant admiration even of the
Philistine; to snuff the incense of adoration on the one hand, and
on the other to feel yourself a member of the choir invisible, the
sweet and solemn company of poets; to own within yourself the
ministry of hope and height. And one step below success, to be

[1] Horace, *Odes* 2.1.6: a work fraught with hazardous risk.

laughed at or softly pitied as the dreamer of ineffectual dreams, the
strummer of impotent music; to be despised alike by the successful
and the unsuccessful; the world if you win,—worse than nothing
if you fail.

> Mediocribus esse poetis
> Non di, non homines, non concessere columnae.[1]

There is no such thing as respectable mediocrity among poets.
Be supreme or contemptible.

And yet we cannot but grieve when we see a poet over whose
feet the stream has flowed, turn back from the brink and make the
great denial; whether from the secret consciousness of aridity, the
drying of the fount of song, or from the imperious temptations of
the busy, ordinary world we cannot say. Somehow we have lost
our poet. It seems that,

> Just for a handful of silver he left us.
> Just for a ribbon to stick in his coat.
> [Browning's 'Lost Leader,' ll. 1–2]

And the singer of an April mood, who might have bloomed year
after year in young and ardent hearts, is buried in the dust of
politics, in the valley of dead bones.

[1] Horace, *Ars Poetica*, l. 372: neither gods, men, nor booksellers will acknowledge middling
poets.

80. J. Stuart's review of Marvell in the Muses' Library Series

1892

In 1892 the editor and biographer George A. Aitken (1860–1917) published a two-volume edition of the poems and satires in the Muses' Library Series (reprinted 1901). His critical comments in the Introduction were, as the reviewer laconically observes, 'not of much account.'

Extract from the *Athenaeum*, No. 3384 (3 September, 1892), pp. 313–14.

Never was reputation worse served by the accident of a particular friendship than Andrew Marvell's. His fame is both distorted and overshadowed by Milton's. The association of the two men in the Latin secretaryship has induced careless or partisan critics to assume an identity, or at least a similarity, in their political opinions, and thus entirely to misread the motive of Marvell's civic action. Edward Phillips's statement as to Milton's security after the Restoration ought to point to a very different conclusion. 'Particularly in the House of Commons,' he says, 'Mr. Andrew Marvell, a member for Hull, acted vigorously in his behalf and made a considerable party for him.' This exercise of influence would have been impossible to an upholder of the divine right of regicide and rebellion. On the other hand, the writer of an article in *Macmillan's Magazine* [see No. 79], cited by Mr. Aitken—who accuses Marvell of inconsistency and an exceedingly base desertion of his party—cannot have sufficiently weighed this evidence, although there is some contemporary evidence to support his opinion. In 'The D. of B.'s Litany' ('Poems on Affairs of State,' ed. 1705, p. 408) the lines occur:—

> From changing old friends for rascally new ones;
> From taking Wildman and Marvel for true ones,
> *Libera nos, &c.*

But the chiefest offender is Mr. Goldwin Smith,[1] who drives the
parallel between the river in Monmouth and the river in Macedon
beyond the limits of reasonable argument. Some of his statements
would be astonishing if they came from any one but Mr. Goldwin
Smith. . . .

Again, when Mr. Goldwin Smith described Marvell as 'a
satellite, paler, yet bright,' of Milton, 'the central orb of that
intellectual lustre which was produced by the union of classical
culture and ancient love of liberty with Puritan enthusiasm'
[II, p. 380, 1908 edn], he ought to have been aware that he was
indulging in fanciful and not very elegant criticism. Happily,
Mr. Aitken's valuable edition is free from such blemishes. He has
issued a faultless text, with careful and extensive annotations. And
he is, we believe, the first of Marvell's biographers who has conquered the temptation to write ecstatic platitudes about the
Miltonic factor, if the expression be permitted, in Marvell's history.
True, the criticism of the poems and satires is not of much account,
because Mr. Aitken refrains from comparisons, which are the salt
of criticism, finding more to interest him in facts about the recluse
student who turned politician. These facts, however, are presented
with skill and tact, in a readable fashion. We have no hesitation
in declaring Mr. Aitken's to be the only life of the poet that can
serve the impartial investigator.

Marvell was thoroughly in touch with the thought of his time,
a man righteous in conduct, with scarce a spark of originality.
He might be fitly described as an honest little fellow; the phrase,
though chosen, is less than choice, yet everything we know of
him establishes its justice. He was not of the race that graduates
in rebellious Liberalism, not was he, in the strictest sense of the
word, a Puritan. Indeed, in many of his poems there is 'clearly
wantonness,' and one of them ('Daphnis and Chloe') is quite as
immoral or non-moral as the average Restoration lyric. But he had
a lively notion of probity and decency both in public and in private
life. At no time did he belong to the Roundheads. Of the Civil War
he wrote: 'I think the cause was too good to have been fought for.
Men ought to have trusted God; they ought and might have trusted
the king in this matter' [RT I, p. 135]. . . . It is easy to see that

---

[1] Smith contributed the prefatory notice on Marvell in the *English Poets* (4 vols, 1880),
edited by T. H. Ward.

Marvell's admiration for Cromwell was but the homage which the reflective temperament almost inevitably renders to the strong man, the man of blood and iron. There is every reason for supposing that his acquiescence in the Protectorate came of a mistaken belief that the institutions established by Cromwell's adroit control of an excited public would outlast both his omnipotent personality and the popular excitement. He had no delusions about divine right nor the inherent sacredness of a republic. As a loyal patriot, he accepted the order of things, and did the best he could for the state and himself. After the Restoration he seems to have fallen into line with the Country party and the older Cavaliers ('Dialogue between Two Horses,' 78–82; 'Last Instructions to a Painter,' 285–294). As he advanced in life he became blunter and more audacious in his speech; but he was always with the moderate section of the opposition, and rarely spoke even severely of the king. The references to Charles in his satires are never maliciously republican, like Rochester's. He attacked Hyde, he had no patience with the reprobate courtiers, he dreaded and mistrusted the Duke of York. But his utmost aspirations would have been satisfied by the king's observance of the Declaration of Breda.

The satires make but indifferent reading—not that 'the meanness of Restoration politics and the dirtiness of Restoration thought' take away from their value, as Mr. Goldwin Smith insinuates. Mr. Aitken has no difficulty in showing their design to be honourable and their manner comparatively temperate. But they are loosely conceived, and something casual and diffuse in execution. The language is vigorous invariably, but Marvell continually lost sight of the central motive and wandered away from his point. There are brilliant passages, smart touches of portraiture, and a curious vein of irony. Setting aside 'Flecnoe' and 'Tom May,' which are merely unreadable, 'The Character of Holland' is the most amusing; but the 'Two Horses' and 'Britannia and Raleigh' show so marvellous an advance in restraint and power as to suggest that their author died before he had 'come to his own.' His poems, likewise, have been often monstrously overrated. In no element do they resemble Milton's. They are the work of a young and not too thoroughly equipped writer, who has some fancy at command, and is largely influenced by the fashions of the day. Often the conceits are no less than ludicrous. When he was old enough to know better, Marvell addressed the king thus:—

And you, great Sir, that with him empire share,
Sun of our world, as he the Charles is there.
['Last Instructions to a Painter,' ll. 955–6]

In one of his best-known works he writes:

The sun himself, of her aware,
Seems to descend with greater care,
And, lest she see him go to bed,
In blushing clouds conceals his head.
['Appleton House,' ll. 661–4]

Nothing could exceed the solemn frivolity of 'Eyes and Tears.'
Yet even his worst poems are worth reading because of stray
lines, 'simple, sensuous, and passionate.'[1] In the midst of lumber-
ing, pointless metaphors the reader sometimes happens upon
the most radiant felicities of diction. But the 'Golden Treasury'
contains all of his work that is worth more than a single reading—
the few poems wherein his taste has attained a complete control
over his delicate and sometimes splendid fancies.

---

[1] Milton, *Of Education, Works* (New York, 1931), IV, p. 286.

81. Sir E.K. Chambers's review of Marvell in the Muses' Library Series

1892

In contrast with No. 80, the review of Aitken's edition by the critic and scholar E. K. Chambers (1866–1954) heralds the true beginnings of positive reassessment of the poetry. There is, first of all, concern for the lyrical poetry to the exclusion of the satires. There is, second, an emphasis on the nature poetry, particularly the Mower poems. Finally, there is an acceptance, when not 'merely fantastical,' of the conceited style.

Extract from the *Academy*, 42 (17 September 1892), pp. 230–1.

The calling of the publisher, no longer merely a trade, begins to take place among the fine arts. Truly this is a thing to be thankful for, more than we are aware. The present book illustrates the blessings thereof. For the better part of the century Marvell was attainable only in the imperfect editions of incapable and ignorant men. So that he was represented to the ordinary reader by selections; and in especial by two ill-understood stanzas of the Horatian Ode, wherein is set forth the theatrical bearing of Charles I., 'the royal actor,' upon his day of execution. About twenty years ago Marvell was edited—badly—by Dr. Grosart. Who, indeed, has escaped being edited—badly—by Dr. Grosart? And Dr. Grosart's edition is moreover a limited issue, a thing dear to the bibliophile, and unspeakably hateful to the lover of literature. . . . For the historical side of his work, which must have meant considerable labour, and for the brief but perfectly sufficient biography, Mr. Aitken deserves great credit. His critical notes are not quite so happy, and at times he seems to have fallen into error by blindly borrowing from Dr. Grosart. And one would have been glad of some more elaborate attempt to appreciate the place of Marvell in English literature. That is a task which an editor has never a right to shirk; and in the present case it was more than usually necessary, for I cannot but think that these volumes will come as a discovery to many who did not quite know the greatness of this half-forgotten poet.

Marvell holds a unique place in the seventeenth century. He stands at the parting of the ways, between the extravagancies of the lyrical Jacobeans on the one hand, and the new formalism initiated by Waller on the other. He is not unaffected by either influence. The modish handling of the decasyllable couplet is very marked here and there. You have it, for instance, in the poem on Blake:

> Bold Stayner leads; this fleet's designed by fate
> To give him laurel, as the last did plate. [ll. 117–18]

And elsewhere, of course, he has conceits which cry aloud in their flagrancy. But his real affinities are with a greater than Waller or Suckling. Milton in those days 'was like a star, and dwelt apart'; but of all who 'called him friend,' Marvell is the one who can claim the most of spiritual kinship. The very circumstances of their lives are curiously similar. Each left poetry for statecraft and polemic: for Milton the flowering time came late; for Marvell, never. And their poetic temper is one: it is the music of Puritanism,—the Puritanism of Spenser and Sidney, not uncultivated, not ungracious, not unsensuous even, but always with the same dominant note in it, of moral strength and moral purity. Marvell is a Puritan; but his spirit has not entered the prison-house, nor had the key turned on it there. He is a poet still, such as there have been few in any age. The lyric gift of Herrick he has not, nor Donne's incomparable subtlety and intensity of emotion; but for imaginative power, for decent melody, for that self-restraint of phrase which is the fair half of art, he must certainly hold high rank among his fellows. The *clear* sign of this self-restraint is his mastery over the octosyllable couplet, a metre which in less skilful hands so readily becomes diffuse and wearisome.

Marvell writes love poems, but he is not essentially a love poet. He sings beautifully to Juliana and Chlora, but they themselves are only accidents in his song. His real passion—a most uncommon one in the seventeenth century—is for nature, exactly as we moderns mean nature, the great spiritual influence which deepens and widens life for us. How should the intoxication of meadow, and woodland, and garden, be better expressed than in these two lines—

Stumbling on melons, as I pass,
Insnared with flowers, I fall on grass. ['The Garden,' ll. 39–40]

unless indeed it be here—

I am the mower Damon. . . .

[Quotes ll. 41–8.]

These mower-idylls, never found in the anthologies, are among the most characteristic of Marvell's shorter poems. I cannot forbear to quote two stanzas from 'The Mower to the Glowworms.'

[Quotes ll. 1–8.]

Observe how Marvell makes of the nightingale a conscious artist, a winged *diva*. Elsewhere he speaks of her as sitting among the 'squatted thorns,' in order 'to sing the trials of her voice.'

I must needs see in Marvell something of a nature-philosophy strangely anticipative of George Meredith. For the one, as for the other, complete absorption in nature, the unreserved abandonment of self to the skyey influences, is the really true and sanative wisdom. Marvell describes his soul, freed of the body's vesture, perched like a bird upon the garden boughs—

Annihilating all that's made
To a green thought in a green shade.

The same idea is to be found in the lines 'Upon Appleton House,' a poem which will repay careful study from all who wish to get at the secret of Marvell's genius. It shows him at his best—and at his worst, in the protracted conceit, whereby a garden, its flowers and its bees, are likened to a fort with a garrison. And here I am minded to enter a plea against the indiscriminate condemnation of conceits in poetry. After all, a conceit is only an analogy, a comparison, a revealing of likeness in things dissimilar, and therefore of the very essence of poetic imagination. Often it illumines, and where it fails it is not because it is a conceit, but because it is a bad conceit; because the thing compared is not beautiful in itself, or because the comparison is not flashed upon you, but worked out with such tedious elaboration as to be 'merely fantastical.' Many of Marvell's conceits are, in effect, bad; the well-known poem, 'On a Drop of Dew,' redeemed though it is by the last line and a half, affords a terrible example.[1] But others are shining successes. Here is one, set in a haunting melody, as of Browning.

[Quotes 'Daphnis and Chloe,' ll. 85–8.]

Next to green fields, Marvell is perhaps happiest in treating of death. His is the mixed mode of the Christian scholar, not all unpaganised, a lover of heaven, but a lover of the earthly life too. There is the epitaph on a nameless lady, with its splendid close:

> Modest as morn, as mid-day bright,
> Gentle as evening, cool as night:
> 'Tis true: but all too weakly said;
> 'Twas more significant. She's dead.
> ['An Epitaph upon—,' ll. 17–20]

There is the outburst on the death of the poet's hero, the great Protector:

> O human glory vain! O Death! O wings!
> O worthless world! O transitory things! [ll. 255–6]

And to crown all, there are these lines, which remind me, for their felicities, their quaintness, and the organ-note in them, of the *Hydriotaphia*:

[Quotes 'To His Coy Mistress,' ll. 21–32.]

I have left myself no room to speak of the Satires. They are not a subject to dwell upon with pleasure. One sees that they were inevitable, that a man of Marvell's strenuous moral fibre, in all the corruption of the Restoration court, could not but break forth into savage invective; yet one regrets them, as one regrets the *Defensio* and *Eikonoklastes*. It may, however, be well to remind anyone, who is tempted by the beauty of Messrs. Lawrence and Bullen's book to buy it for a love-gift to his mistress, that the first volume, containing the Poems, is alone suitable to his purpose.

[1] Indicative of the change in sensibility, cf. the view of Goldwin Smith in *The English Poets*, ed. T. H. Ward (1880): while commending the 'play of intellectual fancy,' he calls the concluding lines with their stroke of 'wit' about the manna 'a sad fall' (1908 reprint, II, p. 382).

82. Richard Garnett on Marvell

1895

Biographer, critic, and minor poet, Richard Garnett (1835–1906) published *The Age of Dryden* in 1895.

Extract from *The Age of Dryden* (1932 reprint), pp. 49–53.

Andrew Marvell was a virtuous man whose good qualities contrast so forcibly with the characteristic failings of his age, that he appears by contrast even more virtuous than he actually was. His integrity made him the hero of legend, for, although the Court would no doubt have been glad to gain him, it is hardly credible that the prime minister should by the king's order have personally waited upon him 'up two pair of stairs in a little court in the Strand.' But the apocryphal anecdote attests the real veneration inspired by his independence in a venal age. Born in the neighbourhood of Hull on March 31st, 1621, he studied at Cambridge, travelled for some years on the Continent, and settled down about 1650 as tutor to the daughter of Lord Fairfax. At this period he wrote his exquisite poem, *The Garden*, and other pieces of a similar character. He also wrote in 1650 the poem on Cromwell's return from Ireland, which may have gained for him in 1653 the appointment of tutor to Cromwell's ward, William Dutton. Other pieces of a like description followed, and in 1657 Marvell became joint Latin secretary with Milton, an office for which Milton had recommended him four years previously. His poem on the Protector's death in the following year is justly declared by Mr. Firth to be 'the only one distinguished by an accent of sincerity and personal affection.'[1] He was elected for Hull to Richard Cromwell's Parliament, and continued to sit for the remainder of his life. He was the last Member of Parliament who received a salary from his constituents, to whose interests he in return attended so

---

[1] C.H. Firth (1857–1936), historian and literary critic, contributed the article on Marvell to the *DNB*.

diligently that upwards of three hundred letters from him upon their concerns and general politics are extant in the Hull archives.

Marvell could scarcely be called a republican. He had been devoted to the Protectorate, and would probably have been easily reconciled to the Restoration if the government had been ably and honestly conducted. In wrath at the general maladministration he betook himself to satires, which circulated in manuscript. At first he attacked Clarendon, but eventually concluded that the only remedy would be the final expulsion of the house of Stuart. In 1672 and 1673 he appeared in print as a prose controversialist with *The Rehearsal Transprosed*, a witty attack on a work by Parker, Bishop of Oxford, wherein, in the author's own words, 'the mischiefs and inconveniences of toleration were represented, and all pretences pleaded in behalf of liberty of conscience fully answered.' He silenced his opponent, and escaped being himself silenced through the interposition of Charles II., whose native good sense and easiness of temper inclined him to toleration, and who promoted the freedom of Nonconformists as a means of obtaining liberty for the Church of Rome. Marvell, however, was not to be reconciled, and in 1677 put forth an anonymous pamphlet to prove, what was but too true, that a design had long been on foot to establish absolute monarchy and subvert the Protestant religion. His sudden death on August 18th, 1678, was attributed to poison, but, according to a physician who wrote some years afterwards, was occasioned by that prejudice of the faculty against Peruvian bark which is recorded by Temple and Evelyn.

As a writer of prose, Marvell is both powerful and humorous, but is not a Junius or a Pascal to impart permanent interest to transitory themes, and make the topics of the day topics for all time.[1] As a poet he ranks with those who have been said to be stars alike of evening and of morning. His earliest and most truly poetical compositions belong in spirit to the period of Charles I., when the strains of the Elizabethan lyric were yet lingering. After passing through a transition stage of manly verse still breathing a truly poetical spirit, but mainly concerned with public affairs, he settles down as a satirist endowed with all the vigour, but, at the same time, with all the prosaic hardness of the Restoration. His

---

[1] Cf. 'Junius must have formed his style, in a great measure, upon that of Marvell' (see No. 51).

most inspired poem, *Thoughts in a Garden*, written under the Commonwealth, and originally composed in Latin, nevertheless rings like a voice from beyond the Civil Wars. Here are the three loveliest of nine lovely stanzas:

[Quotes ll. 33–56.]

'These wonderful verses,' says Mr. Palgrave of the entire poem, 'may be regarded as a test of any reader's insight into the most poetical aspects of poetry.'

As a satirist it is Marvell's error to confound satire with lampoon. He has the *saeva indignatio* [from Swift's epitaph] which makes the avenger, but spends too much of it upon individuals. Occasionally some fine personification gives promise of better things, but the poet soon relapses into mere personalities. This may be attributed in great measure to the circumstances under which these compositions appeared. They could only be circulated clandestinely, and the writer may be excused if he did not labour to exalt what he himself regarded as mere fugitive poetry. The most celebrated of these pieces are the series of *Advices to a Painter*, in which the persons and events of the day are described to an imaginary artist for delineation in fitting, and therefore by no means flattering, colours. It is to Marvell's honour that he succeeds best with a fine subject. When, in his poems on the events of the Commonwealth, he escapes from mere sarcasm and negation, and speaks nobly upon really noble themes, he soars far above the Marvell of the Restoration, though even here his verse is marred by lapses into the commonplace, and by his besetting infirmity of an inability to finish with effect, leaving off like a speaker who sits down rather from the failure of his voice than the exhaustion of his theme. The panegyric on Cromwell's anniversary, and the poem on his death, abound nevertheless with fine, though faulty passages, of which the following may serve as an example.

[Quotes 'On the Death of O. C.,' ll. 255–76.]

83.   An anonymous comment on the poetry

1897

This anonymous comment, stressing Marvell's nature poetry, forecasts a developing appreciation.

Extract from the *Academy*, 51 (1 May 1897), p. 478.

ANDREW MARVELL was a gentleman who wrote with ease; and though the body of his poetical work is of the most slender, his place among the amateur poets, or poets whose primary idea in singing is to please themselves or their friends, is with the highest. He is remarkable chiefly for distinction of intellect; remarkable incidentally in being almost the last poet, until Crabbe and Cowper came, to look at nature for himself. After Marvell the artificial period set in like a frost, and held the fields and lawns with an iron grasp. Marvell's little handful of out-of-door poems—'Upon Appleton House,' 'The Garden,' 'Upon the Hill and Grove at Billborow,' 'The Bermudas'—are as felicitous and debonair as anything in the language. In the presence of yew hedges and box-wood walks, the spreading hands of cedars and the fragrance of roses, the plashings of the fountain and the silent reminder of the sundial, he was sensitive and impressionable to his fingertips: in a garden after his own heart he could annihilate 'all that's made to a green thought in a green shade.' Later in life he fell a victim to the snare of politics, but once he could ask:

> Unhappy! shall we never more
> That sweet militia restore,
> When gardens only had their tow'rs,
> And all the garrisons were flow'rs,
> When roses only arms might bear,
> And men did rosie garlands wear?
> Tulips, in several colours barr'd. . . . [1]

[1] This approving citation of the garden compared with a fortress is to be contrasted with the disapproval of A.C. Benson and E.K. Chambers (Nos 79, 81).

274

[Quotes 'Appleton House,' ll. 329–40.]

Once, in 'The Garden,' Marvell could write:

> Fair Quiet, I have found thee here. . . .

[Quotes ll. 9–16.]

And again:

> Here at the fountain's sliding foot,. . . .

[Quotes ll. 49–53.]

It is sad to think that such a divine loafer as the poet of 'The Garden'—

> The nectarine and curious peach
> Into my hands themselves do reach;
> Stumbling on melons, as I pass,
> Insnar'd with flow'rs, I fall on grass [ll. 37–40]—

should ever have succumbed to faction. But so it was. For the bulk of his later work Marvell courted only the satirical muse. His 'Horatian Ode upon Cromwell's Return from Ireland' is a magnificent exception. No such serious poem was ever handicapped by so abrupt and undignified a metre or came out of the ordeal so triumphantly. The stanzas referring to Charles I. are well known:

[Quotes ll. 57–64.]

Of Marvell's frankly satirical manner these lines from 'The Loyal Scot' are a good example:

> What ethic river is this wondrous Tweed,
> Whose one bank virtue, t'other vice does breed?
> Or what new perpendicular does rise
> Up from her streams continued to the skies,
> That between us the common air should bar,
> And split the influence of every star [ll. 81–6]—

although his best-known effort is the rather too heavy-handed squib entitled 'The Character of Holland.' In a more familiar style is the letter to the learned Dr. Wittie, on the completion of his translation of *Popular Errors*, which shows that Marvell's allegiance to the weed in later life was not less sound than his love of flowers in younger days. He begins:

Our books in growing ranks so numerous be
That scarce one cuttle fish swims in the sea,

by which he means that they all have been captured for ink; and
continues, of the multitude of books:

Sturdier they rise from printing-press's blows,
The more 'tis pressed this Hydra bulkier grows.
Can aconite or plant else known to men
Expel this cacöethes of the pen?
Ind only on our sorrows taking pity
Provides an antidote, dear Dr. Wittie.
Tobacco, useful poison, Ind bestows,
Which more than hellebore drives out our woes.[1]

Marvell, who acted as Milton's secretary, was one of the few
of the poet's contemporaries conscious of the sublimity of *Paradise
Lost*. As the years pass on it is likely that the appreciation of his
own poetry will increase rather than lessen.

84. Alice Meynell's comments on Marvell

1897, 1899

Poet and critic, Mrs Alice Meynell (1874–1922) regularly
contributed an unsigned column entitled 'The Wares of
Autolycus' to the *Pall Mall Gazette* and later became its art
critic. Never one to ignore her earlier (or later) labours, she
used the notes to the poems included in her anthology *The
Flower of the Mind* (1897) in the essay on Marvell of that year.
Later she incorporated the notes to the satires in a second
essay (1899) on Marvell's satiric poetry. A collection of her
'unrepublished essays' has been printed under the title of
The Wares of Autolycus, ed. P. M. Frazer (1965).

---

[1] Translation of the Latin by A.B. Grosart (I, p. 423).

(a)   From the *Pall Mall Gazette*, 14 (14 July 1897), pp. 3–4.

'He earned the glorious name,' says a biographer of Andrew Marvell (editing an issue of that poet's works, which certainly has its faults), 'of the British Aristides' [see No. 33]. The portly dulness of the mind that could make such a phrase, and, having made, award it, is not, in fairness, to affect a reader's thought of Marvell himself nor even of his time. Under correction, I should think that the award was not made in his own age; he did but live on the eve of the day that cumbered its mouth with phrases of such foolish burden and made literature stiff with them. He, doubtless, has moments of mediocre pomp, but even then it is Milton that he touches, and not anything more common; and he surely never even heard a threat of the pass that the English tongue should come to but a little later on.

Andrew Marvell's political rectitude, it is true, seems to have been of a robustious kind; but his poetry, at its rare best, has a 'wild civility,' which might puzzle the triumph of him, whoever he was, who made a success of this phrase of the 'British Artistides.' Nay, it is difficult not to think that Marvell too, who was 'of middling stature, roundish-faced, cherry-cheeked,' a healthy and active rather than a spiritual Aristides, might himself have been somewhat taken by surprise at the encounters of so subtle a muse. He, as a garden-poet, expected the accustomed Muse to lurk about the fountain-heads, within the caves, and by the walks and the statues of the gods, keeping the tryst of a seventeenth-century convention in which there were certainly no surprises. And for fear of the commonplaces of those visits Marvell sometimes outdoes the whole company of garden-poets in the difficult labours of the fancy. The reader treads with him a 'maze' most resolutely intricate, and is more than once obliged to turn back having been too much puzzled on the way to a small, visible, plain, and obvious goal of thought.

And yet this poet two or three times did meet a Muse he had hardly looked for among the trodden paths; a spiritual creature had been waiting behind a laurel or an apple tree. You find him coming away from such a divine ambush a wilder and a simpler man. All his garden had been made ready for poetry, and poetry was indeed there, but in unexpected hiding and in a strange form, looking rather like a fugitive, shy of the poet who was conscious of having her rules by heart, yet sweetly willing to be seen, for all her haste.

For it is only in those well-known poems, 'The Garden,' translated from his own Latin, and 'The Nymph Complaining of the Death of Her Fawn,' in that less familiar piece 'The Mower Against Gardens,' in 'The Picture of T.C. in a Prospect of Flowers,' with a few very brief passages in the course of duller verses, that Marvell comes into veritable possession of his own more interior powers—at least in the series of his garden lyrics. The political poems, needless to say, have an excellence of a different character and a higher degree. They have so much authentic dignity that 'the glorious name of the British Aristides' really seems duller when it is conferred as the earnings of the 'Horatian Ode upon Cromwell's Return from Ireland' than when it inappropriately clings to Andrew Marvell, cherry-cheeked, caught in the tendrils of his vines and melons. He shall be, therefore, the British Aristides in those moments of midsummer solitude; at least, the heavy phrase shall then have the smile it never sought.

Marvell can be tedious in these gardens—tedious with every ingenuity, refinement, and assiduity of invention. When he intends to flatter the owner of the 'Hill and Grove at Billborow,' he is most deliberately silly, not as the eighteenth century was silly, but with a peculiar innocence. Unconsciousness there was not, assuredly, but the artificial phrases of Marvell had never been used by a Philistine, the artifices are freshly absurd, the cowardice before the plain face of commonplace is not vulgar, there is an evident simple pleasure in the successful evasion of simplicity, and all the anxiety of the poet comes to a happy issue before our eyes. He commends the Billborow hill because 'the stiffest compass could not strike' a more symmetrical and equal semi-circle than its form presents, and he rebukes the absent mountains because they deform the earth and affright the heavens. This hill, he says, with a little better fancy, only 'strives to raise the plain.' Lord Fairfax, to whose glory these virtues of the soil are dedicated, and whose own merit they illustrate, is then said to be admirable for the modesty whereby, having a hill, he has also a clump of trees on the top, wherein to sequester the honours of eminence. It is not too much to say that the whole of this poem is untouched by poetry [cf. No. 42].

So is almost that equally ingenious piece, 'Appleton House,' addressed to the same friend. It chanced that Appleton House was small, and out of this plain little fact the British Aristides contrives to turn a sedulous series of compliments with fair success and with a most guileless face. What natural humility in the house-holder who builds in proportion to his body, and is contented like the tortoise and the bird! Further on, however, it appears that the admired house had been a convent, and that to the dis-possessed nuns was due the praise of proportion; they do not get it, in any form, from Marvell. A pretty passage follows, on the wasting of gardens, and a lament over the passing away of some earlier England:

[Quotes ll. 331–2, 335–6.]

Moreover, there is a peaceful couplet about the cattle:

[Quotes ll. 463–4.]

But nothing here is of the really fine quality of 'The Picture of T.C.,' or 'The Garden,' or 'The Nymph Complaining of the Death of Her Fawn.'

In those three the presence of a furtive irony of the gentlest kind is the sure sign that they came of the visitings of the unlooked-for muse aforesaid. Marvell rallies his own 'Nymph,' rallies his own soul for her clapping[1] of silver wings in the solitude of summer trees; and more sweetly does he pretend to offer to the little girl 'T.C.' the prophetic homage of the habitual poets:

[Quotes ll. 15–18, 23–4.]

Charmingly then he asks the child, where she sits painted in the midst of flowers, to 'reform the errors of the spring,' to make that the tulips may have their part of sweetness, 'seeing they are fair'; that violets may have a longer age, and—inevitably—that the roses may be disarmed of thorns. And still more charmingly he warns 'T.C.' to spare the buds in her flower gathering lest an angry Flora, seeing her infants killed, should take the cruel example,

> And, ere we see,
> Nip, in the blossom, all our hopes in thee. [ll. 39–40]

---

[1] The reading 'claps its silver wings' for 'combs' ('The Garden,' l. 54) probably derives from the edition of Cooke followed by Thompson and others though it had appeared earlier in Tonson's *Miscellany* (1716). See n. 11 of the Introduction.

The noble phrase of the 'Horatian Ode' is not recovered again high or low throughout Marvell's book, if we except one single splendid and surpassing passage from 'The Definition of Love.' The hopeless lover speaks:—

> Magnanimous despair alone
> Could show me so divine a thing. [ll. 5–6]

'To His Coy Mistress' is the only piece, not already named, altogether fine enough for an anthology. The Satires are, of course, out of reach for their inordinate length. The celebrated Satire on Holland certainly makes the utmost of the fun to be easily found in the physical facts of the country whose people 'with mad labour fished the land to shore.' The Satire on 'Flecno' makes the utmost of another joke we know of—that of famine. Flecno, it will be remembered, was a poet, and poor; but the joke of his bad verses was hardly needed, so fine does Marvell find that of his hunger. Perhaps there is no age of English satire that does not give forth the sound of that laughter unknown to savages—that craven laughter.

(b) Extract from 'The Fault of the Dutch,' *Pall Mall Gazette*, 68 (3 May 1899), p. 4.

Charles II. has been cheered; the feat is done, the dismay is imagined with joy. But his was a dismal time. Plague, fire, the arrears of pension from the French King remembered and claimed from the restored throne of England, and the Dutch in the Medway—all this was disaster. None the less, having the vanity of new clothes and a pretty figure, did we—especially by the mouth of Andrew Marvell—deride our victors, making sport of the Philistines with a proper national sense of enjoyment of such physical disabilities, or such natural difficulties, or such misfavour of fortune, as may beset the alien.

Especially were the denials of fortune matter for merriment. They are so still; or they were so certainly in the day when a great novelist found the smallness of some South German States to be the subject of unsating banter. The German scenes at the end of 'Vanity Fair,' for example, may prove how much the ridicule of mere smallness, fewness, poverty (and not even real poverty, privation, but the poverty that shows in comparison with the gold of great States, and is properly in proportion) rejoiced the sense of humour in a writer and moralist, who intended to teach mankind to be less worldly. In Andrew Marvell's day they were even more candid. The poverty of privation itself was provocative of the sincere laughter of the inmost man, the true, infrequent laughter of the heart. Marvell, the Horatian, laughed that very laughter—at leanness, at hunger, cold, and solitude— in the face of the world, and in the name of literature, in one memorable satire. I speak of 'Flecno, an English Priest in Rome,' wherein nothing is spared—not the smallness of the lodging, nor the lack of a bed, nor the scantness of clothing, nor the fast.

This basso-rilievo of a man [l. 63]—

personal meagreness is the first joke and the last.

It is not to be wondered at that he should find in the smallness of the country of Holland matter for a cordial jest. But, besides the smallness, there was that accidental and natural disadvantage in regard to the sea. In the Venetians, commerce with the sea, conflict with the sea, a victory over the sea, and the ensuing peace—albeit a less instant battle and a more languid victory— were confessed to be noble; in the Dutch they were grotesque. 'With mad labour,' says Andrew Marvell, with the spirited consciousness of the citizen of a country well above ground and free to watch the labour at leisure, 'with mad labour' did the Dutch 'fish the land to shore':

[Quotes ll. 17–22.]

It is done with a real and jolly wit, and in what admirable couplets!

The fish oft-times the burgher dispossessed,
And sat, not as a meat, but as a guest. [ll. 29–30]

We have lost something more than the delighted laughter of Marvell, more than his practical joke, and more than the heart that was light in so burly a frame—we have lost with these the wild humour that wore so well the bonds of two equal lines, and was wild with so much order, invention, malice, gaiety, polish, equilibrium, and vitality—in a word, the Couplet, the couplet of the past. We who cannot stand firm within two lines, but must slip beyond and between the boundaries, who tolerate the couplets of Keats and imitate them, should praise the day of Charles II. because of Marvell's art, and not for love of the sorry reign. We had plague, fire, and the Dutch in the Medway, but we had the couplet; and there were also the measures of those more poetic poets, hitherto called somewhat slightingly the Cavalier poets, who matched the wit of the Puritan with a spirit simpler and less mocking.

85.   George Saintsbury's comments on Marvell

1898

Journalist, critic, and academician, George Saintsbury (1845–1933) published extensively on English and French literature. His *Short History of English Literature*, published in 1898, was to be reprinted many times.

Extract from *A Short History of English Literature* (New York, 1919), pp. 425–6.

The life of Andrew Marvell and his work both fall into two sharply divided and curiously contrasted sections. In the first he is a quiet student, a passionate lyrical poet of love and nature, and if of Puritan learnings and surroundings, gently inclined to what is noble in the other side; in the second he is, perhaps an austere patriot, certainly a violent politician, and poetically a ferocious lampooner in rough couplets. We may confine ourselves here to his earlier, and as literature better, period. He was born in 1621 at Winestead, not far from Hull, and went early to Cambridge, where he took his Bachelor's but not his Master's degree. He seems to have travelled a good deal, but we find him in 1649 at home, contributing to the collection of elegies on Lord Hastings which saw Dryden's first work, and being the friend of Richard Lovelace. Indeed, the splendid lines on the execution of Charles I., and others, show him as at least partly Royalist at this time. In 1650, however, Fairfax made him his daughter's tutor, and for this reason or that Marvell seems to have changed his politics. He was long resident with his young pupil at Nun Appleton, in Yorkshire, and wrote there much of his most delightful verse. Becoming an admirer of Cromwell and a friend of Milton, he entered Parliament even before the Restoration, and sat for Hull till his death in 1678. For some years he was abroad doing diplomatic work, but latterly he fell more and more into Opposition.

His best, and indeed his only really, poetical work was done before he had reached middle life, and exhibits, with a form individual and in a type more chastened and classical, the best characteristics of the Cavalier poets. The exquisite octosyllables of the long poem on 'Appleton House,' and the shorter and still better known ones on 'The Bermudas' and 'The Nymph regretting the loss of her Fawn,' unite Jonson's art with Herrick's grace. 'The Coronet,' in style between Crashaw and Vaughan, is free from the rococo ornament of the first and the tongue-tied inequality of the second; the passionate magnificence of the Amorists, whom Milton so tastelessly scorned, has no nobler examples than 'To his Coy Mistress,' and still more 'The Definition of Love,' with its splendid beginning—

> My love is of a birth as rare
>   As 'tis for object, strange and high—
> It was begotten of Despair
>   Upon Impossibility;

and the majesty in style of the 'Horatian Ode' (to Cromwell, but containing the lines on his victim) is among the noblest and most individual of the kind in English. Nor can it be said that Marvell, like most of his school and time, wrote unequally; so that it is only curious that he did not write more. But perhaps it is not fanciful to argue that the peculiar and indeed unique perfection of phrase characterising the best poetry of this period involved a kind of mental effort of gestation which could not be repeated very often, and which obliged the poet to be either unequal or else infertile.

86.   H.C. Beeching on the lyrics

1901

H. C. Beeching (1859–1919) was a churchman and a man of letters. His essay with its historical survey of Marvell's *fortuna* signals in his own words 'the recent rise into fame' of the lyric poet. Despite an occasional idiosyncratic judgment (as on the 'Horatian Ode'), he is a sensitive critic.

Extract from the *National Review*, 37 (July 1901), pp. 747–59.

Any one who wished to defend the thesis that our own generation, however it may fall below its predecessors in outstanding poetical genius, is markedly their superior in poetical taste, might find matter for his argument in the recent rise into fame of the lyrical verse of Marvell. It may be interesting to trace the progress of this growth of appreciation.

In 1681, three years after Marvell's death, a well printed folio was brought out by his widow containing all his poetry that existed in manuscript, except the political pieces, which, as the Stuarts were still upon the throne, could not be published with safety. Of this book no second edition was called for. In 1726 a literary hack, one Thomas Cooke, who translated Hesiod, and for attacking Pope was rewarded with immortality:

> From these the world will judge of men and books,
> Not from the Burnets, Oldmixons, and Cookes,
>   [Epistle to Dr. Arbuthnot, ll. 145–6]

issued an edition of Marvell's poems including the political satires, and rests Marvell's fame almost exclusively on political grounds. 'My design,' he says, 'in this is to draw a pattern for all freeborn *Englishmen*, in the life of a worthy Patriot, whose every Action has truely merited to him, with *Aristides*, the surname of the *Just*.' How little capable Cooke was of appreciating any of the distinctive qualities of Marvell's verse may be judged from

284

the poems he singles out for special praise. 'If we have any which may be properly said to come finished from his Hands, they are these, "On Milton's Paradise Lost," "On Blood's Stealing the Crown," and "A Dialogue between two Horses."'

Just fifty years after Cooke's pretty little edition, there appeared another in three great quarto volumes by an editor as little competent to appreciate Marvell's peculiar charm as his predecessor; though he, like Cooke, was a poet in his way. This was Edward Thompson, a captain in the Royal Navy, who was interested in the fame of Marvell, from being himself a native of Hull, and also on the political side, from his friendship with Wilkes. Thompson puts on his title-page some lines from his namesake of *The Seasons*, 'Hail, Independence, Hail,' &c.; and dedicates his volumes to the Mayor and Aldermen of Hull as the 'Friends of Liberty and England'; professing that his labour was undertaken to show his esteem for 'a person who had been a general friend to mankind, a public one to his country, and a partial and strenuous one to the town of Hull.' Thompson's gifts as a critic may be estimated from his assigning to Marvell not only Addison's hymn, 'The Spacious Firmament on High,' which at least is in Marvell's metre, if not in his manner, but also Mallet's 'William and Margaret,' a poem that could not have been written before Allan Ramsay's publications had revived interest in the old Scots ballads. Thompson had found these poems with others in a manuscript book, some part of which he declared to be in Marvell's handwriting; and of this fact he would have been a very competent judge from his familiarity with the many letters of Marvell written to his constituents at Hull, which he printed in his edition. From this invaluable autograph he set up his text. 'Afterwards, as rare things will, it vanished.' But it restored to the world the poem by which Marvell is generally known, 'An Horatian Ode upon Cromwell's Return from Ireland.' I must not speak here about Captain Thompson, but I may perhaps be allowed to say I have come to regard his volumes with much more interest since reading in the *Cornhill Magazine* for May 1868 some extracts from a manuscript journal of his kept in the year 1783–5. The only entry there precisely bearing on our subject is the following, under date 1784, 'A nephew of Emma's [his mistress] was named by me Andrew Marvell; when he comes to reason, the name may inspire him to be virtuous.' This would show, if more evidence were needed, that it was mainly on the political side that Marvell interested the Captain. His own poetical effusions were chiefly squibs and epigrams, and what he well called 'Meretricious Miscellanies.' The list of subscribers to Thompson's volumes tells the same tale. It includes the Duke of G—, the Marquis of Granby, the Earl of Shelburne and other Whig peers, the Lord Mayor of London (Sawbridge), and a dozen Members of Parliament, among them Burke, and such stalwarts as Wilkes and Oliver. It includes, more remarkably, the notorious Rigby, who was said by the wits to have bequeathed by his will 'near half a million of public money.' Learning is represented by that stout republican, Thomas Hollis, and by Daines Barrington the antiquary and naturalist, and correspondent of White of Selborne, who, according to Charles Lamb, was so much the friend of gardens that he paid the gardener at the Temple twenty shillings to poison the sparrows. But literature has only a few names. There is the Rev. Prebendary Mason, his friend the eccentric Dr. Glynn, who once wrote a prize poem, Mrs. Macaulay, and Mr. William Woty. Samuel Johnson, LL.D., is conspicuous by absence. The theatre (for Captain Thompson was himself something of a playwright) contributes David Garrick, Esq., Samuel Foote, Esq., and Mr. Colman; and among other personal friends of the editor is the notorious John Stevenson Hall, better known as Hall Stevenson. This worthy and the Duke of Cumberland (Henry Augustus), who heads the list, may have been attracted by the indelicacy of the satires, hardly by anything else.

Eleven years after Thompson's edition of Marvell, appeared that very interesting book, ominous of the dawn of a new era, *Selected Beauties of Ancient English Poetry*, by Henry Headley, A. B., an enthusiastic young clergyman with genuine taste for the seventeenth-century poets. He revived the memory of Drayton and Daniel, whom he praises with discrimination, quoting from the former the now famous sonnet, 'Since there's no help, come let us kiss and part'; and he has a good word to say for Drummond, Browne, Carew and Crashaw; but Marvell is not mentioned.[1] Four years later, however, Marvell makes his appearance in George Ellis's *Specimens of the Early English Poets*, where he is spoken of as 'an accomplished man who, though *principally* distin-

---

[1] As mentioned in the Introduction, Headley chastizes Johnson for excluding Marvell from the *Lives of the English Poets*, but he does not include him in his own *Select Beauties* ....

guished by his inflexible patriotism, was generally and justly
admired for his learning, his acuteness in controversial writing,
his wit, *and* his poetical talents.' Ellis represents him by extracts
from 'Daphnis and Chloe,' and 'Young Love,' which is much as
if the author of the 'Ancient Mariner' and 'Kubla Khan' should
be represented by the song 'If I had but two little wings.' I do not
recall any reference to Marvell in Coleridge,[1] and Wordsworth
quotes him only as a patriot:

> The later Sidney, Marvell, Harrington,
> Young Vane, and others who called Milton friend. [See No. 40]

It was Charles Lamb who made the discovery of Marvell's merit
as a lyrical poet.[2] In his essay upon the Old Benchers of the Inner
Temple, printed in the *London Magazine* for September 1821, he
quotes, *apropos* of the Temple sun-dial, four stanzas from 'The
Garden,' and says of them that they 'are full, as all his serious
poetry was, of a witty delicacy.' The phrase has become classical,
as it deserves. The most popular anthology of the last half of the
century has been Mr. Palgrave's *Golden Treasury of Songs and Lyrics*,
and this shows, in its later editions, a curious and interesting
growth in appreciation of Marvell. When the first edition appeared,
in 1861, it contained three poems of his, 'The Horatian Ode,'
'The Garden,' and 'The Bermudas.' In 1883, there was added an
extract from 'The Nymph complaining for the Death of her
Fawn,' with a note saying 'Perhaps no poem in this collection is
more delicately fancied, more exquisitely finished'; and in 1891
room was found for 'The Picture of Little T. C. in a Prospect of
Flowers.' With five poems in so small and picked a collection,
Marvell's popular reputation as a lyric poet may be reckoned to
have culminated.

Marvell was born in 1621, the son of a celebrated preacher who
was also master of the Grammar School of Hull, where the boy
was educated. He proceeded to Cambridge, took his degree, and
then travelled in Holland, France, Italy, and Spain. When he

[1] Items 702–8 in Vol. I of the Notebooks, ed. K. Coburn (New York, 1957) include jottings
from the RT.
[2] Although this statement is frequently made even at this late date and Lamb's phrase
'witty delicacy' frequently quoted, the credit, it seems, should go to others, including
Hazlitt (No. 45), Hunt (No. 46), and in particular the anonymous critic in the *Retrospective
Review* (No. 47), followed by John Dove (No. 50) and Hartley Coleridge (No. 52).

returned to England he was engaged by Lord Fairfax as tutor to his daughter Mary, and it is to the time that he spent in retirement in Fairfax's house at Nun Appleton in Yorkshire, perhaps from 1650 to 1653, that we owe the best of his lyrical works. Before this he had written one or two things in rhymed couplets, a preface to Lovelace's *Lucasta*, a copy of verses on Lord Hastings' death, full of wit, and with lines here and there that haunt the memory, like—

> Go stand between the morning and the flowers [l. 5];

and in 1650 was composed the Horatian Ode; but whether any of the lyrics in octosyllables are of an earlier date than these cannot be determined. It will be best, then, to waive all question of chronological precedence, and look at the poems in groups according to their subject. But a word may first be said about the poet's models. He had two; we might call them his good and bad angels. They were John Milton, whose volume of lyrics appeared in 1645, and John Donne, whose poems were not printed during his lifetime, but were widely circulated in manuscript. Donne, one of the most remarkable among seventeenth-century Englishmen of genius, had one of the greatest poetical virtues and two of the greatest poetical vices. His virtue was passion, intensity; his vices were a too cavalier indifference to accent, and a love of quaint and extravagant conceits. Marvell is the pupil of his intensity, and to a certain degree of his extravagance; but he was saved from his careless writing by the study of Milton. The best example of Marvell's work in the manner of Donne is the lyric entitled 'The Fair Singer.' The breathless haste of the rhythm, and the absence of any pause except at the end of the lines, are studied after that master; so is the ingenuity of the idea. The first line of the poem, 'To make a final conquest of all me,' is Donne pure and simple. But even in this poem there is a regularity of measure which betrays the influence of the other school, that of Ben Jonson and Milton:

> I could have fled from one but singly fair;
> My disentangled soul itself might save,
> Breaking the curled trammels of her hair;
> But how should I avoid to be her slave
> Whose subtle art invisibly can wreathe
> My fetters of the very air I breathe! [ll. 7–12]

Of the fantastic and forced images that Marvell copied from Donne it will suffice to offer a single example. In the 'Dialogue between the Soul and the Body' he makes the body say:

> O who shall me deliver whole
> From bonds of this tyrannic soul,
> Which stretched upright impales me so
> That mine own precipice I go! [ll. 11–14]

The poem called 'Eyes and Tears,' which is full of the same sort of thing, is, I suspect, an exercise, the inspiration of which may be traced to the appearance of Crashaw's poem of 'The Weeper' in his volume of 1646. As a rule, Marvell's humour saved him from the worst banalities of this school; as a rule, also, he keeps his fantastic *tours de force* for semi-humorous passages, and often uses these, by way of contrast, to heighten the outburst of passion that follows. Thus, in the poem 'Upon Appleton House,' he compares Fairfax's garden to a fort:

[Quotes ll. 309–20.]

And then, while the reader is still smiling, he finds himself in the midst of a passionate apostrophe to England:

> Oh, thou, that dear and happy isle,
> The garden of the world erewhile,
> Thou Paradise of the four seas
> Which Heaven planted us to please;
> But, to exclude the world, did guard
> With watery, if not flaming, sword,—
> What luckless apple did we taste
> To make us mortal, and thee waste? [ll. 321–8]

The influence of Milton may be traced in the fine sense of form generally, and, in particular, in the use of the octosyllabic couplet. Occasionally we seem to hear an echo of Milton's airy grace, as in the couplet:

> Near this a fountain's liquid bell
> Tinkles within the concave shell.
> ['Clorinda and Damon,' ll. 13–14]

But this is only occasional. Marvell is much more rigid in his rhythms than Milton, and he never attained to Milton's simplicity. That he had read him with care is evident; and there are a few direct reminiscences in the 'First Anniversary,' such as the phrase 'beaked promontories,' and the lines—

the dragon's tail
Swindges the volumes of its horrid flail [ll. 151–2]

and

Unto the kingdom blest of peace and love. [l. 218]

A more interesting reminiscence is the line in 'The Garden'—

Waves in its plumes the various light [l. 56],

which is certainly an echo of the difficult line in 'Il Penseroso,'

Waves at his wings in aery stream [l. 148],

though it throws no light upon its interpretation. But too much must not be made of these imitations. After all, Milton was Milton, and Marvell was Marvell; and what survives to charm us in Marvell is what he gives us of his own. Let me briefly summarise some of the elements in this charm.

The first quality to strike a reader who takes up Marvell's book is his extraordinary terseness. Look, for example, at the poem with which the only good modern edition, that of Mr. G.A. Aitken, opens, 'Appleton House.' The poet wishes to praise the house for not being too big, like most country-houses of the time, and this is how he does it:

Within this sober frame expect
Work of no foreign architect,
That unto caves the quarries drew,
And forests did to pastures hew.

If this were 'transprosed,' it would have to run something as follows: 'Our boasted Italian architects make houses so huge that by drawing the stone for them they hollow out quarries into caves, and cut down whole forests for timber so that they become pastures.' As a part of the same skill it is remarkable in how few strokes he can paint a picture. In this same poem, describing a copse, he says:

Dark all without it knits; within
It opens passable and thin [ll. 505–6],

which gives exactly the difference of impression from without and upon entering. A second notable quality in Marvell's verse is its sensuousness, its wide and deep enjoyment of the world of sense. 'The Garden,' which everybody knows, may stand as the best example of this quality—

> Stumbling on melons as I pass
> Ensnared with flowers, I fall on grass [ll. 39–40]

Marvell is the laureate of grass, and of greenery. A third excellent quality is his humour, to which I have already referred, sometimes showing itself as intellectual wit, or as irony or sarcasm. Still keeping to 'Appleton House,' one may notice the ingenuity of the suggestion of Fairfax's generosity—

> A stately frontispiece of *poor*
> Adorns without the open door [ll. 65–6],

or the deprecation of over-large houses:

> What need of all this marble crust
> To impark the wanton mole [*sic*] of dust;
> That thinks by breadth the world to unite,
> Tho' the first builders failed in height. [ll. 21–4]

Once or twice the humour runs to coarseness when it allies itself with the bitter Puritanism of the time, as in the picture of the nuns defending their house:

> Some to the breach against their foes
> Their wooden saints in vain oppose;
> Another bolder stands at push,
> With their old holy-water brush. [ll. 249–52]

But most characteristic of all the qualities of Marvell's verse is what Lamb well spoke of as his 'witty delicacy'—his delicate invention. The shining and unapproachable instances of this delicacy are 'The Nymph complaining for the death of her Fawn' and 'The picture of little T.C.' The former of these pieces is often hyperbolic in fancy, but the hyperbole fits the pastoral remoteness of the setting; the second needs not even this apology. It is a masterpiece in a *genre* where masterpieces are rare, though attempts are not infrequent. Prior, Waller, and Sedley have tried the theme with a certain success, but their pieces lack the romantic note. 'The Picture of Little T.C.' has this to perfection; it has not a weak line in it, and moves through its five stanzas, each more exquisite than the last, to its admirably mock-serious close:

[Quotes ll. 25–40.]

One other quality of Marvell's lyrical writing remains to be noticed, which is somewhat difficult to fix with a name, unless we call it *gusto*. We imagine him smiling to himself as he writes, smiling at his own fancies, or his own sensuousness, or happy turns. He wrote, we are sure, for his own pleasure quite as much as for ours. I remember the remark being made to me that 'The Bermudas,' for a religious poem, went pretty far in the way of self-indulgence. And so it does. Lastly, it cannot fail to be noted that Marvell was an artist, with an artist's love of making experiments. Perhaps he never attained perfect facility, but he is never amateurish.

Among the various groups into which his lyrical poetry divides itself, the least satisfactory is that whose theme is love. Marvell's love-poetry has, with the exception of one piece, as little passion as Cowley's, while it is as full of conceits. 'The Unfortunate Lover' is probably the worst love-poem ever written by a man of genius. 'The Definition of Love' is merely a study after Donne's 'Valediction.' Cleverer and more original, and somewhat more successful, is 'The Gallery.' The two opposite sides of one long picture-gallery into which the chambers of his heart have been thrown by breaking down partitions are supposed to be covered with portraits of his lady. On the one side she is drawn in such characters as Aurora and Venus; on the other as an enchanter and a murderess.

Marvell was the friend of Milton, and one conjectures that, like his respected friend, he also may have had theories as to the true relation of these sexes which interfered with the spontaneous expression of feeling. There is, nevertheless, one poem in which passion is allowed to take its most natural path, although even in it one feels that the poet is expressing the passion of the human race rather than his own individual feeling; and the passion being, as often in Marvell, masked and heightened by his wit, the effect is singularly striking: indeed, as a love-poem 'To his Coy Mistress' is unique. It could never be the most popular of Marvell's poems, but for sheer power I should be disposed to rank it higher than anything he ever wrote. He begins with hyperbolical protestations to his mistress of the slow and solemn state with which their wooing should be conducted, if only time and space were their servants and not their masters

[Quotes ll. 1–10.]

Each beauty also of face and feature should have its special and age-long praise—

> But at my back I always hear
> Time's winged chariot hurrying near;
> And yonder all before us lie
> Deserts of vast eternity. [ll. 21–4]

> The grave's a fine and private place,
> But none I think do there embrace. [ll. 31–2]

A second division of Marvell's lyric poetry has for its subject religion. The most curious of the religious poems are the pastorals 'Clorinda and Damon,' and 'Thyrsis and Dorinda.' Despite their obvious artificiality I must confess that these poems give me pleasure, perhaps because religious poetry is apt to be shapeless, and these, in point of form, are admirable. It is matter for regret that in the first of the two Marvell should have made the nymph sensual and the swain pious; but the friend of Milton, as I have already suggested, probably shared his low views of the female sex. And then the conversion of the lady is sudden and leaves something to desire in its motive. In 'Thyrsis and Dorinda' the two young things talk together so sweetly of Elysium that they drink opium in order to lose no time in getting there. More genuine in feeling, and more religious in the ordinary sense of the word, are two dialogues: one between the 'Resolved Soul and Created Pleasure,' the other between 'Soul and Body.' The form of the first is noteworthy. The octosyllabic stanzas are alternately unshortened and shortened, the Soul speaking in serious iambics and Pleasure in dancing trochees; and the allurements of sense rise in a well-conceived scale from mere softness through art up to the pleasures of knowledge. The dialogue between Soul and Body is a brilliant duel, each party accusing the other of his proper woes; and except for the one terrible line I quoted above, the poem is an excellent piece of writing. But religious passion sounds a higher and less artificial strain in a pair of odes, the one 'On a Drop of Dew,' in which the soul is compared to the dewdrop upon a leaf, which reflects heaven and is reluctant to coalesce with its environment; the other called 'The Coronet,' an apology for religious poetry on the ground that because it admits art it

ANDREW MARVELL

leaves room for the artist's pride. 'The Coronet' is interesting as
a study in Herbert's manner, and contains one line of exquisite
modesty:

> Through every garden, every mead,
> I gather flowers (my fruits are only flowers). [ll. 5–6]

But the ode 'On a Drop of Dew' is by far the finer. The ideas
are evolved after the manner of Donne, but the rhythm is slower
and more contemplative.

[Quotes ll. 1–30.]

A third and final division of Marvell's lyrics would comprise his
poems upon nature; and here we have Marvell at his best, because
here he lets his passion inspire him. Except in Shakespeare, who
includes 'all thoughts, all passions, all desires' we have but little
passion for nature between Chaucer and Marvell; but in Marvell
the love for natural beauty is not short of passion. Of course his
love is not for wild nature—a feeling which only dates from Gray
and Wordsworth—but for the ordinary country scenes:

> Fragrant gardens, shady woods,
> Deep meadows and transparent floods
> ['Appleton House,' ll. 79–80];

and for these he brings the eye of a genuine lover and, what is
more, of a patient observer. The lines upon 'Appleton House'
are full of observation. He speaks of the 'shining eye' of the
'hatching throstle,' and has a fine imaginative description of the
woodpecker:

[Quotes ll. 539–50.]

In his poem called 'The Garden' Marvell has sung a palinode
that for richness of phrasing in its sheer sensuous love of garden
delights is perhaps unmatchable. At the same time the most
devout lover of gardens must agree with Marvell that even in a
garden the pleasures of the mind are greater than those of the
sense. The poet's thought, as he lies in the shade, can create a
garden for himself far more splendid and also imperishable; as
indeed, in this poem, it has done:

[Quotes ll. 41–56.]

294

Next to 'The Garden' as a descriptive poem must rank the 'Bermudas.' Marvell's 'Bermudas' are not 'still vexed' like Shakespeare's but an earthly paradise. His interest in these islands arose from meeting at Eton, while he was there as tutor to a ward of Cromwell's, a certain John Oxenbridge, who had been one of the exiles thither for conscience sake. The poem is built upon the same plan as 'The Garden'; first, the sensuous delights are described as no one but Marvell could describe them:

[Quotes ll. 17–24.]

And then he passes on, though in this case it must be allowed with much less effect, to the spiritual advantages of the place. We may note in passing that Mr. Palgrave in his 'Golden Treasury' has taken the extraordinary liberty of altering the arrangement of some of the early lines, perhaps through not understanding their construction as they stand. In the folio and all the early editions the lines run as follows:

> What should we do but sing His praise
> That led us through the watery maze,
> Unto an isle so long unknown
> And yet far kinder than our own?
> Where He the huge sea-monsters wracks
> That lift the deep upon their backs,
> He lands *us* on a grassy stage
> Safe from the storms and prelates' rage.

Mr. Palgrave prints lines 5 and 6 before lines 3 and 4, thereby breaking up the arrangement of the line into quatrains, apparently not seeing that 'where' is equivalent to 'whereas,' and that the safety of the exiles is contrasted with the wrecking of the sea-monsters. But to have introduced Marvell's verse to so wide a public should atone to the poet's *manes* for such an injury; especially as the Puck which sits ever upon the pen of commentators has already avenged it by making Mr. Palgrave append to the poem the following note: 'Emigrants supposed to be driven *towards America* by the government of Charles I.' There is no hint in the poem that the 'small boat' was bringing the emigrants across the Atlantic, or that they were describing the newly-discovered islands by the gift of prophecy.

Of the patriotic verse, which in its own way is full of interest, it is impossible to speak in this paper; except of the one poem which

can claim to be a lyric, the 'Horatian ode upon Cromwell's return
from Ireland.' As was said above, this ode was first published in
Captain Thomson's edition, and so must take its stand as Marvell's
only by the weight of internal evidence. But that evidence is
conspicuous in every line. The poem runs on in a somewhat
meandering and self-indulgent course, like all Marvell's longer
poems. But many details are recognisably in Marvell's vein.
The stroke of cleverness about King Charles's head being as
lucky as that which was found when they were digging the foundations of Rome, and the fun he pokes at the Scotch and Irish are
certainly Marvell. So is the view taken that Cromwell made a
great sacrifice in renouncing a private life, which we get also in
Marvell's prose; so is the touch about Cromwell's garden:

> where
> He lived reserved and austere,
> (As if his highest plot
> To plant the bergamot.) [ll. 29–32]

So also is the remarkable detachment from political prejudice, of
which the verses prefixed to the cavalier poet Lovelace's *Lucasta*,
about the same date, afford another instance, a detachment that
would have been impossible for the author of 'Lycidas.' Even
now, in an age which boasts of its tolerant spirit, it gives one a
shock to remember that the stanzas about Charles, which present
the very image of the cavalier saint and martyr, come in a poem
to the honour and glory of the man to whom he owed his death.

[Quotes ll. 57–64.]

These two stanzas are now the only part of the ode that is remembered, and with justice; for the rest of the poem, although in form
and spirit it is Horatian, yet it has little of the *curiosa felicitas* of
Horace's diction to make it memorable.[1] But in these two stanzas
the diction has attained to the happiness of consummated simplicity. They recall the two stanzas at the close of the fifth ode in the
third book in which Horace draws a picture of the martyred
Regulus:

> Atque sciebat, quae sibi barbarus
> Tortor pararet: non aliter tamen

[1] For an opposite assertion, see No. 92.

Dimovit obstantes propinquos,
Et populum reditus morantem,
Quam si clientum longa negotia
Dijudicata lite relinqueret,
Tendens Venafranos in agros
Aut Lacedaemonium Tarentum.[1]

87. An anonymous review article on Marvell's prose style

1902

Reviewing Edward Dowden's volume *Puritan and Anglican* (1900) and Sir Henry Craik's edition of *English Prose Selections* (see No. 15), the anonymous commentator compares Milton's and Marvell's prose styles.

Extract from the *Quarterly Review*, 196 (July 1902), pp. 91, 99.

If we wish to sustain the comparison [between French and English prose writers], we must have recourse to those of our authors who flourished before the Restoration, when England, instead of being, from a literary point of view, almost a province of France, was a powerful and independent nation with a literature almost equal to that of Greece in the age of Pericles. This brings us to the main purpose of our essay. That England held a supreme position in dramatic and lyrical poetry for fifty years in the reigns

---

[1] *Odes* 3.5.49–56:

> Yet when the barb'rous hangman did devise
> For him, he knew: yet he no otherwise
> His remorating kindred did adjourne,
> And all the people stopping his returne,
> Then if, the terme being done, he did withdraw
> From all his clients tedious suits of Law,
> To the Venafran fields taking his way,
> Or to Tarentum of Laconia.
> (Trans. Henry Rider, 1638)

297

of Elizabeth and James I would hardly now be denied. We also wish to show, by a brief review of the earlier seventeenth-century writers, that our finest prose style arose amongst the great Elizabethans, and survived and continuously developed until the reign of Charles II; and that, had no disastrous change then occurred, there would probably have been permanently established in England, not only a style capable of every variety of eloquence, but also a secondary diction, terser and more idiomatic, alert and effective than that which we owe to the labours of Dr. Johnson. To those who study literature apart from history, the time following the death of Shakespeare may seem to be a period of decadence due to the exhaustion of national creative force. But, even as regards poetry, it appears to us to have been an age that in itself was still full of promise; a brilliant dawn that was suddenly overcast with storm-clouds as it was turning into the clear and equable light of day. The Renaissance, with its promise of general culture and fresh developments of the literary spirit, was obscured by the religious and political disturbances arising out of the Reformation.

In order to discern how little Milton's style represented the real development of the prose in his age, we have only to contrast it with Andrew Marvell's. Until the publication of 'Paradise Lost' placed its author beyond all comparison, Milton and Marvell might have ranked together as poets, not in the sense that they were equal, but for the unrivalled perfection which they had each attained in two different kinds of poetry; Milton representing the clearness and simplicity of the older style, and Marvell, with all his wit and gracefulness, the extravagance of a later style that was already antiquated. In the art of prose, however, there had been real improvement; and the positions were reversed—Milton, who adopted the manner of the older writers, being extravagant and obsolete, and Marvell, who used the diction of his day, being clear, direct, and effective.

298

88. W. J. Courthope on 'The First Anniversary'

1903

In his well-known six-volume *History of English Poetry* (1895–1910), W. J. Courthope (1842–1917) presents a very general account of the poetry except for his remarks on 'The First Anniversary.'

Extract from 'Cavalier and Roundhead' in the *History of English Poetry* (1903), III, pp. 312–16.

Marvell continued to be the spokesman of Justice against Fate, and he devoted the finest passage of [the 'Horatian Ode'] to the praise of the leader of the lost cause, in the celebrated lines describing the demeanour of Charles on the scaffold. In the noble conclusion of the *Ode*, recalling Horace's *Qualem ministrum* [*Odes* 4.4], we see that Marvell's admiration for Cromwell is grounded on the greatness of the latter as the representative of England: [quotes ll. 97–120]. This genuine admiration for Cromwell as a man runs through the panegyric on *The First Anniversary of the Government under his Highness the Lord Protector*; and that Marvell's opinions were not inspired by any sympathy with the Parliamentary cause as such is clearly shown in the Cleveland-like lines in which he lashes the Fifth-Monarchy men of the 'Rump':—

> Accursed locusts, whom your king does spit
> Out of the centre of the unbottomed pit;
> Wanderers, adulterers, liars, Münster's rest,
> Sorcerers, atheists, Jesuits possest!
> You, who the Scriptures and the laws deface
> With the same liberty as points and lace;
> O race most hypocritically strict!
> Bent to reduce us to the ancient Pict,
> Well may you act the Adam and the Eve,
> Aye, and the serpent too, that did deceive. [ll. 311–20]

299

There is pathos and nobility in the following description of Cromwell's look in death:—

> I saw him dead: a leaden slumber lies,
> And mortal sleep over those wakeful eyes;
> Those gentle rays under the lids were fled,
> Which through his looks that piercing sweetness shed;
> That port which so majestic was and strong,
> Loose, and deprived of vigour, stretched along;
> All withered, all discoloured, pale and wan,
> How much another thing, no more that man!
> O human glory vain! O Death! O wings!
> O worthless world! O transitory things!
> Yet dwelt that greatness in his shape decayed
> That still, though dead, greater than Death he laid:*
> And in his altered face you something feign
> That threatens Death he yet will live again.
>   ['On the Death of O.C.,' ll. 247–60]

It is highly instructive to compare Marvell's panegyrics on Cromwell with Waller's contemporary verses on the same subject: the capacities of the metaphysical style, as a vehicle for complimentary poetry, are thus brought out by contrast with the more familiar vein of courtly wit which the latter writer was bringing into vogue. Both poets select the same matter for treatment: order brought out of chaos; the subjugation of the Irish and the Scottish nations; the victories of the English navy; the respect paid to the Protector by the European monarchies; Cromwell's private character. Both resort to hyperbole as a necessary condition of poetical flattery. But Waller relies almost entirely on the skilful arrangement of his materials; the propriety of his classical parallels; the lucid and harmonious language in which he brings into relief the points and antitheses of his thought—as in a stanza like the following:—

> To pardon willing and to punish loath,
> You strike with one hand, but you heal with both;
> Lifting up all that prostrate lie, you grieve
> You cannot make the dead again to live.
> ['A Panegyric to my Lord Protector,' ll. 117–20]

---

* This grammatical error occurs more than once in Marvell's poems. See lines on the Death of the Fawn.

With admirable judgment, he reserves the praise of Cromwell's private character for his climax, pretending that an innate moderation would have kept the Protector in his loved retirement, if his great deeds had not been called for by his country's necessities.

Marvell, on the other hand, makes all Cromwell's actions spring out of the grandeur of his character, which he exalts in the opening of his poem. He takes for his model Donne's 'Anniversary,' and, like the founder of the metaphysical school, exhausts his ingenuity in discovering remote analogies and images to express the greatness of his hero. Cromwell, reconstructing the state of England, is likened to Amphion building Thebes by his musical harmony: the poet speculates whether the virtue of the Protector, if his subjects were but docile, might not bring in the Millennium: he likens the feelings of the nation during the Protector's illness to those of the first man on first experiencing the disappearance of the sun. The real greatness of his subject saves his poem from the grotesque disproportion of Donne's 'Anniversary,' but it is far less equally sustained than Waller's *Panegyric*: if in parts it rises into an obscure sublimity beyond what the other was capable of, it sinks in parts to ridiculous bombast, which Waller knew how to avoid. Many lines, for example, are devoted to reflections on a carriage accident which nearly proved fatal to Cromwell, whose runaway horses are feigned to have stopped of their own accord, through a consciousness of the mischief they were doing to their master and the state:

[Quotes ll. 191–200.]

These inequalities in Marvell's thought are reflected in his style. When he is at his best he writes with rare strength and harmony: witness the following lines in which Cromwell is compared to Gideon:—

> When Gideon so did from the war retreat,
> Yet, by the conquest of two kings grown great,
> He on the peace extends a warlike power,
> And Israel, silent, saw him rase the tower,
> And how he Succoth's elders durst suppress
> With thorns and briars of the wilderness.
> No king might ever such a force have done;
> Yet would he not be lord, nor yet his son. [ll. 249–56]

Perhaps more often, however, his constant straining after hyper-

301

bole leads him into elliptical, ambiguous, and obscure modes of expression; as when, describing the influences which prevent Cromwell from achieving the Millennium, he writes:—

> But men, alas! as if they nothing cared,
> Look on, all unconcerned, or unprepared;
> And stars still fall, and still the dragon's tail
> Swinges the volumes of its horrid flail;
> For the great Justice that did first suspend
> The world by sin, does by the same extend.
> Hence that blest day still counterpoisèd wastes,
> The ill delaying what the elected hastes;
> Hence, landing, Nature to new seas is tost,
> And good designs still with their authors lost. [ll. 149–58]

In some respect the career of George Wither resembles that of Marvell. Both were of a sharp satiric genius; both also possessed a vein of pastoral sweetness; both were led by circumstances to side more unhesitatingly with the Republican party in their latter days than in their youth. But Wither was one of those downright and impracticable characters which can never make allowance for their surroundings: hence neither in politics nor in art did he attain to that dignity of expression which is to be admired in the work of Marvell.

89. Stephen Gwynn on the Puritanism of the poet

1904

In a survey of authors who could be classed as 'obligatory,' the poet and critic Stephen Gwynn (1864–1950) includes Marvell only briefly in a chapter devoted to Bunyan and Butler.

Extract from 'Puritanism and the Reaction' in *The Masters of English Literature* (1904), pp. 127–9.

It is characteristic of Milton's orbed isolation that he neither belonged to nor founded a school. Among his intimates was only one man of note in letters, Andrew Marvel, who in the last years of the Protectorate was adjoined to Milton as assistant secretary. Yet, though Marvel belonged to the Puritans in politics and religion he shows nothing of the Puritan in his literature, save in his choice of subjects. Of the three noble lyrics by which he survives, one is the *Horatian Ode* on Cromwell, a second the song of the *Pilgrim Fathers*, 'Where the remote Bermoothes ride In the ocean's bosom unespied.' A third, *The Garden*, betrays more fully his true affinity in literature. Marvel might write stanzas to the author of *Paradise Lost* ('When I behold the poet blind yet bold'), but his own master was the royalist Abraham Cowley. Cowley had succeeded Donne as chief of what has been called the 'metaphysical school'—poets who revelled in strange conceits drawn from unlikely sources of knowledge. There is a trace of this mannerism in these famous lines from *The Garden*:

[Quotes ll. 41–8.]

But as fuller example of this school at its very best may be given this citation from Marvell's lines *To his Coy Mistress*:

[Quotes ll. 1–32.]

But Marvel is in no way typical of the great body of the Puritans. He stands, as Milton does, for the cultured section among them; but their preoccupations were religious rather than political, and Marvel, whose best known works in his own day were satires (now hard to read), did not write of religion. Milton wrote of religion, but from a standpoint of his own, and the poet of *Paradise Regained* attended no place of worship. The true expression of Puritan England is to be found in the writings of John Bunyan, tinker and Baptist preacher, who knew no books but the Bible and Fox's *Book of Martyrs*.

90. Augustine Birrell on Marvell

1905

Although devoting most of his energies to politics, Augustine Birrell (1850–1933) was much admired for his essays on literary topics written in a sprightly and humorous style that became characterized as 'Birrellism.' His volume *Andrew Marvell* appeared in the series 'English Men of Letters' and is largely biographical.

Extract from the final chapter entitled 'Work as a Man of Letters,' *Andrew Marvell* (1905), pp. 225–8, 231–2. (For his earlier remarks [p. 68] on the 'Horatian Ode,' see No. 92, where they are quoted.)

Marvell's work as a man of letters easily divides itself into the inevitable three parts. *First*, as a poet properly so called; *Second*, as a political satirist using rhyme; and *Third*, as a writer of prose.

Upon Marvell's work as a poet properly so called that curious, floating, ever-changing population to whom it is convenient to refer as 'the reading public,' had no opportunity of forming any real opinion until after the poet's death, namely, when the small folio of 1681 made its appearance. This volume, although not containing the *Horatian Ode upon Cromwell's Return from Ireland* or the lines upon Cromwell's death, did contain, saving these exceptions, all the best of Marvell's verse.

How this poetry was received, to whom and to how many it gave pleasure, we have not the means of knowing. The book, like all other good books, had to take its chance. Good poetry is never exactly unpopular—its difficulty is to get a hearing, to secure a *vogue*. I feel certain that from 1681 onwards many ingenuous souls read *Eyes and Tears*, *The Bermudas*, *The Nymph complaining for the Death of her Fawn*, *To his Coy Mistress*, *Young Love*, and *The Garden* with pure delight. In 1699 the poet Pomfret,[1] of whose *Choice* Dr. Johnson said in 1780, 'perhaps no composition in our language has been oftener perused,' and whom Southey in 1807 declared to be 'the most popular of English poets'; in 1699, I say, this poet Pomfret says in a preface, sensibly enough, 'to please everyone would be a New Thing, and to write so as to please no Body would be as New, for even Quarles and Wythers (*sic*) have their Admirers.' So liable is the public taste to fluctuations and reversals, that to-day, though Quarles and Wither are not popular authors, they certainly number many more readers than Pomfret, Southey's 'most popular of English poets,' who has now, it is to be feared, finally disappeared even from the Anthologies. But if Quarles and Wither had their admirers even in 1699, the poet Marvell, we may be sure, had his also.

Marvell had many poetical contemporaries—five-and-twenty at least—poets of mark and interest, to most of whom, as well as to some of his immediate predecessors, he stood, as I must suppose, in some degree of poetical relationship. With Milton and Dryden no comparison will suggest itself, but with Donne and Cowley, with Waller and Denham, with Butler and the now wellnigh forgotten Cleveland, with Walker and Charles Cotton, with Rochester and Dorset, some resemblances, certain influences, may be found and traced. From the order of his mind and his prose style, I should judge Marvell to have been both a reader and a critic of his contemporaries in verse and prose—though of his criticisms little remains. Of Butler he twice speaks with great respect, and his sole reference to the dead Cleveland is kindly. Of Milton we know what he thought, whilst Aubrey tells us that he

[1] John Pomfret (1667–1702), a poetizing divine.

once heard Marvell say that the Earl of Rochester was the only man in England that had the true vein of satire.

Be these influences what they may or must have been, to us Marvell occupies, as a poet, a niche by himself. A finished master of his art he never was. He could not write verses like his friend Lovelace, or like Cowley's *Chronicle* or Waller's lines 'On a Girdle.' He had not the inexhaustible, astonishing (though tiresome) wit of Butler. He is often clumsy and sometimes almost babyish. One has frequently occasion to wonder how a man of business could allow himself to be tickled by such obvious straws as are too many of the conceits which give him pleasure. To attribute all the conceits of this period to the influence of Dr. Donne is but a poor excuse after all. The worst thing that can be said against poetry is that there is so much tedium in it. The glorious moments are all too few. It is his honest recognition of this woeful fact that makes Dr. Johnson, with all his faults lying thick about him, the most consolatory of our critics to the ordinary reading man. 'Tediousness is the most fatal of all faults. ... Unhappily this pernicious failure is that which an author is least able to discover. We are seldom tiresome to ourselves. ... Perhaps no man ever thought a line superfluous when he wrote it' (*Lives of the Poets*. Under *Prior*—see also under *Butler*).

That Marvell is never tiresome I will not assert. But he too has his glorious moments, and they are all his own. In the whole compass of our poetry there is nothing quite like Marvell's love of gardens and woods, of meads and rivers and birds. It is a love not learnt from books, not borrowed from brother-poets. It is not indulged in to prove anything. It is all sheer enjoyment.

[Quotes 'Appleton House,' ll. 609–16; 'The Garden,' ll. 49–53.] ...

Marvell's immediate fame as a true poet was, I dare say, obscured for a good while both by its original note (for originality is always forbidding at first sight) and by its author's fame as a satirist, and his reputation as a lover of 'liberty's glorious feast.' It was as one of the poets encountered in the *Poems on Affairs of State* (fifth edition, 1703) that Marvell was best known during the greater part of the eighteenth century. As Milton's friend Marvell had, as it were, a side-chapel in the great Miltonic temple.

As a prose writer Marvell has many merits and one great fault. He has fire and fancy and was the owner and master of a precise vocabulary well fitted to clothe and set forth a well-reasoned and lofty argument. He knew how to be both terse and diffuse, and can compress himself into a line or expand over a paragraph. He has touches of a grave irony as well as of a boisterous humour. He can tell an anecdote and elaborate a parable. Swift, we know, had not only Butler's *Hudibras* by heart, but was also (we may be sure) a close student of Marvell's prose. His great fault is a very common one. He is too long. He forgets how quickly a reader grows tired. He is so interested in the evolutions of his own mind that he forgets his audience. His interest at times seems as if it were going to prove endless. It is the first business of an author to arrest and then to retain the attention of the reader. To do this requires great artifice.

Among the masters of English prose it would be rash to rank Marvell, who was neither a Hooker nor a Taylor. None the less he was the owner of a prose style which some people think the best prose style of all—that of honest men who have something to say.

91. Three unsigned reviews of Birrell's *Andrew Marvell*

1905, 1906

(a) Extract from the *Times Literary Supplement* (22 September 1905), p. 303.

Each volume of the new issue of the English Men of Letters Series makes the sufficiency of Mr. Morley's original programme increasingly clear; and a counsel of perfection to the publishers would have urged the postponement of their supplementary action for many years. Since, however, the new volumes are coming out with regularity and rapidity, it is idle now to criticize the movement; but we might just remark that among the poets Marvell is the thinnest edge of the wedge yet admitted. We do not see how, logically, we can now escape monographs on Collins and Cowley, Drayton and Shenstone, Prior and Campion, Suckling and Lovelace (to name these only).

We will not ourselves call Mr. Birrell's book disappointing, because we have been convinced from the first that no book suitable for this series could be made from such slender materials as are furnished by the life and labours of Andrew Marvell. But that it must disappoint others is, we fear, inevitable; for Marvell was only in a limited sense an English Man of Letters and Mr. Birrell is here less himself than his many admiring readers will like. . . .

So much for the author of this book. When we come to the subject we find a similar unfitness. Marvell wrote some poetry of unique charm and one ode of the highest distinction and dignity. In addition he wrote some negligible satirical prose pamphlets; a number of satires in verse, a kind of rhymed political journalism; and a series of letters to his constituents describing the progress of Parliament while he was a member. That is all. He had no influence on his contemporaries; he founded no school of verse. If there ever was a poet whose delicate graceful work could be appreciated classically by Mr. Birrell in a short characteristic eassy, it is the poet of 'Appleton House' and 'The Garden,' the 'Coy Mistress,' the 'Horatian Ode,' and the 'Character of the Dutch;' yet here is a monograph extending to 230 pages which has had to be eked out with Samuel Parker, Charles II., Lord Clarendon, General Monk, the Conventicle Bill, No Popery, and all the politics and intrigues of the Restoration—matters which have no bearing on Marvell's literature as we value it, but which have swum into Mr. Birrell's net because Marvell was at heart not an English Man of Letters, but a member of Parliament and a sardonic observer of political life. In these capacities, however, he was never very readable or important. . . .

But the book is not a good one, for it falls between two stools. If it was to deal only with the permanent part of Marvell's charming poetry it is nearly two hundred pages too long; if it was really to explain the politics of his day (which heaven forbid!) it is not long enough.

(b) Extract from a review entitled 'The Poet of Verdure' which appeared in the *Saturday Review*, 100 (7 October 1905), pp. 469–70.

[Birrell's] was just the pen for a book about Marvell—not that Marvell really affords material for anything like a book of two hundred and odd pages. Of Marvell personally only a few glimpses, and those in no sense intimate, survive. The poems, 'full of a witty delicacy,' are of a kind to invite much enjoyment but little comment. The satires in verse were of quite ephemeral merit. His pamphlets, though vigorous and good of their sort, had nothing very extraordinary in an age so prolific of acute argument, and the letters to his Hull constituents, though in point of dignity and restraint they might serve admirably for models to our own members of parliament, can hardly be described as literature. Small wonder if the biographer, thus meagrely provided in respect of the portrait itself, is driven to eke out his picture with a plentiful elaboration of background. For Marvell there was background to spare, and Mr. Birrell has made the most of his opportunities. ... What however has disappointed us very seriously is the scant consideration that Mr. Birrell, with so many blank pages at command, has accorded to the main point— Marvell's serious poetry.

Mr. Birrell astonishes us by the assertion that Marvell 'was never a finished master of his art'; that he could not write verses, for example, like Waller's lines 'On a Girdle.' We know of nothing in Waller (to speak of craftsmanship pure and simple) that can surpass such verses as those on 'The Picture of little T.C. in a Prospect of Flowers.'

[Quotes ll. 25–32.]

As to poetic virtue, comparison of Marvell with a poet like Waller strikes us as almost impossible. They are of two worlds. In Waller, to our ear at all events, the vernal note is at the point of extinction. Waller initiates the period of culture, when poetry ceases to be an impulse and becomes an accomplishment. In Marvell, slight and few as the finer productions of his genius are, the early breath still lingers. Mr. Birrell's remark that 'one has frequently occasion to wonder how a man of business could allow himself to be tickled by such obvious straws as are too many of the conceits which give him pleasure' is not, in our opinion, very discriminating. Wit for its own sake, one must allow, is always tiresome to succeeding generations. Shakespeare's wit is often exceedingly tiresome. But there is all the difference between a wit

that serves (as it served so often, for instance, in the eighteenth
century) by way of substitute for poetic imagination, and a wit
that is the by-product, so to speak, of poetic imagination—a wit
that sprouts by natural excrescence from a full fancy. Elizabethan
wit, though it often irritates us, we regard with a certain indul-
gence, just as we regard the irritating pranks of healthy children.
The pleasure the Elizabethans take in their conceits is simply the
pleasure which Aristotle ascribes to all growing things, as being
pleasantly aware of their own growth. And even in Milton's
generation, when Englishmen had resumed the national habit of
living for other objects than life itself, poems like Marvell's were
put forth in proof that a bough or two was still undried on the
tree of purely English poetry. Two lines only—

> The mind, that ocean where each kind
> Does straight its own resemblance, find
> ['The Garden,' ll. 43–4]

are enough to stamp the intellect of Marvell as part of the indi-
genous renascence, the native muse. We perceive at once the
tendency to 'conceit' which in such a writer as Donne often
overmasters the thought, turning what should be a garden into a
luxuriant wilderness; the intensity of imagination and metaphysical insight that perished with Vaughan; and the English
manner, still pure of Latin influence. Considering that the poem
from which these lines are taken is itself a translation by the author
of his own 'Hortus', we find it very interesting to reflect how
closely Marvell is in touch with two atmospheres. He produces
'An Horatian Ode' which is the true equivalent of Horace just
because it has nothing in common with Horace but the spirit. He
has small antiphonal songs which are really like Theocritus just
because no one could suspect them to be literal translations:

[Quotes 'Second Song,' ll. 17–24.]

Marvell, in fine, though his praise of 'Paradise Lost' is obviously
sincere, himself belongs to an age which thought and felt in
English, however familiar it might be with the language of scholars. Of this age a few notes are to be heard in Milton, it is true,
but only in the early poems, poems written in the country during
the halcyon years which preceded those two decades of wasteful
bigotry that cost us, probably, an English Vergil. With 'Paradise
Lost' we enter that other age of literature—an age that gains from

Latin, no doubt, an imposing dignity and metallic clearness of outline, but only at irrevocable expense of human sympathy and joy. Marvell lived on into this age, and admired 'the verse created, like the theme, sublime' of Miltonic epic, but himself never forsook the green fields of England. The little we know of his political opinions quite confirms the impression his poems leave upon us—the impression of a thoroughly human temperament, an intellect of that highest order which perceives how little of permanent value is to be got, after all, from pressing abstract principles in the teeth of nature and experience. 'Upon considering all, I think the cause was too good to have been fought for. Even as his present Majesty's happy Restoration did itself, so all things else happen in their best and proper time, without any heed of our officiousness' [RT I, p. 135]. These are not the words of a trimmer, or of a comfortable idler. When corruption at Court and slackness in regard of national honour called for words, Marvell carried his just invective to a point of amazing audacity. It was in a poem written to honour Cromwell that Marvell saw fit to include the memorable and glorious stanzas which invest the 'tragic scaffold' with a grandeur supreme alike in history and in verse. The same Marvell devoted his most energetic prose to the cause of religious toleration at a period when only few, besides the King himself, were capable of a larger outlook than petty ecclesiasticism would permit. The work of Marvell had neither quantity nor significance to warrant a regular biography, but this is no disparagement either of his poetic merit or of his symbolic value. Poetically he belongs, in every sense worthily, to the imperishable group of writers who felt beauty at first hand, transmuted what they felt into a genuine possession of the mind, and uttered their mind in the clear spontaneous notes of an age at once profound and simple. Symbolically, he stands for that peculiar type of mind which emerges, in every period of English history, distinct from and superior to the crowd of passions and prejudices which are popularly supposed to constitute the life and motive force of important 'movements'. Minds of this type seldom appear in large print on the page of the historian, but it is these after all which contribute the real and permanent element of progress. Charles I. has no finer monument than the eight lines which Marvell built for him, but Marvell himself was denied a tombstone by the Royalist incumbent of his parish. As poet, he sang the praise of retirement, the refuge from passion which the mind may discover in green alleys and flowery spaces. To politics he carried the secret of that retirement—the philosophy of Nature, which teaches that every truly constructive process is a silent one.

(c) Extract from the *Spectator*, 96 (14 April 1906), pp. 582–3. The reviewer was Lytton Strachey, critic and biographer (1880–1932).

Mr. Birrell's Life of Marvell is a welcome addition to Messrs. Macmillan's well-known series of biographies of 'English Men of Letters.' Marvell, who is now remembered almost solely for his exquisite lyrics, filled in his own day a distinguished place in public life. His contemporaries doubtless thought of him as an eminent politician who had written verses in his youth: we think of him as a great poet who happened to take an interest in politics. Thus the whirligig of Time brings in his revenges. Mr Birrell, however, has evidently attempted to steer clear of these extremes, and to correct our somewhat one-sided vision of a great man who was great on more sides than one. He has aimed at giving a picture of Marvell in his true perspective. He shows him to us by turns as the poet, the Civil servant, the satirist, the Member of Parliament, and the protagonist in ecclesiastical controversy. Amid this great variety of topics Mr. Birrell guides us with a sure and dexterous hand, and with all the sympathy which it is, indeed, only natural that he should feel for a politician who was also a man of letters. Perhaps Mr. Birrell, in his attempt to do justice to the various activities of Marvell, has a little overshot the mark. Now and then his book has more the air of being a history of Restoration politics than a literary biography, and the general impression of Marvell which it leaves upon the reader is rather that of a noble and gifted public character than that of a consummate artist. This is unfortunate, for Marvell was both of these things; and to forget his art is to forget the least mortal part of him. ...

'Poets,' says Mr Birrell, 'like pigeons, have often taken shelter under our public roofs; but Milton, Marvell, and Dryden, all at the same time, form a remarkable constellation. Old Noll', he adds, 'we may be sure, had nothing to do with it.' This assumption is a little unfair to the Lord Protector. But, whatever Cromwell's views may have been with regard to the poetical talents of his subordinates, there can be no doubt about the admiration which Marvell on his side felt for 'The War's and Fortune's son.' In a poem 'Upon the Death of his late Highness, the Lord Protector'—a poem too little known to modern readers—Marvell expressed, in lines more obviously dictated by personal feeling than any in the 'Horatian Ode,' his sense of Cromwell's greatness:

[Quotes ll. 247–8, 251–60.] . . .

In his satires, no less than in the controversial theology of his *Rehearsal Transprosed,* he wrote with an uncompromising fury which expected and allowed no quarter. His object was not to convince his adversary, but to destroy him. And it is this extreme of tone which makes it well-nigh impossible for the modern reader to appreciate this section of Marvell's writings. To do so, one must be able to enter into their fiery spirit with all the vigour of personal partisanship; one must hate the Duchess of Cleveland, one must despise Bishop Parker, with the rage and the scorn of the seventeenth century. For a spectator who cannot take part in the fight the excitement is at best second-hand; but when one is watching Marvell this sort of reflected exhilaration is rarely absent. No one can help warming at the sight of blows so excellently given, and with a relish so obvious and so complete.

The satires offer a curious contrast to the poems of Marvell's youth. It is upon these that his fame rests; and their title to remembrance is their possession of precisely those qualities which the satires most conspicuously lack,—brilliance of expression and beauty of form. Mr. Birrell, it is true, comparing Marvell, to his disadvantage, with Lovelace, Cowley, and Waller, denies that he was a 'finished master of his art.' Of all Mr. Birrell's dicta, this is surely the most surprising. It is difficult to guess what kind of 'finished art' that can be of which Lovelace, Cowley, and Waller were masters, and which Marvell was without. Does Mr Birrell seriously contend that, as a master of words, as a creator of expressions, as a stylist in short, Marvell is inferior to Cowley? Poets, no less than prose writers, may be divided into two classes,—into those pre-eminent for their style, and those pre-eminent for their matter. In English, the most notorious example of a poet without style is Byron, while Milton clearly stands at the head of the opposite school. No one can doubt that Cowley is one of those poets whose claim to distinction rests upon their matter; his elegy on the death of Harvey is a striking instance of literary excellence without literary style, just as 'Lycidas' is a proof that style alone may confer immortality. After reading the former poem it is difficult to remember the expression, and it is impossible to forget the feelings expressed; after reading the latter the expression seems to have absorbed into itself the whole value of the work, so that there is nothing else upon which the mind can dwell. *Pace* Mr. Birrell, Marvell belongs as clearly to the Miltonic type as Cowley does not. His poems possess the crowning quality of style,—their meaning has become an integral and inseparable part of the words by which it is expressed.

[Quotes 'To His Coy Mistress,' ll. 21–4, 37–44.]

It is impossible to think of the sentiments conveyed by these lines expressed in any other form; alter the form, and the meaning itself, like the subtly compounded elixir of an alchemist, vanishes to nothing. Who can deny, after reading 'The Garden,' and 'Bermudas,' and the 'Coy Mistress,' that Marvell was one of the greatest of alchemists, or, in other words, that he was—what Mr. Birrell will not allow him to be—a 'finished master of his art'?

92.   A poet's review of Birrell's edition

1905

The Catholic poet Francis Thompson (1859–1907) is best known for his *Hound of Heaven*. He was a frequent contributor to the *Athenaeum* and the *Academy*, where his review of Birrell appeared anonymously (see the bibliography in his *Literary Criticisms*, ed. Terrence L. Connolly, New York, 1948).

Extract from the *Academy*, 69 (23 September 1905), pp. 976–7.

From the death of Cromwell in 1658 to his own death just twenty years after, Marvell was struggling continuously in the toils of political and religious controversy. The subject-matter of this little book, therefore, is largely contentious; yet, while unravelling the thorny embranglements of the poet's later years—a task which occupies considerably more than half of the volume—his biographer maintains throughout a laudable impartiality, without (need it be added?) for a moment declining into dulness. On one important point, indeed, Mr. Birrell has rendered Marvell a substantial service, namely, in vindicating the memory of the Member for Hull from the two-fold charge of Dissent and Republicanism—an idle imputation already implied by Dryden (who may have been acquainted with Marvell), and assiduously repeated ever since by critics from Dryden's day to our own. Even in Mr. Courthope's 'History of English Poetry' (iii. 307) [see No. 88] it is stated that 'after the Restoration Marvell's political opinions became fixedly Republican.' On the contrary, Mr. Birrell demonstrates from the poet's controversial writings, and, in particular, from his last work, the famous 'Account of the Growth of Popery and Arbitrary Government in England,' that from first to last Andrew Marvell stood for both King and Parliament, and, like his father before him, held fast to the teaching and the discipline of the Reformed Church of England. . . .

If there be any fault to be found with Mr. Birrell's book, it is that he has hardly given adequate space to the consideration of what, when all is said, constitutes Marvell's one, indefeasible title to the name and rank of Man of Letters—his poetry, pastoral, imaginative and political, as distinguished from his later satirical verse. As a poet, Marvell shows affinity with several of his contemporaries: with Donne he revels in subtle imagery and the play of recondite conceits; with Vaughan he shares the passion for Nature, though the beauties he paints with Dutch minuteness are those of the pleasance rather than of the wilderness; while in consummate choiceness and propriety of word and phrase he approaches, if he does not actually rival, Herrick. This *curiosa felicitas* he derives from Horace, to whom also he is indebted for his skill in the poetical treatment of political themes. The famous 'Ode upon Cromwell's Return from Ireland,' first printed, so far as is known, in 1776, appears to have been written in 1650, during the period of Marvell's sojourn at Nunappleton in the position of tutor to the Lady Mary Fairfax. Now at Nunappleton Cromwell was not, writes Mr. Birrell:

a *persona grata* in 1650; for he had no sooner come back from Ireland than
he had stepped into the shoes of the Lord-General Fairfax; and there
were those, Lady Fairfax, I doubt not, among the number, who believed
that the new Lord-General thought it was high time he should be where
Fairfax's 'scruple' at last put him. We may be sure Cromwell's character
was dissected even more than it was extolled at Nunappleton. The
famous 'Ode' is by no means a panegyric, and its true hero is the 'Royal
actor' whom Cromwell, so the poem suggests, lured to his doom. . . .
It is not surprising that this 'Ode' was not published in 1650—if indeed
it was the work of that, and not of a later year. There is nothing either
of the courtier or of the partisan about its stately versification and
sober, solemn thought. Entire self-possession, dignity, criticism of a
great man and a strange career by one well entitled to criticise, are
among the chief characteristics of this noble poem. It is infinitely
refreshing, when reading and thinking about Cromwell, to get as far
away as possible from the fanatic's scream and the fury of the bigot,
whether of the school of Laud or Hobbes. Andrew Marvell knew
Oliver Cromwell alive, and gazed on his features as he lay dead—he
knew his ambition, his greatness, his power, and where that power lay.

In this and many another pleasant passage [of biography], it
must be confessed our author 'has more of Sterne about him than
of Sternhold.' But he quickly 'saddens into excellent sense,' when
he comes to deal with Marvell's career as a practical politician.
His sketch of 'the poor Priapus-king' is a graphic bit of work, and
his account of the fate of Clarendon could not easily be bettered.
On the whole, it may be said that 'Andrew Marvell' holds its own
successfully against any other volume in the new series of Messrs.
Macmillan's 'English Men of Letters.'

93. Albert F. Sieveking on garden poetry

1908

Albert F. Sieveking (1857–1951) published extensively on sports, games, and gardens.

Extract from *Sir William Temple upon the Gardens of Epicurus* (1908), p. xlvi.

As writers in praise of Gardens and Country Life, the palm will, I think, be given by all modern readers to Andrew Marvell. Genuine as is the love of both [Marvell and Cowley] for the country—and to Cowley the desire for retirement and repose was assuredly no pose—Cowley's voice is that of the scholar and the student, and his verse smells of the lamp and grates of the file, while Marvell's song brings the magic of the meadow, the breath of the blowers and new-mown hay, the swish of the scythe, and the lamp of the glow-worm right across the centuries, before our eyes and into our hearts—and we love Marvell's poems, while at the best we can only admire and sympathize, with Cowley's verse.

94. Emile Legouis comments on 'The Death of O.C.'

1912

Academic critic and father of the noted Marvell scholar,
Emile Legouis (1861–1937) is best remembered for an
influential history of English literature written in collaboration with Louis Cazamian. In his lectures on Marvell's
poetry given at the Sorbonne, he praises 'On the Death of
O. C.' as the best of the major poems on Cromwell.

Extract from a résumé (in French) made by René Pruvost,
Revue des cours et conférences (Paris, 1912), p. 229.

[*The First Anniversary*] is not, however, the best piece inspired by
Cromwell. The poem on the death of Cromwell: *On the Death of
his late Highness the lord Protector*, 1658, has a more sure development. It is not only beautiful in its parts, like the preceding, but
in its totality. First and foremost, it is filled with emotion. It seems
that Marvell had moved from a respect for Cromwell, from an
admiration a little distant, to a more tender feeling. In the meantime
he has drawn nearer to Cromwell, and the poem says it. It is an
elegy which addresses itself rather to the man than to the Protector.
It exalts his familiar virtues, his affection, and his goodness.

95.   Edward B. Reed on Marvell's Lyrics

1912

A long-time member of the English department at Yale University, Edward B. Reed (1872–1940) published his *English Lyrical Poetry* in 1912, prompted, he said, because there was at the time no such history.

Extract from *English Lyrical Poetry* (New York, 1967 reprint) pp. 273–8.

The poet who stands nearest Herrick in his love of nature—at times he surpasses him—is Andrew Marvell (1621–1678). He was educated at Trinity College, Cambridge, travelled on the continent, and in 1650 was taken by Lord Fairfax to his Yorkshire estate, to be the tutor of his daughter. Here, in the retirement of the country, Marvell composed his finest poems *Upon Appleton House*, the *Horatian Ode*, *The Garden*, *On a Drop of Dew*, and in all probability, *The Nymph Complaining for the Death of her Fawn*. Fairfax delighted in poetry, but could not write it, though he made many attempts. Undoubtedly he encouraged Marvell, but the young tutor's lyric period was a brief one. As Milton's colleague in the Latin secretaryship, and later, as member of Parliament from Hull, he became absorbed in politics; in place of nature poems, he wrote verse satires, brutally frank, or pamphlets full of vigorous, ironical prose. English history gained a patriot at a time when honesty and courage seemed forgotten virtues; the English lyric is the poorer since it possesses not the achievement, but the promise of Andrew Marvell.

If Herrick avoided Donne's influence, Marvell shows it most plainly. He never mentions Donne's name; he does not imitate any one poem, or even lift any phrase, but the spirit of Donne is in many a line. At times he can be as fantastic as any of the metaphysical poets:

> Tears (watery shot that pierce the mind,)
> And sighs (Love's cannon filled with wind;)
> ['Appleton House,' ll. 715–16]

319

and the Dean of St. Paul's might have written such stanzas as:

> My love is of a birth as rare
>   As 'tis, for object, strange and high;
> It was begotten by Despair,
>   Upon Impossibility. . . .
>
> As lines, so love's oblique, may well
>   Themselves in every angle greet:
> But ours, so truly parallel,
>   Though infinite, can never meet
> ['Definition of Love,' ll. 1–4, 25–8]

As a rule Marvell's conceits are quaint and charming rather than extravagant and grotesque. We see this in such a couplet as

> And stars show lovely in the night,
> But as they seem the tears of light ['Eyes and Tears,' ll. 43–4]

and better in these stanzas from *The Mower to the Glow Worms*:

> Ye living lamps, by whose dear light
> The nightingale does sit so late,
> And studying all the summer night,
> Her matchless songs does imitate;
>
> Ye country comets, that portend
> No war nor prince's funeral,
> Shining unto no higher end
> Than to presage the grass's fall. [ll. 1–8]

Such verses show plainly what Lamb has called the 'witty delicacy' of Marvell.

The themes of Marvell are not those of Donne; he lacked the romantic temperament and writes coldly of women. Only one of his love poems is worthy of him; it has something of Donne's wit, and far more important, fine moments of imagination and passion, for Marvell is continually hinting at greater things. His *Coy Mistress* has the same theme as Herrick's *Corinna*, but not Herrick's art. Contrasted with this poem, Marvell's octosyllabics are rough and unfinished; his humor seems out of keeping and too grotesque. He tells his coy love that the days haste away; if there were time

> I would
> Love you ten years before the flood,
> And you should, if you please, refuse
> Till the conversion of the Jews.

Then, in this quaint tirade, he pauses and cries with an intensity of emotion which Herrick never expressed:

[Quotes ll. 21–4, 41–4.]

Never again does this mood seize him; instead of love poems, he writes verses to children, 'young beauties of the woods.'

If Marvell forsook the greatest lyric theme of all, he at least brought new ones to English verse. Through the Elizabethan period, when Italian influence was supreme, the patriotism of the Italian sonneteers was never imitated; we have no sonnets, no odes to England or to English leaders, whereas the Italian poets took the deepest interest in the political fortunes of their towns or provinces. Marvell considered Cromwell to be the savior of his country; moved by the sincerest admiration for him he became his laureate. Where other poets flattered subserviently, he praised boldly and, on the whole, justly, though he is not free from certain absurd touches of adulation. We can hardly call his elegy on Cromwell a lyric, for it is rather a descriptive poem, rising at times to a Miltonic diction:

> When up the armed mountains of Dunbar
> He marched, and through deep Severn, ending war [ll. 45–6],

with lines that move with the rugged strength of Cromwell's Ironsides:

> Thee, many ages hence, in martial verse
> Shall the English soldier, ere he charge, rehearse [ll. 277–8];

but his *Horatian Ode upon Cromwell's Return from Ireland* falls well within our province. It is one of the most successful attempts to reproduce in English the effect of Horace's close-knit stanzas. Abandoning the experiment of forcing English thought into a Latin metre—a *tour de force* which diverts the reader's mind from the substance of the poem—he uses his own difficult measure with such success that we forget his metrical skill in admiring the

321

nobility of thought and the dignity of expression as he praises
the man

> Who from his private gardens, where
> He lived reservèd and austere
>   (As if his highest plot
>   To plant the bergamot;)
>
> Could by industrious valour climb
> To ruin the great work of time,
>   And cast the kingdoms old,
>   Into another mould. [ll. 29–36]

It is more than a century before the English lyric can equal this.

Turning to Marvell's nature poems, we find their spirit astonish-
ingly modern; he views nature not as an artist but as a lover. He
belonged to his generation, for he was the poet of meadows and
woods, and with Howell regarded mountains as 'hook-shouldered
excrescences.' Summer was his season; the warm earth with its
flowers and fruits, his delight; he says little of sky or clouds. Keen
in his observation, nature is to him an end; his descriptions are not
ornaments to his poems. There is all the languor and luxury of a
summer's day in the tropical richness of his *Garden*. Here and in his
Nymph Complaining for the Death of her Fawn, he has the sensuousness of Keats. 'I stood tip-toe upon a little hill' is more delicate; it
has a greater wealth of detail and a finer finish; but its spirit differs
in no wise from that of Marvell's verses.

But Marvell sees more than the loveliness of the earth; he has a
touch of that transcendentalism that characterizes our modern
conception of nature. Overpowered by the beauty about him he
cries, in Wordsworth's spirit:

> Thrice happy he, who, not mistook,
> Hath read in Nature's mystic book! ['Appleton House,' ll. 583–4]

He becomes a part of the life around him: he confers with birds
and trees; he casts aside the 'body's vest'; his soul flies into the
boughs and

> There, like a bird, it sits and sings,
> Then whets and combs its silver wings. ['The Garden,' ll. 53–4]

The visible world disappears, and the mind creates other regions
for itself

>Annihilating all that's made
>To a green thought in a green shade. [ll. 47–8]

No other English poet had approached nature in this spirit.

Marvell's poems are lyrical because of the intensity of his feeling; even those poems which he has entitled songs do not suggest a musical accompaniment. His verse is too compact, too overladen with thought and emotion for the lute's melody of

>lesser intervals, and plaintive moan
>Of sinking semitone.

The lyric is becoming more and more an art form, independent of music. We see this in the song of the English emigrants in the *Bermudas*, a poem worth all the pages of Tom Moore's lyrical description of these islands.

96. Francis L. Bickley on the quality of Marvell's poetry

1913

In addition to his work for the Victoria County Histories and the Historical MSS. Commission, Francis L. Bickley (1885–19—) has written extensively on literary subjects.

From *North American Review*, Boston-New York, 197 (February 1913), pp. 234–45.

Modern criticism—with an ardor sometimes disproportioned to its theme—has been a busy maker of reputations. We grow more catholic, seeing that art is a house of many mansions; but toleration has not been the only motive at work. In the trade of letters competition grows ever keener, and the tradesman's best chance of profit lies in the display of strange wares. So poets who have long

ANDREW MARVELL

languished in obscurity have been brought with a flourish to the
light. Some of them surely must have blinked beneath its unexpected beams.

Not that the literary discoverer is a bad citizen. All men who
have lived are interesting more or less, and that some have written
verse does not necessarily diminish their interest. To have rescued
the seventeenth century from the dark night cast over it by the
eighteenth is a pious and admirable work: by no means the least
noble manifestation of the nineteenth century's vaunted progress.
It is only that to hail every calf-bound duodecimo raked from the
two-penny box as a precious casket of genius is to set our minor
poets too low a standard. But the pseudo-great, ancient or modern,
will soon sink into a decent oblivion.

So it comes about that there are few poets who can claim that
they lack at least their due meed of worship. But there are just
one or two who have listened in vain, if not for the trumpet, at
least for the answering shout. Andrew Marvell is one of them.
He is possibly the most under-valued of our poets.

True, he has his place, with many a lesser man, in the *Muses'
Library* [ed. G. A. Aitken, 1892, see Nos 80, 81], and so can be
bought for a florin. Dr. Grosart, an enthusiast but a pedant,
edited him completely, prose and verse, in four bulky and inaccessible volumes, the hundred possessors whereof must needs be
muscular as well as wealthy. Somewhat tardily the Ministry has
honored him with admission to the *English Men of Letters*; but
Mr. Birrell, while writing an admirable biography of the politician
and satirist, pecks but cautiously at criticism of the artist. The
new *Cambridge History*, though discreetly appreciative, gives him
a curious position as a kind of make-weight in a chapter devoted
to Bunyan.

If Marvell were merely of the rank and file of his age, such
recognition would be enough. The modern discovery of such
charming singers as Waller and Carew and Suckling is an excellent
thing, if only as a symptom that we have at last got free from the
stupendous solemnity of the romantic revival and are not utterly
engulfed in the solemnity of modern problems; that we have
learned that greatness and gravity are not identical in art. But we
should not lay too great a stress on these men's importance. Give
them a tray in the window as good specimens of Ben's progeny,
but don't put them in the central showcase to jostle their betters.

324

Marvell, however, is in quite another class than Carew or Suckling. Yet, in the matter of editing, appreciation, and so forth, he has had much the same treatment. In this he has been unfairly used. One other man, roughly of his era, is roughly his equal. At an Elysian banquet of poets of the Cavalier and Puritan age Herrick and Marvell should be set on either hand of John Milton, their president. Herrick has his due. For a time forgotten, then recognized for a pretty singer, he has now his place in the van of the English lyrists. It is admitted that if one considers the 'Nativity Ode' a better poem than the 'Nightpiece to Julia,' it is a matter of taste rather than of weight and measure. Herrick is of the elect. But Marvell must still take his chance with the ruck.

One does not desire to establish him among the mighty. But he has certain qualities which call for wider recognition. All but very few of the poets whom we honor are only great in moments more or less frequent. Coleridge, who touched perfection in 'Kubla Khan,' was the author of I know not what dreariness. Longfellow, who doddered at such inordinate length, was a great poet when he wrote 'My Lost Youth.' Marvell is another of the intermittent great. He might be compared with Marlowe. He is as far below Milton as Marlowe is below Shakespeare. The Elizabethan produced much gaudy fustian, the Puritan elaborated many empty conceits. But each scaled sudden heights, each had his moments of insight. Marlowe once saw Helen more clearly than any Greek. Marvell, the Puritan (some said the Republican), had a nobler vision of Charles than was vouchsafed to the most loyal Cavalier. In lines among the few of his that have become common quotation he re-created the King in the high-handed way of the great artist; in the way of Wordsworth with Chatterton, of Swinburne with François Villon.

[Quotes the 'Horatian Ode,' ll. 57–64.]

This directness of statement, an absolute rightness of touch based on an absolute sureness of vision, is a high virtue in poetry and one of the rarest. Poets the loftiest in spirit and the wealthiest in words have almost or altogether lacked it. The poets of the romantic revolt, for instance, with all their splendor, achieved it only at long intervals; for in their attitude something of the argumentative was implied which made against this divine certitude. Yet it is a quality of the romantics. The eighteenth century, which stated its opinions in couplets, knew nothing of this or any other poetic quality except the art of getting a high polish on their phrases. But Milton, the truest classic among our poets, also lacked the gift of sudden inevitability. No English poet comes anywhere near him in general perfection. None says what he wants to say with so calm and melodious an assurance. But he misses just the final something. This, as Matthew Arnold held, is the difference between classic and romantic. The classic with his watchful art, his nine years' solicitude, makes his work as perfect as hand and brain can contrive. The romantic contents himself with faulty work while he waits—I will not say the inspiration— but the impulse to expression which seems transcendental in its aptitude.

Marvell partook of the nature both of the classic and of the romantic. In some poems he has the romantic's faults and rare triumphs or the faults without the triumphs. In others he is wholly classic in his chaste and chiseled accuracy. Once, at least, he is both in one poem. 'The Horatian Ode upon Cromwell's Return from Ireland' will, according to Dean Trench [see No. 70], 'give a truer notion of the kind of greatness which he [Horace] achieved than could, as far as I know, be obtained from any other poem in our language.' It is indeed a stately panegyric of a man whose opinions and achievements the poet respected. But when he has to speak of a man whose opinions he dislikes, but whose personality is one of those which fascinate the imaginative in their own despite, a sudden wave of enthusiasm uplifts him and impels him to the magic of the lines quoted.

This mixture of classical and romantic was common enough in the Renaissance poets. But whereas by Marvell's time the classical was fast gaining ground, Marvell was more romantic not only than his contemporaries, but than the majority of his predecessors. He sounds certain notes which will not be heard again in English literature until the days of Coleridge and Shelley. Shakespeare's 'wood-notes wild,' Herrick's songs of country pleasures, have not that intimacy with impersonal nature which makes Marvell seem so modern.

Divers influences shaped Marvell. He was educated at the Hull Grammar School under his father, a good scholar who grounded him in the classics, and at Trinity College, Cambridge. He wrote verses both Latin and Greek. He knew his Horace, as we have seen, and also his Catullus. Sparrows and fawns can hardly be called akin, but the pets of Lesbia and of Marvell's nymph might at least have come from the same fanciers:

[Quotes 'The Nymph,' ll. 41–6.]

These lines can scarcely be the work of one who did not remember

> Nam mellitus erat, suamque norat
> Ipsam tam bene quam puella matrem.
> Nec sese a gremio illius movebat,
> Sed circumsiliens modo huc modo illuc
> Ad solam dominam usque pipiebat.[1]

Marvell, like most of his fellows, felt the influence of Donne's potent personality. Conceit was a fashion which it took a stronger man than he to ignore. There are conceits in his verse in plenty, as when he says that 'Jubal tuned Music's Jubilee,' and writes of 'music, the mosaic of the air.' Nor need we admire such things. There is no need to school our historical sense to appreciate Donne when our sense of beauty has Johnson and Herrick and Milton ready to hand. Donne was a man of daring conceptions which he only marred by his tricksy style. There is a dateless language which has been written by all the greatest poets and calls for no chronological posturing to feel at ease with it. Those who do not use that language are the less worthy of our homage. They may have much in them that is admirable, but undue exaltation of such men of their age as Donne and Sir Thomas Browne is sentimental antiquarianism.

Marvell, however, had a natural directness of expression which largely counteracted these crooked influences. He who could write the last four lines of 'Bermudas'—

> Thus sang they, in the English boat,
> An holy and a cheerful note;
> And all the way, to guide their chime,
> With falling oars they kept the time—

was hardly the man seriously to disfigure any large proportion of his work with tortuous conceits. Still, many of his poems are of the 'metaphysical' order. 'The Match,' 'Mourning,' and others

---

[1] Catullus 3.6–10: For honey-sweet he was, and knew his mistress as well as a girl knows her own mother. Nor would he stir from her lap, but hopping now here, now there, would still chirp to his mistress alone. (Trans. F. W. Cornish, Loeb Classical Library, 1912.)

are overweighted with the faults of the school. But sometimes when Marvell has had conceptions of the Donnesque order and translated them into Donne's symbolism, he has in the actual writing purified them with his own simplicity. The result is a poem as vast, picturesque, and lucid as 'To his Coy Mistress,' which contains the lines,

> But at my back I always hear
> Time's winged chariot hurrying near.

This is the second of the 'familiar quotations' from Marvell, but the whole passage (a third part of the poem) is of equal felicity. It has almost all the virtues and almost none of the faults of a phase of English poetry of which it is a typical example:

[Quotes ll. 21–32.]

It cannot be claimed that the language of this is dateless, but its topical flavor does not weigh heavier than the idea, which is an universal one. Similarly composed are 'Daphnis and Chloe,' so old-fashioned in its conception, so modern in its astringent humor, and the less satisfactory 'Definition of Love' with its magnificent beginning:

> My love is of a birth as rare
>   As 'tis, for object, strange and high;
> It was begotten by Despair,
>   Upon Impossibility.

'Daphnis and Chloe' is, unfortunately, too long to quote in full and too climactic to quote in part, but there is probably no poem of Marvell's which gives one greater joy to read.

Lightness, the one thing lacking in our nineteenth-century great; butterfly-winged in Shakespeare's songs and in Herrick; the predominant virtue of the Caroline singers, varying from sheer faery to sheer frivolity; not quite gone (though sadly materialized) even at the Restoration; last heard in Prior; this lightness often makes Marvell's verse charming. 'Daphnis and Chloe,' though wasp rather than butterfly, is at any rate winged; and winged and stingless are the dainty dialogues between Clorinda and Damon, Thyrsis and Dorinda, Hobbinol, Phillis, and Tomalin (for Mary Cromwell's Wedding), and Ametas and Thestylis at their hay-rope. This last is short as well as sweet:

[Quotes the poem.]

It is a slight note, but one the world did ill to lose. It was sounded by no light scorner of the realities, but by a man immersed in affairs and earnestly concerned with the problems of religion and government. Love, the state, and the soul came alike to the ready lyre of the seventeenth century; and Marvell was as varied in his themes as any, and more varied in his touch than most. The form so prettily used for pastoral colloquy was transformed into the vehicle of sound if not very original moralizing in the dialogues between the Resolved Soul and Created Pleasure and between the Soul and the Body. The fine lines called 'Bermudas,' referring to the emigrants driven thither by Laud, were inspired by Marvell's hatred of Episcopalian tyranny, though he was ever a faithful, if independent, son of the Established Church.

Love is seen in many ways; never more beautifully than in the allied and exquisite poems 'The Picture of Little T. C. in a Prospect of Flowers' and 'Young Love.' Political interests produced, if they did not perfect, the 'Horatian Ode' and called forth some pages of dignified couplets on the Protector's death and Blake's victory at Santa Cruz. After the Restoration they seduced the poet to satire; but Marvell, though his was the better cause, has left nothing that lives with 'Hudibras' and 'Absalom and Achitophel.' His satires, inspired by a fine enthusiasm—shame at the Dutch in the Medway, horror of the corruption at Court—are written with tremendous vigor and often in language unsuited to the nice modern ear. They served their turn. But they have neither Dryden's finality and dignity nor the babbling wit which makes Butler still readable because he is so easy to read.

The finest of Marvell's poems in decasyllabic couplets is that prefixed to the 1674 edition of 'Paradise Lost.' It is a noble tribute from a poet to his friend and superior, is an excellent piece of criticism, and has a sting in its tail for Dryden. It may here be noted that at one time Milton, Dryden, and Marvell were all working in the same office of the Council of State. Not even when Mr. [H. A.] Dobson and Mr. [Edmund] Gosse were concocting rondeaux at the Board of Trade (as Mr. [Max] Beerbohm has portrayed them) was so much poetic talent ever gathered into a government office before or since.

But apart from exceptional passages, such as the royal stanzas of the 'Horatian Ode,' the quality which separates Marvell from his contemporaries and lifts him, as it were, right over the eighteenth century is his almost mystical *rapport* with nature.

It is true that there are no stark mountain-tops or troubled seas in his work; his is the kindlier nature of the garden. It was an age of garden-lovers. Bacon, Cowley, and Temple spanned the century. Marvell, as literary horticulturalist, makes a worthy fourth. The garden looms large in his poems. Cromwell comes 'from his private gardens' to his great work. The poet had every opportunity of cultivating the taste. He was born at Winstead in Holderness. 'Roses still riot in Winstead,' says Mr. Birrell, 'the fruit-trees are as many as in the seventeenth century.' The garden of Hull Grammar School was famous; so was that at Nunappleton House, where Marvell lived as tutor to Fairfax's daughter and probably wrote most of his poetry. Thus the poet wandered from garden to garden, learning their secret.

The garden may be the antithesis of nature. But the garden which Marvell loved was not so. It was no place of balanced *parterres* and clipped hedges, but a spot where the earth's fruitfulness is intensified rather than selected.

[Quotes 'The Garden,' ll. 34-40.]

'My fruits are only flowers,' he says elsewhere, but here in his garden poem *par excellence* the fruits are plentiful enough. The last two lines are suggestive of a tropical forest. In one poem, indeed, he goes so far as to inveigh against the gardener's art; but this is one of a charming series for which Damon the Mower is made responsible and in any case does not amount to more than an indictment of too much artifice. Marvell's garden was a 'delicious solitude' of rich grass and fruitful trees. Above all, it was a green place.

In 'The Nymph Complaining for the Death of her Fawn' he describes a girl's delightful pleasaunce—

> So with roses overgrown,
> And lilies, that you would it guess
> To be a little wilderness;

and for a score of lines he rings the changes on white and pink, reminding one of Jacopo del Sellaio's Venus in the National Gallery.

I have through every garden been
Amongst the red, the white, the green ['Eyes and Tears,' ll. 17–18],

he writes elsewhere; but in the famous 'Garden,'

> No white nor red was ever seen
> So amorous as this lovely green. [ll. 17–18]

Taken by themselves, these lines suggest nothing more than a feeling for color. It is only when one has read right through Marvell's work that one realizes the intense significance which green things had for him. Time and again the word occurs, as substantive or adjective, and always with a curious pregnancy. One does not credit him with the definite vagueness, or the vague definition, of a modern symbolist; but it is obvious that *green* was his shorthand for something he could not quite describe, an ecstasy which came on him among grass and moss and trees. It colors his couplets on Appleton House and invests a long and rather tedious poem with a certain glamour. 'The nursery of all things green' he calls Eden, the mother of gardens. Elusive, colorless things, shadows, and thoughts are green for him. In 'The Garden' the overripe, too solid stanza about apples and melons is followed by his most subtle and suggestive lines:

> Meanwhile the mind, from pleasure less,
> Withdraws into its happiness:
> The mind, that ocean where each kind
> Does straight its own resemblance find:
> Yet it creates, transcending these,
> Far other worlds, and other seas,
> Annihilating all that's made
> To a green thought in a green shade. [ll. 41–8]

One might search Shelley and Meredith in vain for a more perfect expression of the mystical union between man and nature. The next stanza is more explicit:

[Quotes ll. 49–56.]

This idea of metamorphosis occurs also in 'Appleton House':

[Quotes ll. 561–8.]

There is nothing very remarkable about either of these two passages. They might be mere flights of fancy. But taken in

331

connection with the rest of Marvell's work, read while his sudden
flashes of insight are remembered (one of which, indeed, the first
immediately follows), they appear as attempts at an intellectual
description of the experiences of a wonderful imaginative sympathy. An understanding which is more than mere aptitude for
simile went to the making of such lines as,

> He hangs in shades the orange bright,
> Like golden lamps in a green night ['Bermudas,' ll. 17–19],

or

> While the youthful hue
> Sits on thy skin like morning dew. ['To His Coy Mistress,' ll. 33–4]

This imaginative quality is by no means omnipresent in Marvell's
poetry, but it is there in sufficient volume to be a strong element
in the final impression which that poetry leaves; and it links him
with Marlowe and Shakespeare on the one hand, with Coleridge
and Shelley on the other, rather than with those who were of his
own age and in many external characteristics his kin.

His poems were little more than an episode in Marvell's busy
life, and he did not even publish them. It was not until three years
after his death that a volume of his verse was given to the world. All
his best work was probably done while he was in the pleasant and
stimulating company of the Fairfaxes. His latter days were almost
songless. Affairs claimed him. First as Milton's assistant in the
Latin secretaryship, and then for eighteen years as a silent but
conscientious member of Parliament, he had little time for strolling
in green garden ways.

His pen was by no means dry. The weekly letters which he wrote
to his constituents at Hull are valuable documents for the parliamentary history of the period. After the Restoration he used much
black and bitter ink in satire and controversy. He was the most
brilliant journalist of the Country Party. But though 'The Rehearsal
Transprosed' and 'The Last Instructions to a Painter' are still
interesting, they are journalism and nothing higher. The lines on
Milton are the noblest work of his later years, but even they have
the taint of party feeling.

It is obvious that Marvell was extremely sensitive to his environment. He was not one of those who can write of roses in
Grub Street. In the thick of politics he became perforce a pamphleteer; it was only on the shaded lawns of Appleton that he could

be a poet. His poems are as few as his years of rural peace. But if this responsiveness to his surroundings conditioned and limited his production, it was also precisely that which gave to what he did write its intimate magic.

97. Isaac Rosenberg comments on 'To His Coy Mistress'

1917

An experimental and 'war poet,' Isaac Rosenberg (1890–1918) had a short career. His collected works—poetry, prose, letters, and some drawings—were published in 1937 with a foreword by Siegfried Sassoon. In a letter to (Sir) Edward Marsh, postmarked 27 May 1917, he comments somewhat hazily on 'To His Coy Mistress.'

Extract from the *Collected Works*, ed. G. Bottomley and D. Harding (1937), pp. 316–17.

My Dear Marsh,
.... Mr. [Laurence] Binyon has often sermonised lengthily over my working on two different principles in the same thing and I know how it spoils the unity of a poem. But if I couldn't before, I can now, I am sure plead the absolute necessity of fixing an idea before it is lost, because of the situation its concieved [*sic*] in. Regular rythms [*sic*] I do not like much, but of course it depends on where the stress and accent are laid. I think there is nothing finer than the vigorous opening of Lycydas [*sic*] for music; yet it is regular. Now I think if Andrew Marvell had broken up his rythms more he would have been considered a terrific poet. As it is I like his poem urging his mistress to love because they have not a thousand years to love in and he can't afford to wait. (I forget the name of the poem) well I like it more than Lycydas.

333

98. A. Clutton-Brock on
Marvell and Vaughan

1918

Critic and journalist, A. Clutton-Brock (1868–1924) contributed an unsigned review-essay on Sir Francis Meynell's
edition of Marvell and Vaughan to the *Times Literary Supplement*, 1 August, 1918; he then reprinted it in a collection of his
essays.

Extract from *More Essays on Books* (1921), pp. 134–42, 145–8.

It was a happy idea of Mr. Meynell's to put some poems of Marvell
and Vaughan together in one volume and to call it *The Best of Both
Worlds*. The very title is a light thrown on the virtues of these two
poets, on their likeness and on the difference between them.
Marvell is of this world; Vaughan of the other; but each gives us
the best of his own world because he is not shut up in it. There is
no worldliness in Marvell, no other-worldliness in Vaughan.
Between them, they prove that there is a quality common to both
worlds because it is common to them. It was, indeed, the virtue
of their age to be aware of this common quality. Many then thought
and felt in terms of both worlds; and neither religion nor science
had set up a partition between them. There has never been a time
in which so many men, not poets by profession, have attained to
the highest excellence in poetry. It is not that, like the Elizabethans,
they had the knack of pretty songs or were governed by a fine convention of art. The best amateur poetry of the seventeenth century
escapes from convention and dares the utmost absurdities in its
freedom; but the most absurd of them, [Edward] Benlowes
himself, can think with the beauty of passion and feel with the
precision of thought. Writing of a private music-meeting, he says:

> Sure it was no time to pray,
> The deities themselves then being all at play. ['A Poetic Descant,'
>   ll. 62–3]

How could the quality of some music be better expressed? It is holy, but with the holiness of gods at play. It might have been written by Mozart about his own music, had Mozart been a poet. All the poets of that age, from Milton downwards, see in music the link between the two worlds. They are of a society in which men will at any moment gather, from fighting or controversy or love-making or politics, into a quiet room to make music or listen to it. The other world, for them, is not something to which you pay formal compliments in church, or which you try to disprove with the envy of those who have never seen it; it is acknowledged, because known, by all; it shapes gardens as it shapes music and verse; and at any moment they could escape into its peace.

They did indeed make the best of both worlds, because they had not cut them off from each other, because to them beauty was a common quality of both. Heaven was not all mists nor earth all mud. Vaughan speaks of the other world in terms of this one; and Marvell of this in the terms of the other. . . .

Marvell, too, through his intimacy with earth, was intimate with heaven. The worldling is one who sees nothing of the other world because he sees nothing of this. Thinking of everything in terms of something else, he is always glancing over his shoulder to discover what others are looking at. For him the world is like a waiting-room at Clapham Junction, where he never catches any train, but waits for pleasure or success that never comes, seeing nothing because he is always waiting. But Marvell, who had both pleasure and success, who must have enjoyed life if ever a man did, waited for nothing, but found his happiness in the garden where he was. At first it seems to be a happiness of pure sense:

[Quotes 'The Garden,' ll. 33–40.]

But the very intensity of sense, being enjoyed by the mind no less than the body, awakens the spirit to its own delight:

[Quotes ll. 49–56.]

The very theme of this poem is that passing of sense into spirit which its art actually accomplishes. They are not two different and hostile things as they seem to the ascetic or the materialist, both frightened fools; but rather different degrees of intensity. The poem itself is all sense, only before the theme has possessed the

poet; the mind, out of the very intensity of its delight in all that the
senses pour into it,—

> Creates, transcending these,
> Far other worlds and other seas;
> Annihilating all that's made
> To a green thought in a green shade. [ll. 45–8]

So Shelley said of the poet:—

> He will watch from dawn to gloom
> The lake-reflected sun illume
> The yellow bees in the ivy-bloom,
> Nor heed nor see what things they be;
> But from these create he can
> Forms more real than living man,
> Nurslings of immortality.
> [*Prometheus Unbound*, I. 743–9]

It needed a Shelley, in his time, to see such things and to say them;
and to many of his time, and ours, his words seem mere musical
nonsense. But in Marvell's age many saw them and said them;
and they were known to be truth. Marvell was a member of Parliament, a man of affairs; yet he had the faith, the very experience, of
Shelley, and expressed it in a more matter-of-fact, more concrete,
way, because it was not a private faith or experience of his own but
common to many. The very fanatics of that age were politicians
and soldiers too; they banded together and, instead of writing
pamphlets or poems published privately, tried to practise what
they preached; they seized land on St. George's Hill at Weybridge,
and there went naked and ate no flesh. Shelleys in action were
common and talked a religious language which, because it was
religious, was the language of other men and understood by them.
So their action, because it was religious, was but the action, carried
further, of other men and understood by them. They were saints,
not cranks, even if troublesome saints.

Marvell was not a saint or troublesome; but he talks the language, even when he trifles, of the extreme poets. The theme of
his lines to his coy mistress was worked to death by triflers of
succeeding generations; it had been worked to death generations
before. But for him, even while he still seemed to trifle with it, it
was an opening to all the spaces of time and eternity. The figures
of the lover and his mistress are like the little, modish figures of

Fragonard, which move us because their wistful frivolity is set in a vast landscape of cloudy golden trees and infinite avenues. There are these avenues in Marvell's poem:—

> Had we but world enough and time,
> This coyness, lady, were no crime—

he begins like any trifling versifier, but for the phrase 'world enough and time.' That phrase controls the poem; and he passes at once into immensities:

[Quotes ll. 3–10.]

There follows the couplet wonderful in sound and sense—

> My vegetable love should grow
> Vaster than empires and more slow—

a couplet that makes one think of pumpkins and eternity in one breath, preparing for the great stroke of the poem—

> But at my back I always hear
> Time's winged chariot hurrying near;
> And yonder all before us lie
> Deserts of vast eternity.

At the end we are left wondering at this art, more like the painter's than the poet's, which can conjure everything out of nothing by its very quality. In spite of the difference of theme it is the quality of Vaughan's:—

> I saw eternity the other night,
> Like a great ring of pure and endless light,
> All calm as it was bright ['The World,' ll. 1–3]—

the quality of minds that know both worlds and always see one in the other.

But Marvell, the poet of this world felt to the utmost, has more of the wisdom of this world than Vaughan, and is more fit for anthologies. Most of his good poems are good all through, artfully contrived, full of audacities on the verge of absurdity and delighting us with their hairbreadth escape from it.

When Vaughan reaches a certain intensity of feeling both worlds become one to him, as they do to Shelley, to Augustine, to Marvell even. For all these the opposition of spirit and sense is one that happens through failure. All those oppositions with which the mind of man is troubled are but the result of failure to live always at a height reached sometimes; and what troubles them is not the opposition, but the failure to rise above it. Vaughan is more troubled than Marvell; for Marvell believed in the natural man and in a simple, easy way of life. If only men would cultivate their gardens, they might enjoy the happiness which life offers them with both hands.

[Quotes 'The Garden,' ll. 1–8.] . . .

The great over-weening nuisances of the world are merely dull of sense; their energy is blind and furious because they do not know how to enjoy. Napoleon was 'the unamusable.' That is the wisdom which Marvell does not preach but sings. No poet is less sensual than he is; for he knows that sensuality is mere dullness of sense. Pure sense for him has the disinterestedness of spirit in it and becomes spirit as it grows more intense. That is how one world turns into the other and how the best of both becomes one. If you have the sense of beauty, which is a sense, your spirit is aware of the spirit of beauty. So he says to the Nuns of Appleton House [*sic*]—

> I see the angels, in a crown,
> On you the lilies showering down;
> And round about you glory breaks,
> That something more than human speaks.
> All beauty when at such a height
> Is so already consecrate. [ll. 141–6]

See beauty with enough intensity and you see that it is holy. You need all your sense to be aware of spirit.

But, we may be sure, Marvell would not have denied the more troubled and straining doctrine of Vaughan. The language of this world which he spoke was, because of its beauty, kin to Vaughan's language of the other world; there are birds and flowers in Vaughan's Paradise as in Marvell's garden. The same perversity makes a man blind to both; for he is blind to the other world because he is blind to this one. Therefore it is well to read these poets together, and to remember that they lived in a time of trouble like our own, a trouble as bitter as ours, though with a different bitterness. Then, as now, men seemed to make the worst of both worlds, because they could see neither. They lived, as they live, in a nonsense world of their own making; and the poets shatter it more gently, but not less surely, than the prophets. For they show us the true world of sense, which in their art is one. That relation which is beauty is of both worlds; whenever you see beauty as it is—

> ... round about you glory breaks,
> That something more than human speaks.
> All beauty when at such a height
> Is so already consecrate. [ll. 143–6]

These poets, whether they trifle or agonize, are a prophecy of the human mind when it shall have learned its true business, to be aware of the one world of beauty, and to act according to its awareness. The hero rushes into the nonsense world that he may force it into sense; the poet also has his own cure for it. He is the sun shining on the obstinate traveller; he tells us that we have only to cast away the cloak of our own blindness and we shall see reality.

99. H.M. Margoliouth on Marvell and his contemporaries

1919

Academician and later distinguished editor of Marvell's poems and letters, H. M. Margoliouth (1887–1959) published the two-part essay on Marvell anonymously. He is identified as its author by Legouis, *André Marvell* (Paris-London, 1928), p. 480.

(a) 'Marvell and Cowley,' *Saturday Review*, 127 (7 June 1919), pp. 550–1.

With a few exceptions, and those not of the first importance, the poems of Andrew Marvell were first printed in 1681. But practically all were written in the decade 1649–1658, and they owe more hints than is generally known to the work of contemporaries and immediate predecessors. It is, of course, to be expected that there should be reminiscences of Shakespeare and Jonson, and Marvell's close familiarity with 'Lycidas' among the other works of Milton, at first his patron and afterwards his protégé, is obvious enough. But readers who find Marvell's charm unfailing but could still ask with Pope,

> Who now reads Cowley?

can hardly be aware of the suggestions which Marvell drew from Cowley's 'Mistress' and built up into great poetry.

Cowley's 'Mistress: or, Several Copies of Love-Verses,' was first published in 1647. It would be rash to say that Marvell was unfamiliar with any of these poems before publication, for Cowley had been the precocious genius of that age and he and Marvell were scholars of Trinity, Cambridge together, being elected in 1637 and 1638 respectively; and this may be one reason why Marvell, familiar though he was with most of the numerous volumes of poems which thronged to the press on the cessation of fighting in 1646, was familiar above all with 'The Mistress.'

Perhaps the most striking instance to bring forward is that of Marvell's opening lines 'To his Coy Mistress.' If only Time would allow, he would consent to as slow a wooing as might be:

[Quotes ll. 13–18, 21–4.]

Not for nothing had Cowley, in 'My Dyet,' written:

> On a *Sigh* of Pity I a year can live,
>   One *Tear* will keep me twenty at least,
>   Fifty a gentle *Look* will give;
> An hundred years on one *kind word* I'll feast;
>   A thousand more will added be,
> If you an *Inclination* have for me;
> And all beyond is vast Eternity. [st. 3]

Cowley is here trying a difficult metre and Marvell an easy one; but that does not alter the fact that, if the merit of suggestion is Cowley's, the merit of accomplishment is Marvell's. To begin with, there is all the difference between them which, to use Cole-ridge's vocabulary, exists between the product of Fancy and that of Imagination, and then Marvell develops the last line of 'The Dyet' into that wonderfully solemn quatrain, sounding a note as though blown with subdued breath on the trumpet of the Dweller in the Innermost—a note familiar to the Marvellian, who comes upon it even in a poem on weeping, that trite and sometimes nauseating subject of the Caroline poets,

> How wide they dream! The *Indian* slaves
> That sink for Pearl through Seas profound,
> Would find her Tears yet deeper Waves
> And not of one the bottom sound. ['Mourning,' ll. 29–32]

The conceit in the third line jars one, but it is the true note and it indicates that the true *afflatus* had come on the poet, a 'ditty of no tone' had been piped to his spirit, for the whole feeling of the poem changes, and instead of the 'conceited' and 'metaphysical' nonsense of which it has hitherto consisted, it ends simply and surprisingly:

> I yet my silent Judgment keep,
> Disputing not what they believe:
> But sure as oft as Women weep,
> It is to be suppos'd they grieve.

Marvell grew up under the influence of the conceit. On the whole it was not a good influence. Usually he has to escape from it into poetry, but sometimes he subdues and makes poetry of it.

> My soul is of a birth as rare
> As 'tis for object strange and high:
> It was begotten by despair
> Upon Impossibility. ['Definition of Love,' ll. 1–4]

It is not fanciful to see here a reminiscence of Cowley's poem 'Impossibilities,' for Marvell's last stanza,

> Therefore the Love which us doth bind
> But Fate so enviously debars,
> Is the Conjunction of the Mind,
> And Opposition of the Stars,

is clearly not unrelated to Cowley's third verse,

341

So thy *Heart* in *Conjunction* with mine,
  Shall our own fortunes regulate;
And to our *Stars themselves* prescribe a Fate. [st. 3]

The contrast of sentiment here is noticeable and instinctive, Cowley, indeed, though the lesser poet, is the greater love poet. 'Impossibilities' is a fine poem; the lines quoted are as sturdy as those of Henley's which they suggest; and it has a beautiful ending. Marvell's love poetry, where chiefly Cowley's influence is to be noted, is small in bulk and lacks cumulative evidence of sincerity, how great soever are the individual merits of 'To his Coy Mistress' and 'The Fair Singer,' not to mention isolated lines and stanzas elsewhere. The writer of 'Bermudas,' 'The Garden' and 'An Horation Ode' does not live as a poet of love, but as a master of words, a maker of a sweet and solemn music and a revealer of the greatness of men and their actions.

One more passage from 'The Mistress' must be quoted, though there are others which can be found for the looking, for by it we are able to clinch the restoration of a line in Marvell that has gone wrong from its first printing to the present day. The first piece printed in the original (1681) issue of Marvell's poems is 'A Dialogue, Between The Resolved Soul, and Created Pleasure.' It is an attractive poem in two parts in which Pleasure first attacks the soul by offering inducements to each of the five senses, to that of touch, for instance, by suggesting that the 'Lord of Earth' should

On these soft downy Pillows lye,
Whose soft Plumes will thither fly. [ll. 19–20]

To which the almost Shelleian reply is

My gentler Rest is on a Thought. [l. 23]

After each sense has been attacked and the attack rebuffed, there is an interval in which the Soul is encouraged to persevere, and then Pleasure tries again by offers of Beauty, Wealth, Power and Knowledge, and again the attack is beaten off. The offer of Beauty comes first and appears thus in the original edition:

All this fair, and cost, and sweet,
  Which scatteringly doth shine,
Shall within one Beauty meet,
  And she be only thine.

342

Two things are clear here. One is the meaning—all these attractions which were presented to each sense separately shall be combined in a single Beauty. The other is that something has gone wrong with the word 'cost.' Marvell's next editor ('Hesiod' Cooke in 1726) cut the Gordian knot and printed

> All that's costly, fair, and sweet,

which is not only a hopelessly unscholarly correction, but misses half the meaning. All succeeding editors have followed him, yet it is clear that 'cost' (with a long s) is only a misprint, and not a very bad one, for 'soft,' which harks back to the 'downy Pillows.' Any doubt is dispelled when we turn to Cowley and in a poem called 'The Soul,' a title shorter than but similar to Marvell's, read first an appeal to each sense in turn and then these lines:

> If all things that in *Nature* are
> Either soft, or sweet, or fair,
> Be not in Thee so '*Epitomiz'd*.' [ll. 17–19]

Apart from 'The Mistress,' there is one point of comparison between Marvell and Cowley not to be overlooked. In his Essay 'Of Obscurity,' the latter translated into twenty-six turgid lines a thirteen-line passage from a chorus in Seneca's 'Thyestes.' Marvell englished the same into fourteen lines beginning:—

> Climb at *Court* for me that will,

using a metre which may be considered the exact equivalent in our language of Seneca's, giving a perfect and almost literal translation, and yet creating a little poem that contains no hint of foreign origin. A full comparison of it with Seneca and with Cowley well repays interest, but it may be mere coincidence that both English poets translated the same passage. Cowley's Essays were published in 1668, after his death, and, if it is not a coincidence, Marvell either knew 'Of Obscurity' long before its publication or wrote his own lines after 1668.[1] The latter is on several grounds almost impossible.

(b) 'Marvell and Other Contemporaries,' *Saturday Review*, 128 (19 July 1919), pp. 55–6.

---

[1] Also translated in 1676 by Sir Matthew Hale, *Contemplations, Moral and Divine*, and in 1684 by John Norris of Bemerton, *Poems and Discourses*.

From Cowley we turn to the older poet who shared with him such great contemporary reputation and such posthumous decline, Edmund Waller. He, too, was a Cambridge man, but he had 'gone down' many years before the time of Cowley or Marvell. But the latter was extremely well acquainted with Waller's 'Battle of the Summer Islands,' first published in 1645. The 'Summer Islands' are the Bermudas. The subject was not suggested to Marvell by this poem, which, after an account of the Islands, goes on to describe a fight with two stranded whales. Marvell's subject, the arrival of Puritan exiles at this western Paradise, was suggested by his residence as tutor to a ward of Cromwell at the house of the Oxenbridges, who had twice visited the Bermudas *Religionis causa*. But he drew largely on Waller for his description of the islands, and almost begins with an allusion to the subject of Waller's poem:—

> Where he the huge Sea-Monsters wracks,
> That lift the Deep upon their Backs,
> He lands *us* on a grassy stage. [ll. 9–11]

The italics of *us* are our own, but the emphasis and contrast with the 'huge Sea-Monsters' is often missed.

Then Marvell writes,

> He gave us this eternal spring,
> Which here enamels everything

with a felicity at least equal to that of his original

> For the kind spring, which but salutes us here,
> Inhabits there, and courts them all the yeare. [I. 40–1]

In the same way Marvell goes on to his well-known description of the fruits of the islands and the ambergris of the sea, which was nearly all in Waller before him; but Marvell translates it all into poetry, where Waller gave little better than a catalogue or at most an attractive menu.

It is interesting, while on this subject, to notice, even though the instances are rather trifling, that Marvell twice more drew on 'The Battle of the Summer Islands,' once before and once after writing 'Bermudas.' The earlier instance is in the poem 'Upon the Hill and Grove at Bill-borow,' where he borrows the phrase 'Groves of Pikes' [III. 54], and later in the lines which he addressed to Cromwell on Blake's victory off Teneriffe, where, after a description of Teneriffe very much in the manner of Waller's account of the Bermudas, he breaks off,

> But whilst I draw that Scene, where you ere long
> Shall conquests act, your present are unsung [ll. 65–6],

just as Waller broke off,

> But while I doe these pleasing dreames indite,
> I am diverted from the promis'd fight. [I. 73–4]

Marvell wrote this poem on Blake's victory fresh from reading the broadside publication of Waller's lines on the victory won a few months earlier off San Lucar, near Cadiz. The two poems will repay a close comparison, though it will not bring out Marvell's strongest points, for in spite of those passages in his 'Poem on the Death of Oliver Cromwell,' where the true note is struck, he is not happiest with the decasyllabic couplet. Most noticeably in the poem on Blake's victory he borrows Waller's view of the Spanish treasure which was sunk in these two battles:—

> What Earth in her dark bowels could not keep
> From greedy hands, lies safer in the deep,
> Where *Thetis* kindly do's from mortals hide,
> Those seeds of Luxury, Debate, and Pride,
> ['Of a War with Spain, and a Fight at Sea,' ll. 71–4]

wrote Waller, and Marvell echoed him with,

> Their Gallions sunk, their wealth the sea does fill,
> The only place where it can cause no Ill [ll. 151–2],

and a few lines later,

> And in one War the present age may boast,
> The certain seeds of many Wars are lost. [ll. 159–60]

How Waller's 'Instructions to a Painter,' followed by Denham's, lured or led Marvell into the path of political satire is another story. Many of the satires and lampoons ascribed to him are not by his hand; those which are certainly his have all the wit, but not much of the delicacy of Lamb's famous phrase. But that Marvell could always dispense with delicacy in our sense of the word is proved by what is very probably his earliest extant work in English, the very clever poem on 'Fleckno, an English Priest at Rome.' It is strange that, as a writer, he should have been known exclusively as the author of satires or of witty prose; that even in Wordsworth's day his name survived in company with those of Algernon Sidney and James Harrington [see No. 40] as that of a stalwart republican (which he was not); and that his poetry properly so-called should not have been printed till after his death, and, in spite of three eighteenth century editions, should not have been 'discovered' till the nineteenth.

The boom in publication at the end of the main fighting of the civil war included not only Cowley's 'Mistress,' but all or most of the work of Crashaw, Henry Vaughan, Herrick and Lovelace. It also included (1647) Cleveland's 'Rebel Scot,' which long afterwards gave a title to Marvell's 'Loyal Scot.' With Lovelace Marvell was, of course, acquainted. He was among many who wrote complimentary verses introducing Lovelace's volume entitled 'Lucasta' (1649), and he had in mind the lines of the 'Dialogue. Lucasta, Alexis,'

> Love nee're his Standard when his Hoste he sets,
> Creates alone fresh-bleeding Bannerets [ll. 15–16],

when he wrote at the end of 'The Unfortunate Lover,'

> a Lover drest
> In his own Blood does relish best.
> This is the only *Banneret*
> That ever Love created yet.

From Crashaw Marvell took little. He is one of the best known exponents of the 'tear' motive and may have given Marvell a hint of phraseology in 'Eyes and Tears.' Vaughan shares with Marvell, though in a less degree, a fondness for the adjectives 'green' and 'shady,' and it can hardly be fortuitous that Marvell's description in 'Tom May's Death' of Ben Jonson in the Elysian Fields, where

> in the dusky Laurel shade
> Amongst the Chorus of old Poets laid [ll. 14–15]

he rules over 'the Learned throng,' can be so exactly paralleled by Vaughan's lines (published 1646) 'To my Ingenuous Friend, R. W.':—

First, in the shade of his owne bayes,
Great BEN they'le see, whose sacred Layes,
The learned Ghosts admire, and throng,
To catch the subject of his Song. [ll. 29–32]

We will conclude with a slightly earlier poet, Thomas Carew, whose poems were first collected in 1640, a year after his death. Here the connection is not so striking or obvious as in the case of Cowley or Waller, but where one instance might fail to carry conviction, several make it fairly certain that the earlier and lesser poet did act by way of suggestion on Marvell. Marvell in 'Young Love' says that

Common Beauties stay fifteen,

and Carew was fond of the expression 'Common Beauties.'[1] Marvell, perhaps, borrows from Carew the name Celia for his pupil, Mary Fairfax. Marvell's Daphnis unsuccessfully woos Chloe, for he

Knew not that the Fort to gain
Better 'twas the Siege to raise. [ll. 19–20]

Carew, in 'Conquest by Flight,' had declared, though with a different moral, that

only they
Conquer love that run away. [ll. 15–16]

Marvell in his charming lines on 'The Picture of Little T. C. in a Prospect of Flowers,' where—like Francis Thompson, though with a difference—he goes on to think of the child as she will be, speaks of her in a phrase of Carew's as 'This Darling of the Gods,'[2]

whose chaster Laws
The wanton Love shall one day fear,
And, under her command severe
See his Bow broke [ll. 11–14],

as Carew, in 'A New Year's Gift. To the Queen,' had addressed her as

[1] For example, 'Ingrateful Beauty Threat'ned,' l. 4, and 'To A. L. Persuasions to Love,' l. 14.
[2] 'Upon the King's Sickness,' l. 37.

347

Thou great Commandress, that doest move
Thy Scepter o'r the Crown of Love,
And through his Empire with the Awe
Of Thy chaste beames, doest give the Law. [ll. 1–4]

Finally, Carew's poem, 'To my Friend G. N. from Wrest,'
contains a long passage which cannot but have been in Marvell's
mind or before his eyes when he wrote his description of Appleton
House. Both houses are homely and hospitable, both have dis-
pensed with the ambitious architect. In the house Carew describes

In stead of Statues to adorn their wall,
They throng with living men, their merry Hall. [ll. 33–4]

At Appleton House,

A Stately *Frontispice of Poor*
Adorns without the open Door:
Nor less the Rooms within commends
Daily new *Furniture of Friends.*
The House was built upon the Place
Only as a *Mark of Grace*;
And for an *Inn* to entertain
Its *Lord* awhile, but not remain. [ll. 65–72]

At Appleton House Marvell was in his poetic prime. Here he
wrote his poems of garden and country, and here his master
Fairfax, taking Marvell's lines metaphorically and using Marvell's
metre and cadences, wrote of his house as may still be read in his
own handwriting:—

Thinke not ô Man that dwells herein
This House's a stay, but as an Inne
Which for Convenience fittly stands
In way to one nott made with hands.
But if a time here thou take Rest,
Yett thinke Eternity's the Best.
['Upon the New-built House at Appleton']

100. H. J. Massingham on Marvell's poetry

1919–1921

Motivated in part because it was the 'most neglected' period in English literature, the journalist and writer H. J. Massingham (1888–1952) published an anthology of seventeenth-century verse in 1919. He included in it eleven of Marvell's poems, in whole or in excerpts, but, interestingly enough, he excluded 'Bermudas' because it was so well known. In 1921 he published an unsigned essay on Marvell which was then reprinted, with minor changes, in the *Tercentenary Tributes*. His autobiography *Remembrance* appeared in 1941.

(a)   Note on 'To His Coy Mistress' from *A Treasury of Seventeenth-Century English Verse* (1919), pp. 354–5.

A perfect example of Marvell's 'witty delicacy.' Being a beautiful composite of various emotions all playing into one another's hands, it is more. Perfect gallantry, pathos, irony, reflective melancholy, reverence, buoyancy, passion, tact are all contained in a style of matchless purity and fitness. Wonderful too is the way the slight playful tone of the poem, like the plashing of a stream, expands into a river of full harmony!

> My vegetable love should grow
> Vaster than empires, and more slow.

Marvell, like Vaughan, is unique. They both have a special and most precious note among our poets.

(b)   Extract from 'Andrew Marvell,' *Nation and Athenaeum*, 2 April 1921, pp. 20–1.

Marvell, indeed, has had a topsy-turvy reputation. Up to quite modern times, men have honoured him as the political purist who opposed a vain and lonely integrity to the demoralization of affairs after the Restoration, who was almost the only honest MP in a House stuffed with trimmers, careerists, place-hunters, and profiteers, who was a consistent Radical constitutionalist under a despotism, and saved Milton at personal risk from being excluded from the Bill of Indemnity, and pay for his apology for Charles's execution with his own. His lyrics were the amenities embroidered upon the toga of public probity, whereas nowadays we view the former as the seamless garment clothing a firm and gracious temper, a richly composite personality, of which his politics were less the expression than the material. His satires, lampoons, and invectives, with their fierce, contemptuous dignity unsoured by prejudice or personal malignity, and, except in pieces like 'The Character of Holland' (driven by a spate of literary high spirits channelled by wit), nearly always motived by a disinterested passion for tolerance, justice, charity, and principle, occupy us for his sake rather than their own, as an index to a character which directed a whole man made up of many parts. Put him beside Waller, whom the 'Cambridge History' commends for his 'constitutional liberalism,' and for being 'a party to the *via media*,' smooth titles which fit Marvell well enough. Waller, in fact, was a Coalition Liberal, a politic amphibian adjusted to the mastery of all elements, a meteorological expert of such dexterous parts that he could sense a change of wind and be ever prompt to set his sails by it. In the 1664 edition of his poems, his elegy upon the death of the Lord Protector occurs next door to his panegyric 'Upon His Majesty's Happy Return,' and his discreet courtship of 'Sacharissa' (aptly named)—the daughter of the Earl of Leicester—carried into a domestic triumph a public career sufficiently distinguished for its ingenuities.

Marvell himself steered these same perilous waters. He was a Cromwellian who never fought in the Civil War, a monarchist who denounced the corruptions of kingship, a servant of two hostile parties, and a factionary of neither, a politician who did his best for both worlds. But we no more think of doubting Marvell's honor than his poetic genius, and if he was strangely compounded both of Puritan and Cavalier, he was a whole man—*integer vitae*—who fused the best qualities of them both. When he writes to his constituents [*sic*]—'Parliament was never so embarrassed beyond recovery. We are all venal cowards except some few,'[1] we silently

---

[1] The letter (14 April 1670) was, in fact, addressed to his nephew William Popple (*Letters*, p. 317).

assume the exception and take him wholeheartedly at his own valuation—'I shall, God willing, maintain the same incorrupt mind and clear conscience, free from faction or any self-ends, which I have, by His grace, hitherto preserved' [*Letters*, p. 177]—because in his public, equally with his poetic fruits, we recognize by an intuitive appreciation that he nothing common did or mean.

As a Member of Parliament, Marvell was not much more than a back-bencher, shrewd and incorruptible. In poetry he is as unique as John Clare [see No. 49], in the sense that he is matchless, not in greatness, but in individual quality. But the same compositeness, the same poise and balance, appear in his poetics as his politics, and in similar conditions. His poetry accurately reflects the transition between the metaphysical and the Augustan schools, and yet holds these incompatibles as perfectly as he reconciled the Puritan and the Cavalier as a man, and Republicanism and Monarchism as a public servant, because he was both and neither, but a personal third into which they melted in harmony. By analysis, Marvell's poems are full of contraries. His porcelain-like artificiality, for instance, is obvious:

> I could have fled from one but singly fair:
> My disentangled soul itself might save,
> Breaking the curled trammels of her hair,
> But how should I avoid to be her slave
> Whose subtil art invisibly can wreathe
> My fetters of the very air I breathe?
> ['The Fair Singer,' ll. 7–12]

Yet, outside Vaughan, he was the only seventeenth-century poet to bespeak Nature to her face:—

> Thrice happy he, who, not mistook,
> Hath read in Nature's mystic book.
> ['Appleton House,' ll. 583–4]

In 'Upon Appleton House' he writes on the 'Hewel' (yaffle)—'He walks still upright from the root, Meas'ring the timber with his foot; And all the way to keep it clean, Doth from the bark the woodmoths glean' [ll. 539–42]; on the thrush: 'And through the hazels thick espy The hatching throstle's shining eye' [ll. 531–2]; 'And where I language want, my signs The bird upon the bough divines' [ll. 571–2], and such intimacy is a stranger to the age.

Another poetic mark of his is (in the 'Manners makyth ...'
sense) mannerliness, now tender, now playful, now ironical, now
gallant, now reflective, and sometimes, as in 'To His Coy Mistress,'
all of them and more:

> Had we but world enough, and time,
> This coyness lady, were no crime. ...
> My vegetable love should grow
> Vaster than empires, and more slow [ll. 1–2, 11–12],

and so on in that wonderfully precise and disciplined command of
the rather diffuse octosyllabic couplet in the enchanting use of
which he outshone all his contemporaries. This mannerliness is a
very subtle privilege of Marvell's. It is more than 'witty delicacy,'
than elegance, than grace or comeliness, just as his metrical chimes
are more than sensuously grateful to the ear. At its most fugitive,
it possesses an imaginative gravity, which brings news and sound
of the eternal concords. Marvell has been too readily summed up
as the poetic epicure. Yet again, endowed as he is with this quality,
so supremely that it comes unconsciously to his hand, a poet, too,
of the lawn rather than the field, of the cultivated than the hedge
rose, a poet with little passion, there is more than a hint of a sudden
wildness in him. Again 'The Coy Mistress':—

> Let us roll all our strength and all
> Our sweetness up into one ball
> And tear our pleasures with rough strife
> Thorough the iron gates of life.
> Thus, though we cannot make our sun
> Stand still, yet we will make him run [ll. 41–6];

in:—

> Bind me, ye woodbines, in your twines,
> Curl me about, ye gadding vines,
>   ['Appleton House,' ll. 609–10]

like a bound of the heart, and in the intoxicated surrender of
personal identity in the famous Garden poem.

These incongruities could easily be multiplied, but the total
impression of the poems is of their completeness. In politics it is
one kind of integrity, in poetry another. If by analysis he can be
separated into heterogeneous parts, by synthesis all his best
poems are resolved into a final unity. This is the more striking

because, being a poet of the transition, his poetic self-fulfilment is, as it were, dimorphic. Marvell is often very near the eighteenth century, and his pastorals (not to mention his polished later satires) walk on the edge of that chasm of personification which swallowed poetry up for nearly a hundred years—'And virgin Trebles wed the manly Base' ['Music's Empire,' l. 10]—one foot is over. The frustrations of the seventeenth-century Metaphysical School in its heroic ambition to touch, if only by the fingertips, the great original of the lesser spiritual illuminations which both guide and distract the heart of man, were bound to lead to the well-bred generalities of the Augustans. The word, being incompletely made flesh, lost it in the end altogether, and poetry, unable to express the abstract by the form of the concrete and particular, sacrificed both to the prosaic habit of general terms. Thus Marvell is at times pure seventeenth century:—

> My Love is of a birth as rare
>   As 'tis for object strange and high;
> It was begotten by Despair
>   Upon Impossibility. ['Definition of Love,' ll. 1–4]

There is the queer throb of that magical cadence, which, as Professor Saintsbury truly says, has never, except fragmentarily, been rediscovered since its loss. The lines 'On a Drop of Dew' engrave all the mysticism of the age, and Marvell had a flair for the conceit which his wit and workmanship usually turned to the happiest account. Thus poised in a middle way between two literary ages which contradicted each other more flatly than ever Republican did Monarchist, he kept his head between the two.

Reconciliation, then, is a good word for Marvell; he went about his world rubbing out frontiers. Varicoloured as were his life and work, he was an artist in blends. And, confounding the sharpest division of all, that between political and poetic truth, he wrote

[Quotes 'Appleton House,' ll. 321–34.]

101. Sir Herbert Grierson on the metaphysical lyric

1921

The first professor of English at Aberdeen University and later successor to Saintsbury at Edinburgh, Sir Herbert Grierson (1866–1960) did much to stimulate interest in the metaphysical poets with his two-volume edition of Donne and other works.

Extract from the Introduction to *Metaphysical Lyrics and Poems of the Seventeenth Century* (Oxford, 1921), pp. xxix–xxxi, xxxvii–xxxviii, reprinted by permission of Oxford University Press.

It was among the younger generation of Courtiers that Donne found the warmest admirers of his paradoxical and sensual audacities as a love-poet, as it was the divines who looked to Laud and the Court for Anglican doctrine and discipline who revered his memory, enshrined by the pious Izaak Walton, as of a divine poet and preacher. The 'metaphysicals' were all on the King's side. Even Andrew Marvell was neither Puritan nor Republican. 'Men ought to have trusted God,' was his final judgement on the Rebellion, 'they ought to have trusted the King with the whole matter' [*RT I*, p. 135]. They were on the side of the King, for they were on the side of the humanities; and the Puritan rebellion, whatever the indirect constitutional results, was in itself and at the moment a fanatical upheaval, successful because it also threw up the John Zizka of his age; its triumph was the triumph of Cromwell's sword.

[Quotes the 'Horatian Ode,' ll. 115–20.]

To call these poets the 'school of Donne' or 'metaphysical' poets may easily mislead if one takes either phrase in too full a sense. It is not only that they show little of Donne's subtlety of

354

mind or 'hydroptic, immoderate thirst of human learning,' but they want, what gives its interest to this subtle and fantastic misapplication of learning,—the complexity of mood, the range of personal feeling which lends such fullness of life to Donne's strange and troubled poetry. His followers, amorous and courtly, or pious and ecclesiastical, move in a more rarefied atmosphere; their poetry is much more truly 'abstract' than Donne's, the witty and fantastic elaboration of one or two common moods, of compliment, passion, devotion, penitence. It is very rarely that one can detect a deep personal note in the delightful love-songs with which the whole period abounds from Carew to Dryden. The collected work of none of them would give such an impression of a real history behind it, a history of many experiences and moods, as Donne's Songs and Sonnets and the Elegies, and, as one must still believe, the sonnets of Shakespeare record. Like the Elizabethan sonneteers they all dress and redress the same theme in much the same manner, though the manner is not quite the Elizabethan, nor the theme. Song has superseded the sonnet, and the passion of which they sing has lost most of the Petrarchian, chivalrous strain, and become in a very definite meaning of the words, 'simple and sensuous.' And if the religious poets are rather more individual and personal, the personal note is less intense, troubled and complex than in Donne's Divine Poems; the individual is more merged in the Christian, Catholic or Anglican.

But the strongest personality of all is Andrew Marvell. Apart from Milton he is the most interesting personality between Donne and Dryden, and at his very best a finer poet than either. Most of his descriptive poems lie a little outside my beat, though I have claimed The Garden as metaphysical,

> Annihilating all that's made
> To a green thought in a green shade [ll. 47–8],

and I might have claimed The Nymph and the Faun had space permitted. But his few love poems and his few devotional pieces are perfect exponents of all the 'metaphysical' qualities—passionate, paradoxical argument, touched with humour and learned imagery:

> As lines, so loves oblique, may well
>   Themselves in every angle greet:
> But ours so truly parallel,

Though infinite, can never meet;
['Definition of Love,' ll. 25–8]

and above all the sudden soar of passion in bold and felicitous image, in clangorous lines:

[Quotes 'To His Coy Mistress,' ll. 21–32.]

These lines seem to me the very roof and crown of the metaphysical love lyric, at once fantastic and passionate. Donne is weightier, more complex, more suggestive of subtle and profound reaches of feeling, but he has not one single passage of the same length that combines all the distinctive qualities of the kind, in thought, in phrasing, in feeling, in music; and Rochester's most passionate lines are essentially simpler, less metaphysical.

When wearied with a world of woe,
['Absent from thee,' l. 9]

might have been written by Burns with some difference. The best things of Donne and Marvell could only have been composed—except, as an imitative *tour de force*, like [Sir William] Watson's

Bid me no more to other eyes—[1]

in the seventeenth century. But in that century there were so many poets who could sing, at least occasionally, in the same strain. Of all those whom Professor Saintsbury's ardent and catholic but discriminating taste has collected there is none who has not written too much indifferent verse, but none who has not written one or two songs showing the same fine blend of passion and paradox and music. The 'metaphysicals' of the seventeenth century combined two things, both soon to pass away, the fantastic dialectics of mediaeval love poetry and the 'simple, sensuous' strain which they caught from the classics—soul and body lightly yoked and glad to run and soar together in the winged chariot of Pegasus. Modern love poetry has too often sacrificed both to sentiment.

[1] Line 1 of 'The Protest,' published in the *Daily Chronicle*, 1 September 1894, reprinted in *Odes and Other Poems*, 1894.

102. Cyril Falls on the tercentenary of Marvell's birth

1921

Known for his writings on military topics, Cyril Falls (1888-1971) published his essay on Marvell in April 1921. It was later incorporated in the *Tercentenary Tributes*.

Extract from 'Andrew Marvell,' *Nineteenth Century and After*, No. 530 (April 1921), pp. 630–3, 637–42.

Andrew Marvell marks the close of an era. Having produced him, Mother England, that had been of late so fecund of poets, fell barren or nigh barren for a while. In the thirty years that preceded his birth were born, to name but the greatest, Herrick, Herbert, Randolph, Waller, Milton, Suckling, Butler, Crashaw, Lovelace and Cowley, of whom Waller and Butler alone outlived him. In the next thirty, nay in the next sixty, years there appears but one great poet, Dryden. There is not another the equal of Waller, least of the company of the elders. . . .

Followed a long and leisurely Grand Tour, which embraced France, Holland, Italy and Spain. In its couse he met Flecknoe, born, if ever man was, to be a butt, and wrote a hateful satire to mark the occasion—hateful because, however dull and stupid a man may be, his poverty and his hunger are unpleasant subjects for mockery. On his return he showed some sympathy with royalism by a blistering poem on the death of Thomas May, and by declaring his friendship for the prince of Cavalier poets, Richard Lovelace, then fallen on evil times. . . .

Marvell's lyrical poetry belongs to his youth, but on the principle of keeping the good wine till last we may leave it for a moment to consider his other work. His verse satire and his prose have each a certain importance, but he would be a very minor and uninteresting figure if they were all he had left. The Marvell of the lyrics and he of the satires are different poets, belonging to different ages.

357

He cannot be said to bridge those ages, as do Waller and Cowley. His early work is definitely in one; his later in the other. In the former he is a genuine 'Fantastic,' true son of Dr. John Donne. The last of that strange Italian gilding that gives such subtle beauty to all the age of Elizabeth, James and the First Charles, is worn away when he quits country for town. The satires are Restoration in spirit.... The most famous is *The Last Instructions to a Painter about the Dutch Wars*, 1667. Marvell had sung the praises of Blake, and was furious at the shameful degeneracy of English naval power. The title was taken from Waller's eulogy of the Duke of York's naval victory off Harwich. Denham, whose wife had become the Duke's mistress, had been the first to turn the idea to satire. Marvell begins by whipping St. Albans, and then the Duchess of York, daughter of the man he hated worse than poison, the Chancellor Clarendon. His biographers have tumbled over themselves in their efforts to palliate these atrocious assaults— for there are many others—on this far from estimable lady. It is the privilege of biographers to eulogise their subjects and abuse their subjects' enemies, but nothing they can write alters the fact that Marvell's lines on poor 'Nan Hyde' are venomous and disgusting. Follows a bitter attack on the House of Commons, and then at last the poem rises to a high order of merit. With a biting pen Marvell describes our unpreparedness, the sailing of De Ruyter up the Thames, the capture of our ships, the impotence of Monk ashore:

> (As if, alas! we ships, or Dutch had horse) [l. 482];

breaking out finally into a splendid rage:

> Black day, accursed! ...

[Quotes ll. 737–56.]

The longest of the lyrical poems, *Upon Appleton House*, is not among the best. It is perhaps as much narrative as lyrical. It contains a tedious history of how the estate came into the hands of the Fairfaxes. But here and there in the latter part are instances of that keen observation of nature and of that passionate nature-worship in which Marvell is not only unique in his day but which he is the earliest English poet to evince. The lines that follow are a fair example of the first. They could in that age have been written by none but him:

[Quotes ll. 529–50.]

That line 'the hatching throstle's shining eye' has a tenderness that seems to belong to a later period, and might have been culled from the work of a living poet, Mr. Ralph Hodgson.* The latter characteristic, that of nature-worship, shines out in the following famous passage:

[Quotes ll. 609–20.]

These lines illustrate singularly well my statement that Marvell looks upon nature without spectacles. It is hard to think of any other poet before the days of Wordsworth in such complete harmony and such close communion with nature. We can see the young poet—most unromantic in appearance according to conventional standards, with his 'roundish-faced, cherry-cheeked' head and his 'pretty strong-set' body—walking in the park and woods with his little pupil, giving a corner of his intelligence to her talk, and with the rest of it drinking in the beauty and peace of his surroundings.

Influences of Donne and some resemblances to Milton have been traced in Marvell's poetry. There is another poet of the generation previous to his whom in some of his moods he recalls —George Herbert. He was religious, but always and before all a sturdy Protestant of the Reformation. His mysticism is a Protestant mysticism. It is not fanciful to suppose that at certain moments, moments of revulsion from the world, he approached the point of view of that recluse, so colourless beside Crashaw, who yet remains the most typically English of devotional poets. *The Coronet* and *A Dialogue between the Soul and Body* are the examples of this side of his poetical genius. The latter is somewhat harsh and laboured, but the former has charming lines, and, despite its conceits, a heart-felt sense of devotion:

[Quotes ll. 1–16.]

The *Horatian Ode* shares with *Bermudas, The Nymph complaining for the Death of her Fawn, To His Coy Mistress, The Picture of Little T. C. in a Prospect of Flowers,* and *The Garden,* the chief fame and the chief merit of Marvell's poems. All except the third, apparently omitted in an access of prudery which is simply incomprehensible

* *The Last Blackbird; and Other Lines* (1907); and *Poems* (1917).

to us, are included in the *Golden Treasury*, and are perhaps as well
known as any five lyrical poems by any one of our poets. It is, in
fact, on this sextet above all that Marvell is adjudged a great poet,
not in that narrow sense in which we declare Chaucer, Shakespeare,
Milton, Wordsworth, Keats and Shelley to be the great poets of
England, but in the wider and more usual sense in which we
speak of some five-and-twenty great English poets. The more
closely we examine these poems and compare them with the
product of other poets of that age and of the next hundred and
fifty years, the more highly shall we value them. Their charm is
not altogether a lively charm. Marvell cannot sing a song such as
Lovelace and Davenant achieve in their happiest moments, still
less such as Herrick and Carew trill out joyously time and time
again. With the poets in question the art of pure singing dies, not
to be reborn—and then as a more complicated, less inevitable
art—till the days of Shelley and Byron. But, placid as it is, it is
also limpid and extremely delicate. The poet conjures up every
now and then visions of pure beauty that match those of Spenser.
Some of these jewels are known to all, but they will bear quotation
yet once again. In *Bermudas* occurs the beautiful passage.

[Quotes ll. 17–24.]

There is extraordinary intensity in these lines. The 'golden lamps
in a green night' is the supreme mastery of words, and appears
to bring the imagination of the painter to the aid of that of the
poet. They can be matched by stanzas from *The Garden*. This is a
translation of a Latin poem of Marvell's. The original has a fine
Horatian flavour, but it is the greater softness of the English
tongue which gives these stanzas their extraordinary fascination.

[Quotes stt. 5–6, then:]

> Here at the fountain's sliding foot,
> Or at some fruit-tree's mossy root,
> Casting the body's vest aside,
> My soul into the boughs does glide:
> There, like a bird, it sits and sings,
> Then whets and combs its silver wings,
> And, till prepared for longer flight,
> Waves in its plumes the various light.

Here is another expression, 'a green thought in a green shade,'

that, though it might in a modern appear precious, is delightful
in Marvell because it comes to him naturally and because it is so
exquisitely in tune with the sentiments of the preceding lines.
The third, fourth, fifth and sixth lines of the last stanza quoted
are the poetry of pure enchantment. They represent one of those
magic moments that no poet, however great, has very often, and
that none but a great poet compasses ever. This is perhaps the
most perfect of all Marvell's poems.

The Nymph and the Fawn is best described by the adjective, used
in its best sense, pretty. It is intentionally so. The poem is put into
the mouth of a very young girl, and is shot through with a child's
delicate fancies. Probably it was written for Moll Fairfax, and with
her picture in the poet's mind. So fascinating is it that we do not
pause to inquire how the fawn's 'foot' could be 'more white and
soft' than the hand of its mistress! It takes all the poet's art to save
this poem from too much sweetness, but that art succeeds by a
refusal to force the note. The combined simplicity and colour of
the phrases will be noted in these lines:

[Quotes ll. 71–86.]

That is the feminine side of Marvell. How masculine he can be
in his most lyrical moments is shown by these lines from *His Coy
Mistress*, which it is pleasant to compare with those just quoted:

[Quotes ll. 33–46.]

Andrew Marvell is a man of contrasts. To all but a few students
he is to-day the author of the delightful lyrical poems that I have
been last considering. Yet to himself they were but an interlude in
his life. He turned his back upon that 'happy garden-state,' threw
himself into the world of politics and diplomacy and satire. It is
as if Mr. Walter de la Mare were suddenly to appear as 'Anti-waste'
candidate, to go on political missions to China, and to write
leading articles in the daily Press against the Government. Doubtless he was inspired by a high sense of duty, but we can ill spare,
for a few stinging attacks on a dynasty dead and gone, for a volume
of dull letters to constituents and interminable speeches before
his barbaric majesty the Tsar of Muscovy, the rightful successors
to *The Garden* and *Bermudas*. He cut himself off from lyrical poetry
by his own action almost as completely as Keats was cut off by
premature death. He remains a great poet; he might have had to
be numbered with our greatest.

103. T.S. Eliot on the tercentenary of Marvell's birth

1921

By virtue of his later status as poet and critic, the essay by T. S. Eliot (1888–1965) may properly be said to cap the initial reassessment of Marvell's poetry. Its far-ranging and pervasive influence determined the trend of much subsequent criticism.

Written initially for the *Times Literary Supplement*, the essay was reprinted in the *Tercentenary Tributes* and Eliot himself reprinted it twice: in the *Hogarth Essays: Homage to John Dryden* (1927), and again in *Selected Essays* (1932). Yet only two years after writing it, he had modified his attitude considerably, if the review of the Nonesuch edition of Marvell is to be taken as an indication. Though its publication goes beyond the limits of the dates for this volume, the review is included here not because of any intrinsic value for assessing the *fortuna* of Marvell's poetry but because it affords an ironic, if somewhat oblique, insight into the literary views of the most influential of twentieth-century critics on Marvell.

From *Selected Essays*, New York, 1932, pp. 278–90. This version drops one or two of the learned allusions.

The tercentenary of the former member for Hull deserves not only the celebration proposed by that favoured borough, but a little serious reflection upon his writing. That is an act of piety, which is very different from the resurrection of a deceased reputation. Marvell has stood high for some years; his best poems are not very many, and not only must be well known, from the *Golden Treasury* and the *Oxford Book of English Verse*, but must also have been enjoyed by numerous readers. His grave needs neither rose nor rue nor laurel; there is no imaginary justice to be done; we may think about him, if there be need for thinking, for our own benefit, not his. To bring the poet back to life—the great, the perennial, task of criticism—is in this case to squeeze the drops of the essence of two or three poems; even confining ourselves to these, we may find some precious liquor unknown to the present age. Not to determine rank, but to isolate this quality, is the critical labour. The fact that of all Marvell's verse, which is itself not a great quantity, the really valuable part consists of a very few poems indicates that the unknown quality of which we speak is probably a literary rather than a personal quality; or, more truly, that it is a quality of a civilization, of a traditional habit of life. A poet like Donne, or like Baudelaire or Laforgue, may almost be considered the inventor of an attitude, a system of feeling or of morals. Donne is difficult to analyse: what appears at one time a curious personal point of view may at another time appear rather the precise concentration of a kind of feeling diffused in the air about him. Donne and his shroud, the shroud and his motive for wearing it, are inseparable, but they are not the same thing. The seventeenth century sometimes seems for more than a moment to gather up and to digest into its art all the experience of the human mind which (from the same point of view) the later centuries seem to have been partly engaged in repudiating. But Donne would have been an individual at any time and place; Marvell's best verse is the product of European, that is to say Latin, culture.

Out of that high style developed from Marlowe through Johnson (for Shakespeare does not lend himself to these genealogies) the seventeenth century separated two qualities: wit and magniloquence. Neither is as simple or as apprehensible as its name seems to imply, and the two are not in practice antithetical; both are conscious and cultivated, and the mind which cultivates one may cultivate the other. The actual poetry, of Marvell, of Cowley, and of Milton, and of others, is a blend in varying proportions. And we must be on guard not to employ the terms with too wide a comprehension; for like the other fluid terms with which literary criticism deals, the meaning alters with the age, and for precision we must rely to some degree upon the literacy and good taste of the reader. The wit of the Caroline poets is not the wit of Shakespeare, and it is not the wit of Dryden, the great master of contempt, or of Pope, the great master of hatred, or of Swift, the great master of disgust. What is meant is some quality which is common to the songs in *Comus* and Cowley's Anacreontics and Marvell's Horatian Ode. It is more than a technical accomplishment, or the vocabulary and syntax of an epoch; it is, what we have designated tentatively as wit, a tough reasonableness beneath the slight lyric grace. You cannot find it in Shelley or Keats or Wordsworth; you cannot find more than an echo of it in Landor; still less in Tennyson or Browning; and among contemporaries Mr. Yeats is an Irishman and Mr. Hardy is a modern Englishman—that is to say, Mr. Hardy is without it and Mr. Yeats is outside of the tradition altogether. On the other hand, as it certainly exists in Lafontaine, there is a large part of it in Gautier. And of the magniloquence, the deliberate exploitation of the possibilities of magnificence in language which Milton used and abused, there is also use and even abuse in the poetry of Baudelaire.

Wit is not a quality that we are accustomed to associate with 'Puritan' literature, with Milton or with Marvell. But if so, we are at fault partly in our conception of wit and partly in our generalizations about the Puritans. And if the wit of Dryden or of Pope is not the only kind of wit in the language, the rest is not merely a little merriment or a little levity or a little impropriety or a little epigram. And, on the other hand, the sense in which a man like Marvell is a 'Puritan' is restricted. The persons who opposed Charles I and the persons who supported the Commonwealth were not all of the flock of Zeal-of-the-land Busy or the United Grand Junction Ebenezer Temperance Association. Many of them were gentlemen of the time who merely believed, with considerable show of reason, that government by a Parliament of gentlemen was better than government by a Stuart; though they were, to that extent, Liberal Practitioners, they could hardly foresee the tea-meeting and the Dissidence of Dissent. Being men of education and culture, even of travel, some of them were exposed to that spirit of the age which was coming to be the French spirit of the age. This spirit, curiously enough, was quite opposed to the tendencies latent or the forces active in Puritanism; the contest does great damage to the poetry of Milton; Marvell, an active servant of the public, but a lukewarm partisan, and a poet on a smaller scale, is far less injured by it. His line on the statue of

Charles II, 'It is such a King as no chisel can mend,'[1] may be set off against his criticism of the Great Rebellion: 'Men ... ought and might have trusted the King' [RT I, p. 135]. Marvell, therefore, more a man of the century than a Puritan, speaks more clearly and unequivocally with the voice of his literary age than does Milton.

This voice speaks out uncommonly strong in the *Coy Mistress*. The theme is one of the great traditional commonplaces of European literature. It is the theme of *O mistress mine*, of *Gather ye rosebuds*, of *Go, lovely rose*; it is in the savage austerity of Lucretius and the intense levity of Catullus. Where the wit of Marvell renews the theme is in the variety and order of the images. In the first of the three paragraphs Marvell plays with a fancy which begins by pleasing and leads to astonishment.

> Had we but world enough and time,
> This coyness, lady, were no crime,
> ... I would
> Love you ten years before the Flood,
> And you should, if you please, refuse
> Till the conversion of the Jews;
> My vegetable love should grow
> Vaster than empires and more slow. [ll. 1–2, 7–12]

We notice the high speed, the succession of concentrated images, each magnifying the original fancy. When this process has been carried to the end and summed up, the poem turns suddenly with that surprise which has been one of the most important means of poetic effect since Homer:

> But at my back I always hear
> Time's wingèd chariot hurrying near,
> And yonder all before us lie
> Deserts of vast eternity. [ll. 21–4]

A whole civilization resides in these lines:

> Pallida Mors aequo pulsat pede pauperum tabernas,
> Regumque turris.[2]

---

[1] From *The Statue in Stocks-Market*, l. 56, a poem of dubious authorship, ascribed to Marvell only on the authority of Captain Thompson.

[2] Horace, *Odes* I. 4.13–14; Pale death with same foot knocks at the bowers/Of the poore men, and at the Princes towers. (Trans. Henry Rider, 1638)

And not only Horace but Catullus himself:

> Nobis, cum semel occidit brevis lux,
> Nox est perpetua una dormienda.[1]

The verse of Marvell has not the grand reverberation of Catullus's Latin; but the image of Marvell is certainly more comprehensive and penetrates greater depths than Horace's.

A modern poet, had he reached the height, would very likely have closed on this moral reflection. But the three strophes of Marvell's poem have something like a syllogistic relation to each other. After a close approach to the mood of Donne,

> then worms shall try
> That long-preserved virginity. . .
> The grave's a fine and private place,
> But none, I think, do there embrace [ll. 27–8, 32–3],

the conclusion,

> Let us roll all our strength and all
> Our sweetness up into one ball,
> And tear our pleasures with rough strife,
> Thorough the iron gates of life. [ll. 41–4]

It will hardly be denied that this poem contains wit; but it may not be evident that this wit forms the crescendo and diminuendo of a scale of great imaginative power. The wit is not only combined with, but fused into, the imagination. We can easily recognize a witty fancy in the successive images ('my *vegetable* love,' 'till the conversion of the Jews'), but this fancy is not indulged, as it sometimes is by Cowley or Cleveland, for its own sake. It is structural decoration of a serious idea. In this it is superior to the fancy of *L'Allegro*, *Il Penseroso*, or the lighter and less successful poems of Keats. In fact, this alliance of levity and seriousness (by which the seriousness is intensified) is a characteristic of the sort of wit we are trying to identify. It is found in

> Le squelette était invisible
> Au temps heureux de l'art paien!
> [*Emaux et Camées*, 'Bûchers et Tombeaux,' ll. 1–2]

---

[1] Catullus, 5.5–6: But, soone as once set is our little light,/Then must we sleepe an ever-during night. (Trans. Thomas Campion, 1601.)

of Gautier, and in the *dandysme* of Baudelaire and Laforgue.
It is in the poem of Catullus which has been quoted, and in the
variation by Ben Jonson:

> Cannot we deceive the eyes
> Of a few poor household spies?
> 'Tis no sin love's fruits to steal,
> But that sweet sin to reveal,
> To be taken, to be seen,
> These have sins accounted been.
>
> [*Volpone*, III. vii. 176–7, 180–3]

It is in Propertius and Ovid. It is a quality of a sophisticated
literature; a quality which expands in English literature just at the
moment before the English mind altered; it is not a quality which
we should expect Puritanism to encourage. When we come to
Gray and Collins, the sophistication remains only in the language,
and has disappeared from the feeling. Gray and Collins were
masters, but they had lost that hold on human values, that firm
grasp of human experience, which is a formidable achievement
of the Elizabethan and Jacobean poets. This wisdom, cynical
perhaps but untired (in Shakespeare, a terrifying clairvoyance),
leads toward, and is only completed by, the religious comprehension; it leads to the point of the 'Ainsi tout leur a craqué dans la
main' of [Flaubert's] Bouvard and Pécuchet..

The difference between imagination and fancy, in view of this
poetry of wit, is a very narrow one. Obviously, an image which
is immediately and unintentionally ridiculous is merely a fancy.
In the poem *Upon Appleton House*, Marvell falls in with one of these
undesirable images, describing the attitude of the house toward
its master:

> Yet thus the leaden house does sweat,
> And scarce endures the master great;
> But, where he comes, the swelling hall
> Stirs, and the square grows spherical [ll. 49–52],

which, whatever its intention, is more absurd than it was intended
to be. Marvell also falls into the even commoner error of images
which are over-developed or distracting; which support nothing
but their own misshapen bodies:

And [*sic*] now the salmon-fishers moist
Their leathern boats begin to hoist;
And, like Antipodes in shoes,
Have shod their heads in their canoes. [ll. 769–72]

Of this sort of image a choice collection may be found in Johnson's
Life of Cowley. But the images in the *Coy Mistress* are not only witty,
but satisfy the elucidation of Imagination given by Coleridge:

This power ... reveals itself in the balance or reconcilement of opposite
or discordant qualities: of sameness, with difference; of the general,
with the concrete; the idea with the image; the individual with the
representative; the sense of novelty and freshness with old and familiar
objects; a more than usual state of emotion with more than usual order;
judgment ever awake and steady self-possession with enthusiasm and
feeling profound or vehement [*Biographia Literaria*, XIV].

Coleridge's statement applies also to the following verses, which
are selected because of their similarity, and because they illustrate
the marked caesura which Marvell often introduces in a short line:

The tawny mowers enter next,
Who seem like Israelites to be
Walking on foot through a green sea ...
　　　　['Appleton House,' ll. 388–90]

And now the meadows fresher dyed,
Whose grass, with moister colour dashed,
Seems as green silks but newly washed ... [ll. 626–8]

He hangs in shades the orange bright,
Like golden lamps in a green night ... ['Bermudas,' ll. 17–18]

Annihilating all that's made
To a green thought in a green shade ... ['The Garden,' ll. 47–8]

Had it lived long, it would have been,
Lilies without, roses within. ['The Nymph,' ll. 91–2]

The whole poem, from which the last of these quotations is drawn
(*The Nymph and the Fawn*), is built upon a very slight foundation,
and we can imagine what some of our modern practitioners of
slight themes would have made of it. But we need not descend to
an invidious contemporaneity to point the difference. Here are
six lines from *The Nymph and the Fawn*:

> I have a garden of my own,
> But so with roses overgrown
> And lilies, that you would it guess
> To be a little wilderness;
> And all the spring-time of the year
> It only lovèd to be there. [ll. 71-6]

And here are five lines from *The Nymph's Song to Hylas* in the *Life and Death of Jason*, by William Morris:

> I know a little garden close
> Set thick with lily and red rose.
> Where I would wander if I might
> From dewy dawn to dewy night,
> And have one with me wandering. [IV. 577-81]

So far the resemblance is more striking than the difference, although we might just notice the vagueness of allusion in the last line to some indefinite person, form, or phantom, compared with the more explicit reference of emotion to object which we should expect from Marvell. But in the latter part of the poem Morris divaricates widely:

> Yet tottering as I am, and weak,
> Still have I left a little breath
> To seek within the jaws of death
> An entrance to that happy place;
> To seek the unforgotten face
> Once seen, once kissed, once reft from me
> Anigh the murmuring of the sea. [IV. 602-8]

Here the resemblance, if there is any, is to the latter part of *The Coy Mistress*. As for the difference, it could not be more pronounced. The effect of Morris's charming poem depends upon the mistiness of the feeling and the vagueness of its object; the effect of Marvell's upon its bright, hard precision. And this precision is not due to the fact that Marvell is concerned with cruder or simpler or more carnal emotions. The emotion of Morris is not more refined or more spiritual; it is merely more vague: if any one doubts whether the more refined or spiritual emotion can be precise, he should study the treatment of the varieties of discarnate emotion in the *Paradiso*. A curious result of the comparison of Morris's poem with Marvell's is that the former, though it appears

369

to be more serious, is found to be the slighter; and Marvell's
Nymph and the Fawn, appearing more slight, is the more serious.

> So weeps the wounded balsam; so
> The holy frankincense doth flow;
> The brotherless Heliades
> Melt in such amber tears as these. [ll. 95–8]

These verses have the suggestiveness of true poetry; and the
verses of Morris, which are nothing if not an attempt to suggest,
really suggest nothing; and we are inclined to infer that the
suggestiveness is the aura around a bright clear centre, that you
cannot have the aura alone. The day-dreamy feeling of Morris is
essentially a slight thing; Marvell takes a slight affair, the feeling
of a girl for her pet, and gives it a connexion with that inexhaustible
and terrible nebula of emotion which surrounds all our exact and
practical passions and mingles with them. Again, Marvell does
this in a poem which, because of its formal pastoral machinery,
may appear a trifling object:

> CLORINDA. Near this, a fountain's liquid bell
> Tinkles within the concave shell.
> DAMON. Might a soul bathe there and be clean,
> Or slake its drought? ['Clorinda and Damon,' ll. 13–16]

where we find that a metaphor has suddenly rapt us to the image
of spiritual purgation. There is here the element of *surprise*, as
when Villon says:

> Necessité faict gens mesprendre
> Et faim saillir le loup des boys ['Le Testament,' ll. 167–8],

the surprise which Poe considered of the highest importance,
and also the restraint and quietness of tone which make the surprise possible. And in the verses of Marvell which have been
quoted there is the making the familiar strange, and the strange
familiar, which Coleridge attributed to good poetry.

The effort to construct a dream-world, which alters English
poetry so greatly in the nineteenth century, a dream-world utterly
different from the visionary realities of the *Vita Nuova* or of the
poetry of Dante's contemporaries, is a problem of which various
explanations may no doubt be found; in any case, the result makes

a poet of the nineteenth century, of the same size as Marvell, a more trivial and less serious figure. Marvell is no greater personality than William Morris, but he had something much more solid behind him: he had the vast and penetrating influence of Ben Jonson. Jonson never wrote anything purer than Marvell's *Horatian Ode*; this ode has that same quality of wit which was diffused over the whole Elizabethan product and concentrated in the work of Jonson. And, as was said before, this wit which pervades the poetry of Marvell is more Latin, more refined, than anything that succeeded it. The great danger, as well as the great interest and excitement, of English prose and verse, compared with French, is that it permits and justifies an exaggeration of particular qualities to the exclusion of others. Dryden was great in wit, as Milton in magniloquence; but the former, by isolating this quality and making it by itself into great poetry, and the latter, by coming to dispense with it altogether, may perhaps have injured the language. In Dryden wit becomes almost fun, and thereby loses some cantact with reality; becomes pure fun, which French wit almost never is.

> The midwife placed her hand on his thick skull,
> With this prophetic blessing: Be thou dull ...
> [*Absalom and Achitophel*, Pt. II, 476–7]

> A numerous host of dreaming saints succeed,
> Of the true old enthusiastic breed. [Pt. I, 529–30]

This is audacious and splendid; it belongs to satire beside which Marvell's Satires are random babbling, but it is perhaps as exaggerated as:

> Oft he seems to hide his face,
> But unexpectedly returns,
> And to his faithful champion hath in place
> Bore witness gloriously; whence Gaza mourns
> And all that band them to resist
> His uncontrollable intent.
> [*Samson Agonistes*, ll. 1749–54]

How oddly the sharp Dantesque phrase 'whence Gaza mourns' springs out from the brilliant contortions of Milton's sentence!

371

Who from his private gardens, where
He lived reservèd and austere,
   (As if his highest plot
   To plant the bergamot)

Could by industrious valour climb
To ruin the great work of Time,
   And cast the kingdoms old
   Into another mold. . . .

The Pict no shelter now shall find
Within his parti-coloured mind,
   But, from this valour sad,
   Shrink underneath the plaid:
     ['Horatian Ode,' ll. 29–36; 105–8]

There is here an equipoise, a balance and proportion of tones, which, while it cannot raise Marvell to the level of Dryden or Milton, extorts an approval which these poets do not receive from us, and bestows a pleasure at least different in kind from any they can often give. It is what makes Marvell a classic; or classic in a sense in which Gray and Collins are not; for the latter, with all their accredited purity, are comparatively poor in shades of feeling to contrast and unite.

We are baffled in the attempt to translate the quality indicated by the dim and antiquated term wit into the equally unsatisfactory nomenclature of our own time. Even Cowley is only able to define it by negatives:

Comely in thousand shapes appears;
   Yonder we saw it plain; and here 'tis now,
   Like spirits in a place we know not how.
                      ['Ode: Of Wit,' ll. 6–8]

It has passed out of our critical coinage altogether, and no new term has been struck to replace it; the quality seldom exists, and is never recognized.

In a true piece of Wit all things must be
   Yet all things there agree;
As in the Ark, join'd without force or strife,
All creatures dwelt, all creatures that had life.

> Or as the primitive forms of all
> (If we compare great things with small)
> Which, without discord or confusion, lie
> In that strange mirror of the Deity. [ll. 57–64]

So far Cowley has spoken well. But if we are to attempt even no more than Cowley, we, placed in a retrospective attitude, must risk much more than anxious generalizations. With our eye still on Marvell, we can say that wit is not erudition; it is sometimes stifled by erudition, as in much of Milton. It is not cynicism, though it has a kind of toughness which may be confused with cynicism by the tender-minded. It is confused with erudition because it belongs to an educated mind, rich in generations of experience; and it is confused with cynicism because it implies a constant inspection and criticism of experience. It involves, probably, a recognition, implicit in the expression of every experience, of other kinds of experience which are possible, which we find as clearly in the greatest as in poets like Marvell. Such a general statement may seem to take us a long way from *The Nymph and the Fawn*, or even from the *Horatian Ode*; but it is perhaps justified by the desire to account for that precise taste of Marvell's which finds for him the proper degree of seriousness for every subject which he treats. His errors of taste, when he trespasses, are not sins against this virtue; they are conceits, distended metaphors and similes, but they never consist in taking a subject too seriously or too lightly. This virtue of wit is not a peculiar quality of minor poets, or of the minor poets of one age or of one school; it is an intellectual quality which perhaps only becomes noticeable by itself, in the work of lesser poets. Furthermore, it is absent from the work of Wordsworth, Shelley, and Keats, on whose poetry nineteenth-century criticism has unconsciously been based. To the best of their poetry wit is irrelevant:

> Art thou pale for weariness
> Of climbing heaven and gazing on the earth,
> Wandering companionless
> Among the stars that have a different birth,
> And ever changing, like a joyless eye,
> That finds no object worth its constancy?
> [Shelley, 'To the Moon,' ll. 1–6]

We should find it difficult to draw any useful comparison between these lines of Shelley and anything by Marvell. But later poets, who would have been better for Marvell's quality, were without it; even Browning seems oddly immature, in some way, beside Marvell. And nowadays we find occasionally good irony, or satire, which lack wit's internal equilibrium, because their voices are essentially protests against some outside sentimentality or stupidity; or we find serious poets who are afraid of acquiring wit, lest they lose intensity. The quality which Marvell had, this modest and certainly impersonal virtue—whether we call it wit or reason, or even urbanity—we have patently failed to define. By whatever name we call it, and however we define that name, it is something precious and needed and apparently extinct; it is what should preserve the reputation of Marvell. *C'était une belle âme, comme on ne fait plus à Londres.*

Note: Extract from a review of *Miscellaneous Poems* (Nonesuch Press, 1923) in the *Nation and Athenaeum*, 33 (29 September 1923), p. 809. It is to be noted that here Eliot describes Henry King as 'greater' than Marvell.

A year or two ago, after the City of Hull, with more gratitude than most cities, had commemorated the tercentenary of a Parliamentarian who had served his constituency well, there appeared a memorial volume which did more credit to the City which subventioned it than to the writers whose critical essays on Andrew Marvell were there assembled.[1] From such a collection some genuine agreement, or definite difference, concerning the place and significance in English literature of the author celebrated, ought to transpire: but it never does. Critics almost invariably treat a writer, on such solemn occasions, as if it were impiety to recognize that any other authors have existed, or have had any relation to the subject of the eulogy. Exactly the points which it is their business to ponder, and on which their consensus or discord would have some interest and value, are avoided; the critics neither agree nor disagree: they expatiate upon their own whimsies and fancies. Now, a poet must be very great, very individual indeed, for us to be more or less safe in isolating him in this way; and even then we have only the part of a true appreciation. And Marvell and his contemporaries are not in this class. There is no one of them who is a safe model for study, in the

[1] A quite valid estimate of the *Tercentenary Tributes*, in which his own essay appeared. Edited by the City Librarian of Hull, the volume includes only two other items (Nos 100, 102) which provide extracts worthy of being reprinted.

sense that Chaucer, that Pope, is a safe model. For they are all more or less fantastical. This is no censure; there is no reason why a poet should not be as fantastical as possible, if that is the only way for him. But fantasticality must be that proper to its age, and the fantastic which may be a proper expression for our own will not be the fantastic of any other. Our conceits cannot be those of Marvell; they will spring, equally genuine, from a different impulse, from a different level of feeling.

Marvell is, without doubt, a very conceited poet. In a conceit two things very different are brought together, and the spark of ecstasy generated in us is a perception of power in bringing them together. It is, in my opinion, a conceit of the very finest order when Marvell says, of a spring of clear water:—

> Might a soul bathe there and he clean?
> Or slake its drought? ['Clorinda and Damon,' ll. 15–16]

Our pleasure is in the suddenness of the transference from material to spiritual water. But when Shakespeare says—

> She looks like sleep
> As she would catch another Antony
> In her strong toil of grace,
> [*Antony and Cleopatra*, V. ii. 347–9]

it is not a conceit. For instead of contrast we have fusion: a restoration of language to contact with things. Such words have the inevitability which make them appropriate to be spoken by any character. And when a greater than Marvell—Bishop King—says—

> But hark! my pulse, like a soft drum,
> Beats my approach, tells thee I come,
> ['The Exequy,' ll. 111–12]

that also is a conceit. If the drum were left out it would cease to be a conceit—but it would lose the valuable associations which the drum gives it. But when Dante says—

> Qual si fe Glauco, al gustar della erba,
> [*Il Paradiso*, I. 68]

or—

> l'impresa
> Che fe Nettuno ammirar l'ombra d'Argo,
> [*Il Paradiso*, XXXIII. 95–6]

375

or the best known—

> si ver noi aguzzevan le ciglia,
> come vecchio sartor fa nella cruna,' [*Inferno*, XV. 20–1]

these are not conceits. They have a rational necessity as well as suggestiveness, they are, like the words of Shakespeare above, an *explication* of the meaning.

A conceit is not to be something practised by the poet and despised by the critic; it has its place; for a purpose, for a poet, for a whole age, it may be the proper thing. And we must understand that the conceits which seem to us to fail are formed by exactly the same method as the conceits which seem to us to succeed. For that understanding we must read the whole of Marvell. But we must not only read the whole of Marvell; we must read Cleveland as well. And for this reason, and for others, and for the simple pleasure in a well-made book, we hope that the Nonesuch Press will continue their editions of seventeenth-century poets.

Bibliography

Either by references, selections, or introductions, these works provide materials on Marvell's reputation.

CAREY, JOHN (ed.), *Andrew Marvell*, Penguin Critical Anthologies, Harmondsworth, 1969.

DUNCAN, J. E., *The Revival of Metaphysical Poetry*, Minneapolis, Minnesota, 1959; reprinted New York, 1969.

GROSART, A. B. (ed.), *The Complete Works in Verse and Prose of Andrew Marvell*, 4 vols, Fuller Worthies Library, 1872–5.

LEGOUIS, PIERRE, *André Marvell: poète, puritain, patriot*, Paris—London, 1928. This is the most comprehensive and valuable survey of Marvell's reputation. The revised English version (Oxford, 1965; reprinted 1968), although it reduces the number of historical references, adds some new ones.

THOMPSON, EDWARD (ed.), *The Works of Andrew Marvell*, 3 vols, 1776.

WILDING, MICHAEL (ed.), *Marvell*, Modern Judgements, 1969.

Index

This Index is divided into three sections: I. Marvell's works including attributed and *dubia*; II. General (authors, periodicals, etc.); III. Authors with attributed similarities to Marvell or influence on him.

II. GENERAL (AUTHORS, PERIODICALS, ETC.)

III. AUTHORS WITH ATTRIBUTED SIMILARITIES TO MARVELL OR INFLUENCE ON HIM

III. AUTHORS WITH ATTRIBUTED SIMILARITIES TO MARVELL OR INFLUENCE ON HIM

THE CRITICAL HERITAGE SERIES

GENERAL EDITOR: B. C. SOUTHAM

Volumes published and forthcoming

MATTHEW ARNOLD:

THE POETRY	Carl Dawson
JANE AUSTEN	B. C. Southam
SAMUEL BECKETT	L. Graver and R. Federman
WILLIAM BLAKE	G. E. Bentley Jr
THE BRONTËS	Miriam Allott
BROWNING	Boyd Litzinger and Donald Smalley
ROBERT BURNS	Donald A. Low
BYRON	Andrew Rutherford
THOMAS CARLYLE	Jules Paul Seigel
CHAUCER 1385–1837	Derek Brewer
CHAUCER 1837–1933	Derek Brewer
CLARE	Mark Storey
CLOUGH	Michael Thorpe
COLERIDGE	J. R. de J. Jackson
WILKIE COLLINS	Norman Page
CONRAD	Norman Sherry
FENIMORE COOPER	George Dekker and John P. McWilliams
CRABBE	Arthur Pollard
STEPHEN CRANE	Richard M. Weatherford
DEFOE	Pat Rogers
DICKENS	Philip Collins
JOHN DONNE	A. J. Smith
DRYDEN	James and Helen Kinsley
GEORGE ELIOT	David Carroll
WILLIAM FAULKNER	John Bassett
HENRY FIELDING	Ronald Paulson and Thomas Lockwood
FORD MADOX FORD	Frank MacShane
E. M. FORSTER	Philip Gardner
GEORGIAN POETRY 1911–1922	Timothy Rogers
GISSING	Pierre Coustillas and Colin Partridge
GOLDSMITH	G. S. Rousseau
THOMAS HARDY	R. G. Cox
HAWTHORNE	J. Donald Crowley
ALDOUS HUXLEY	Donald Watt
IBSEN	Michael Egan